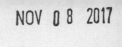

RLD
GER

DAISUKE ASHIHARA

MANGA

13

SHONEN JUMP MANGA EDITION

WORLD TRIGGER DATA BASE

BORDER

An agency founded to protect the city's peace from Neighbors.

S-Rank Black Trigger Users (i.e. Tsukihiko Amo)

A-Rank (Elite) — Away teams selected from here (Arashiyama, Miwa squads)

Promoted in Rank Wars

B-Rank (Main force) — Agents on defense duty must be at least B-Rank (Tamakoma-2)

Promoted at 4,000 solo points

C-Rank (Trainees) — Use trainee Triggers only in emergencies (Izuho Natsume)

TRIGGER

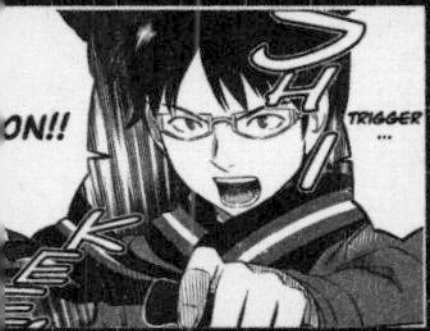
TRIGGER ...
ON!!

A technology created by Neighbors to manipulate Trion. Used mainly as weapons, Triggers come in various types.

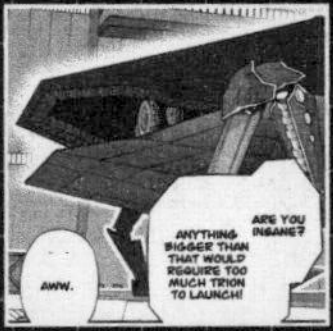
ARE YOU INSANE?
ANYTHING BIGGER THAN THAT WOULD REQUIRE TOO MUCH TRION TO LAUNCH!
AWW.

◀ A miss ships also run Trion

POSITIONS

Border classifies them into three groups: Attacker, Gunner and Sniper.

Attacker

Close-range attacks. Weapons include: close-range Scorpions that are good for surprise attacks, the balanced Kogetsu sword, and the defense-heavy Raygust.

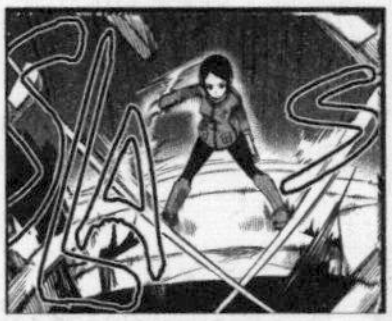

Gunner

Shoots from mid-range. There are several types of bullets, including multipurpose Asteroids, twisting Vipers, exploding Meteors, and tracking Hounds. People who don't use gun-shaped Triggers are called Shooters.

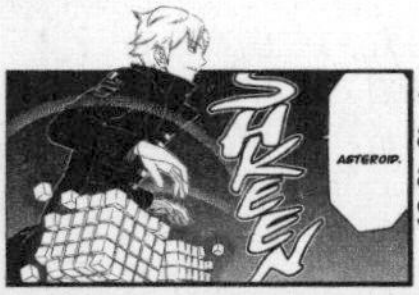
ASTEROID.

◀ Osamu and Izumi are Shooters.

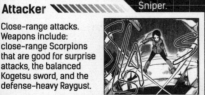

Sniper

Fires from a long distance. There are three sniping rifles: the well-balanced Egret, the light and easy Lightning, and the powerful but unwieldy Ibis.

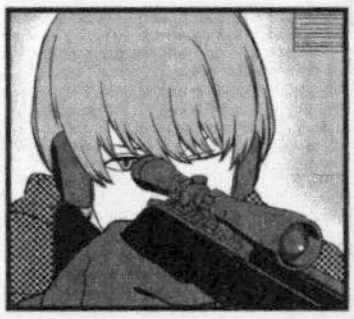

Operator

Supports combatants by relaying information such as enemy positions and abilities.

RANK WARS

Practice matches between Border agents. Promotions in Border are based on good results in the Rank Wars and defense duty achievements.

B-Rank agents are split into top, middle, and bottom groups. Three to four teams fight in a melee battle. Defeating an opposing squad member earns you one point and surviving to the end nets two points. Top teams from the previous season get a bonus.

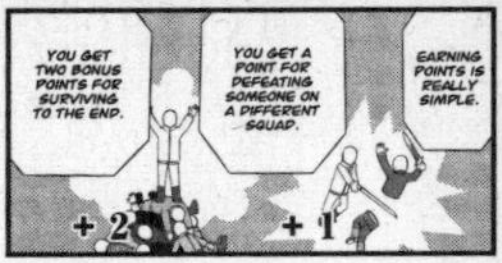
EARNING POINTS IS REALLY SIMPLE.
YOU GET A POINT FOR DEFEATING SOMEONE ON A DIFFERENT SQUAD.
+ 1
YOU GET TWO BONUS POINTS FOR SURVIVING TO THE END.
+ 2

A-Rank

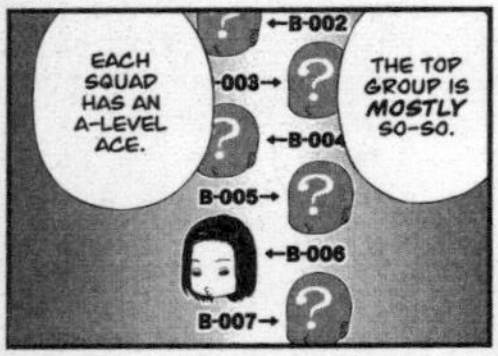
THE TOP GROUP IS *MOSTLY* SO-SO.
B-002
-003
B-004
B-005
B-006
B-007
EACH SQUAD HAS AN A-LEVEL ACE.

B-Rank middle groups have set strategies. Top groups all have an A-Rank level ace.

Top two B-Rank squads get to challenge A-Rank.

The lowest-ranked team in each match gets to pick the stage.

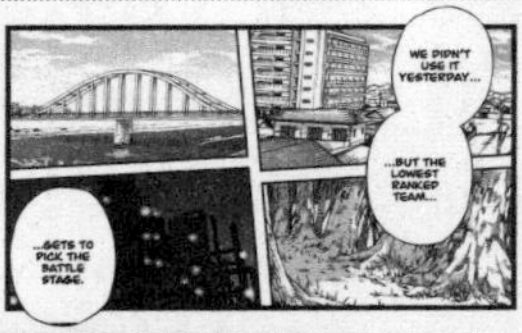
WE DIDN'T USE IT YESTERDAY...
...BUT THE LOWEST RANKED TEAM...
...GETS TO PICK THE BATTLE STAGE.

B-Rank

Agents ▶ (B-Rank and above) can't fight trainees (C-Rank) for points.

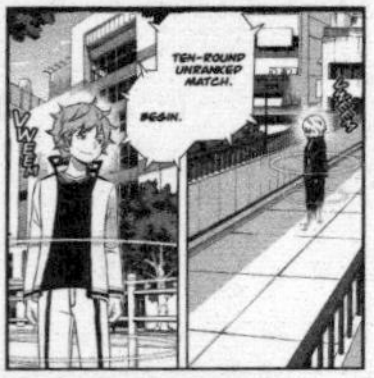
TEN-ROUND UNRANKED MATCH.
BEGIN.

C-Rank Wars are fought through solo matches. Beating someone with more points than you gets you a lot of points. On the other hand, beating someone with fewer points doesn't get you as many.

C-Rank

STORY

About four years ago, a Gate connecting to another dimension opened in Mikado City, leading to the appearance of invaders called Neighbors. After the establishment of the Border Defence Agency, people were able to return to their normal lives.

Osamu Mikumo is a junior high student who meets Yuma Kuga, a Neighbor. Yuma is targeted for capture by Border, but Tamakoma branch agent Yuichi Jin steps in to help. He convinces Yuma to join Border instead, then gives his Black Trigger to HQ in exchange for Yuma's enlistment. Now Osamu, Yuma and Osamu's friend Chika work toward making A-Rank together.

Aftokrator, the largest military nation in the Neighborhood, begins another large-scale invasion! Border succeeds in driving them back, but over thirty C-Rank trainees are kidnapped in the process. Border implements more plans for away missions to retrieve the missing Agents.

Tamakoma-2 enters the Rank Wars for a chance to be chosen for away missions. They win a fierce battle in the third round against Suzunari-1 and Nasu Squads, but Osamu becomes painfully aware of his lack of skill. Before the fourth round against the top B-Rank squads, Ninomiya and Kageura Squads,

WORLD TRIGGER CHARACTERS

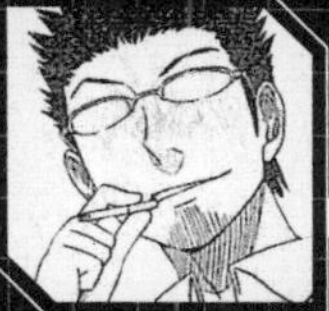

TAKUMI RINDO

Tamakoma Branch Director.

TAMAKOMA BRANCH

Understanding toward Neighbors. Considered divergent from Border's main philosophy.

TAMAKOMA-2

Tamakoma's B-Rank squad, aiming to get promoted to A-Rank.

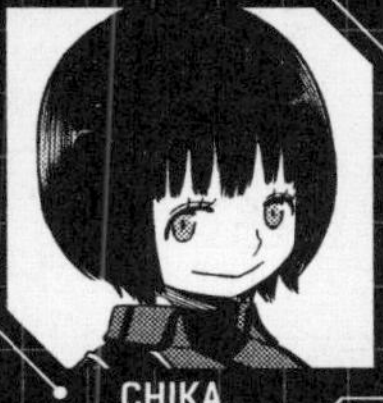

CHIKA AMATORI

Osamu's childhood friend. She has high Trion levels.

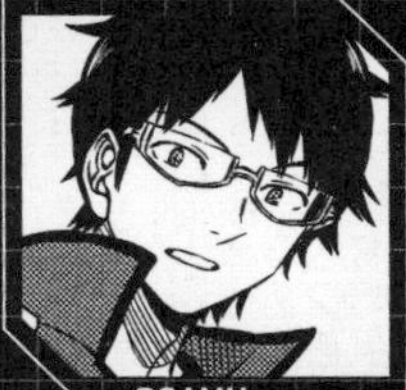

OSAMU MIKUMO

Ninth-grader who's compelled to help those in trouble. Captain of Tamakoma-2 (Mikumo squad).

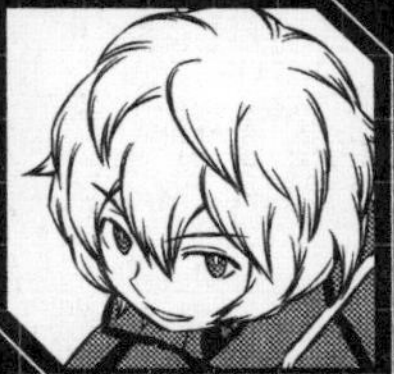

YUMA KUGA

A Neighbor who carries a Black Trigger.

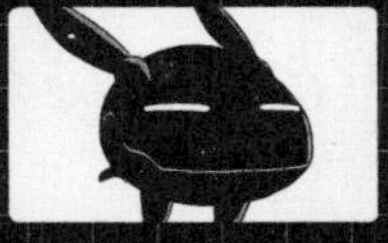

REPLICA

Yuma's chaperone. Missing after recent invasion.

TAMAKOMA-1

Tamakoma's A-Rank squad.

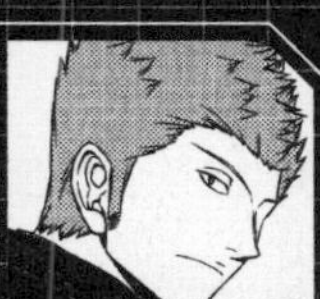

REIJI KIZAKI

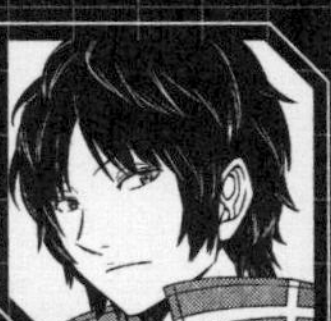

KYOSUKE KARASUMA

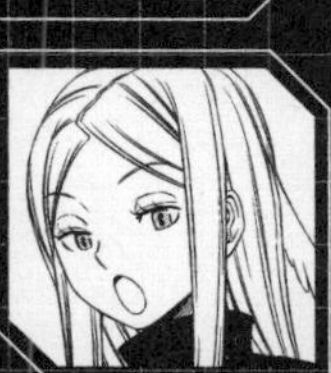

KIRIE KONAMI

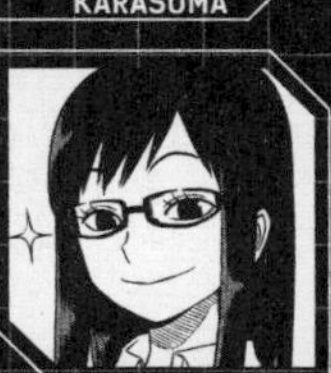

SHIORI USAMI

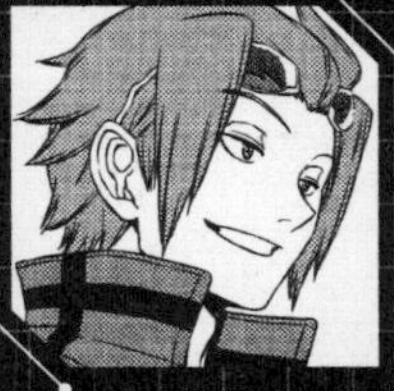

YUICHI JIN

Former S-Rank Black Trigger user. His Side Effect lets him see the future.

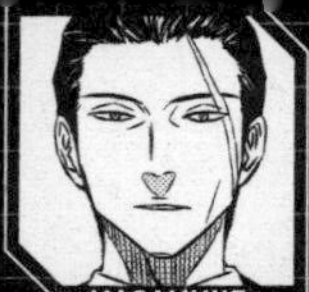

MASAMUNE KIDO

HQ Commander.

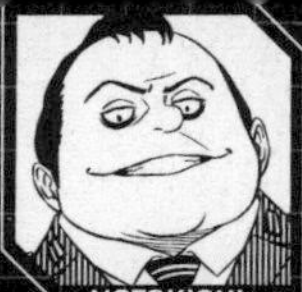

MOTOKICHI KINUTA

R&D Director.

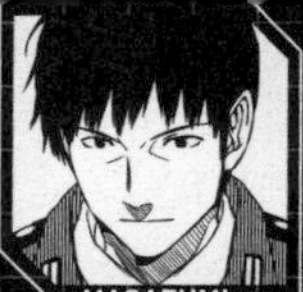

MASAFUMI SHINODA

HQ Director and Defense commander.

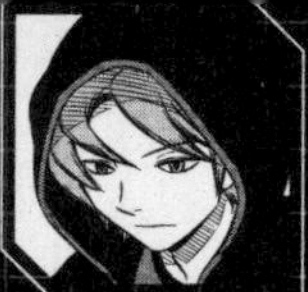

HYUSE

Neighbor from Aftokrator left behind in the invasion.

A-RANK AGENTS

ARASHIYAMA SQUAD

Border HQ A-Rank #5 squad.

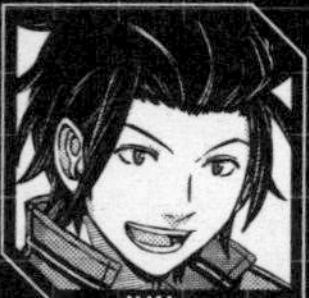

JUN ARASHIYAMA

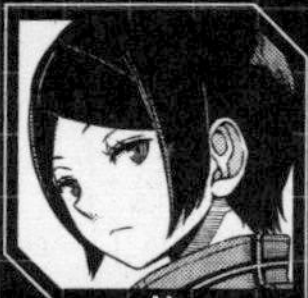

AI KITORA

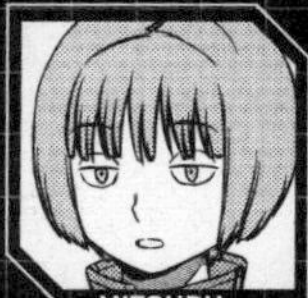

MITSURU TOKIEDA

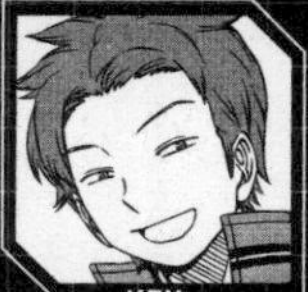

KEN SATORI

TACHIKAWA SQUAD

Border HQ A-Rank #1 squad.

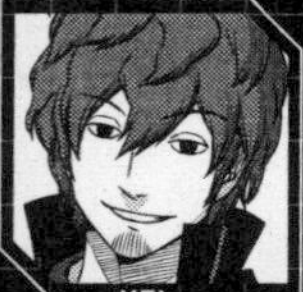

KEI TACHIKAWA

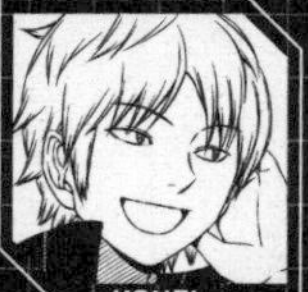

KOHEI IZUMI

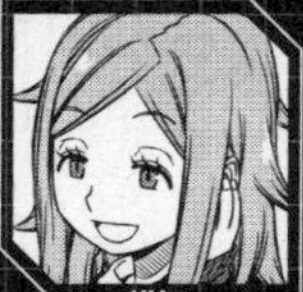

YU KUNICHIKA

B-RANK AGENTS

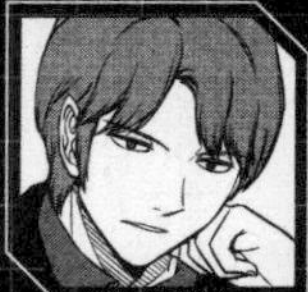

MASATAKA NINOMIYA

Ninomiya squad #1 Shooter.

AZUMA SQUAD

Border HQ B-Rank #7 squad.

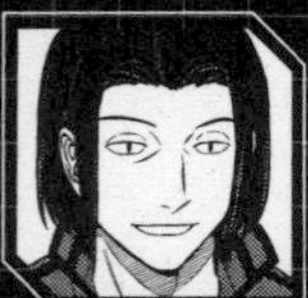

HARUAKI AZUMA

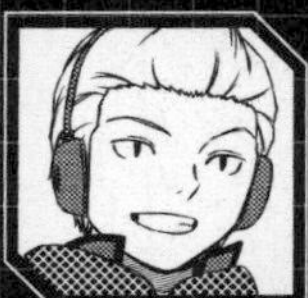

NOBORU KOARAI

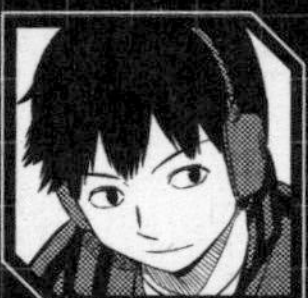

TSUNEYUKI OKUDERA

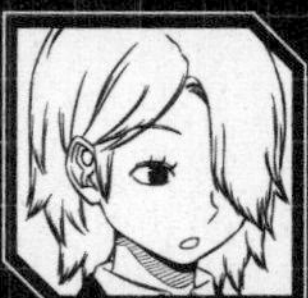

MAKO HITOMI

WORLD TRIGGER
CONTENTS

13

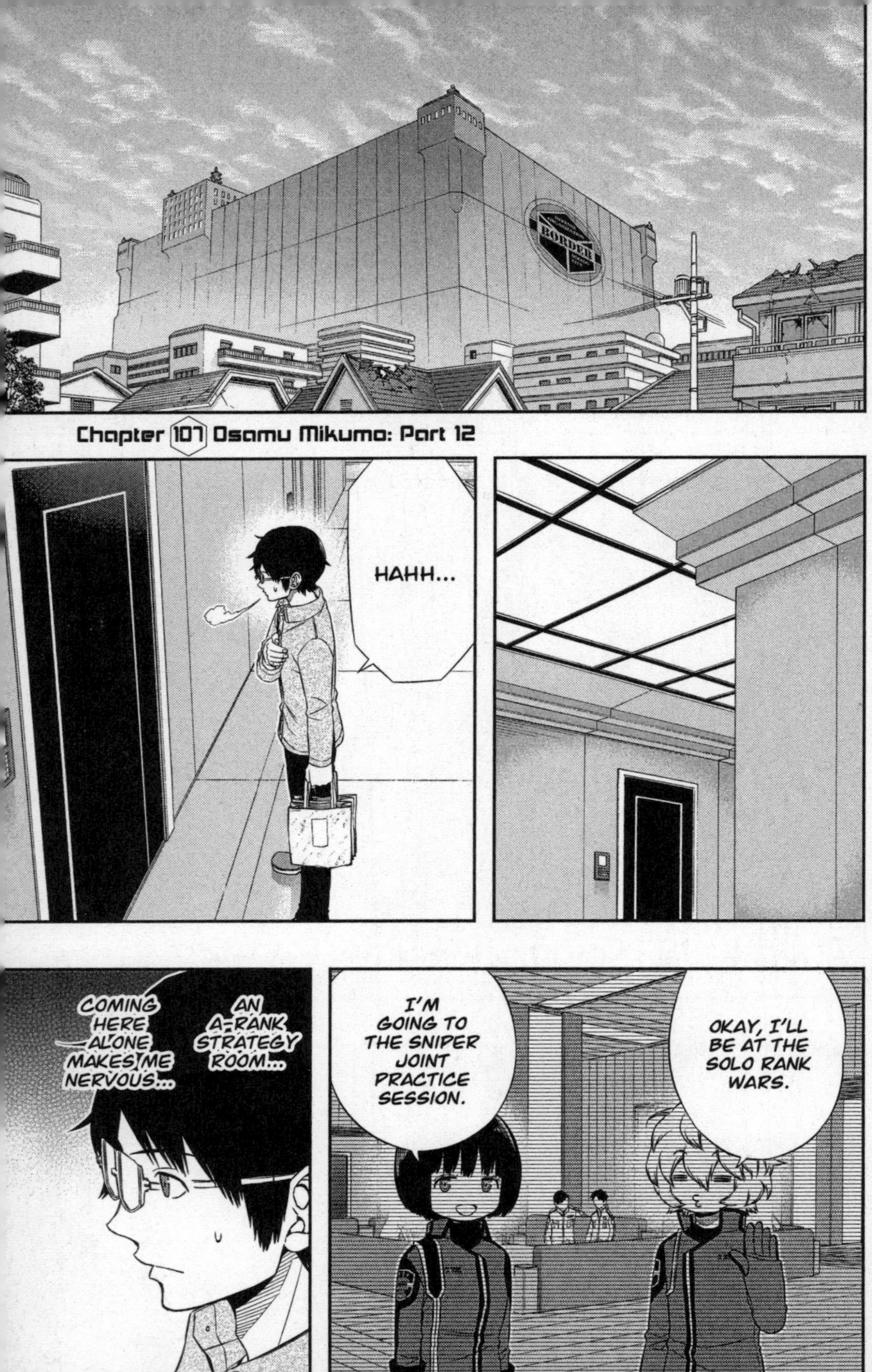
BORDER
Chapter 107 Osamu Mikumo: Part 12
HAHH...
OKAY, I'LL BE AT THE SOLO RANK WARS.
I'M GOING TO THE SNIPER JOINT PRACTICE SESSION.
AN A-RANK STRATEGY ROOM...
COMING HERE ALONE MAKES ME NERVOUS...

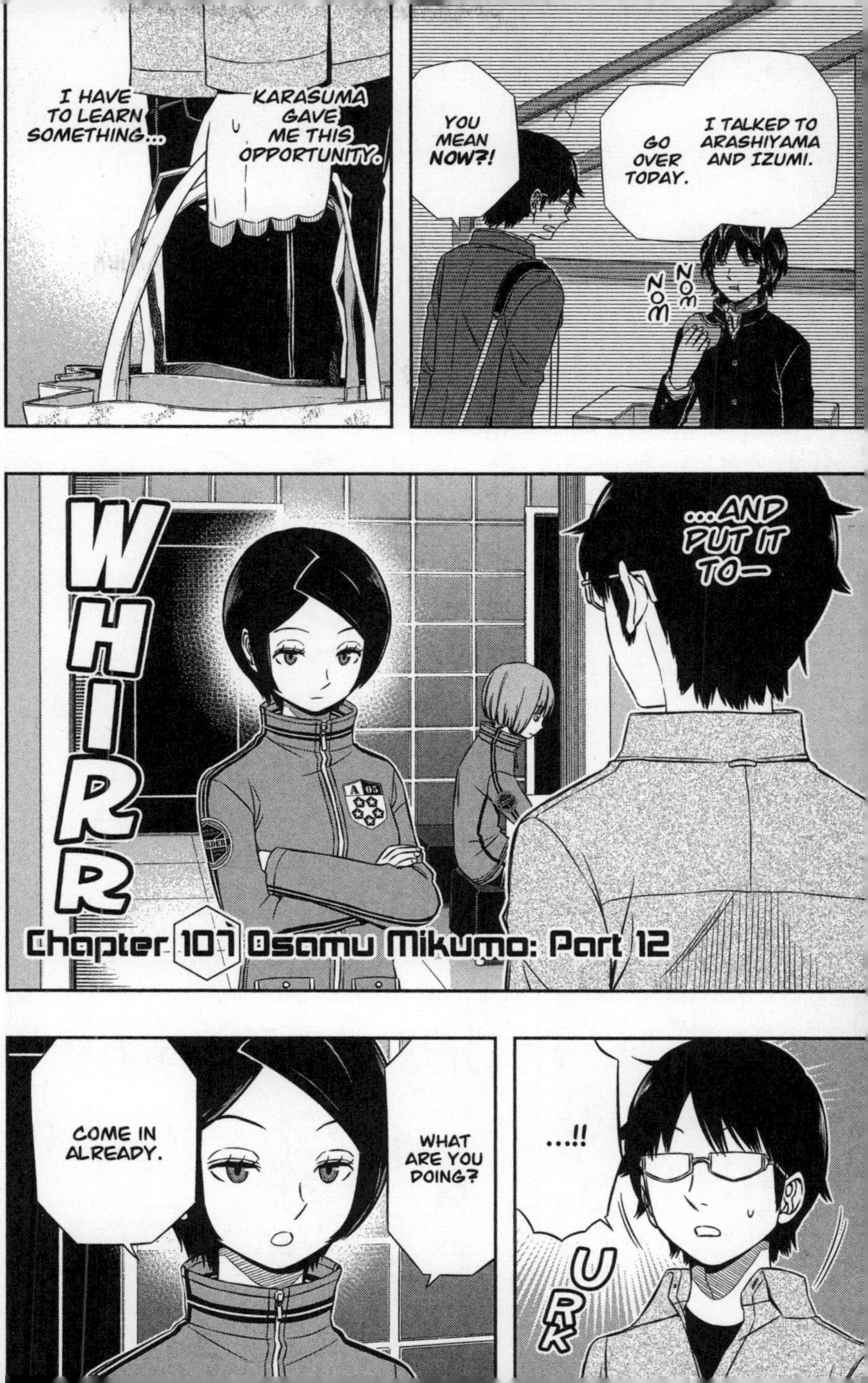
I TALKED TO ARASHIYAMA AND IZUMI.
GO OVER TODAY.
NOM NOM
YOU MEAN NOW?!
KARASUMA GAVE ME THIS OPPORTUNITY.
I HAVE TO LEARN SOMETHING...
...AND PUT IT TO—
WHIRR
Chapter 107 Osamu Mikumo: Part 12
...!!
URK
WHAT ARE YOU DOING?
COME IN ALREADY.

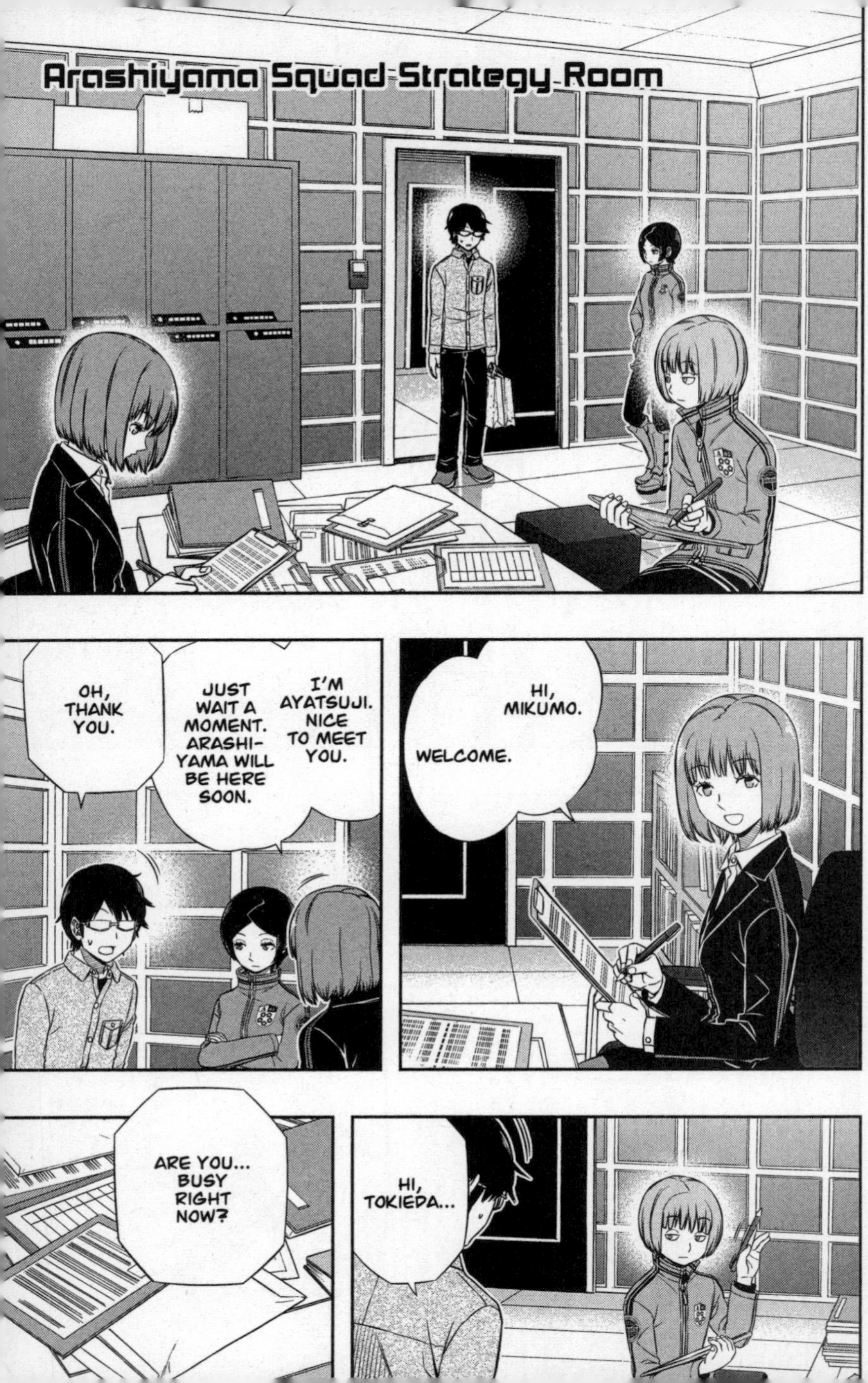
Arashiyama Squad Strategy Room
HI, MIKUMO.
WELCOME.
I'M AYATSUJI. NICE TO MEET YOU.
JUST WAIT A MOMENT. ARASHIYAMA WILL BE HERE SOON.
OH, THANK YOU.
HI, TOKIEDA...
ARE YOU... BUSY RIGHT NOW?

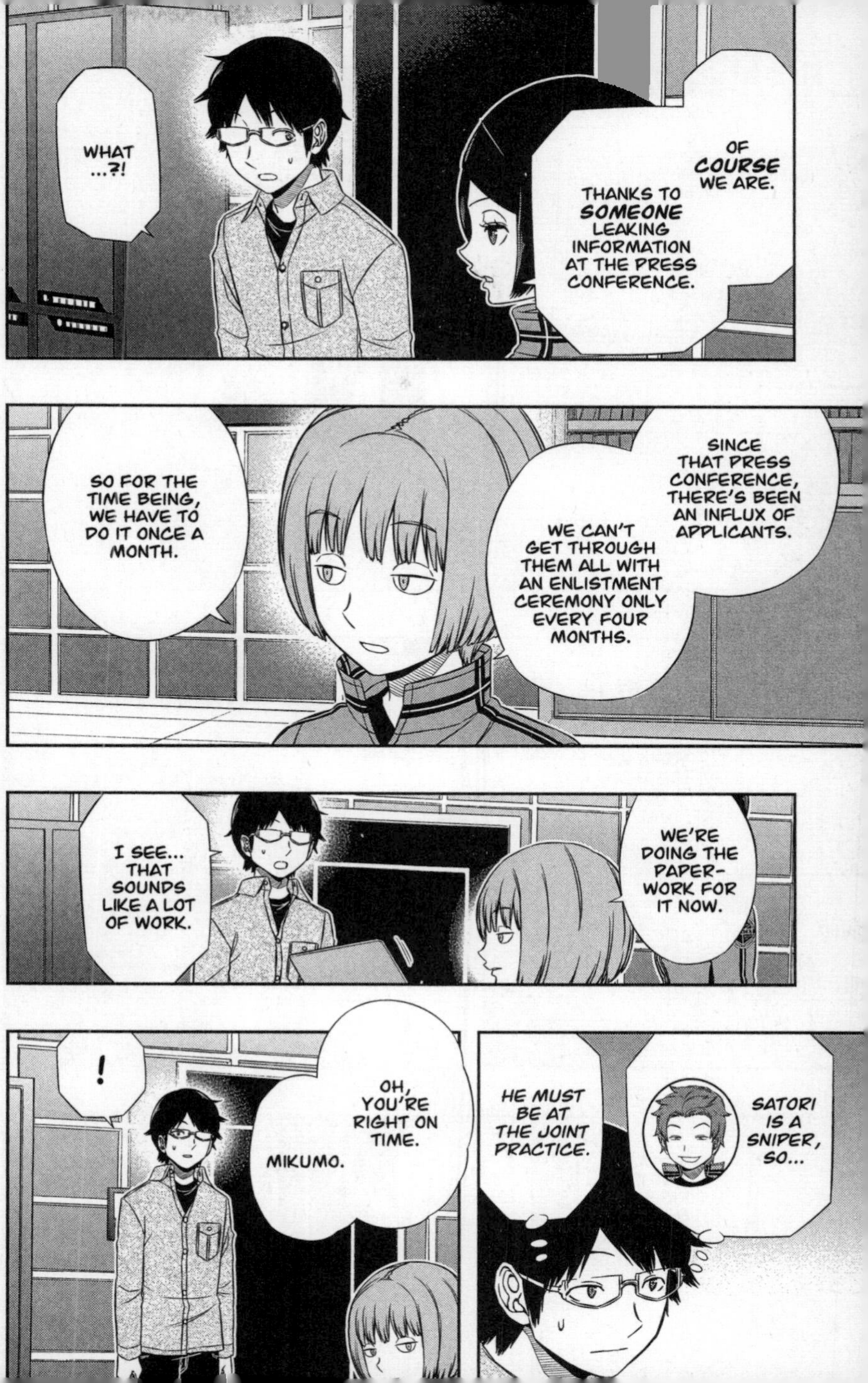
OF COURSE WE ARE.
THANKS TO SOMEONE LEAKING INFORMATION AT THE PRESS CONFERENCE.
WHAT ...?!
SINCE THAT PRESS CONFERENCE, THERE'S BEEN AN INFLUX OF APPLICANTS.
WE CAN'T GET THROUGH THEM ALL WITH AN ENLISTMENT CEREMONY ONLY EVERY FOUR MONTHS.
SO FOR THE TIME BEING, WE HAVE TO DO IT ONCE A MONTH.
WE'RE DOING THE PAPER-WORK FOR IT NOW.
I SEE... THAT SOUNDS LIKE A LOT OF WORK.
SATORI IS A SNIPER, SO...
HE MUST BE AT THE JOINT PRACTICE.
OH, YOU'RE RIGHT ON TIME.
MIKUMO.
!

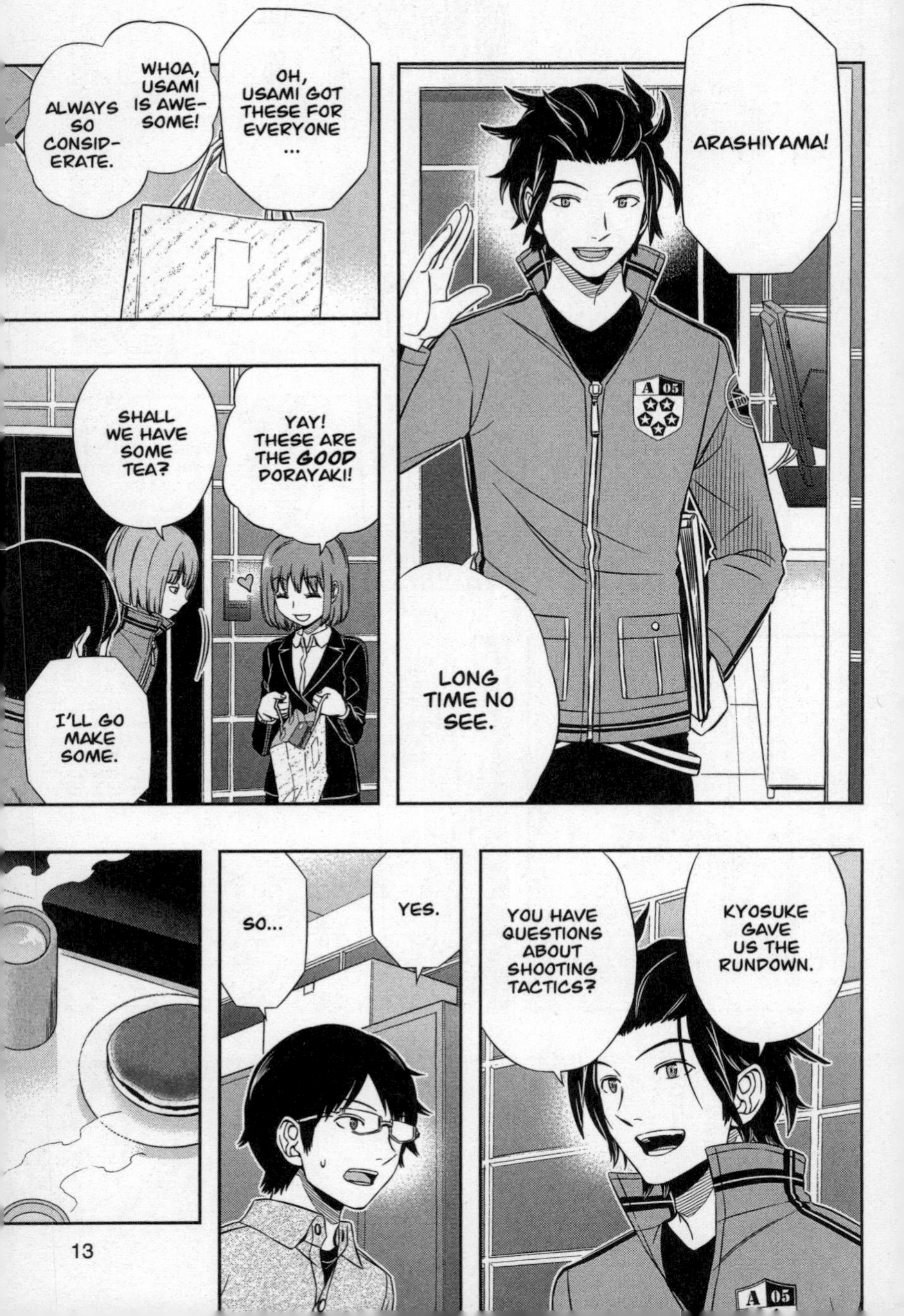
ARASHIYAMA!
LONG TIME NO SEE.
OH, USAMI GOT THESE FOR EVERYONE...
WHOA, USAMI IS AWE-SOME!
ALWAYS SO CONSID-ERATE.
YAY! THESE ARE THE GOOD DORAYAKI!
SHALL WE HAVE SOME TEA?
I'LL GO MAKE SOME.
KYOSUKE GAVE US THE RUNDOWN.
YOU HAVE QUESTIONS ABOUT SHOOTING TACTICS?
YES.
SO...

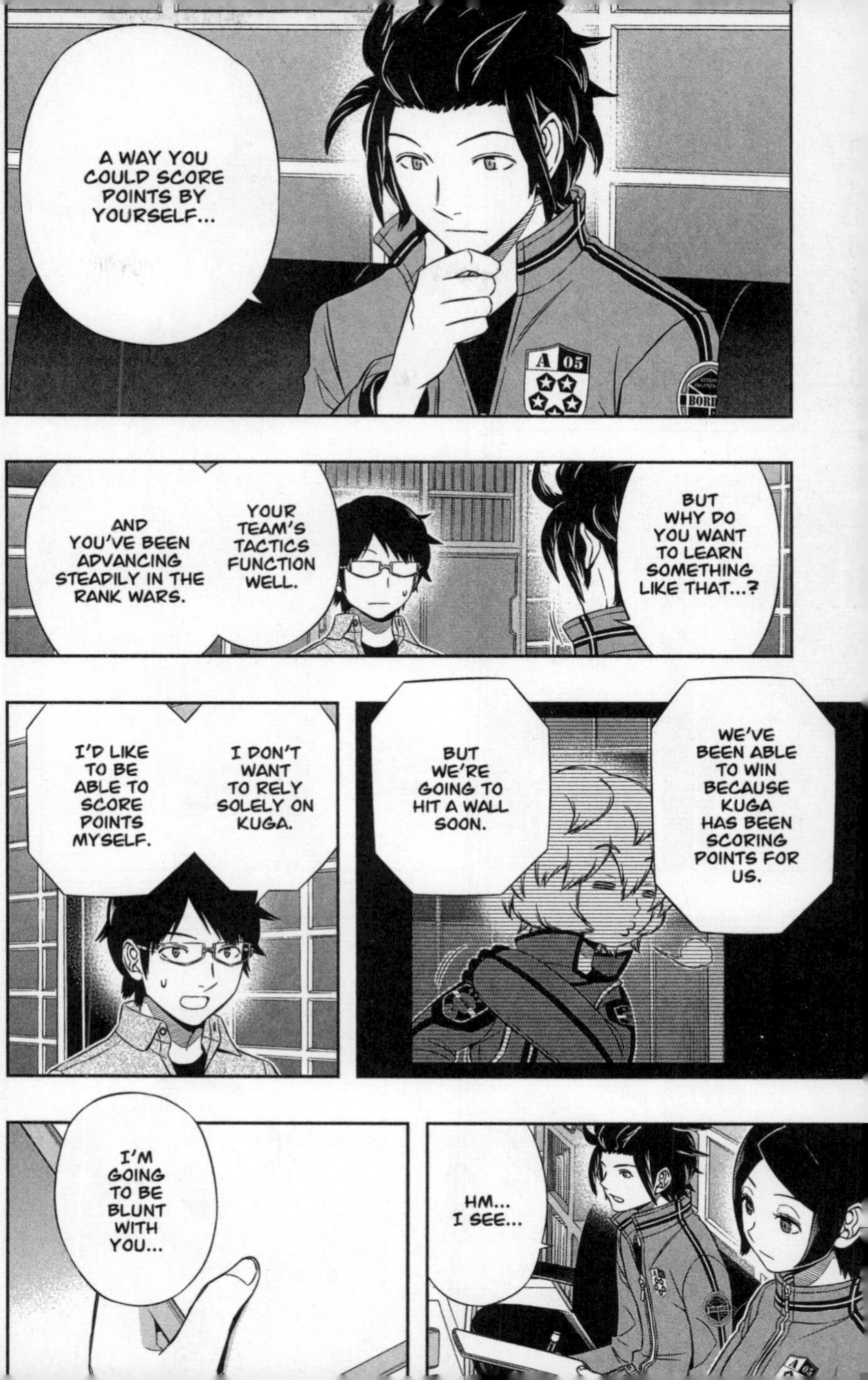
A WAY YOU COULD SCORE POINTS BY YOURSELF...
BUT WHY DO YOU WANT TO LEARN SOMETHING LIKE THAT...?
YOUR TEAM'S TACTICS FUNCTION WELL.
AND YOU'VE BEEN ADVANCING STEADILY IN THE RANK WARS.
WE'VE BEEN ABLE TO WIN BECAUSE KUGA HAS BEEN SCORING POINTS FOR US.
BUT WE'RE GOING TO HIT A WALL SOON.
I DON'T WANT TO RELY SOLELY ON KUGA.
I'D LIKE TO BE ABLE TO SCORE POINTS MYSELF.
HM... I SEE...
I'M GOING TO BE BLUNT WITH YOU...

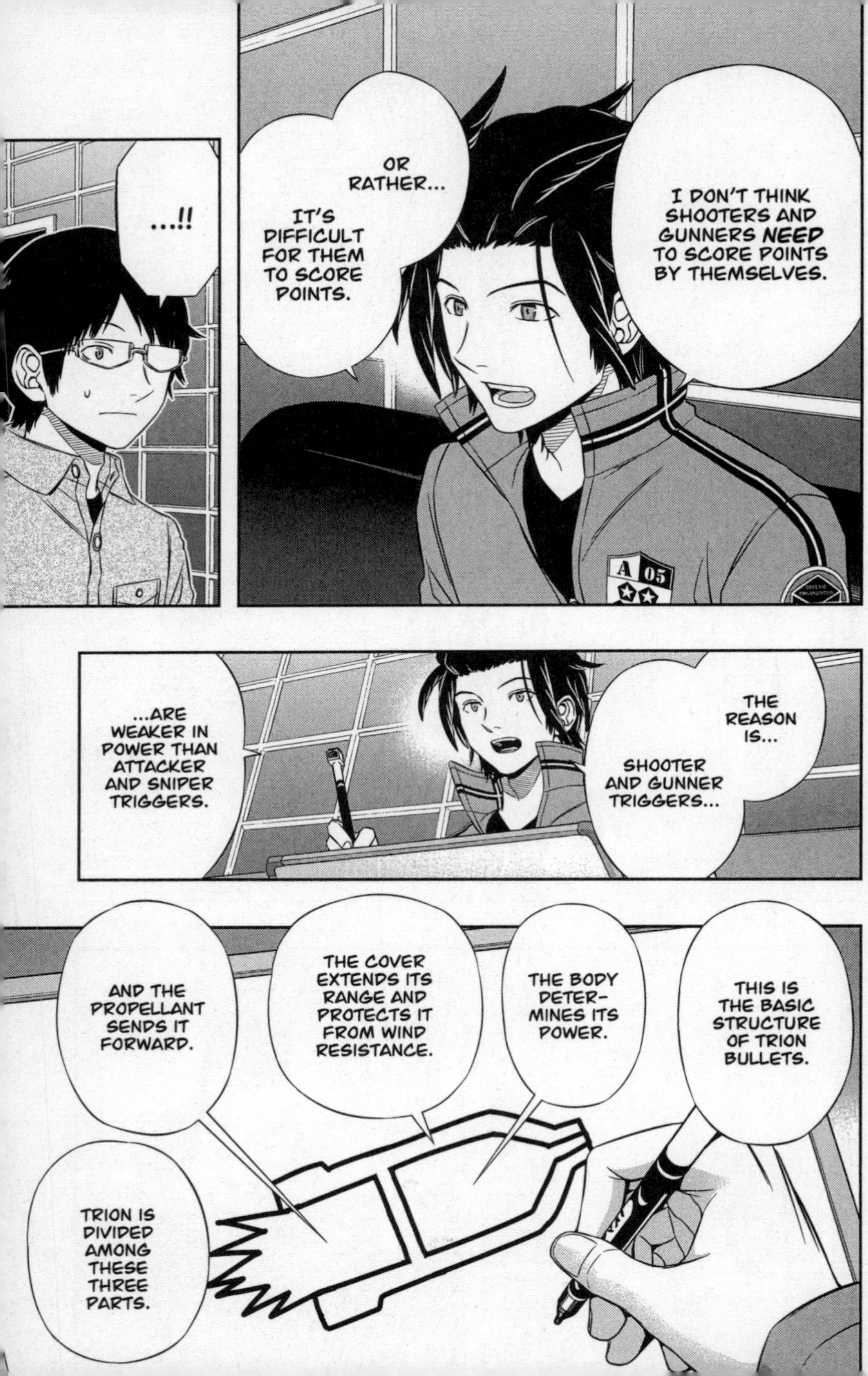
I DON'T THINK SHOOTERS AND GUNNERS NEED TO SCORE POINTS BY THEMSELVES.
OR RATHER...
IT'S DIFFICULT FOR THEM TO SCORE POINTS.
...!!
THE REASON IS...
SHOOTER AND GUNNER TRIGGERS...
...ARE WEAKER IN POWER THAN ATTACKER AND SNIPER TRIGGERS.
THIS IS THE BASIC STRUCTURE OF TRION BULLETS.
THE BODY DETER-MINES ITS POWER.
THE COVER EXTENDS ITS RANGE AND PROTECTS IT FROM WIND RESISTANCE.
AND THE PROPELLANT SENDS IT FORWARD.
TRION IS DIVIDED AMONG THESE THREE PARTS.

SO ATTACKERS CAN GET CLOSER THAN EVER BEFORE.

AND SHIELDS HAVE A HIGHER PERFORMANCE RATE THESE DAYS.

...THEY'RE WEAKER THAN BLADE TRIGGERS THAT FOCUS SOLELY ON USING TRION FOR POWER.

SINCE YOU'RE USING TRION FOR BOTH RANGE AND BULLET SPEED...

| Asteroid | Range | Speed | Power |
| Kogetsu | Hardness | Power | |

...SHE COULDN'T HAVE WON WITHOUT SUPPORT FROM HER TEAMMATES...

IN YOUR MATCH A COUPLE DAYS AGO...

...IF NASU HAD BEEN FORCED TO DIRECTLY FACE OFF AGAINST KO OR YUMA...

...AND YOU CAN PINPOINT YOUR ATTACKS.

WELL...

YOU CAN ATTACK FROM AFAR...

WHAT DO YOU THINK ARE THE STRENGTHS OF A SHOOTING TRIGGER?

SO, ANYWAY...

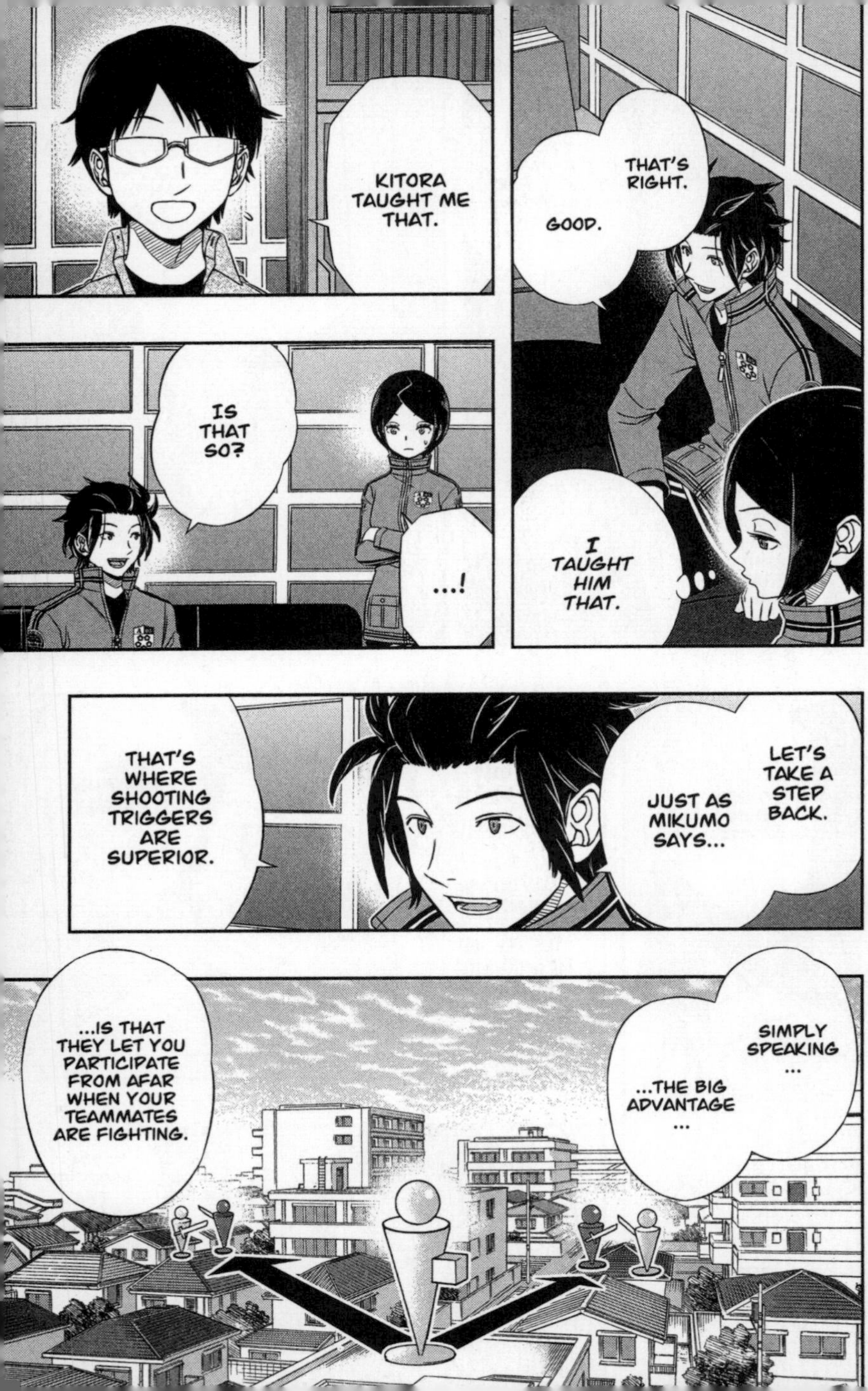
THAT'S RIGHT.
GOOD.
I TAUGHT HIM THAT.
KITORA TAUGHT ME THAT.
IS THAT SO?
...!
LET'S TAKE A STEP BACK.
JUST AS MIKUMO SAYS...
THAT'S WHERE SHOOTING TRIGGERS ARE SUPERIOR.
SIMPLY SPEAKING ...
...THE BIG ADVANTAGE ...
...IS THAT THEY LET YOU PARTICIPATE FROM AFAR WHEN YOUR TEAMMATES ARE FIGHTING.

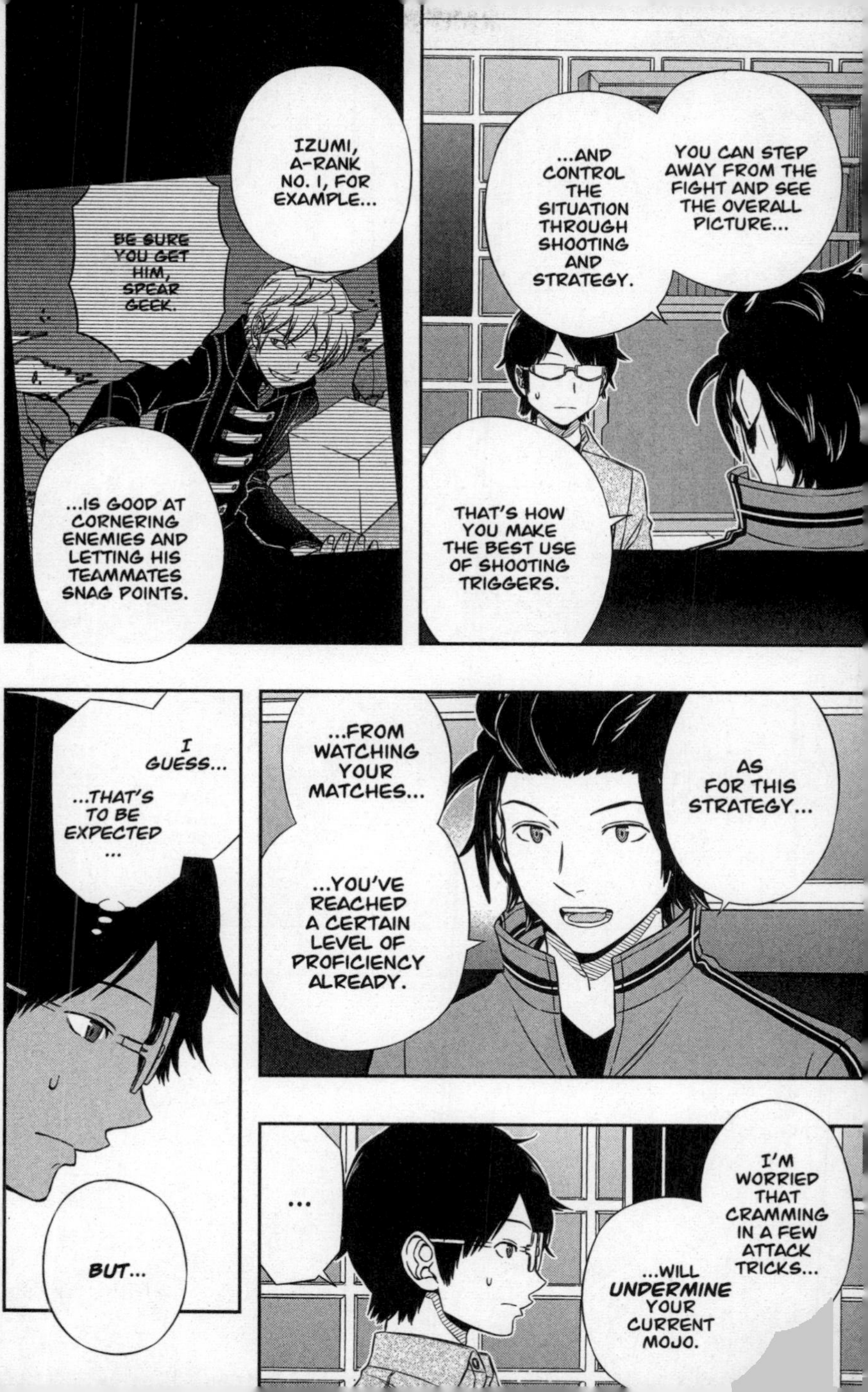
YOU CAN STEP AWAY FROM THE FIGHT AND SEE THE OVERALL PICTURE...
...AND CONTROL THE SITUATION THROUGH SHOOTING AND STRATEGY.
THAT'S HOW YOU MAKE THE BEST USE OF SHOOTING TRIGGERS.
IZUMI, A-RANK NO. 1, FOR EXAMPLE...
BE SURE YOU GET HIM, SPEAR GEEK.
...IS GOOD AT CORNERING ENEMIES AND LETTING HIS TEAMMATES SNAG POINTS.
AS FOR THIS STRATEGY...
...FROM WATCHING YOUR MATCHES...
...YOU'VE REACHED A CERTAIN LEVEL OF PROFICIENCY ALREADY.
I'M WORRIED THAT CRAMMING IN A FEW ATTACK TRICKS...
...WILL *UNDERMINE* YOUR CURRENT MOJO.
...
I GUESS...
...THAT'S TO BE EXPECTED...
BUT...

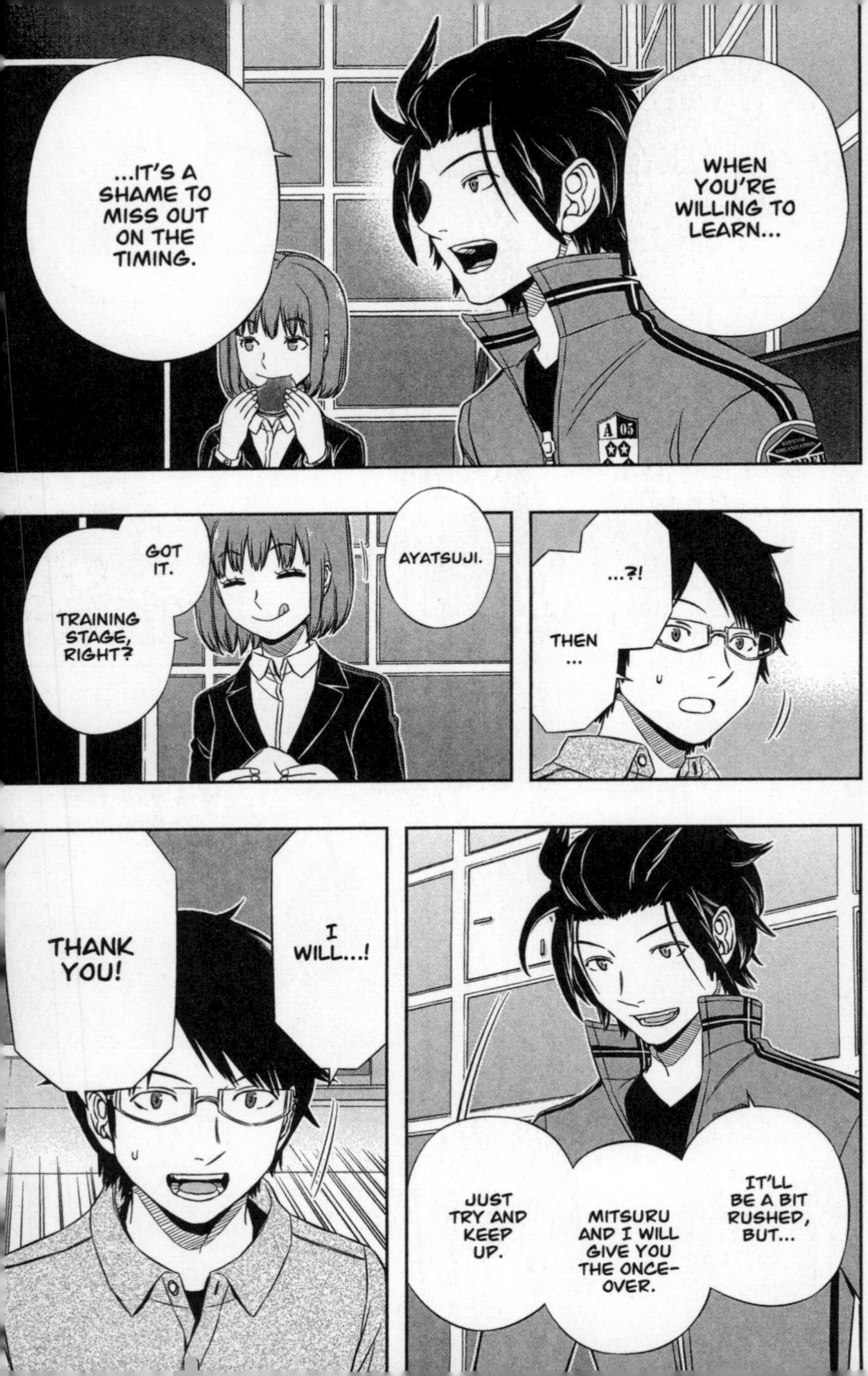
WHEN YOU'RE WILLING TO LEARN...
...IT'S A SHAME TO MISS OUT ON THE TIMING.
...?!
THEN ...
AYATSUJI.
GOT IT.
TRAINING STAGE, RIGHT?
IT'LL BE A BIT RUSHED, BUT...
MITSURU AND I WILL GIVE YOU THE ONCE-OVER.
JUST TRY AND KEEP UP.
I WILL...!
THANK YOU!

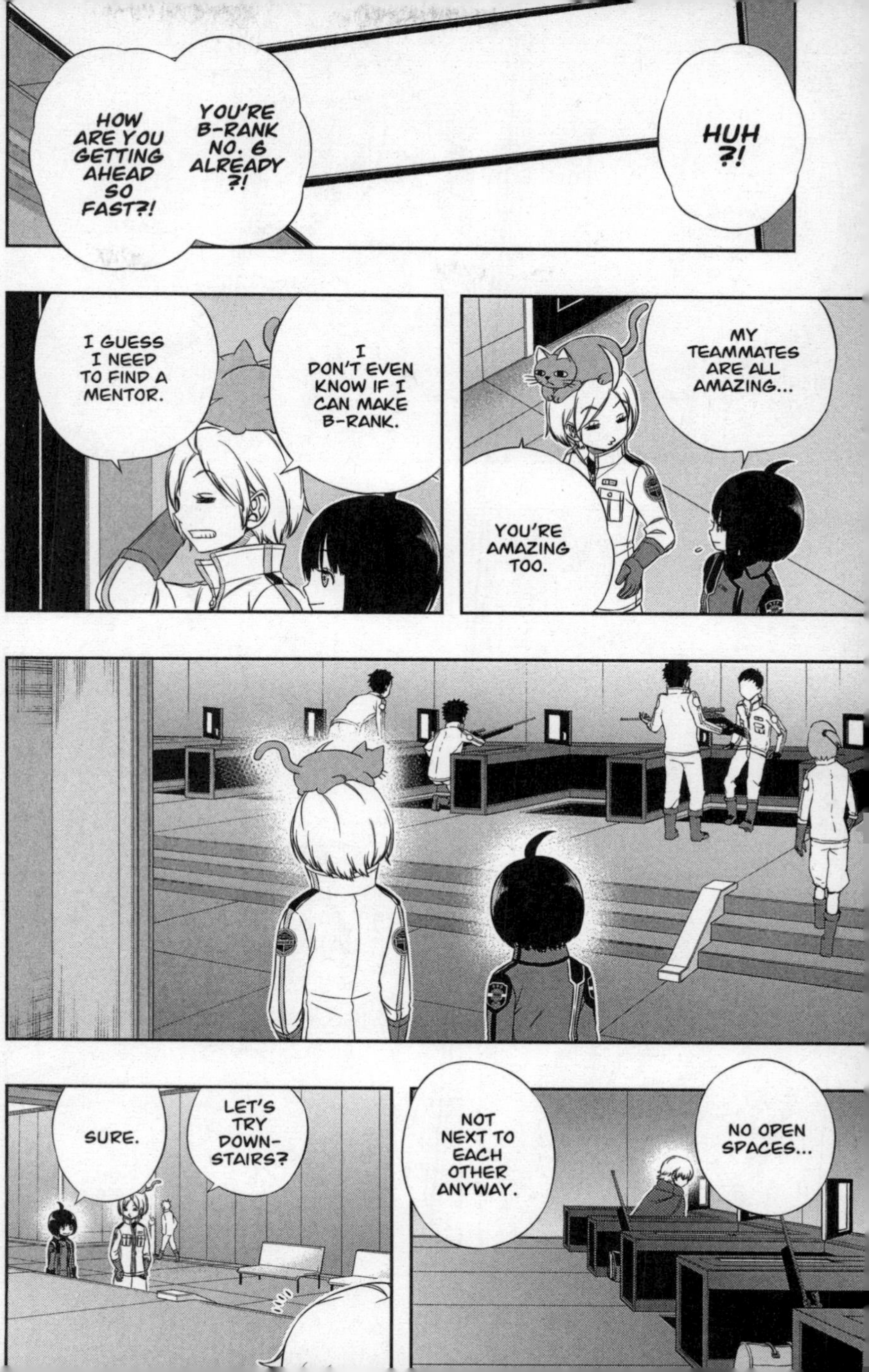
HUH ?!
YOU'RE B-RANK NO. 6 ALREADY ?!
HOW ARE YOU GETTING AHEAD SO FAST?!
MY TEAMMATES ARE ALL AMAZING...
YOU'RE AMAZING TOO.
I DON'T EVEN KNOW IF I CAN MAKE B-RANK.
I GUESS I NEED TO FIND A MENTOR.
NO OPEN SPACES...
NOT NEXT TO EACH OTHER ANYWAY.
LET'S TRY DOWN-STAIRS?
SURE.

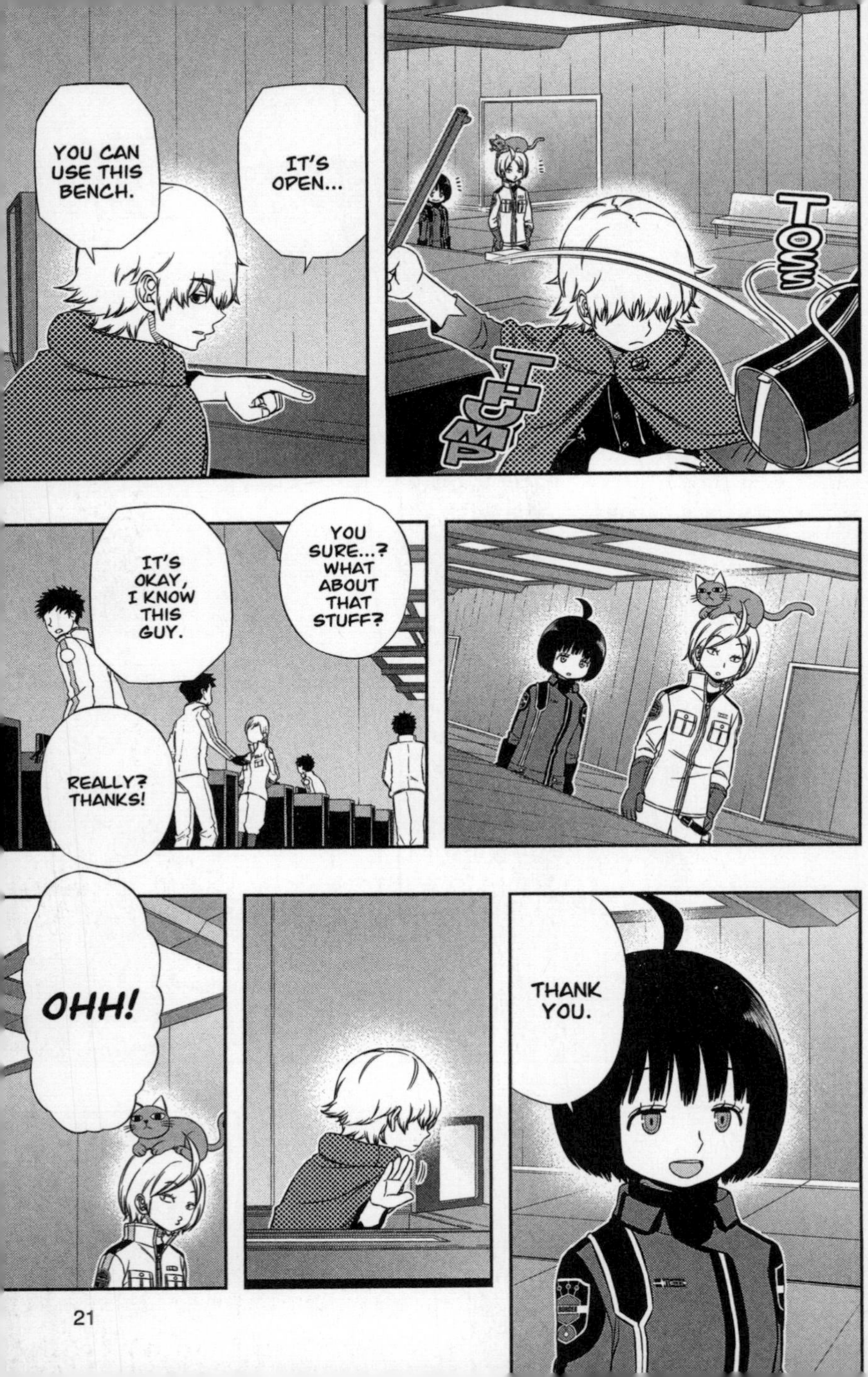
TOSS
THUMP
IT'S OPEN...
YOU CAN USE THIS BENCH.
YOU SURE...? WHAT ABOUT THAT STUFF?
IT'S OKAY, I KNOW THIS GUY.
REALLY? THANKS!
THANK YOU.
OHH!

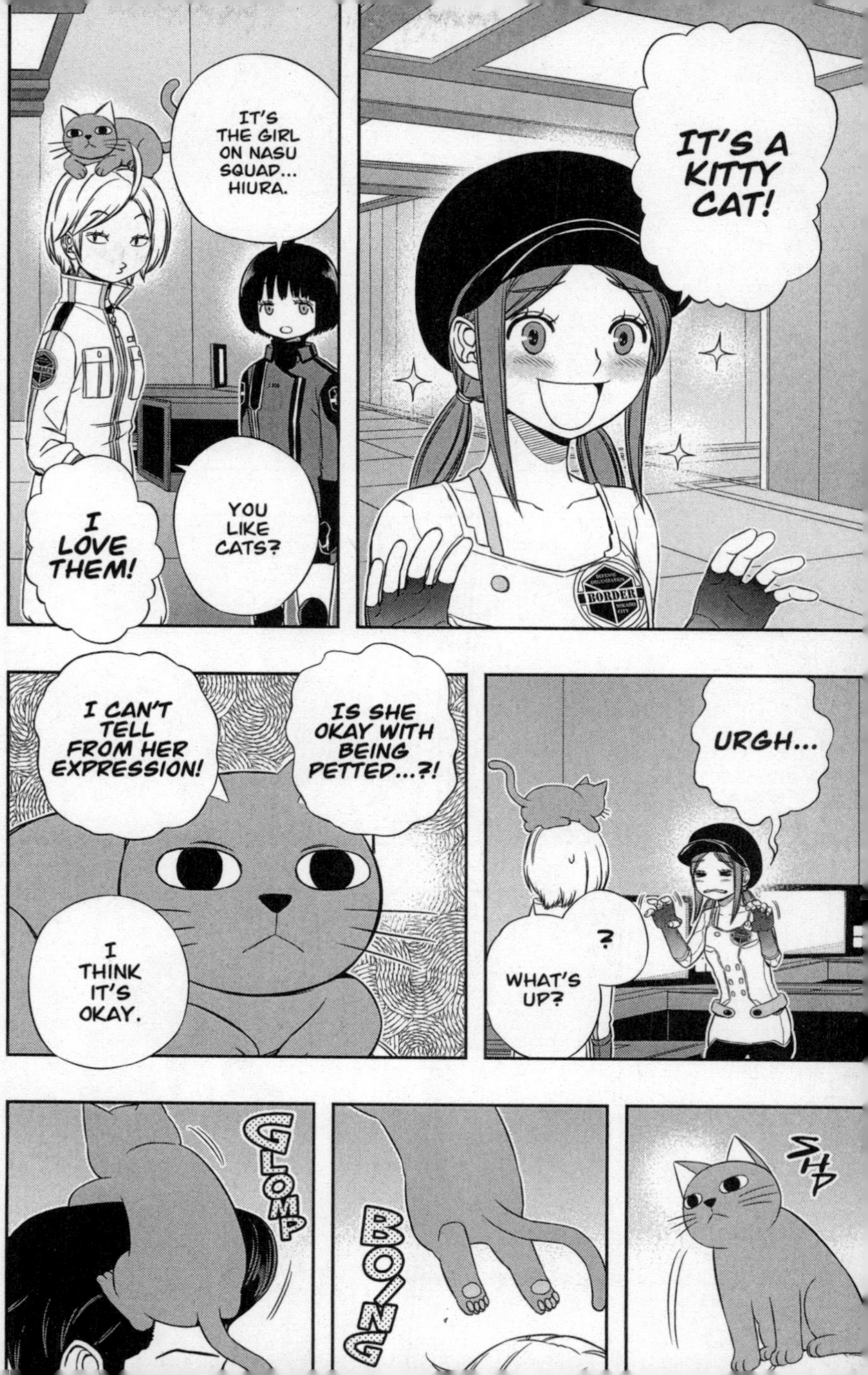
IT'S A KITTY CAT!
IT'S THE GIRL ON NASU SQUAD... HIURA.
YOU LIKE CATS?
I LOVE THEM!
URGH...
?
WHAT'S UP?
IS SHE OKAY WITH BEING PETTED...?!
I CAN'T TELL FROM HER EXPRESSION!
I THINK IT'S OKAY.
SHP
BOING
GLOMP

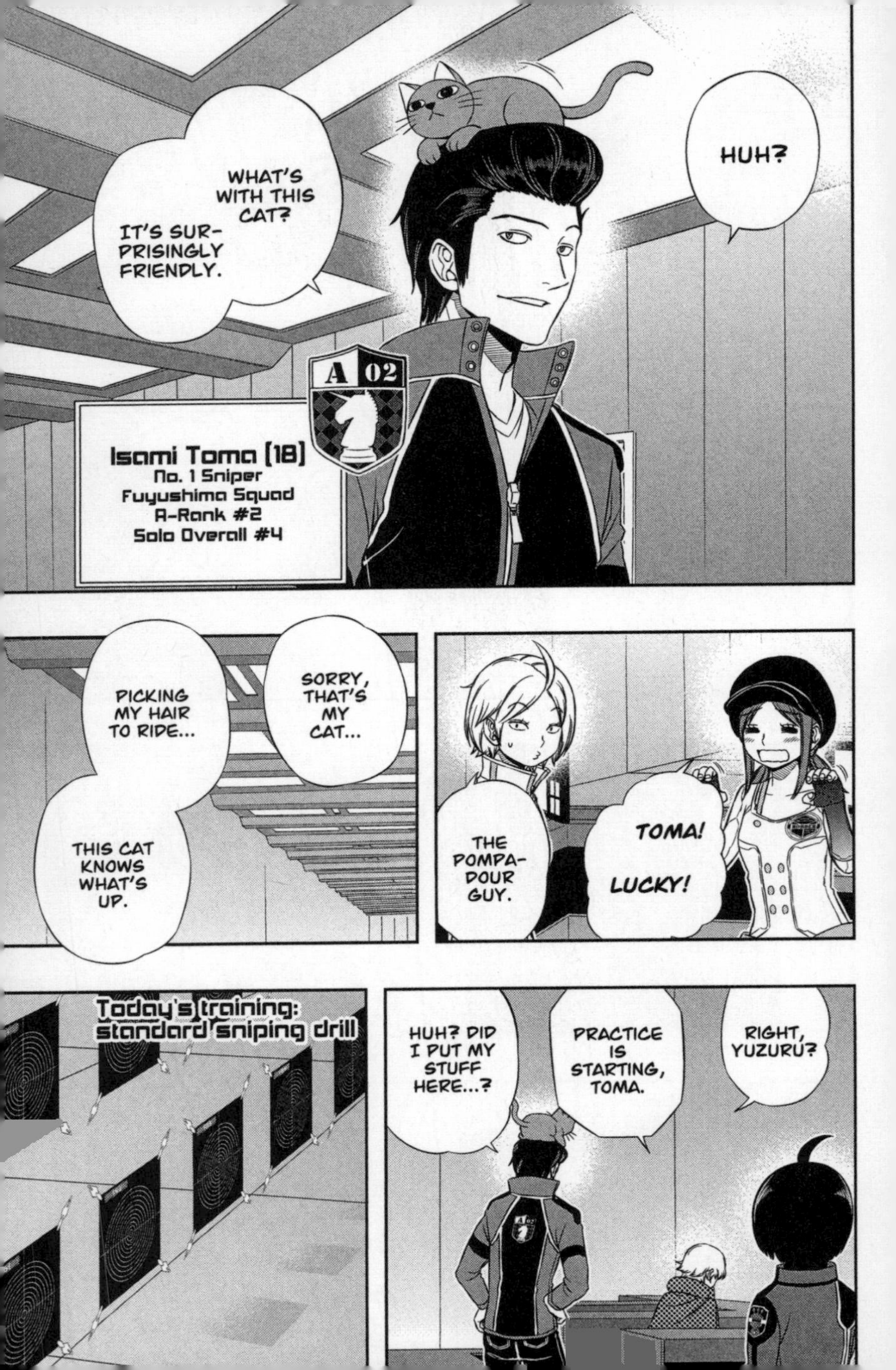
HUH?
WHAT'S WITH THIS CAT?
IT'S SUR-PRISINGLY FRIENDLY.
A 02
Isami Toma [18]
No. 1 Sniper
Fuyushima Squad
A-Rank #2
Solo Overall #4
TOMA!
LUCKY!
THE POMPA-DOUR GUY.
SORRY, THAT'S MY CAT...
PICKING MY HAIR TO RIDE...
THIS CAT KNOWS WHAT'S UP.
RIGHT, YUZURU?
PRACTICE IS STARTING, TOMA.
HUH? DID I PUT MY STUFF HERE...?
Today's training: standard sniping drill

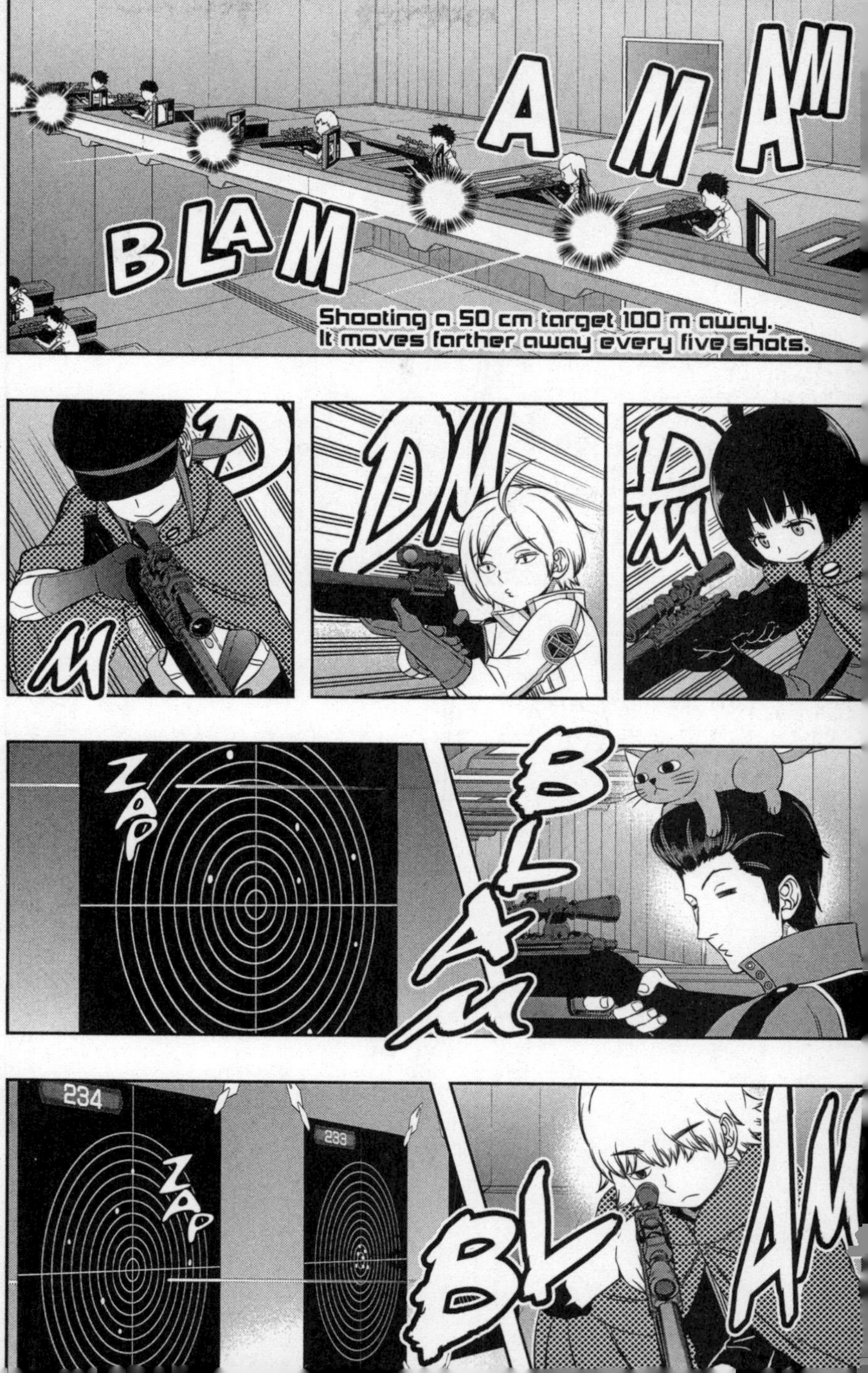

AMAM
BLAM
Shooting a 50 cm target 100 m away.
It moves farther away every five shots.
DM
DM
DM
BLAM
ZAP
BLAM
233
ZAP
234

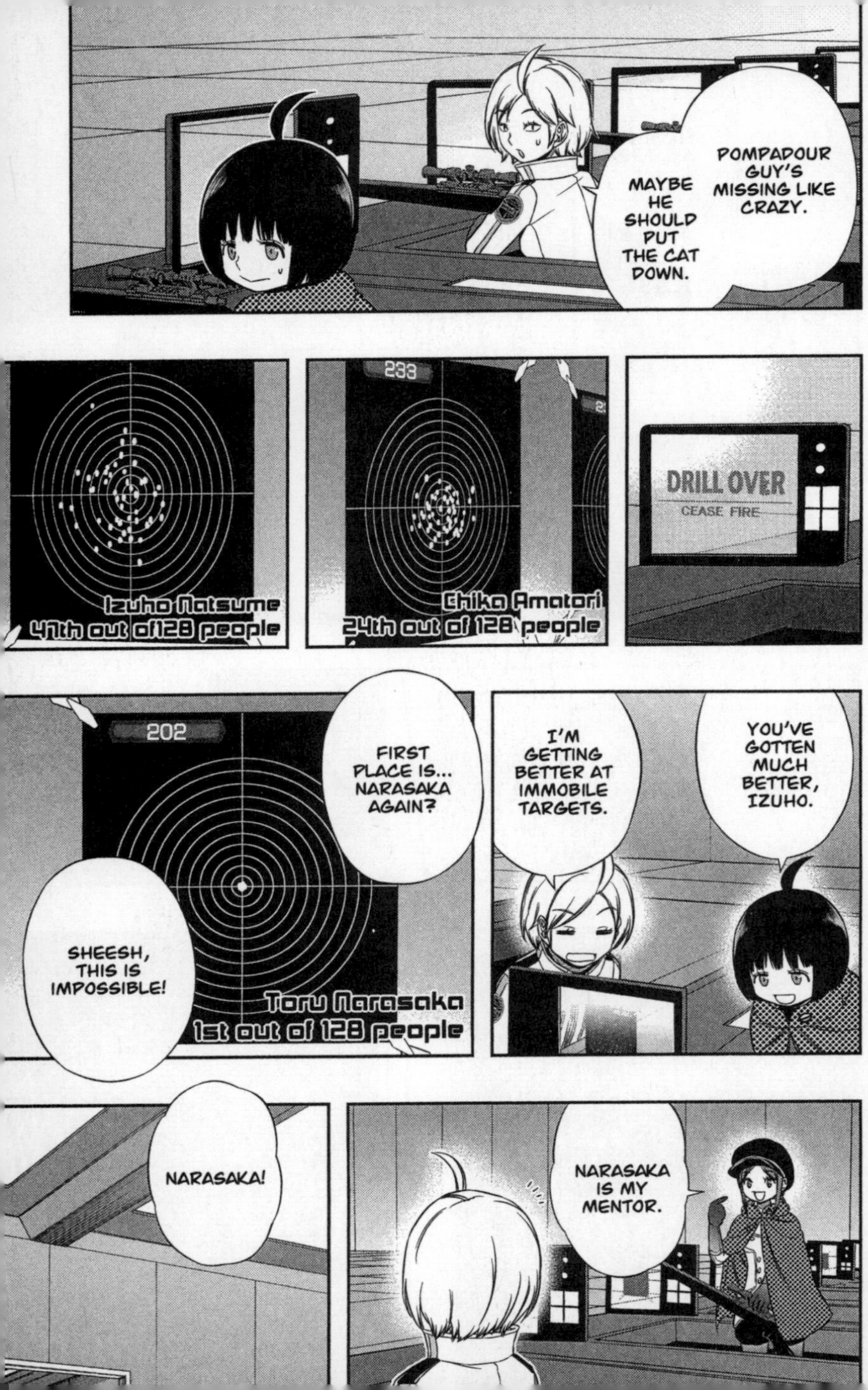
POMPADOUR GUY'S MISSING LIKE CRAZY.
MAYBE HE SHOULD PUT THE CAT DOWN.
DRILL OVER
CEASE FIRE
233
Chika Amatori
24th out of 128 people
Izuho Natsume
47th out of128 people
YOU'VE GOTTEN MUCH BETTER, IZUHO.
I'M GETTING BETTER AT IMMOBILE TARGETS.
FIRST PLACE IS... NARASAKA AGAIN?
202
Toru Narasaka
1st out of 128 people
SHEESH, THIS IS IMPOSSIBLE!
NARASAKA IS MY MENTOR.
NARASAKA!

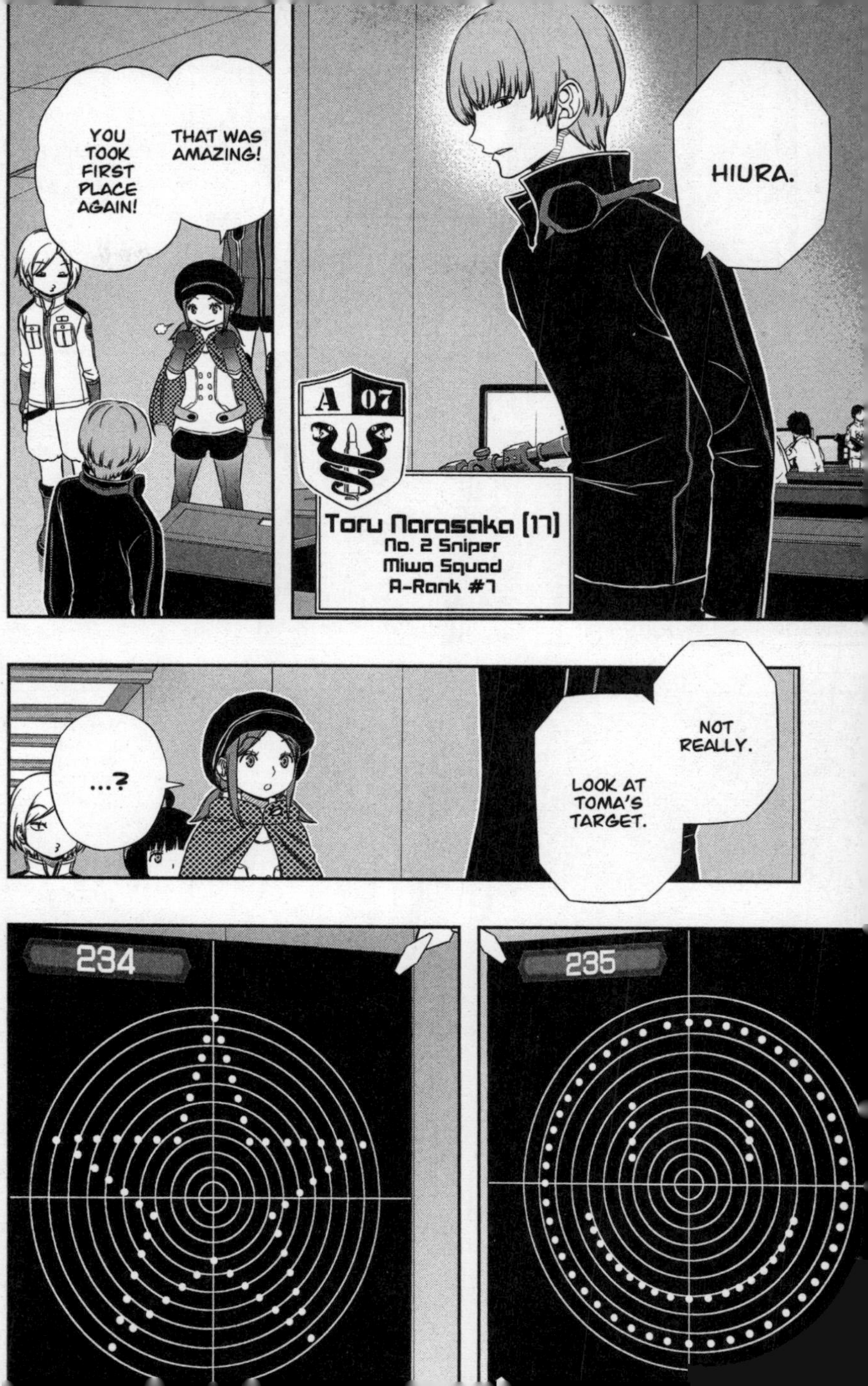
HIURA.
Toru Narasaka [17]
No. 2 Sniper
Miwa Squad
A-Rank #7
THAT WAS AMAZING!
YOU TOOK FIRST PLACE AGAIN!
NOT REALLY.
LOOK AT TOMA'S TARGET.
...?
235
234

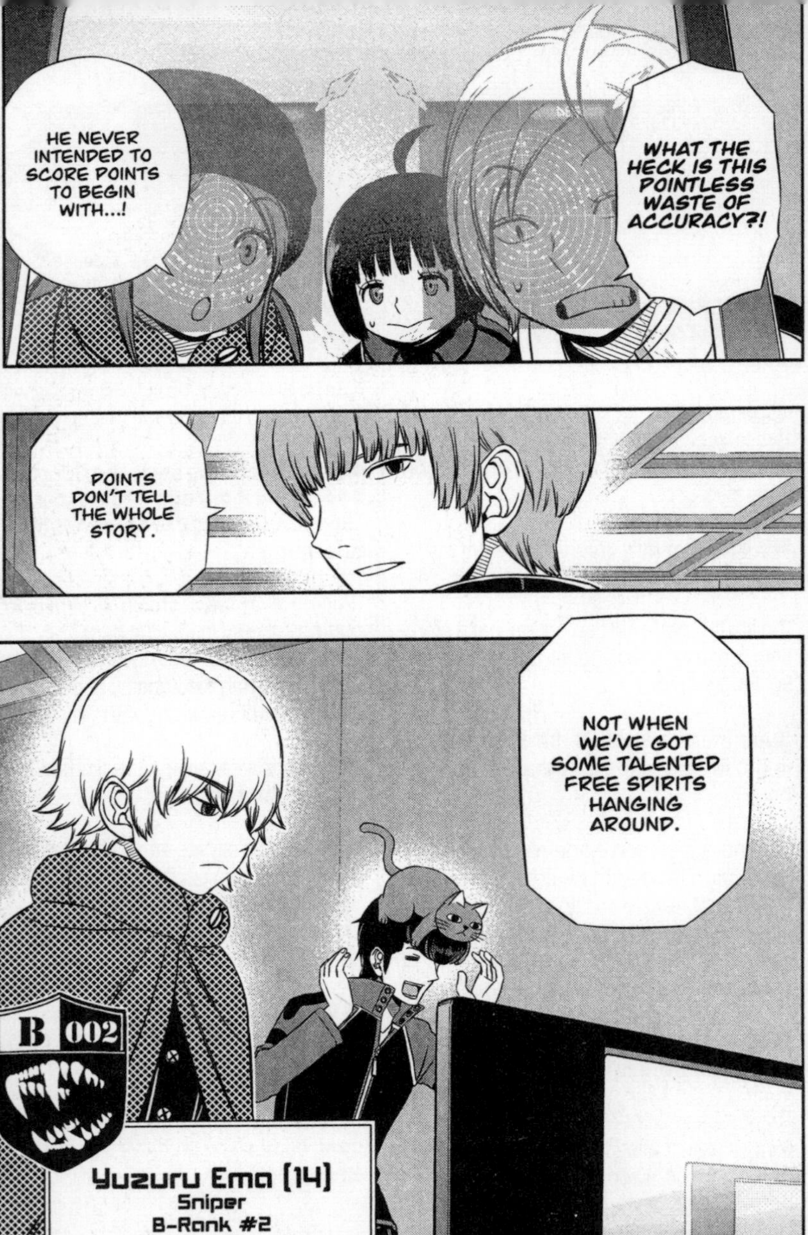

WHAT THE HECK IS THIS POINTLESS WASTE OF ACCURACY?!
HE NEVER INTENDED TO SCORE POINTS TO BEGIN WITH...!
POINTS DON'T TELL THE WHOLE STORY.
NOT WHEN WE'VE GOT SOME TALENTED FREE SPIRITS HANGING AROUND.
B 002
Yuzuru Ema (14)
Sniper
B-Rank #2
Kageura Squad

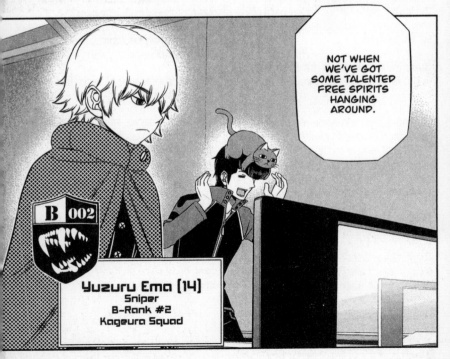

Q&A: Part 10

Finally...

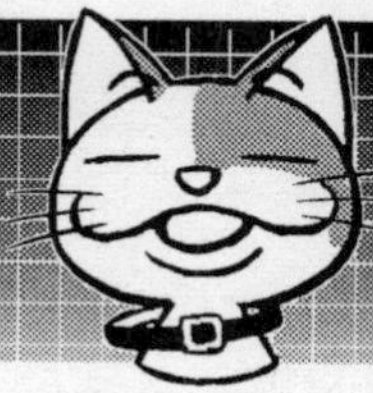

■In general, do people who use Trion bodies not need to sleep but still need food?

All people who use Trion bodies need rest. This is because the brain gets tired and the Trion gland doesn't recover while the Trion body is in use.

■Is the Raygust's shield mode a separate Trigger?

The shield mode isn't an option, but a standard feature of the Raygust. It doesn't take up a Trigger slot.

■Are there individual differences in the time it takes to rebuild a Trion body?

The more Trion someone has (meaning more Trion is used in battle), the bigger the cost of reconstructing the combat body, so it takes longer. Chika takes a long time while Osamu can return to battle in a relatively short time (1–2 hours).

■What do agents do on days off when they don't have missions or school?

They practice in individual Rank Wars, study logs, get absorbed in their hobbies, get depressed, sleep, think about what to do with their money, get overwhelmed by assignments, play, dance, visit graves and daydream about people they like.

■Was Satori punished for the hole Chika shot through the wall with the Ibis?

Azuma and Arashiyama followed up with Mr. Kinuta, so it ended with a slap on the wrist.

■How is "putting away the Scorpion and taking it out again" different from "dematerializing the Kogetsu and reforming it"?

"Putting away the Scorpion" is similar to putting Kogetsu in its scabbard. The Scorpion is lighter and doesn't get in the way. Dematerializing the Kogetsu is deactivating the sword entirely along with the scabbard.

■From how far away can Sniper Triggers hit their targets?

For immobile targets and using the Egret, precise shooters such as Narasaka and Hanzaki can probably hit a target from 1 kilometer away. The Ibis and the Lightning have shorter ranges.

■Yuma doesn't have to sleep since his body is made out of Trion (chapter 94) but does he get hungry?

He needs nutrients for life support for his dying body, so he probably eats more than other people.

■ I sometimes answer questions I get in my fan mail on my official Twitter feed. The more followers I get, the happier my new editor gets! **World Trigger Official Twitter Account: @W_Trigger_off**

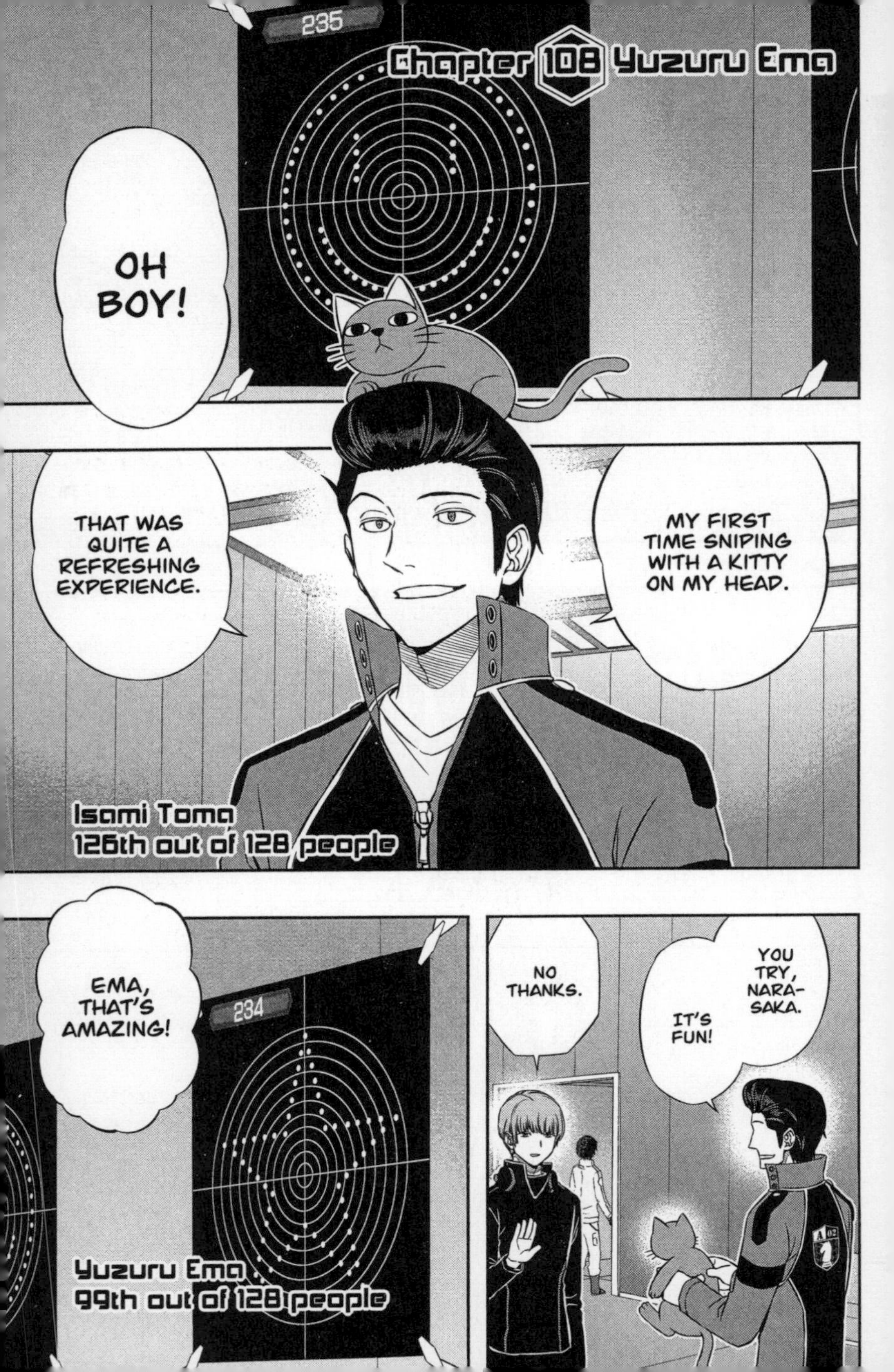
235
Chapter 108 Yuzuru Ema
OH BOY!
MY FIRST TIME SNIPING WITH A KITTY ON MY HEAD.
THAT WAS QUITE A REFRESHING EXPERIENCE.
Isami Toma
126th out of 128 people
YOU TRY, NARA-SAKA.
IT'S FUN!
NO THANKS.
EMA, THAT'S AMAZING!
234
Yuzuru Ema
99th out of 128 people

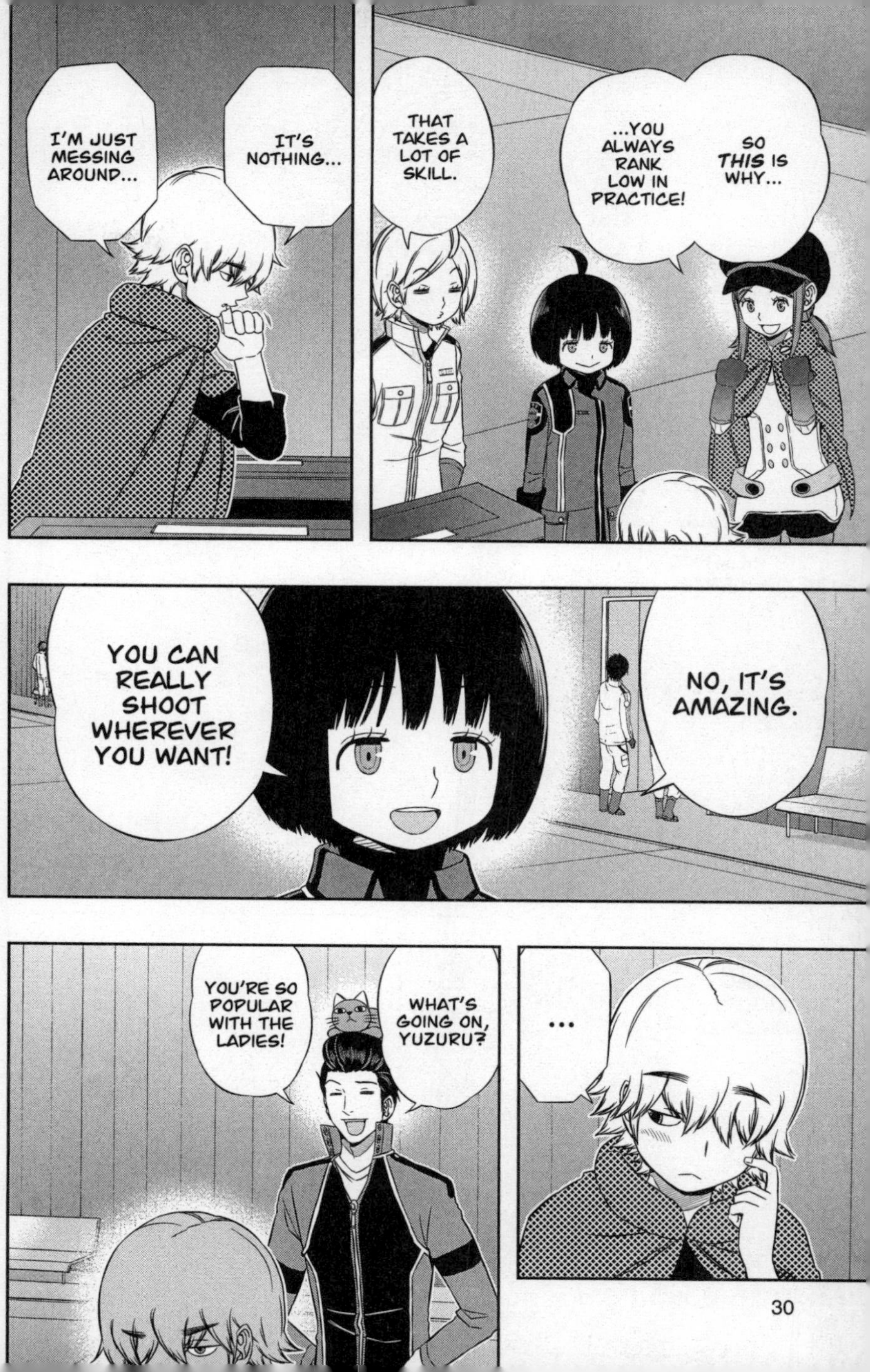
SO THIS IS WHY...
...YOU ALWAYS RANK LOW IN PRACTICE!
THAT TAKES A LOT OF SKILL.
IT'S NOTHING...
I'M JUST MESSING AROUND...
NO, IT'S AMAZING.
YOU CAN REALLY SHOOT WHEREVER YOU WANT!
...
WHAT'S GOING ON, YUZURU?
YOU'RE SO POPULAR WITH THE LADIES!

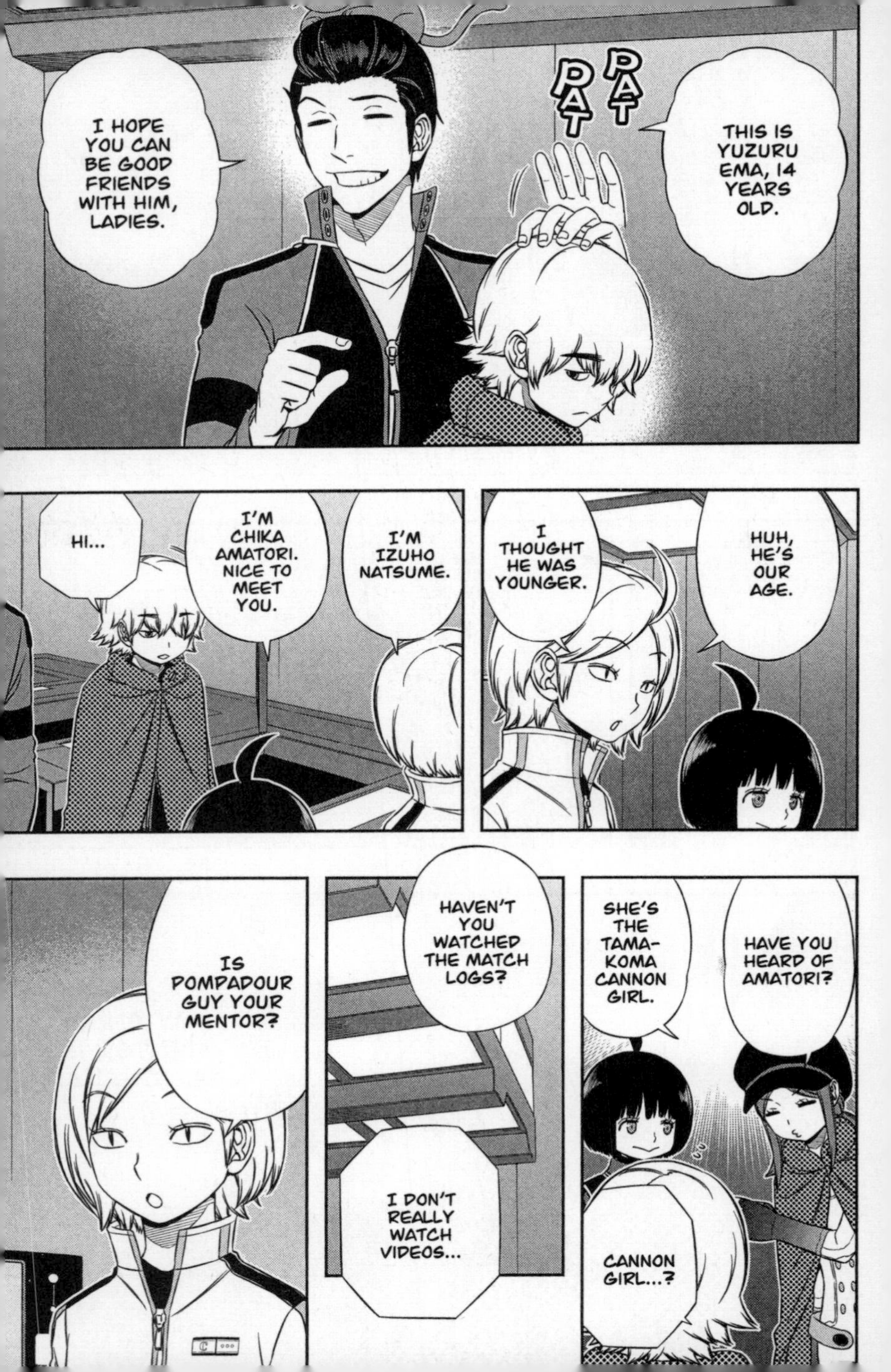
PAT PAT
THIS IS YUZURU EMA, 14 YEARS OLD.
I HOPE YOU CAN BE GOOD FRIENDS WITH HIM, LADIES.
HUH, HE'S OUR AGE.
I THOUGHT HE WAS YOUNGER.
I'M IZUHO NATSUME.
I'M CHIKA AMATORI. NICE TO MEET YOU.
HI...
HAVE YOU HEARD OF AMATORI?
SHE'S THE TAMA-KOMA CANNON GIRL.
CANNON GIRL...?
HAVEN'T YOU WATCHED THE MATCH LOGS?
I DON'T REALLY WATCH VIDEOS...
IS POMPADOUR GUY YOUR MENTOR?

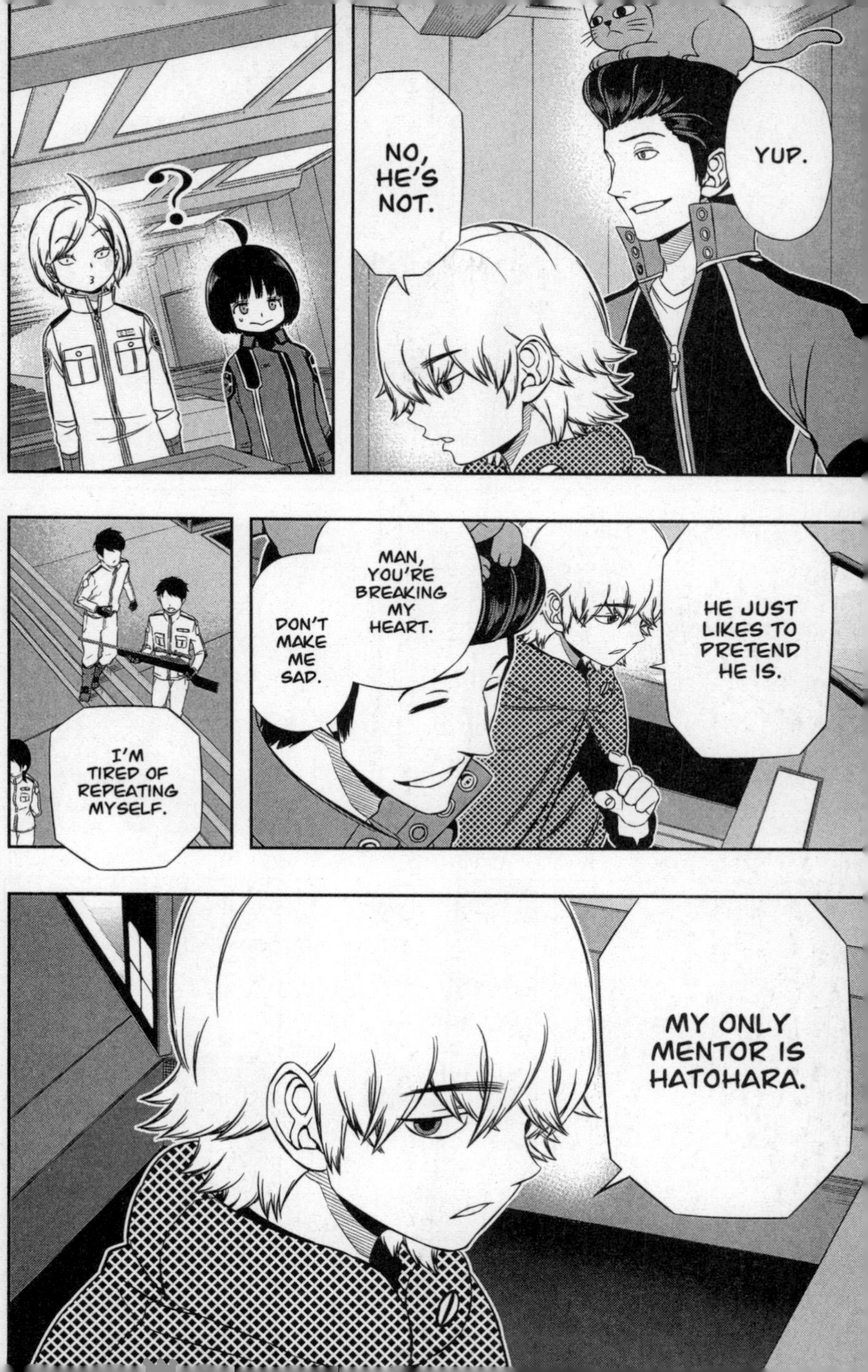
YUP.
NO, HE'S NOT.
?
HE JUST LIKES TO PRETEND HE IS.
MAN, YOU'RE BREAKING MY HEART.
DON'T MAKE ME SAD.
I'M TIRED OF REPEATING MYSELF.
MY ONLY MENTOR IS HATOHARA.

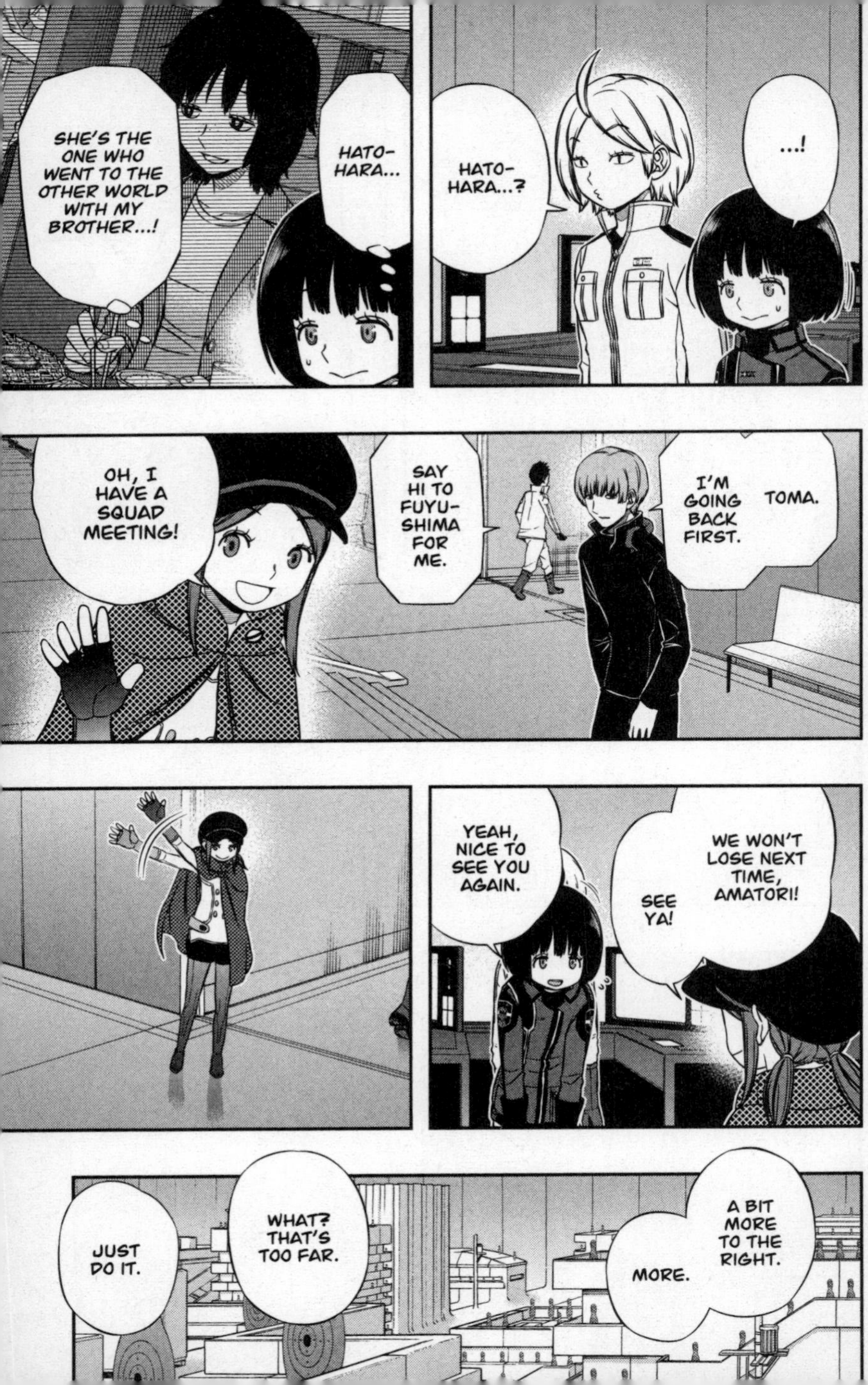
...!
HATO-HARA...?
HATO-HARA...
SHE'S THE ONE WHO WENT TO THE OTHER WORLD WITH MY BROTHER...!
TOMA.
I'M GOING BACK FIRST.
SAY HI TO FUYU-SHIMA FOR ME.
OH, I HAVE A SQUAD MEETING!
WE WON'T LOSE NEXT TIME, AMATORI!
SEE YA!
YEAH, NICE TO SEE YOU AGAIN.
A BIT MORE TO THE RIGHT.
MORE.
WHAT? THAT'S TOO FAR.
JUST DO IT.

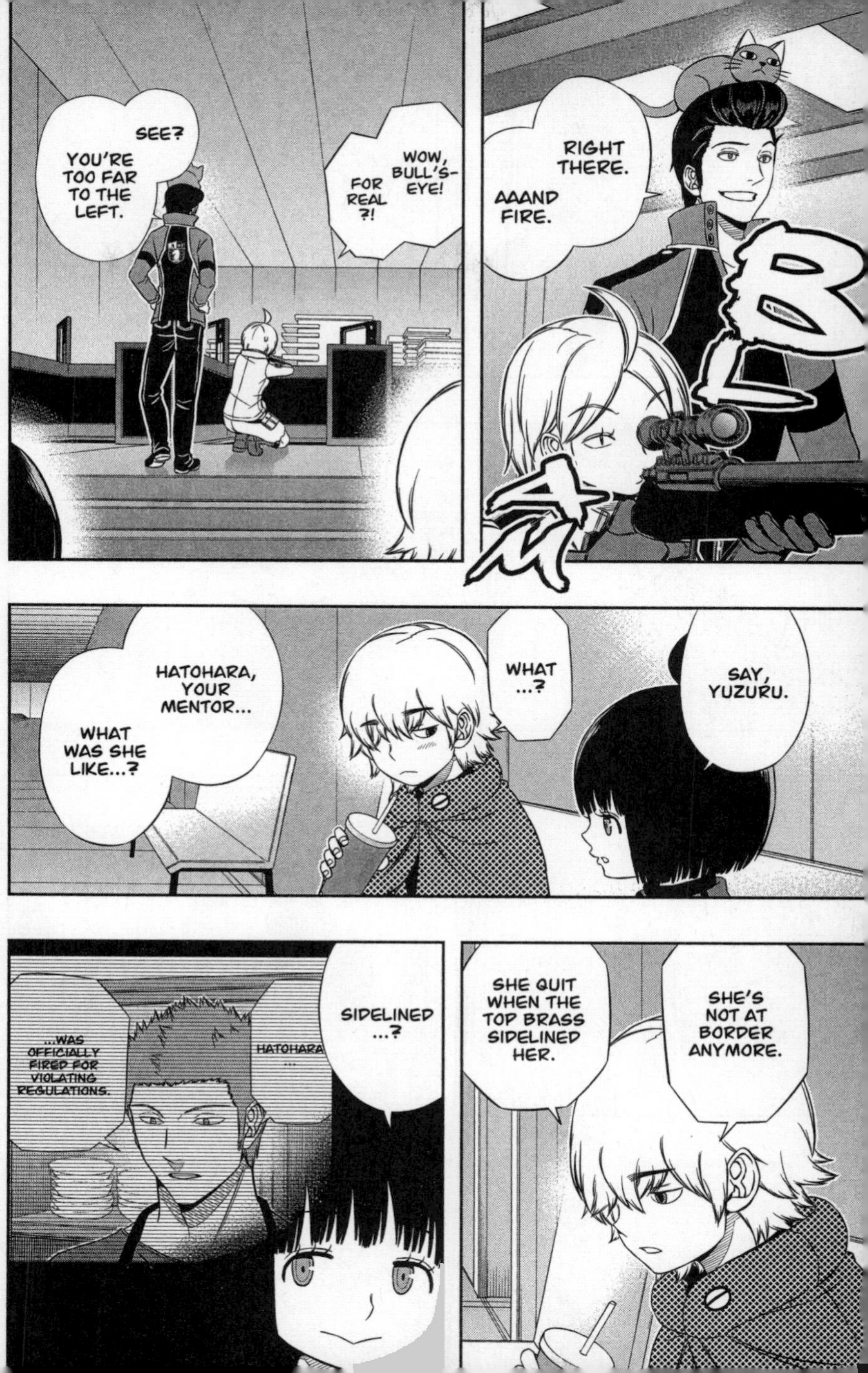
RIGHT THERE.
AAAND FIRE.
WOW, BULL'S-EYE!
FOR REAL?!
SEE?
YOU'RE TOO FAR TO THE LEFT.
SAY, YUZURU.
WHAT...?
HATOHARA, YOUR MENTOR...
WHAT WAS SHE LIKE...?
SHE'S NOT AT BORDER ANYMORE.
SHE QUIT WHEN THE TOP BRASS SIDELINED HER.
SIDELINED...?
HATOHARA...
...WAS OFFICIALLY FIRED FOR VIOLATING REGULATIONS.

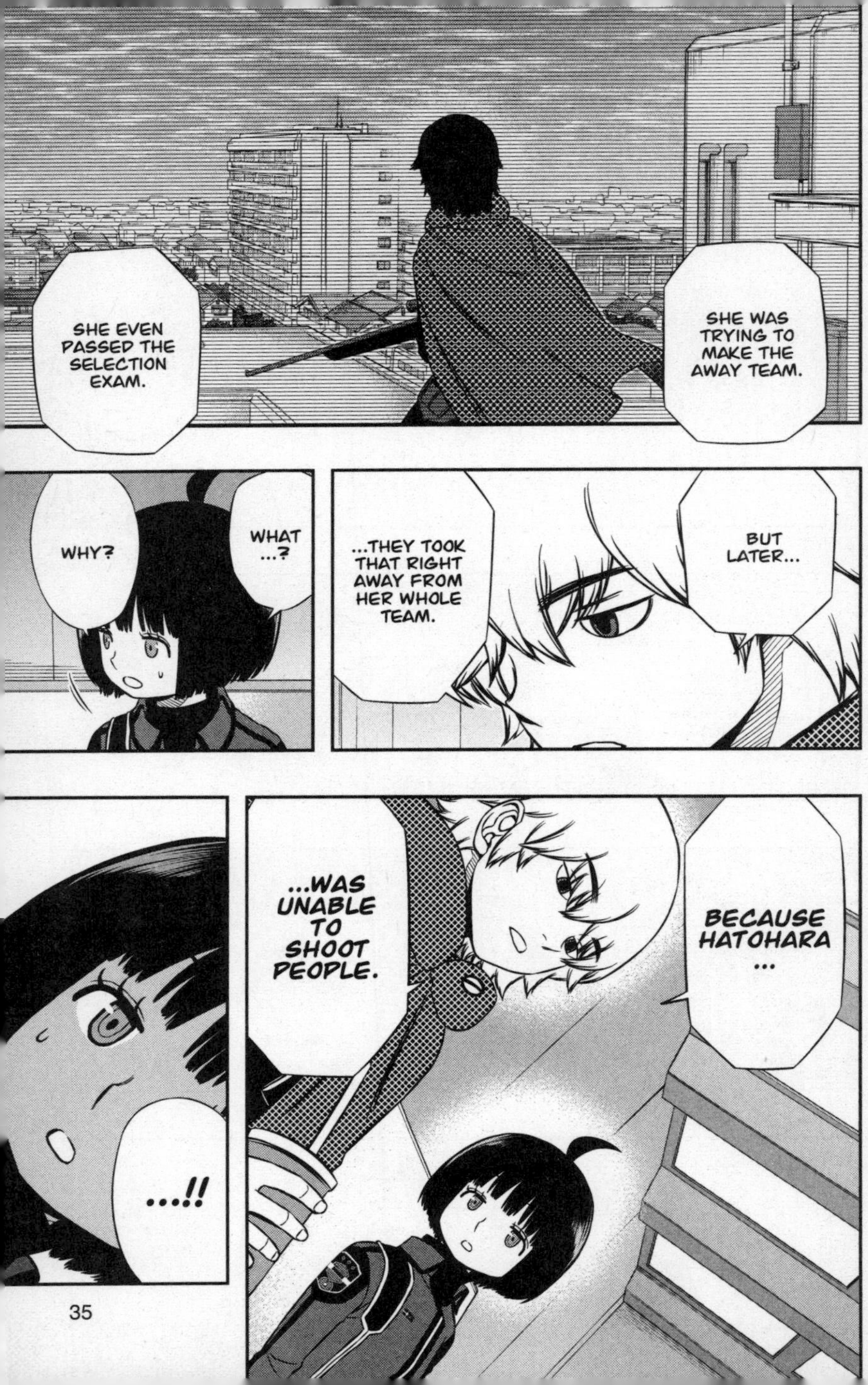
SHE WAS TRYING TO MAKE THE AWAY TEAM.
SHE EVEN PASSED THE SELECTION EXAM.
BUT LATER...
...THEY TOOK THAT RIGHT AWAY FROM HER WHOLE TEAM.
WHAT ...?
WHY?
BECAUSE HATOHARA ...
...WAS UNABLE TO SHOOT PEOPLE.
...!!

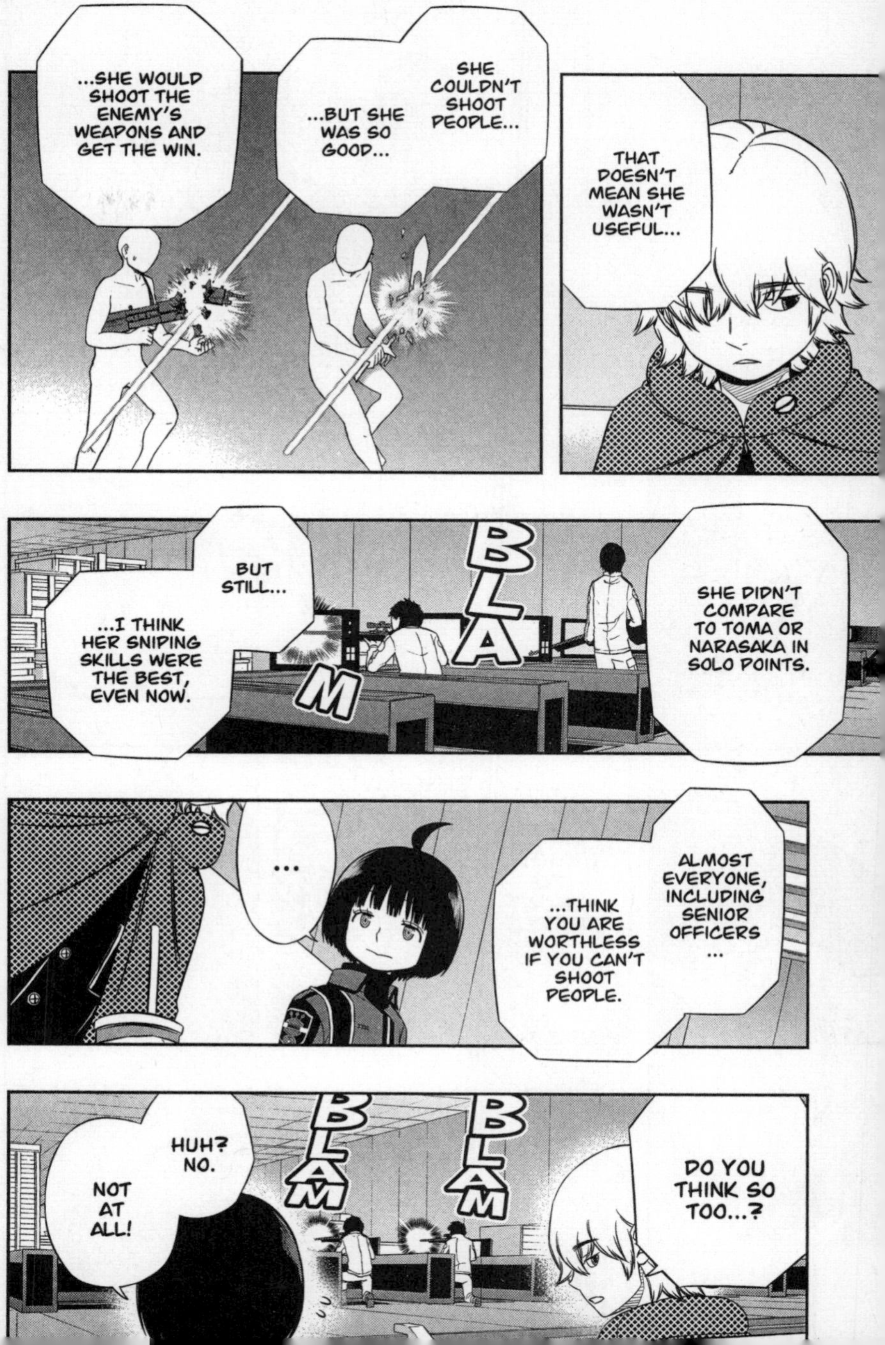
THAT DOESN'T MEAN SHE WASN'T USEFUL...
SHE COULDN'T SHOOT PEOPLE...
...BUT SHE WAS SO GOOD...
...SHE WOULD SHOOT THE ENEMY'S WEAPONS AND GET THE WIN.
SHE DIDN'T COMPARE TO TOMA OR NARASAKA IN SOLO POINTS.
BLAM
BUT STILL...
...I THINK HER SNIPING SKILLS WERE THE BEST, EVEN NOW.
ALMOST EVERYONE, INCLUDING SENIOR OFFICERS ...
...THINK YOU ARE WORTHLESS IF YOU CAN'T SHOOT PEOPLE.
...
DO YOU THINK SO TOO...?
BLAM
BLAM
HUH? NO.
NOT AT ALL!

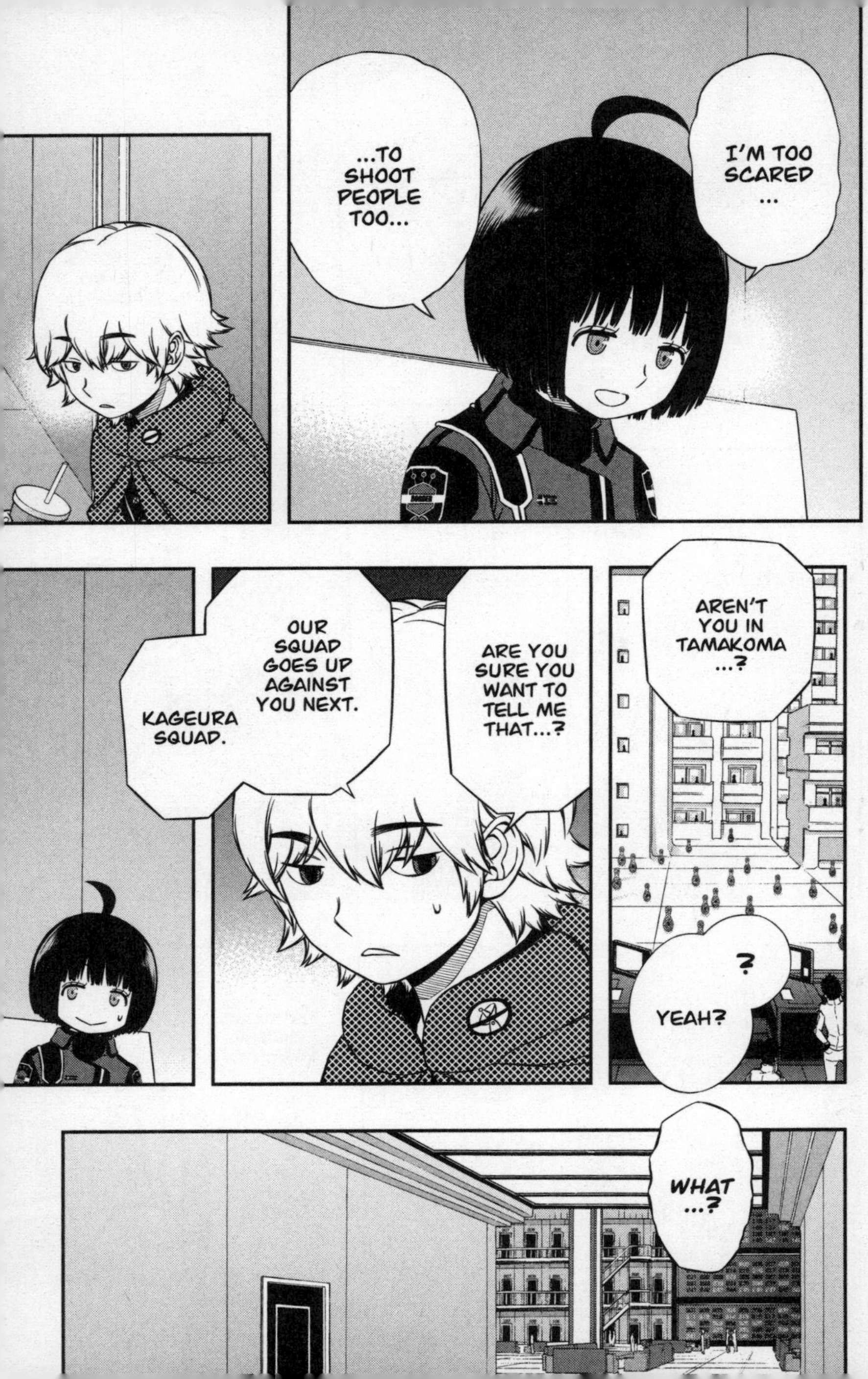
I'M TOO SCARED ...
...TO SHOOT PEOPLE TOO...
AREN'T YOU IN TAMAKOMA ...?
?
YEAH?
OUR SQUAD GOES UP AGAINST YOU NEXT.
KAGEURA SQUAD.
ARE YOU SURE YOU WANT TO TELL ME THAT...?
WHAT ...?

| KUGA | ✗◯◯✗◯ | ◯✗✗✗◯ | ✗✗✗◯✗ |
| MURAKAMI | ◯✗✗◯✗ | ✗◯◯◯✗ | ◯◯◯✗◯ |

AND YOU'RE NO. 4, RIGHT MURAKAMI?

TACHIKAWA IS THE NO. 1 ATTACKER...

KAZAMA IS NO. 2.

HE'S 20TH BUT HE'S BETTER THAN YOU?

HMM...?

NO, KAGE IS 20TH OR SO.

SO THEN THIS KAGEURA IS NO. 3?

THOSE FOUR ARE THE ONLY ATTACKERS I CAN'T BEAT.

TACHIKAWA, KAZAMA, KAGE, AND...

HE IS.

...I HAVEN'T FOUGHT HER MUCH, BUT...

KONAMI.

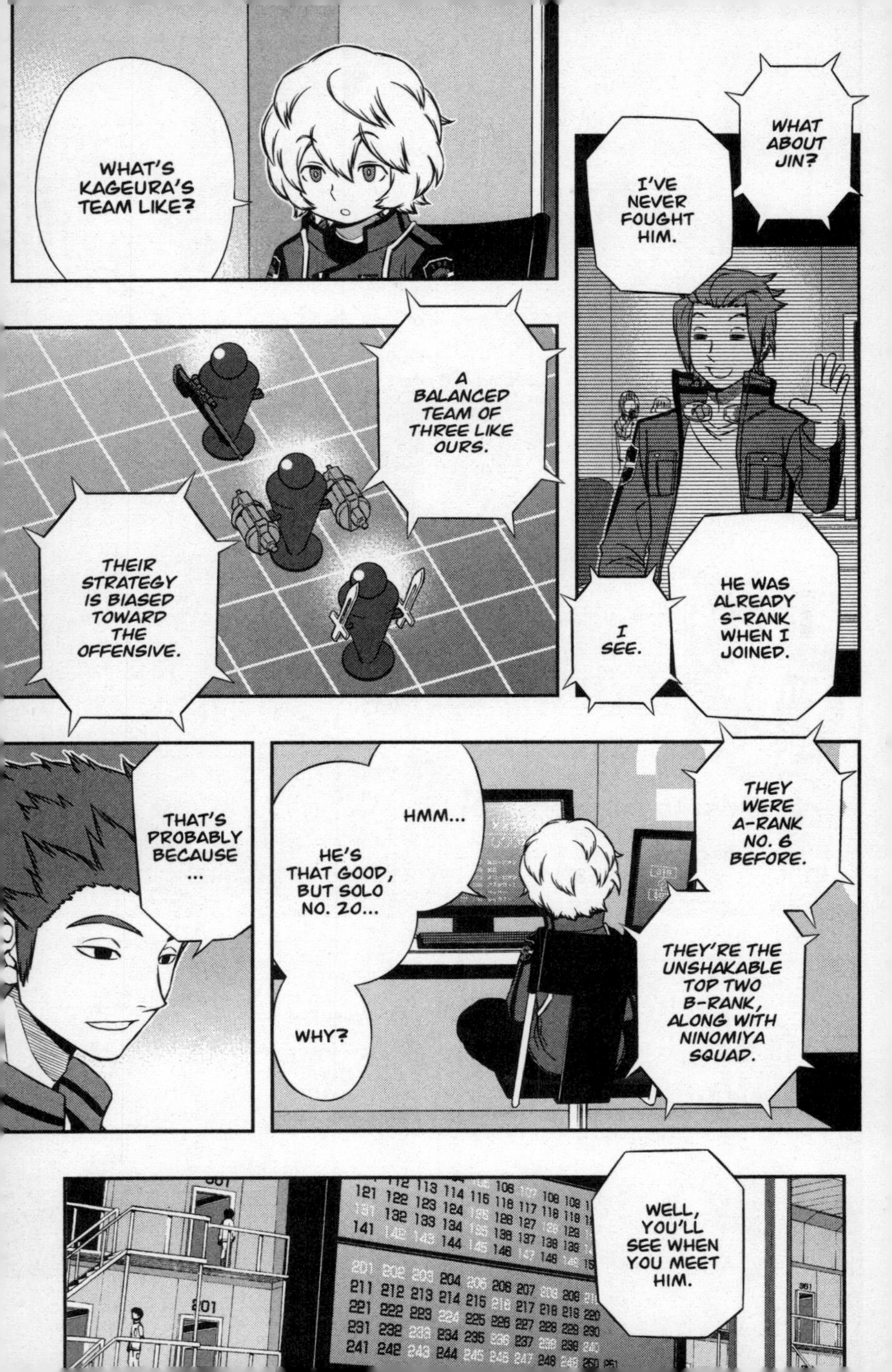
WHAT ABOUT JIN?
I'VE NEVER FOUGHT HIM.
HE WAS ALREADY S-RANK WHEN I JOINED.
I SEE.
WHAT'S KAGEURA'S TEAM LIKE?
A BALANCED TEAM OF THREE LIKE OURS.
THEIR STRATEGY IS BIASED TOWARD THE OFFENSIVE.
THEY WERE A-RANK NO. 6 BEFORE.
THEY'RE THE UNSHAKABLE TOP TWO B-RANK, ALONG WITH NINOMIYA SQUAD.
HMM...
HE'S THAT GOOD, BUT SOLO NO. 20...
WHY?
THAT'S PROBABLY BECAUSE...
WELL, YOU'LL SEE WHEN YOU MEET HIM.

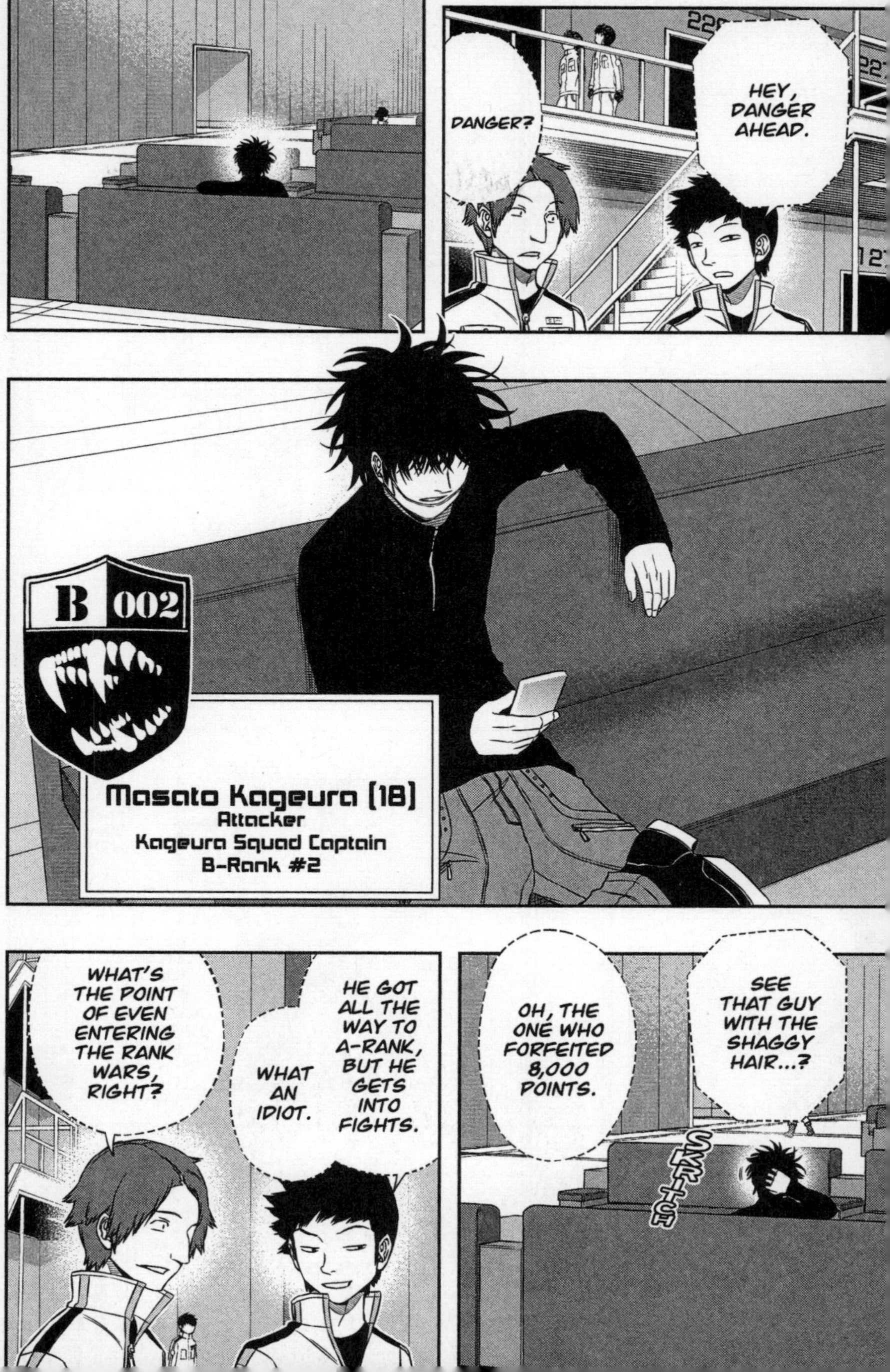
HEY, DANGER AHEAD.
DANGER?
B 002
Masato Kageura (18)
Attacker
Kageura Squad Captain
B-Rank #2
SEE THAT GUY WITH THE SHAGGY HAIR...?
OH, THE ONE WHO FORFEITED 8,000 POINTS.
SKRITCH
HE GOT ALL THE WAY TO A-RANK, BUT HE GETS INTO FIGHTS.
WHAT AN IDIOT.
WHAT'S THE POINT OF EVEN ENTERING THE RANK WARS, RIGHT?

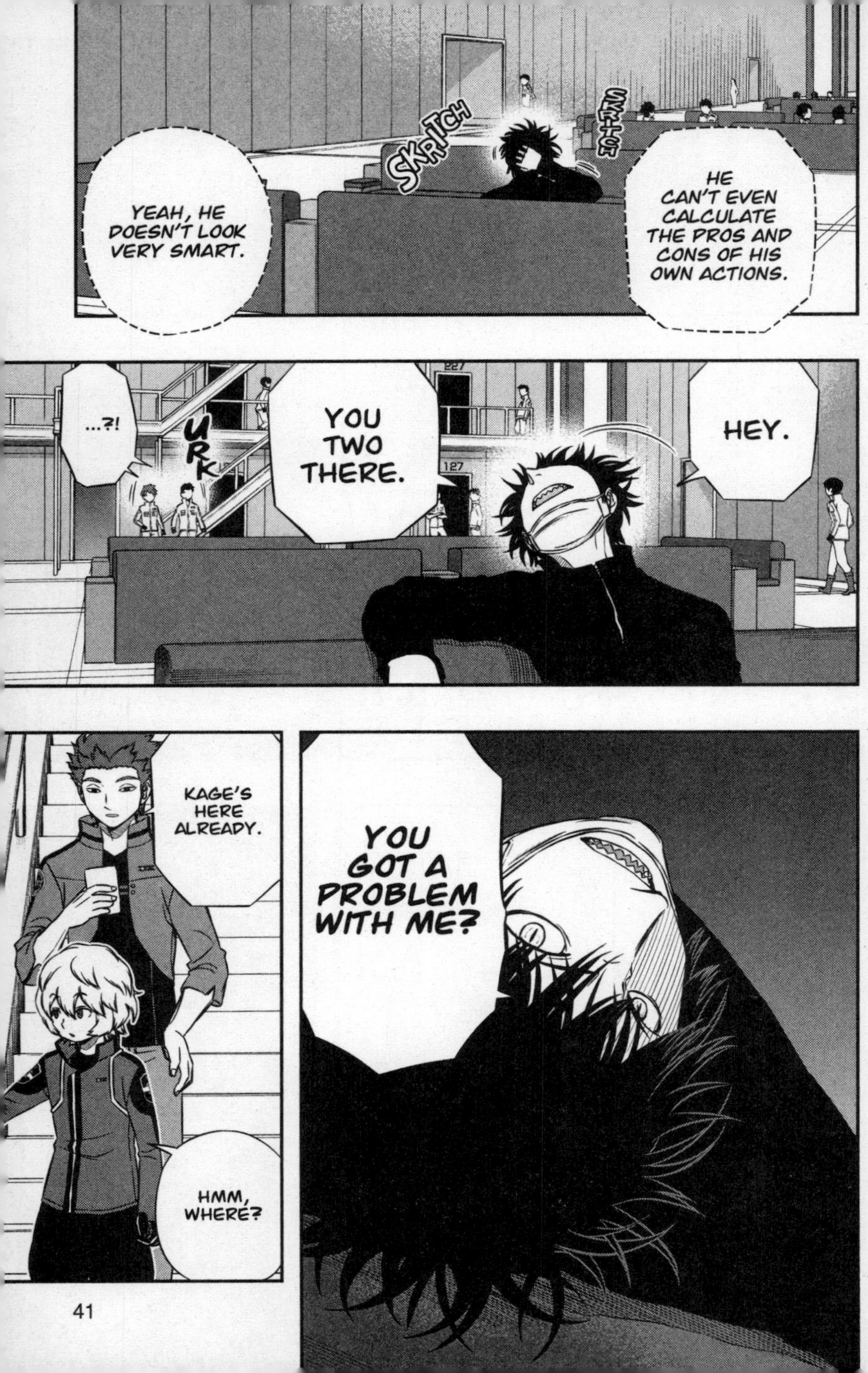
SKRITCH
SKRITCH
HE CAN'T EVEN CALCULATE THE PROS AND CONS OF HIS OWN ACTIONS.
YEAH, HE DOESN'T LOOK VERY SMART.
HEY.
YOU TWO THERE.
URK
...?!
YOU GOT A PROBLEM WITH ME?
KAGE'S HERE ALREADY.
HMM, WHERE?

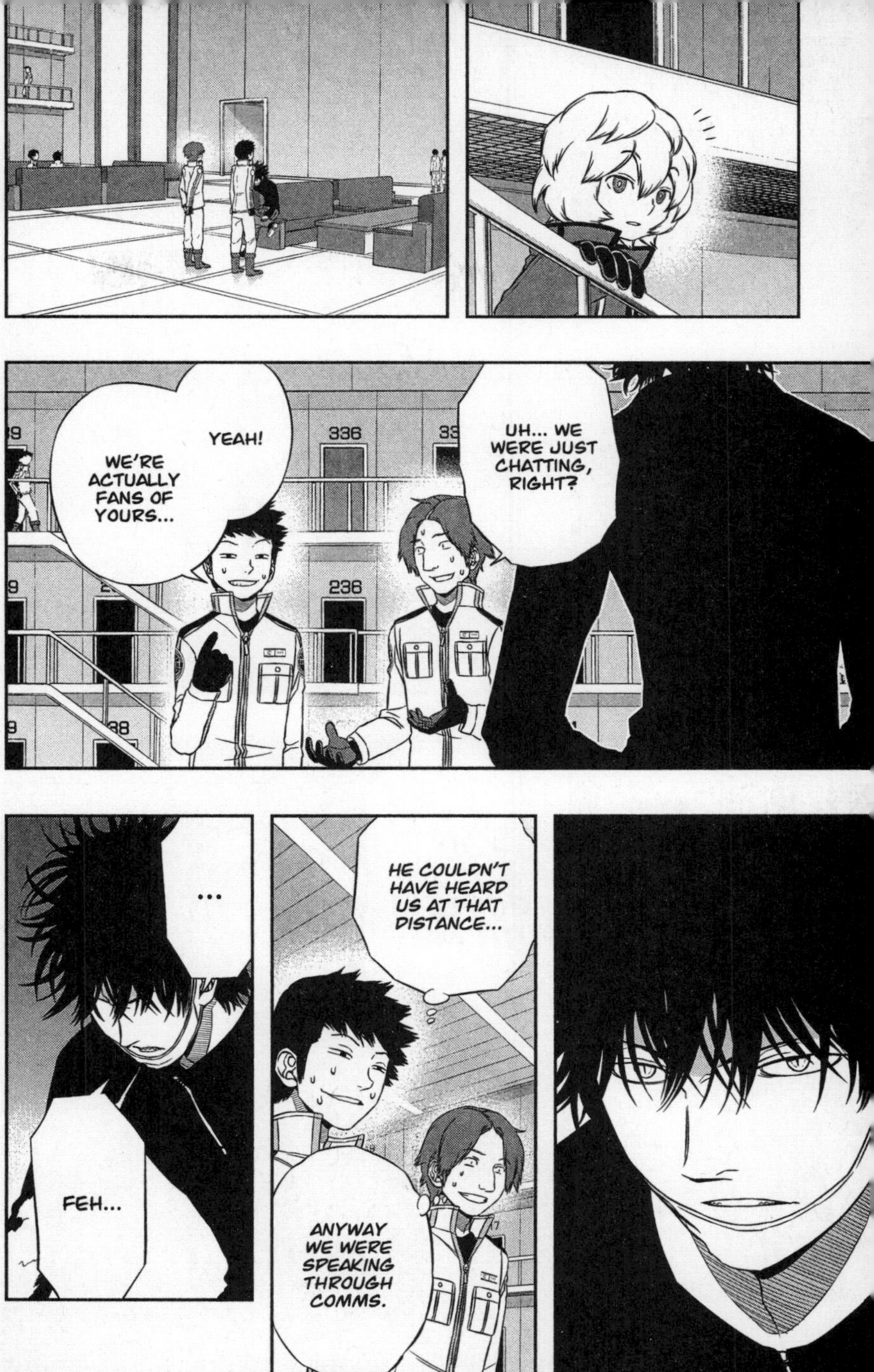
UH... WE WERE JUST CHATTING, RIGHT?
YEAH!
WE'RE ACTUALLY FANS OF YOURS...
HE COULDN'T HAVE HEARD US AT THAT DISTANCE...
ANYWAY WE WERE SPEAKING THROUGH COMMS.
...
FEH...

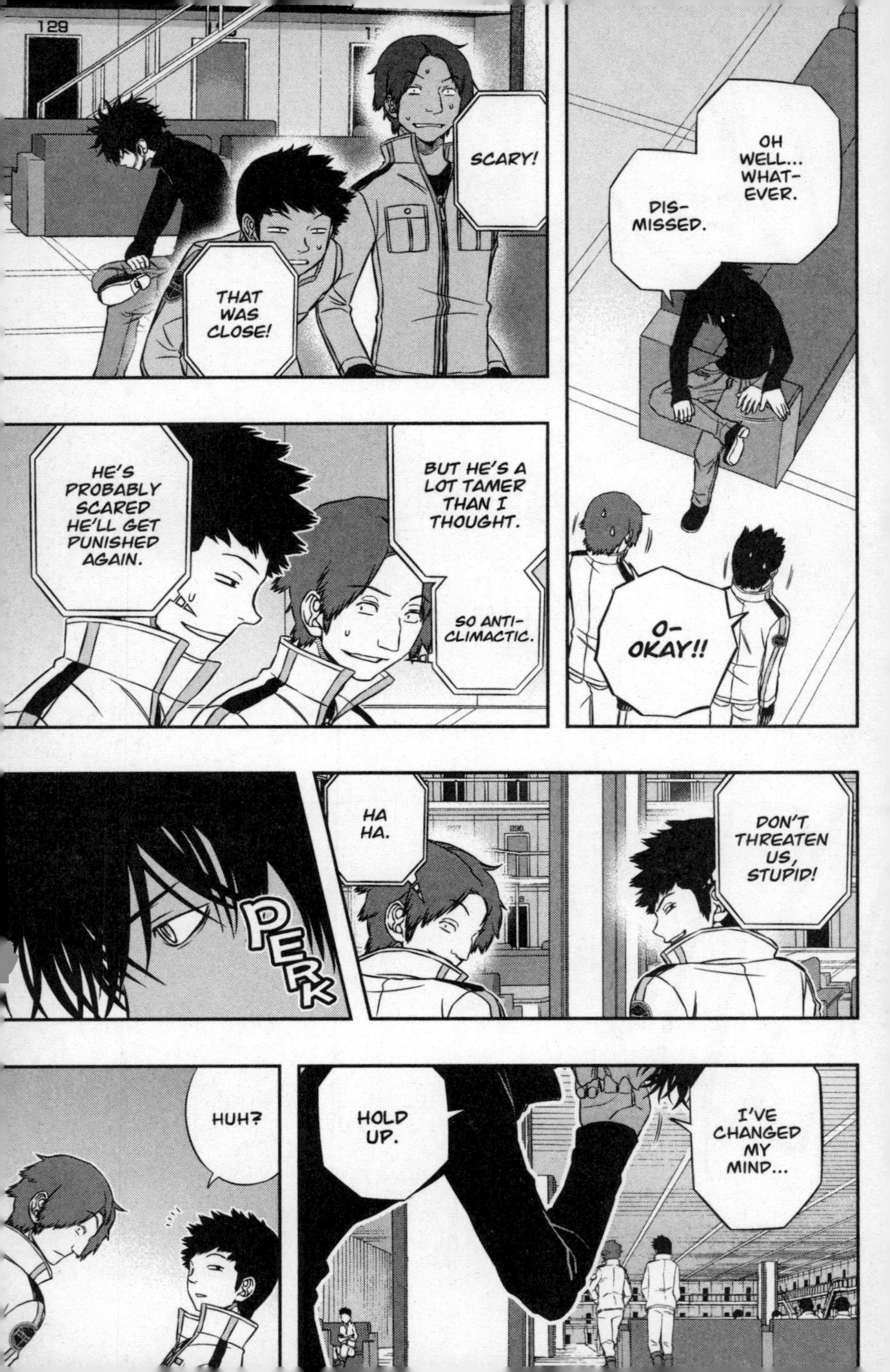
OH WELL... WHATEVER.
DIS-MISSED.
O-OKAY!!
SCARY!
THAT WAS CLOSE!
BUT HE'S A LOT TAMER THAN I THOUGHT.
SO ANTI-CLIMACTIC.
HE'S PROBABLY SCARED HE'LL GET PUNISHED AGAIN.
DON'T THREATEN US, STUPID!
HA HA.
PERK
I'VE CHANGED MY MIND...
HOLD UP.
HUH?

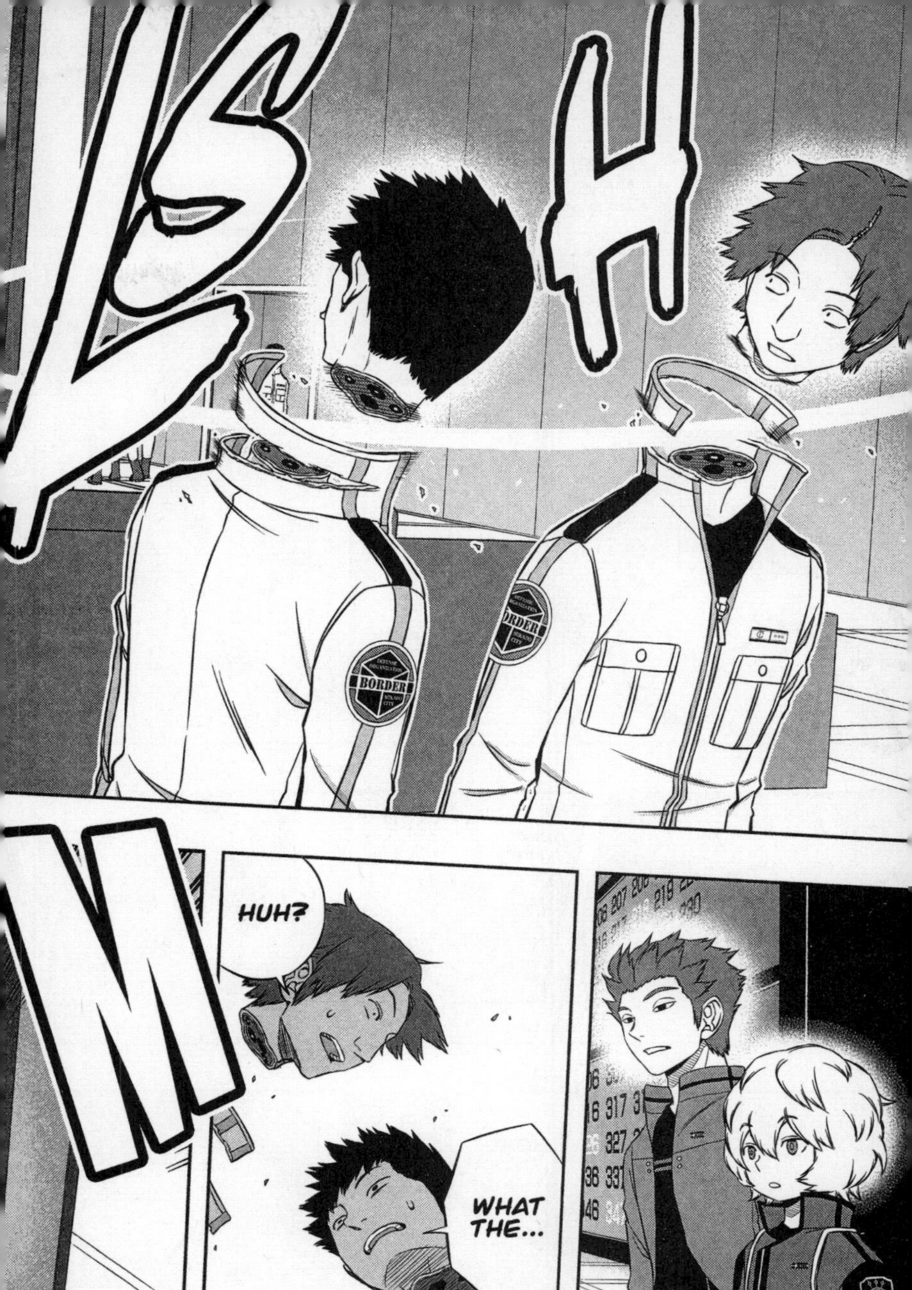
KSHM
HUH?
WHAT THE...

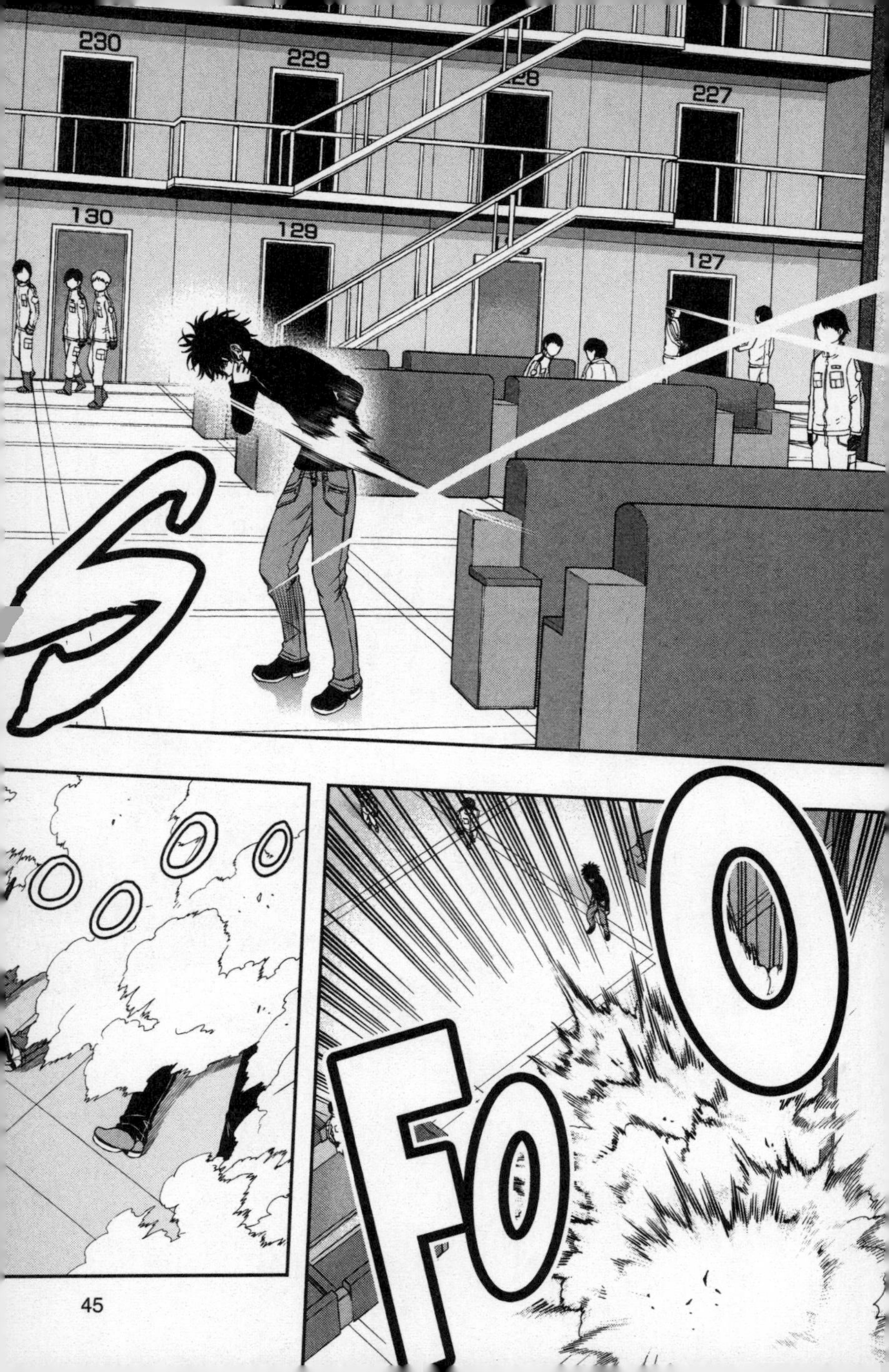
227
229
230
127
129
130
S
FOO
OOOOO

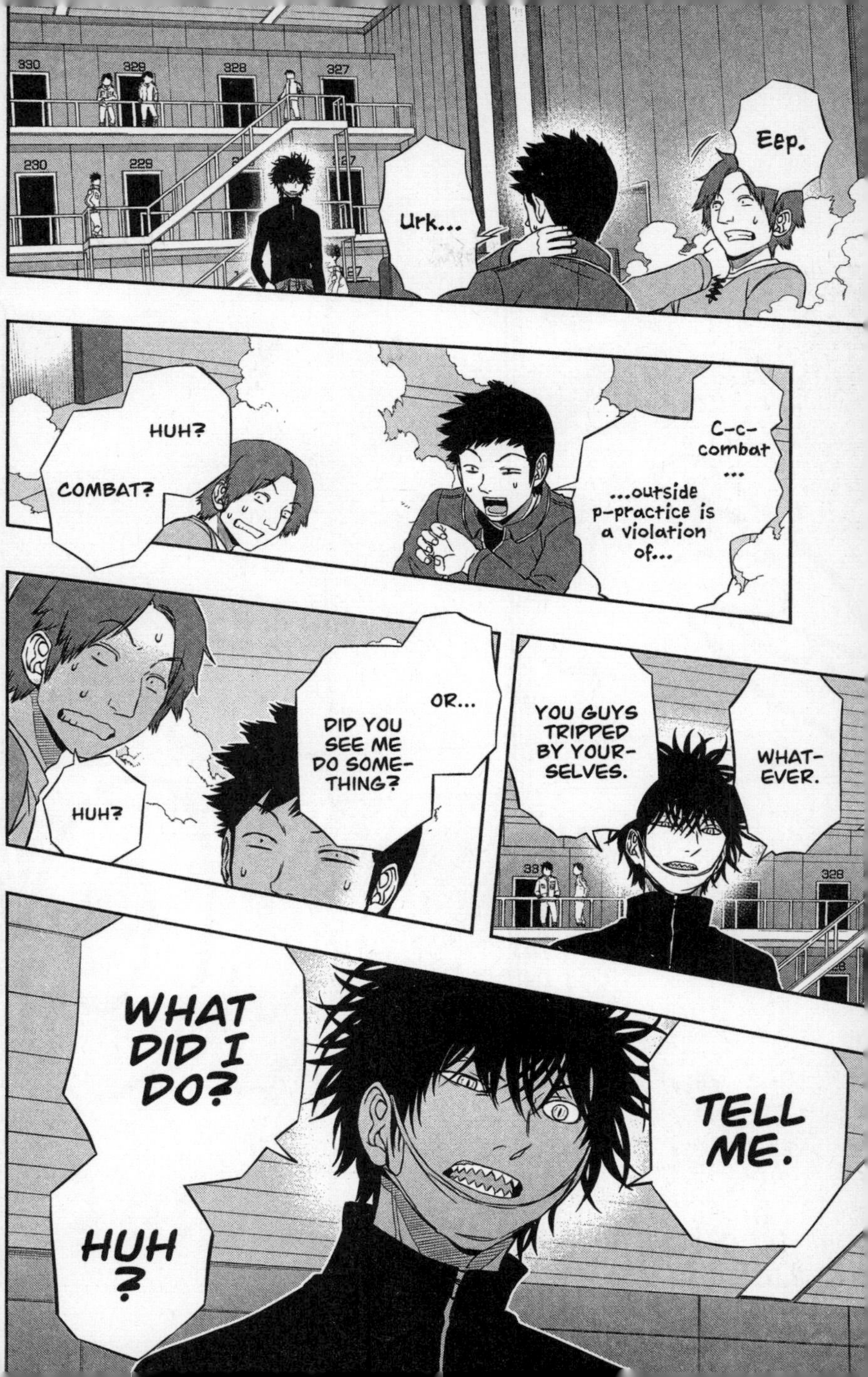
Eep.
Urk...
C-c-combat...
...outside p-practice is a violation of...
HUH?
COMBAT?
WHAT-EVER.
YOU GUYS TRIPPED BY YOUR-SELVES.
OR...
DID YOU SEE ME DO SOME-THING?
HUH?
TELL ME.
WHAT DID I DO?
HUH?

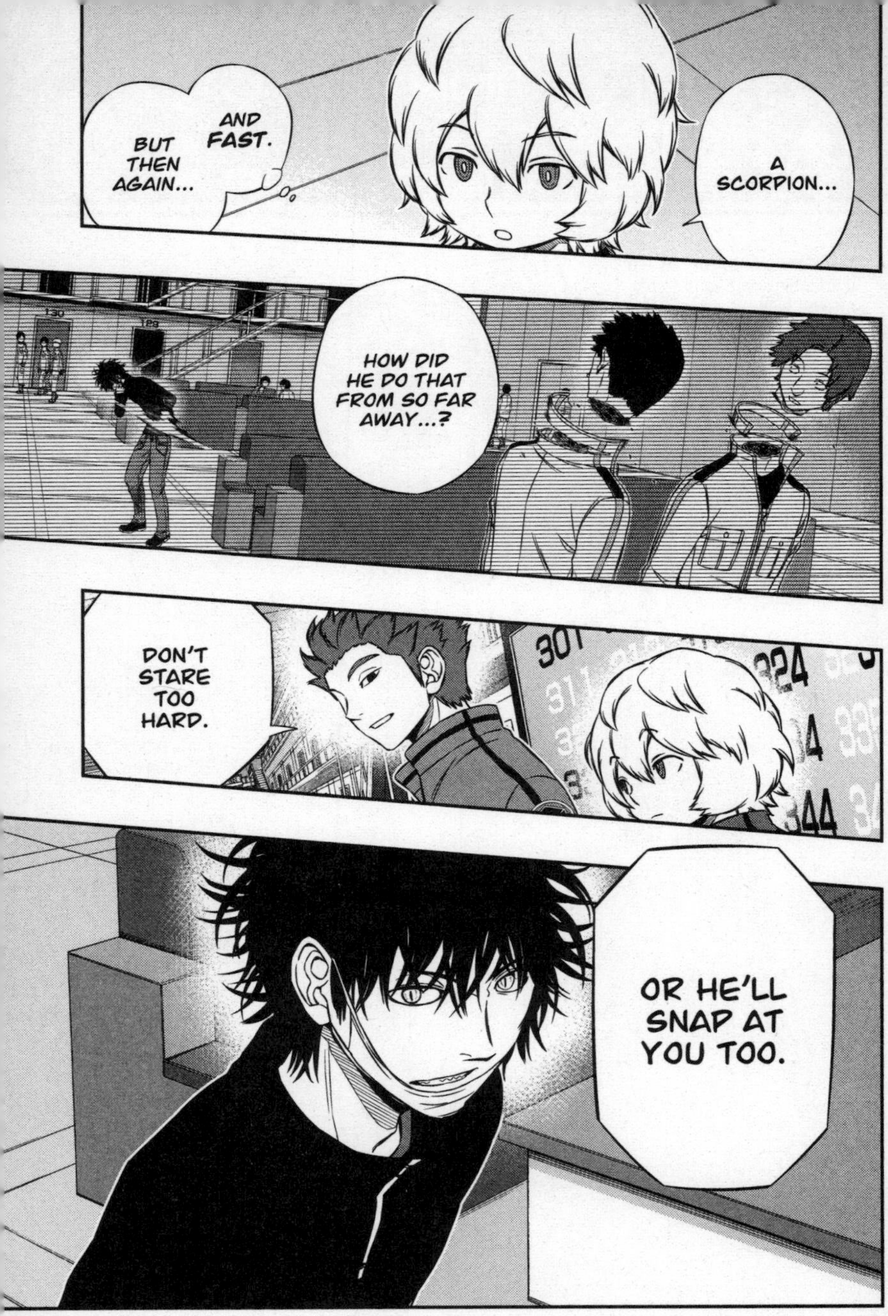
A SCORPION...
AND FAST.
BUT THEN AGAIN...
HOW DID HE DO THAT FROM SO FAR AWAY...?
DON'T STARE TOO HARD.
OR HE'LL SNAP AT YOU TOO.

Arashiyama Squad Strategy Room

A-Rank strategy rooms are a little bigger than B-Rank rooms, with a kitchenette and a small additional room.

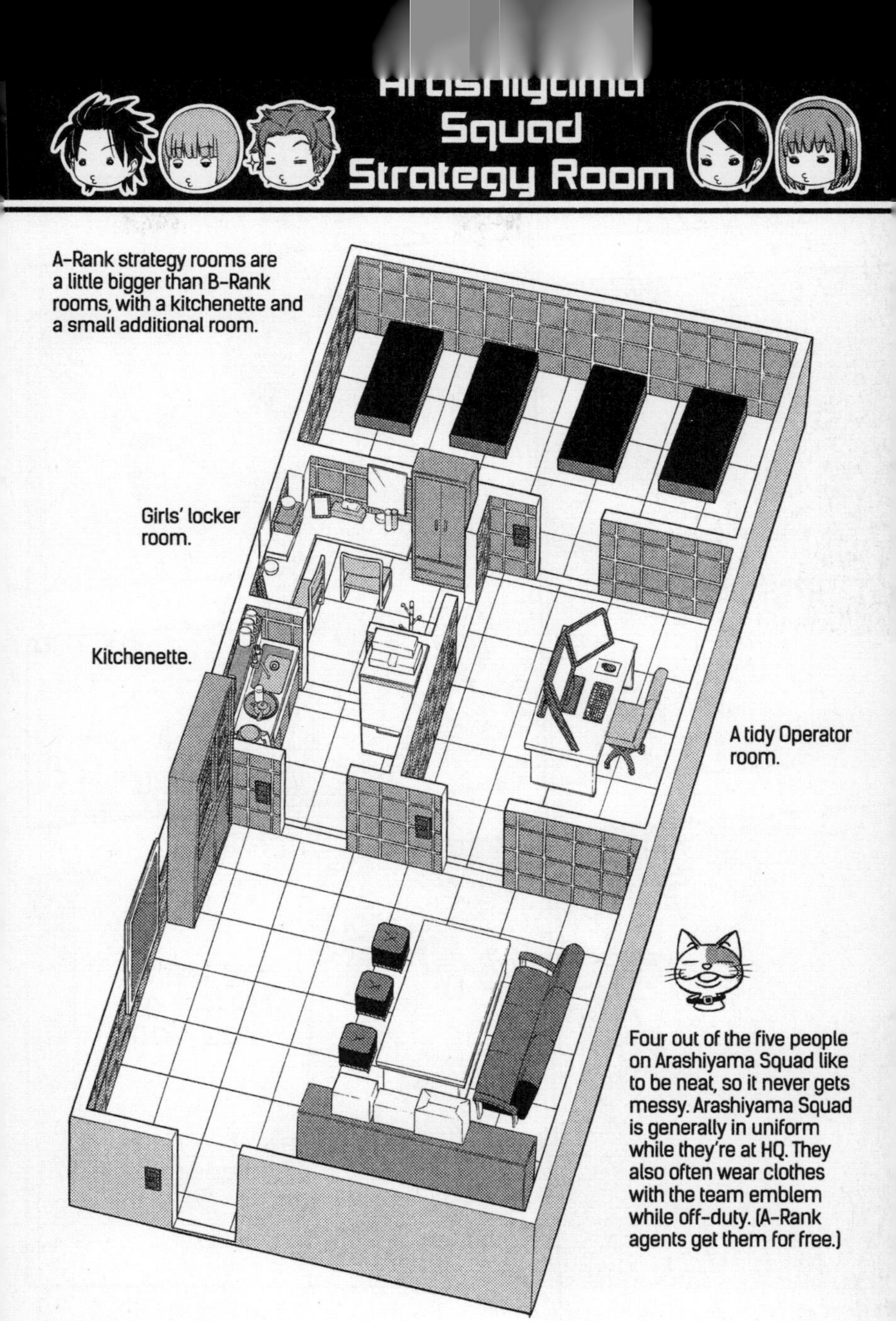

Girls' locker room.

Kitchenette.

A tidy Operator room.

Four out of the five people on Arashiyama Squad like to be neat, so it never gets messy. Arashiyama Squad is generally in uniform while they're at HQ. They also often wear clothes with the team emblem while off-duty. (A-Rank agents get them for free.)

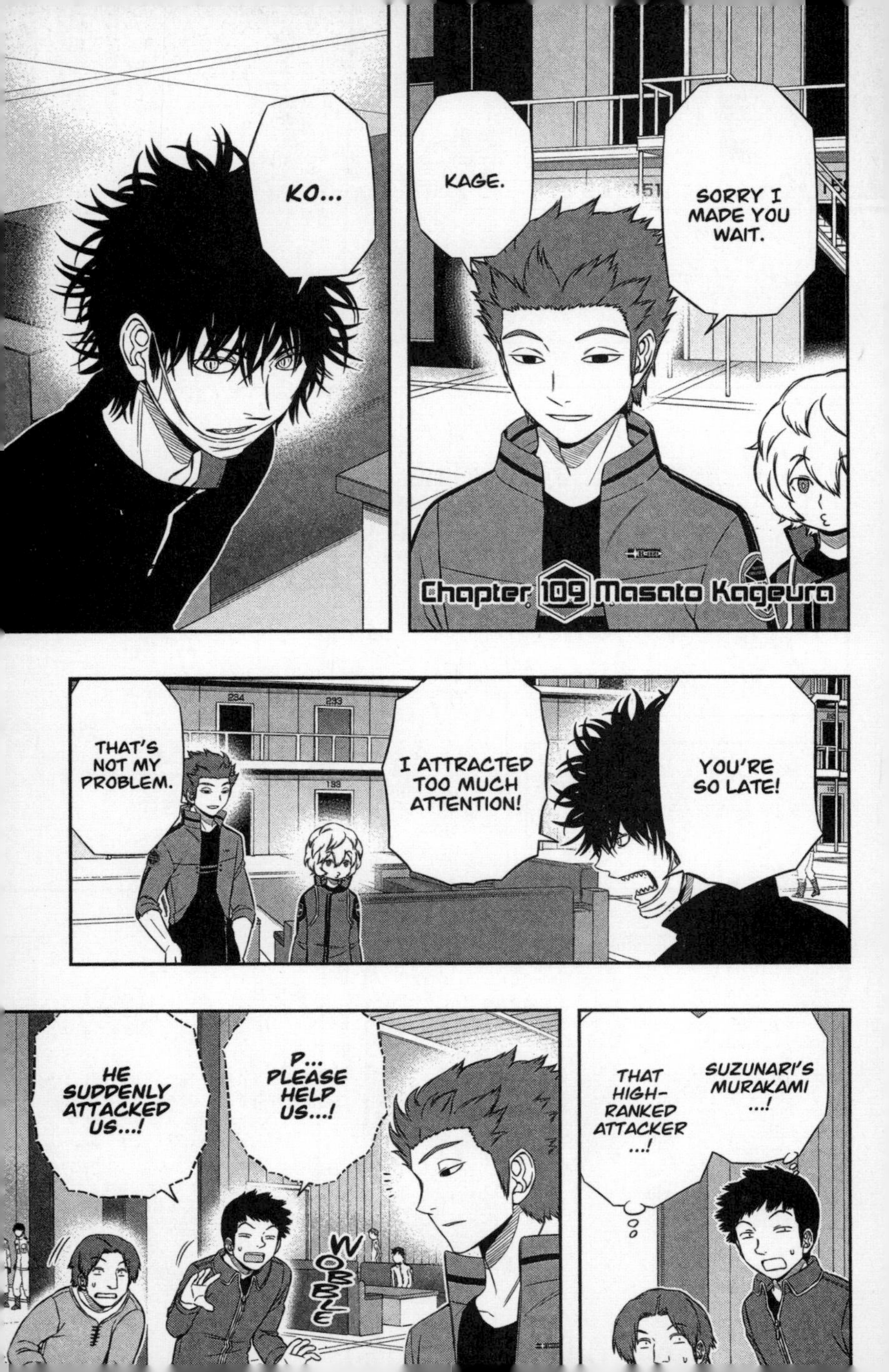
SORRY I MADE YOU WAIT.
KAGE.
Chapter 109 Masato Kageura
KO...
YOU'RE SO LATE!
I ATTRACTED TOO MUCH ATTENTION!
THAT'S NOT MY PROBLEM.
SUZUNARI'S MURAKAMI ...!
THAT HIGH-RANKED ATTACKER ...!
P... PLEASE HELP US...!
HE SUDDENLY ATTACKED US...!
WOBBLE

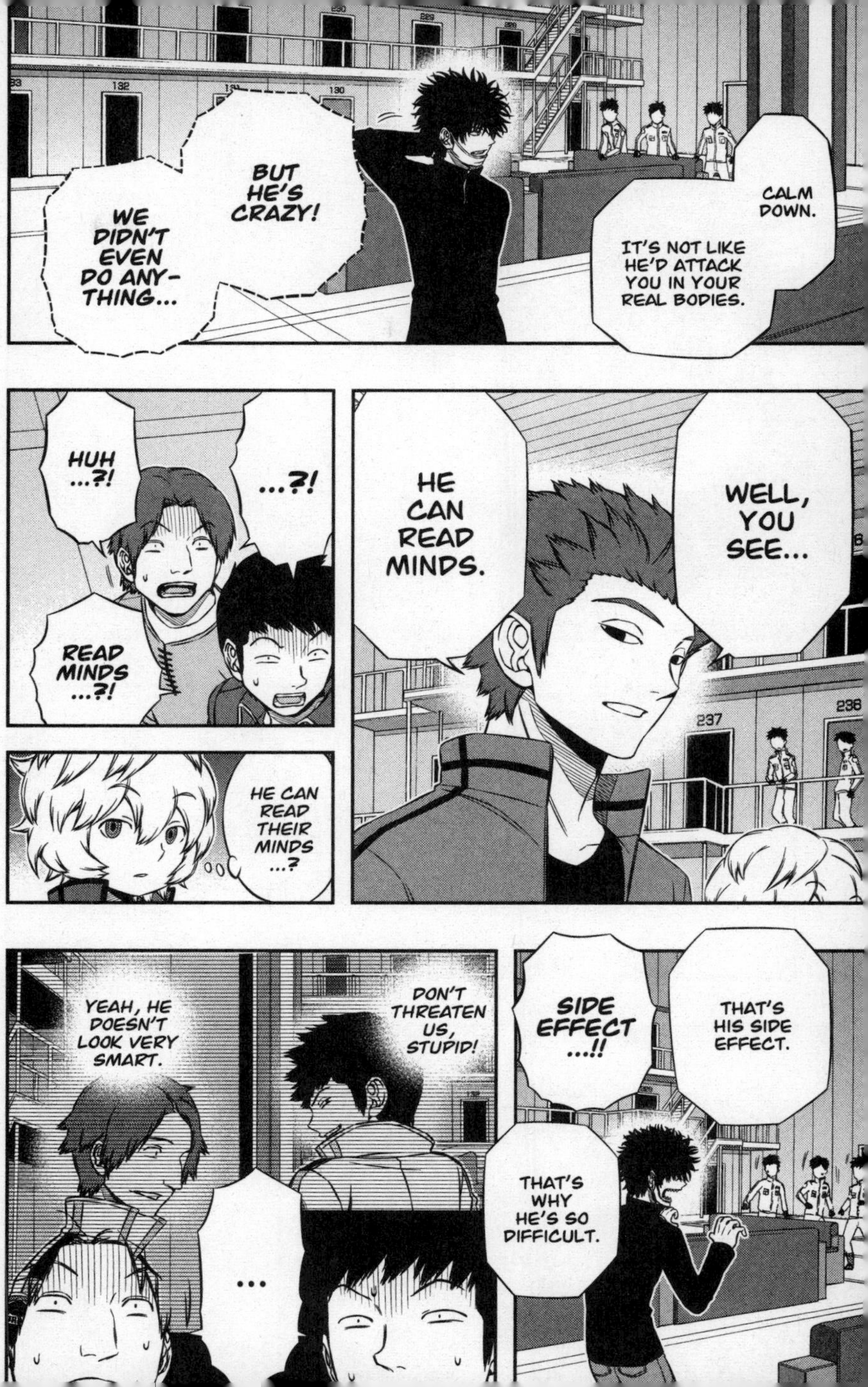
CALM DOWN.
IT'S NOT LIKE HE'D ATTACK YOU IN YOUR REAL BODIES.
BUT HE'S CRAZY!
WE DIDN'T EVEN DO ANY-THING...
WELL, YOU SEE...
HE CAN READ MINDS.
...?!
HUH ...?!
READ MINDS ...?!
HE CAN READ THEIR MINDS ...?
THAT'S HIS SIDE EFFECT.
SIDE EFFECT ...!!
THAT'S WHY HE'S SO DIFFICULT.
DON'T THREATEN US, STUPID!
YEAH, HE DOESN'T LOOK VERY SMART.
...

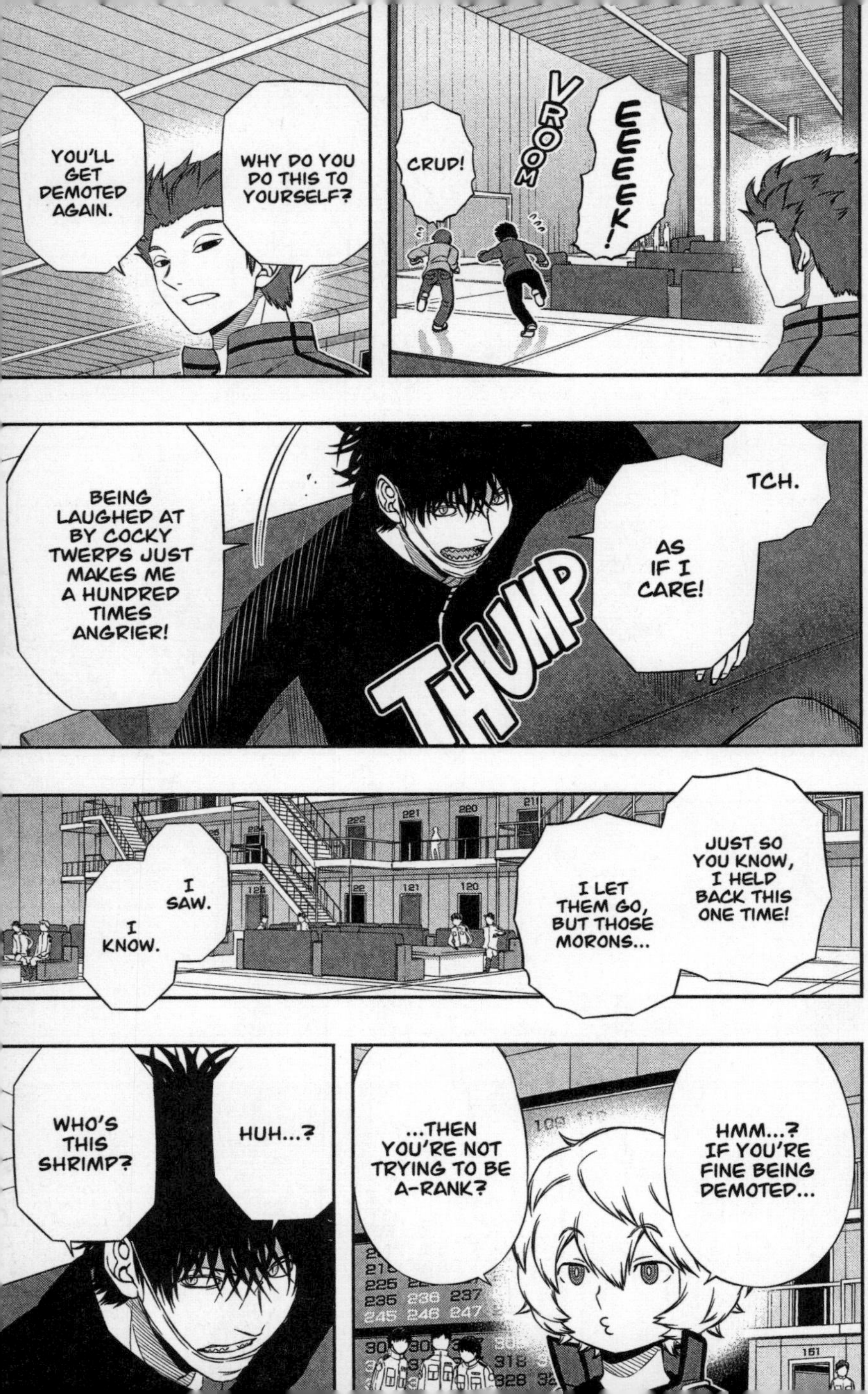
EEEEK!
VROOM
CRUD!
WHY DO YOU DO THIS TO YOURSELF?
YOU'LL GET DEMOTED AGAIN.
TCH.
AS IF I CARE!
THUMP
BEING LAUGHED AT BY COCKY TWERPS JUST MAKES ME A HUNDRED TIMES ANGRIER!
JUST SO YOU KNOW, I HELD BACK THIS ONE TIME!
I LET THEM GO, BUT THOSE MORONS...
I SAW.
I KNOW.
HMM...? IF YOU'RE FINE BEING DEMOTED...
...THEN YOU'RE NOT TRYING TO BE A-RANK?
HUH...?
WHO'S THIS SHRIMP?

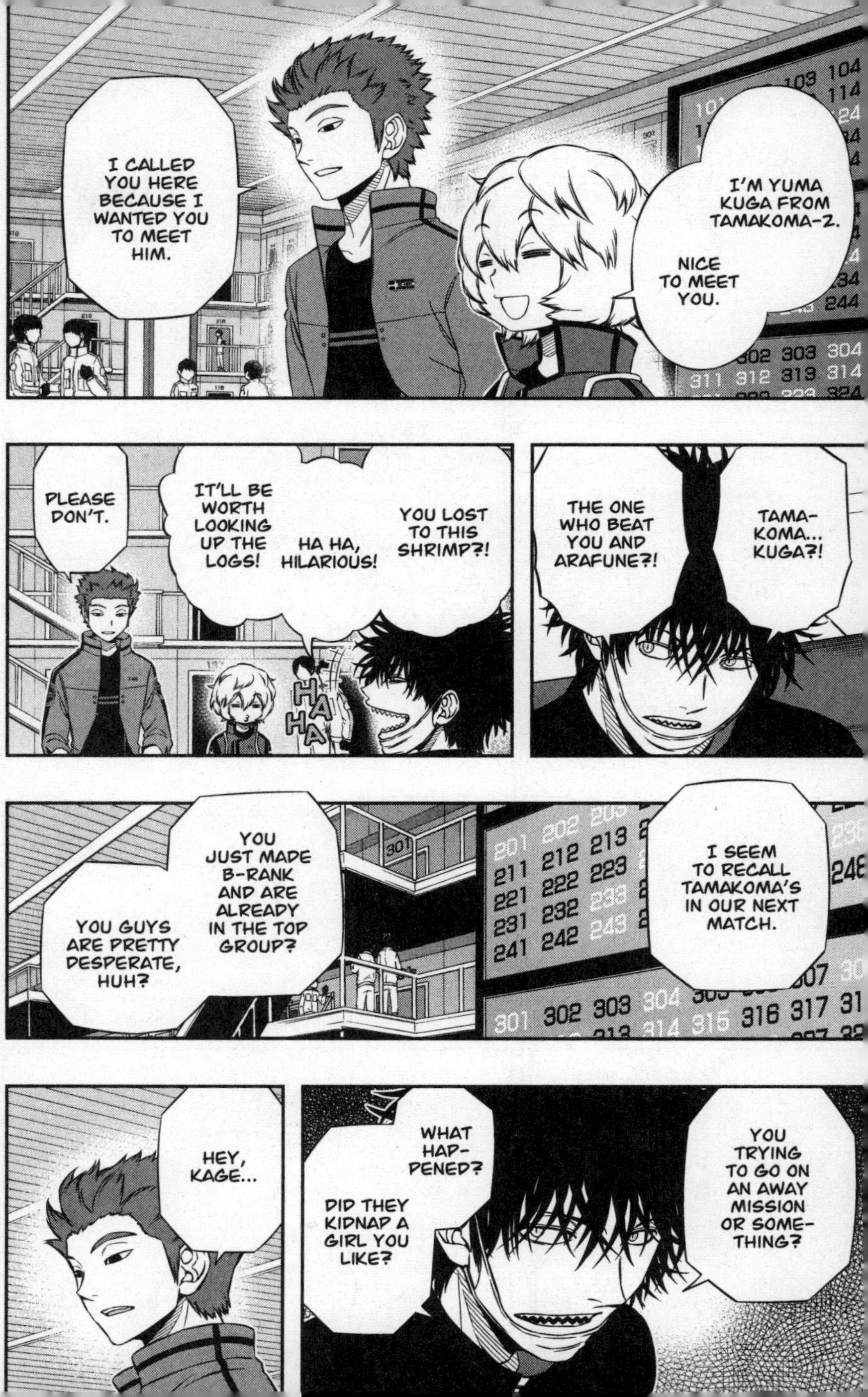
I'M YUMA KUGA FROM TAMAKOMA-2.
NICE TO MEET YOU.
I CALLED YOU HERE BECAUSE I WANTED YOU TO MEET HIM.
TAMA-KOMA... KUGA?!
THE ONE WHO BEAT YOU AND ARAFUNE?!
YOU LOST TO THIS SHRIMP?!
HA HA, HILARIOUS!
IT'LL BE WORTH LOOKING UP THE LOGS!
HA HA
PLEASE DON'T.
I SEEM TO RECALL TAMAKOMA'S IN OUR NEXT MATCH.
YOU JUST MADE B-RANK AND ARE ALREADY IN THE TOP GROUP?
YOU GUYS ARE PRETTY DESPERATE, HUH?
YOU TRYING TO GO ON AN AWAY MISSION OR SOMETHING?
WHAT HAP-PENED?
DID THEY KIDNAP A GIRL YOU LIKE?
HEY, KAGE...

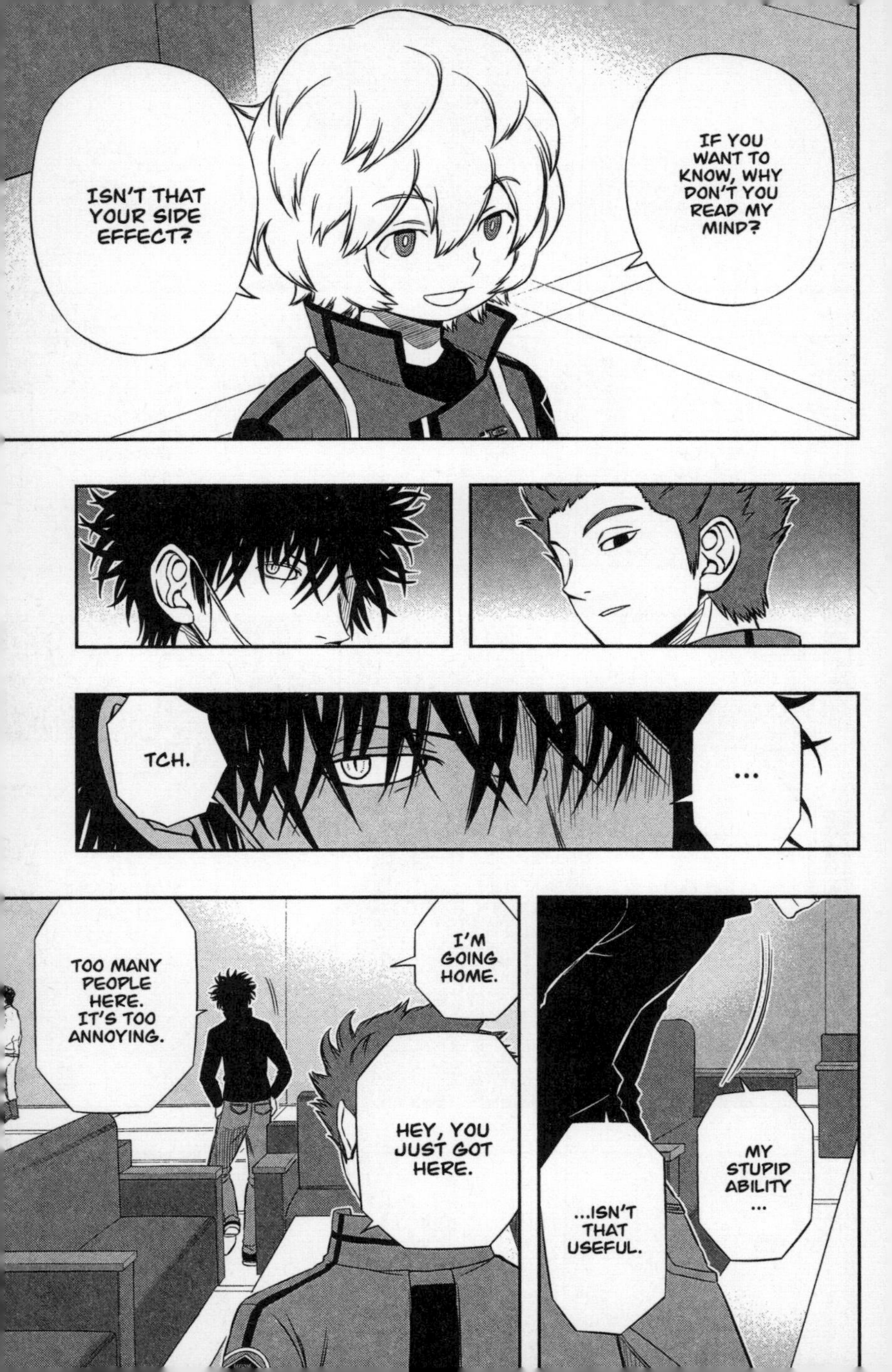
IF YOU WANT TO KNOW, WHY DON'T YOU READ MY MIND?
ISN'T THAT YOUR SIDE EFFECT?
...
TCH.
MY STUPID ABILITY ...
...ISN'T THAT USEFUL.
I'M GOING HOME.
TOO MANY PEOPLE HERE. IT'S TOO ANNOYING.
HEY, YOU JUST GOT HERE.

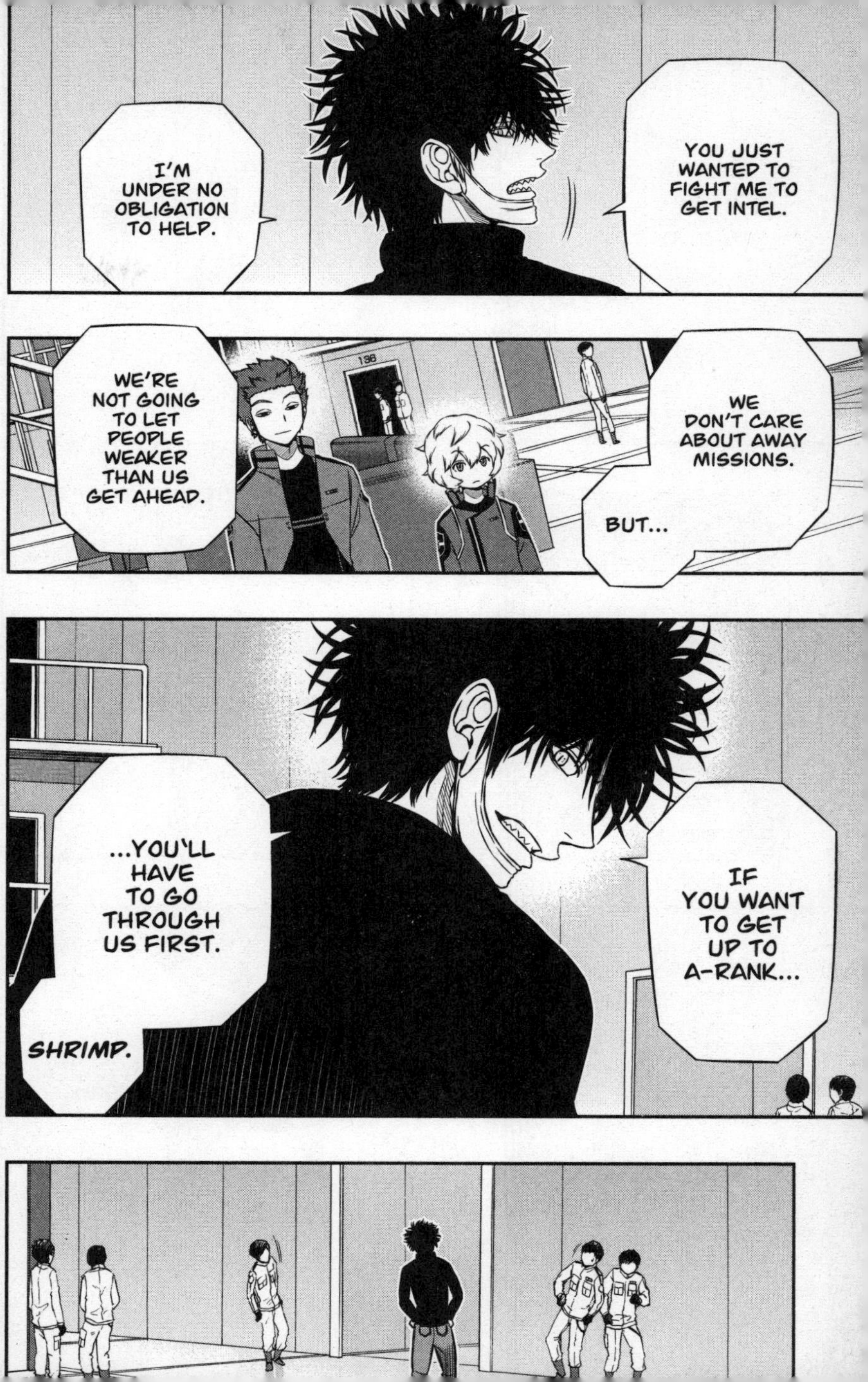
YOU JUST WANTED TO FIGHT ME TO GET INTEL.
I'M UNDER NO OBLIGATION TO HELP.
WE DON'T CARE ABOUT AWAY MISSIONS.
BUT...
WE'RE NOT GOING TO LET PEOPLE WEAKER THAN US GET AHEAD.
IF YOU WANT TO GET UP TO A-RANK...
...YOU'LL HAVE TO GO THROUGH US FIRST.
SHRIMP.

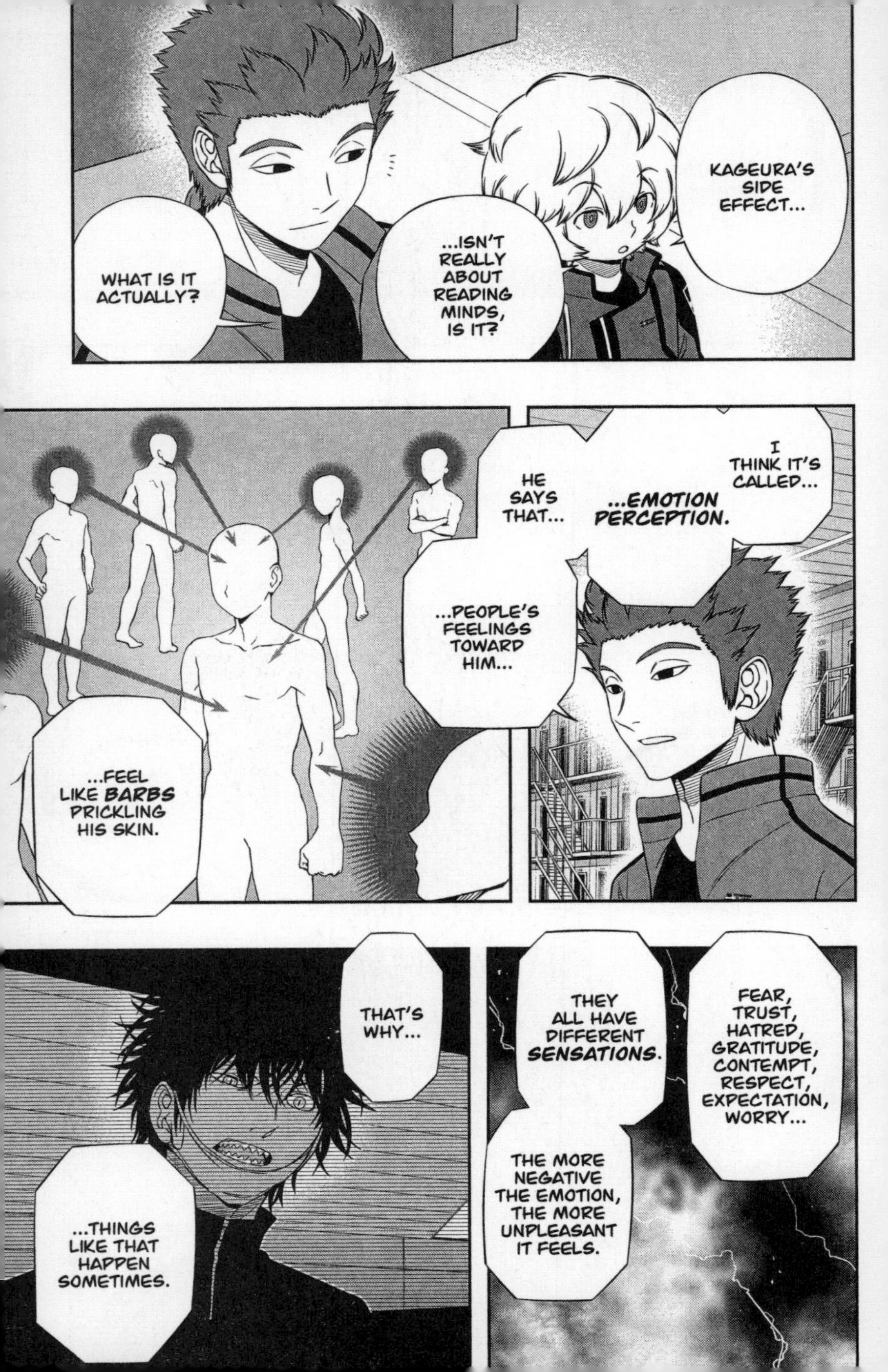
KAGEURA'S SIDE EFFECT...
...ISN'T REALLY ABOUT READING MINDS, IS IT?
WHAT IS IT ACTUALLY?
I THINK IT'S CALLED...
...EMOTION PERCEPTION.
HE SAYS THAT...
...PEOPLE'S FEELINGS TOWARD HIM...
...FEEL LIKE BARBS PRICKLING HIS SKIN.
FEAR, TRUST, HATRED, GRATITUDE, CONTEMPT, RESPECT, EXPECTATION, WORRY...
THEY ALL HAVE DIFFERENT SENSATIONS.
THE MORE NEGATIVE THE EMOTION, THE MORE UNPLEASANT IT FEELS.
THAT'S WHY...
...THINGS LIKE THAT HAPPEN SOMETIMES.

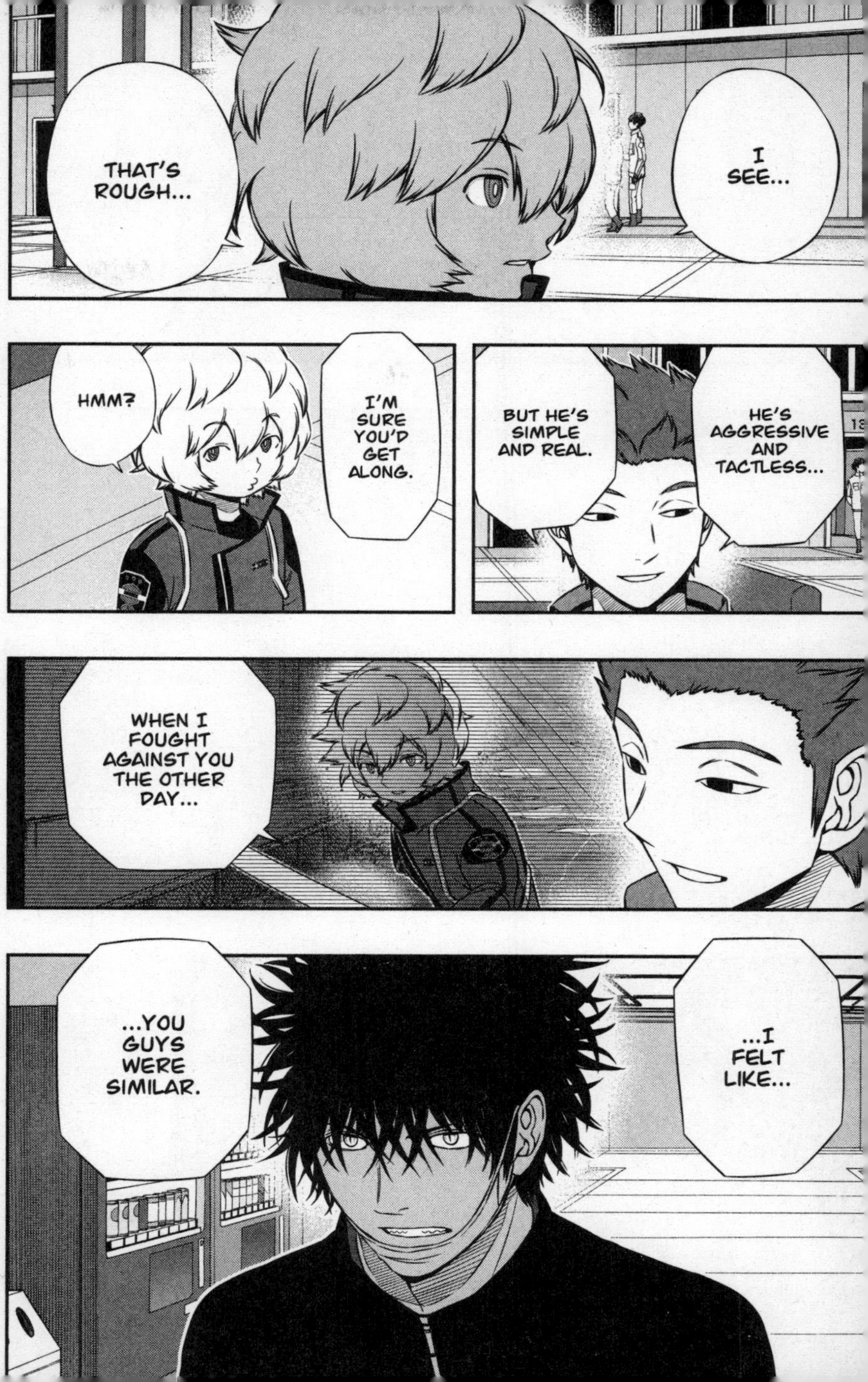
I SEE...
THAT'S ROUGH...
HE'S AGGRESSIVE AND TACTLESS...
BUT HE'S SIMPLE AND REAL.
I'M SURE YOU'D GET ALONG.
HMM?
WHEN I FOUGHT AGAINST YOU THE OTHER DAY...
...I FELT LIKE...
...YOU GUYS WERE SIMILAR.

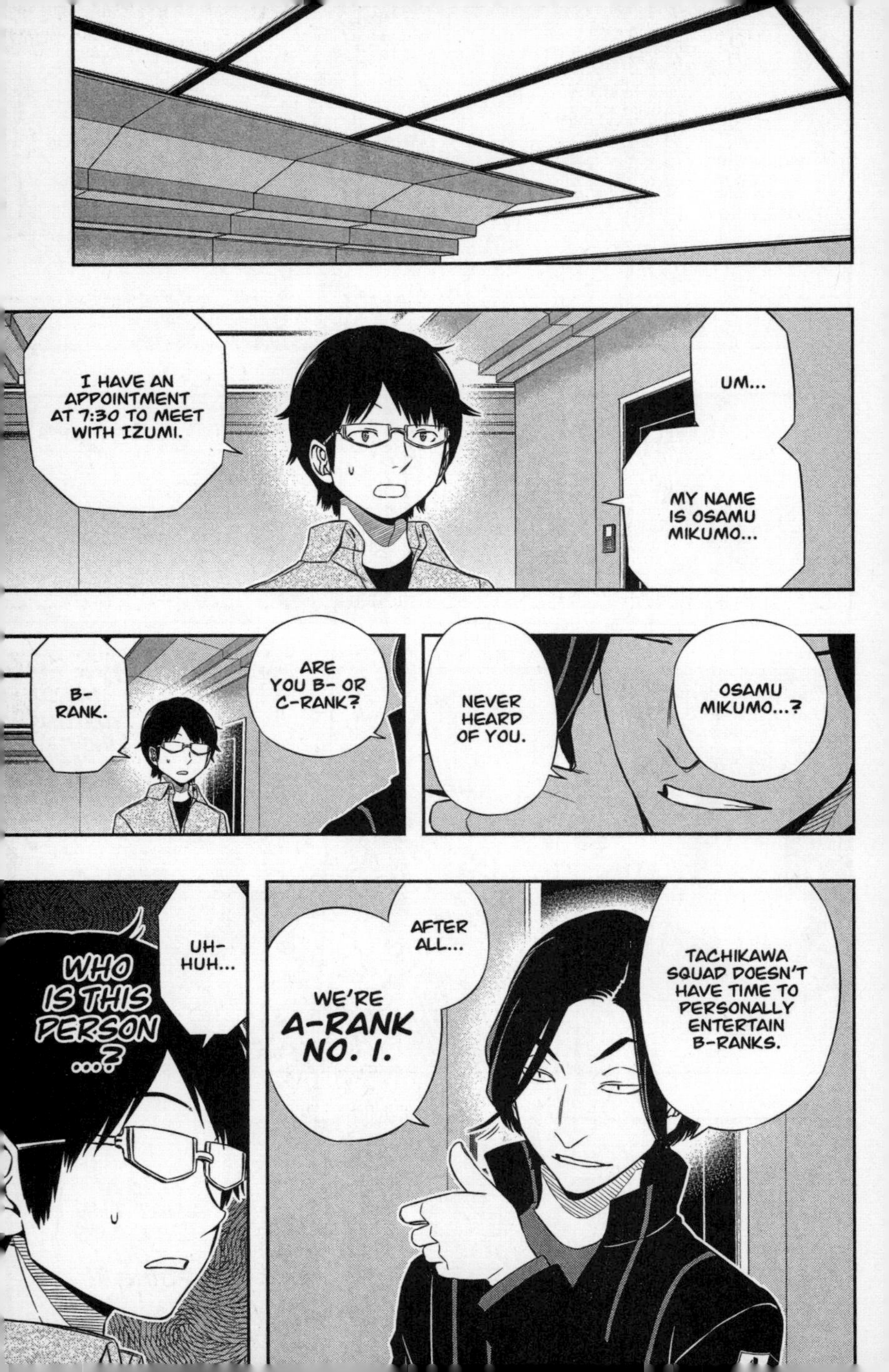
UM...
MY NAME IS OSAMU MIKUMO...
I HAVE AN APPOINTMENT AT 7:30 TO MEET WITH IZUMI.
OSAMU MIKUMO...?
NEVER HEARD OF YOU.
ARE YOU B- OR C-RANK?
B-RANK.
TACHIKAWA SQUAD DOESN'T HAVE TIME TO PERSONALLY ENTERTAIN B-RANKS.
AFTER ALL...
WE'RE A-RANK NO. 1.
UH-HUH...
WHO IS THIS PERSON...?

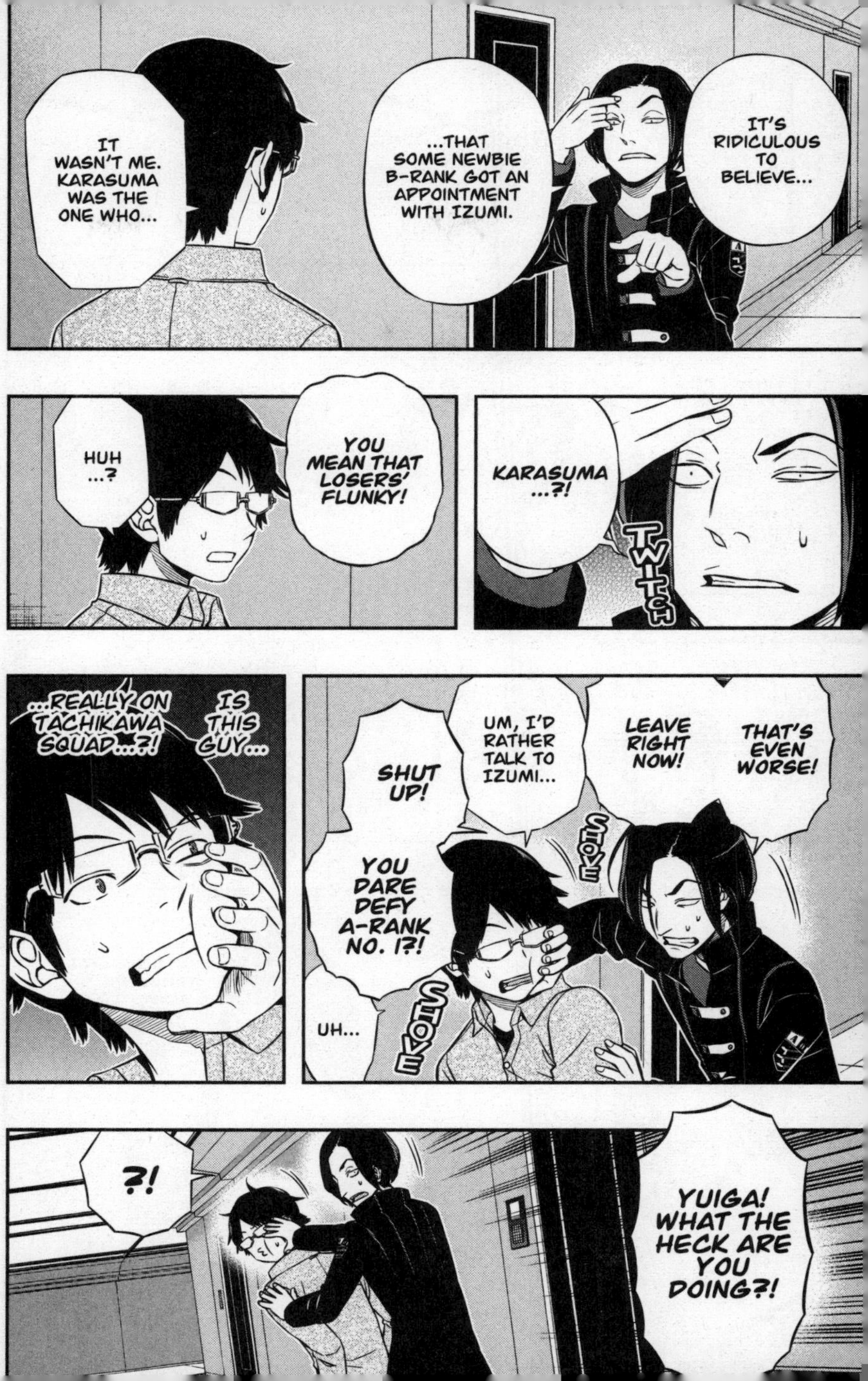
IT'S RIDICULOUS TO BELIEVE...
...THAT SOME NEWBIE B-RANK GOT AN APPOINTMENT WITH IZUMI.
IT WASN'T ME. KARASUMA WAS THE ONE WHO...
KARASUMA ...?!
TWITCH
YOU MEAN THAT LOSERS' FLUNKY!
HUH ...?
THAT'S EVEN WORSE!
LEAVE RIGHT NOW!
UM, I'D RATHER TALK TO IZUMI...
SHOVE
SHUT UP!
YOU DARE DEFY A-RANK NO. 1?!
SHOVE
UH...
IS THIS GUY...
...REALLY ON TACHIKAWA SQUAD...?!
YUIGA! WHAT THE HECK ARE YOU DOING?!
?!

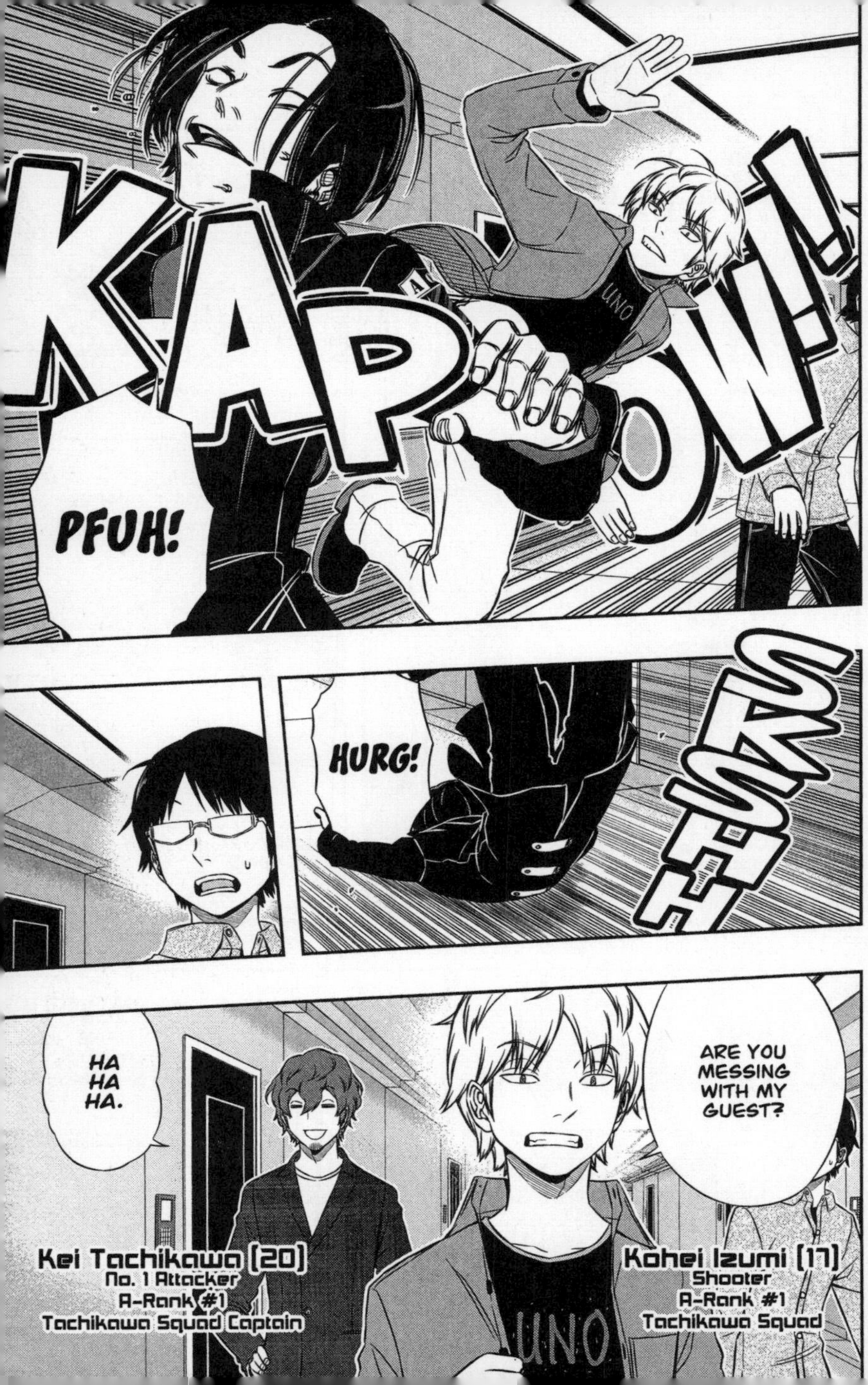
KAPOW!
PFUH!
SKSHH
HURG!
ARE YOU MESSING WITH MY GUEST?
HA HA HA.
Kohei Izumi (17)
Shooter
A-Rank #1
Tachikawa Squad
Kei Tachikawa (20)
No. 1 Attacker
A-Rank #1
Tachikawa Squad Captain

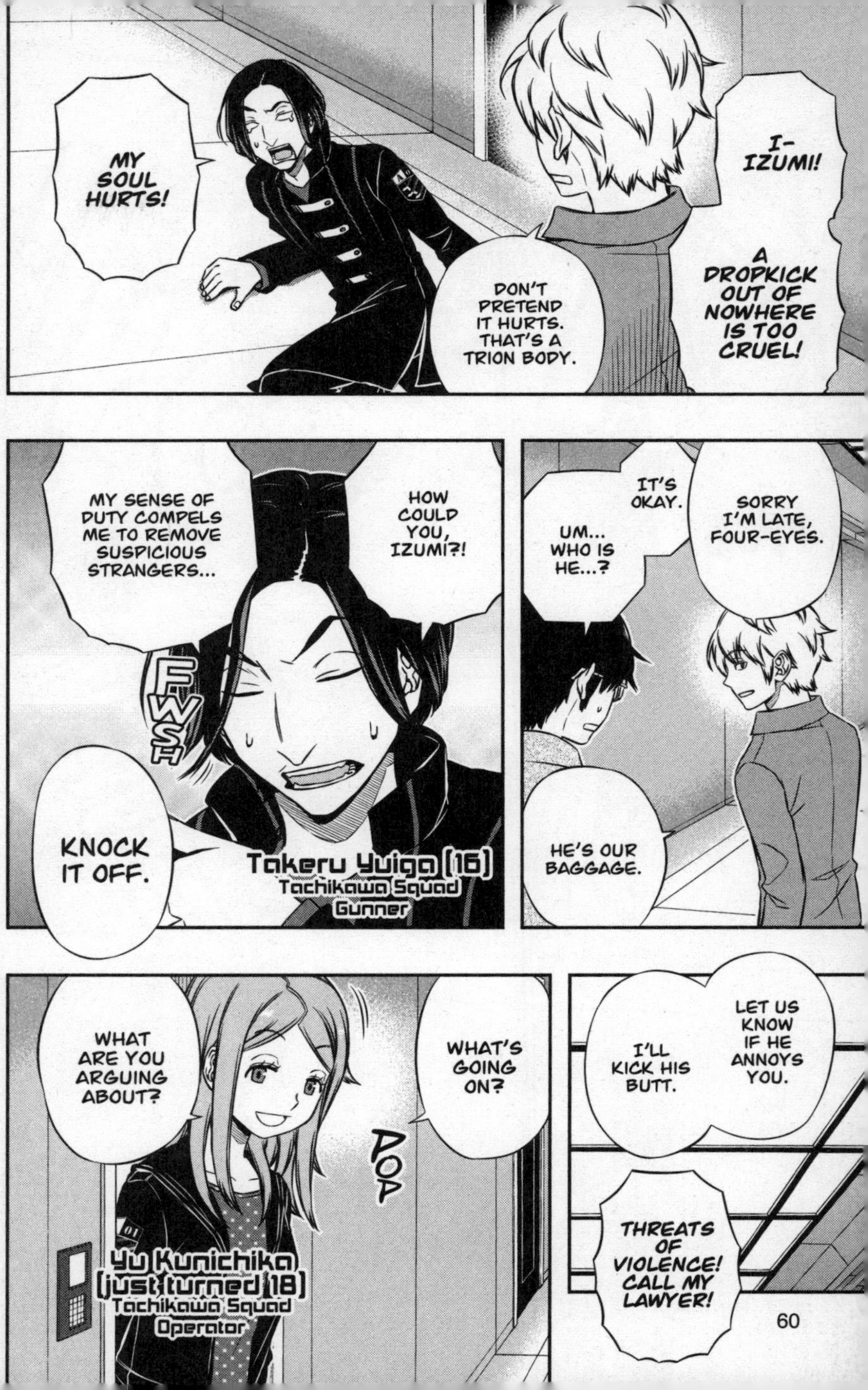
I- IZUMI!
A DROPKICK OUT OF NOWHERE IS TOO CRUEL!
DON'T PRETEND IT HURTS. THAT'S A TRION BODY.
MY SOUL HURTS!
SORRY I'M LATE, FOUR-EYES.
IT'S OKAY.
UM... WHO IS HE...?
HE'S OUR BAGGAGE.
HOW COULD YOU, IZUMI?!
MY SENSE OF DUTY COMPELS ME TO REMOVE SUSPICIOUS STRANGERS...
FWSH
Takeru Yuiga [16]
Tachikawa Squad Gunner
KNOCK IT OFF.
LET US KNOW IF HE ANNOYS YOU.
I'LL KICK HIS BUTT.
THREATS OF VIOLENCE! CALL MY LAWYER!
WHAT'S GOING ON?
POP
WHAT ARE YOU ARGUING ABOUT?
Yu Kunichika [just turned 18]
Tachikawa Squad Operator

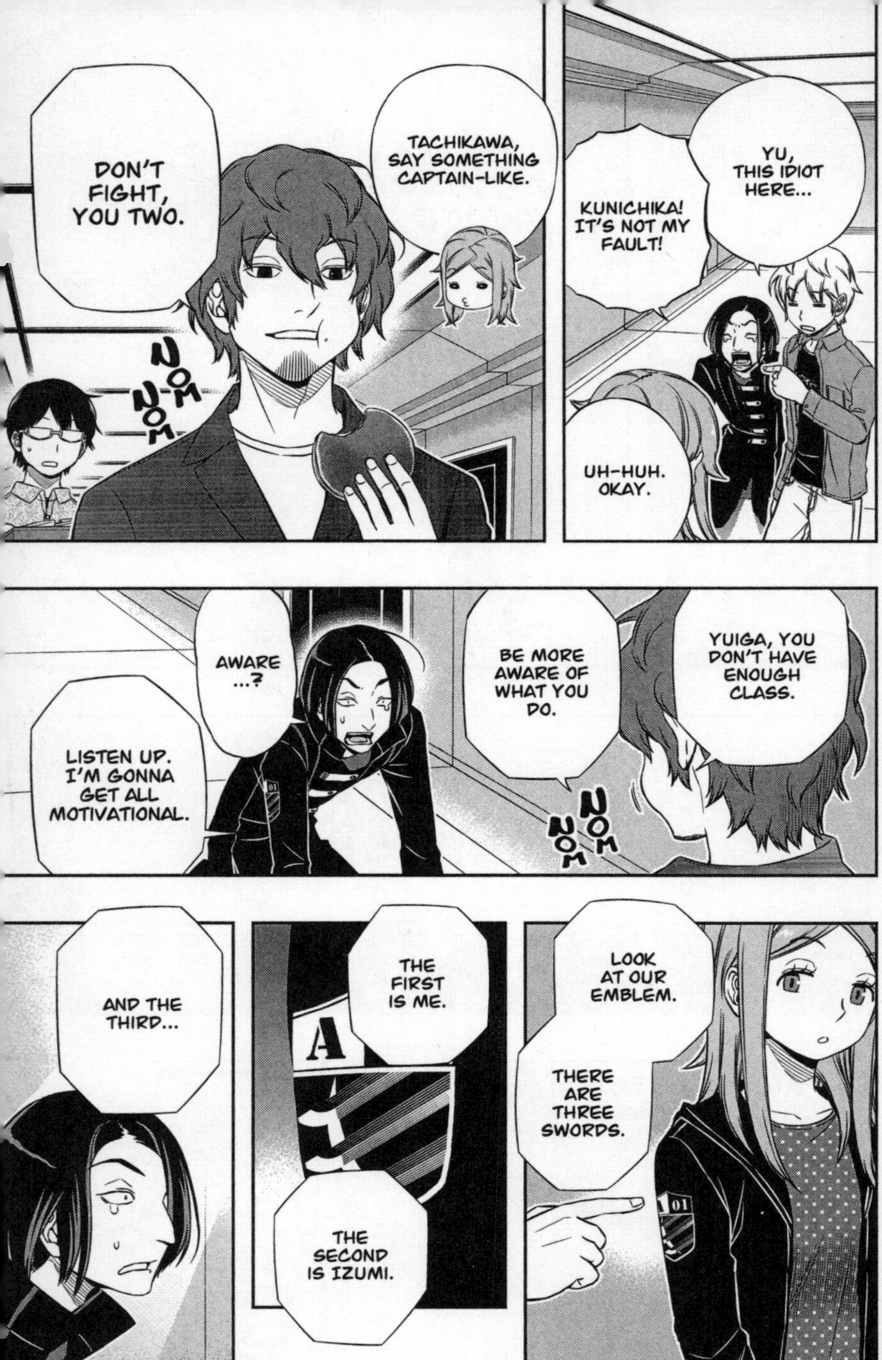
YU, THIS IDIOT HERE...
KUNICHIKA! IT'S NOT MY FAULT!
UH-HUH. OKAY.
TACHIKAWA, SAY SOMETHING CAPTAIN-LIKE.
DON'T FIGHT, YOU TWO.
NOM NOM NOM
YUIGA, YOU DON'T HAVE ENOUGH CLASS.
BE MORE AWARE OF WHAT YOU DO.
NOM NOM NOM
AWARE ...?
LISTEN UP. I'M GONNA GET ALL MOTIVATIONAL.
LOOK AT OUR EMBLEM.
THERE ARE THREE SWORDS.
THE FIRST IS ME.
THE SECOND IS IZUMI.
AND THE THIRD...

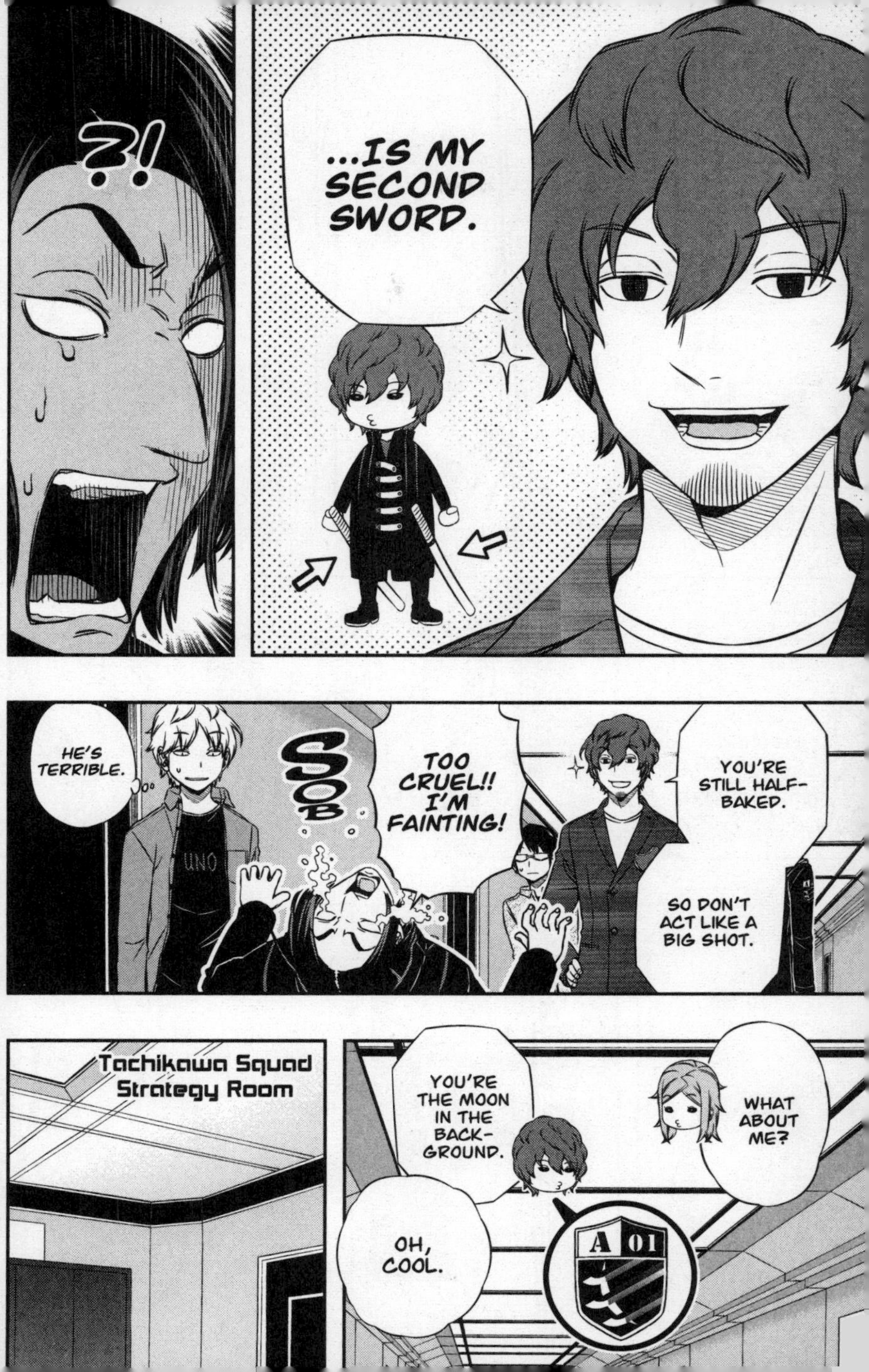
...IS MY SECOND SWORD.
?!
YOU'RE STILL HALF-BAKED.
SO DON'T ACT LIKE A BIG SHOT.
TOO CRUEL!! I'M FAINTING!
SOB
HE'S TERRIBLE.
WHAT ABOUT ME?
YOU'RE THE MOON IN THE BACK-GROUND.
OH, COOL.
A 01
Tachikawa Squad Strategy Room

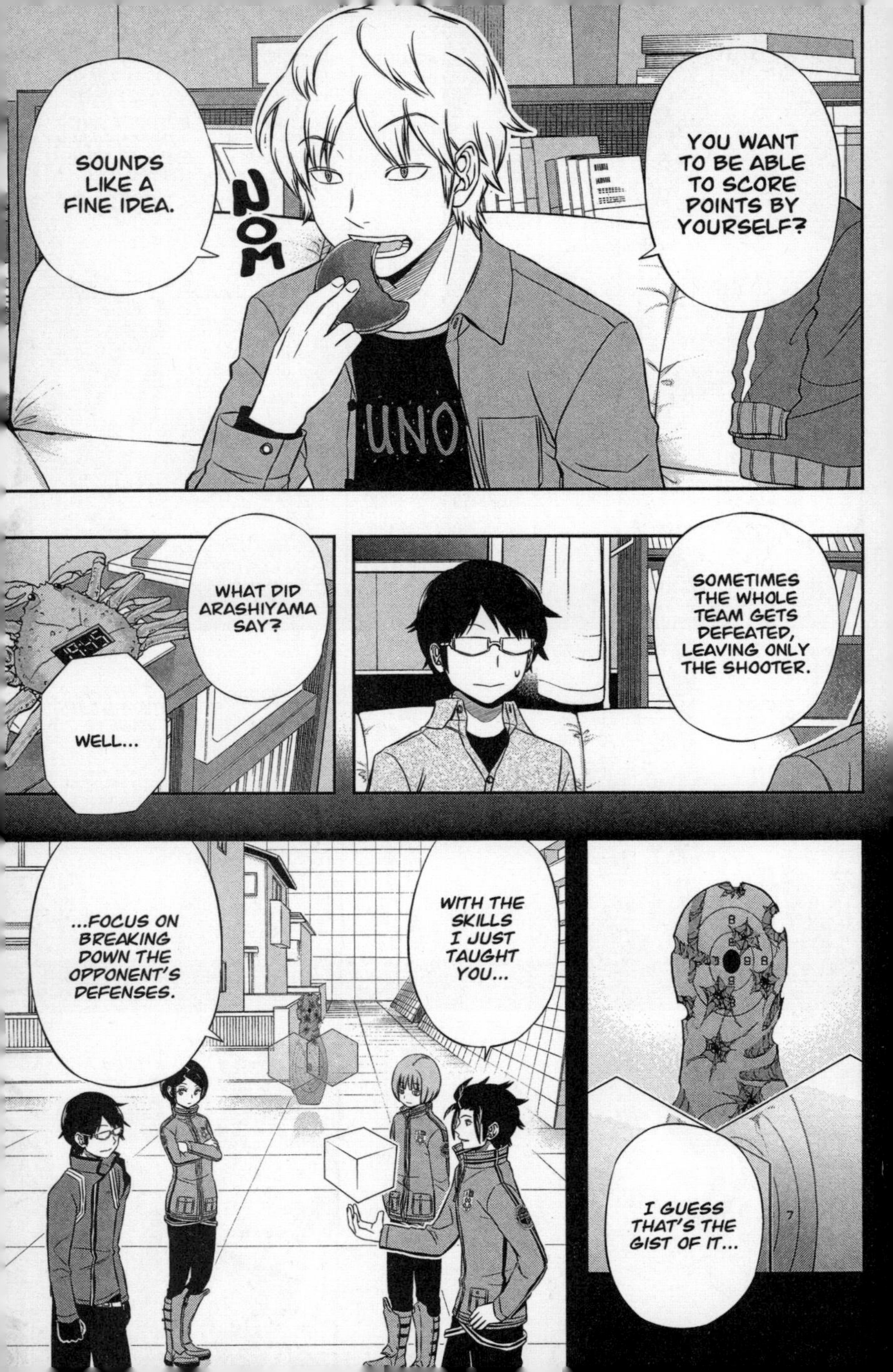
YOU WANT TO BE ABLE TO SCORE POINTS BY YOURSELF?
NOM
UNO
SOUNDS LIKE A FINE IDEA.
SOMETIMES THE WHOLE TEAM GETS DEFEATED, LEAVING ONLY THE SHOOTER.
WHAT DID ARASHIYAMA SAY?
WELL...
I GUESS THAT'S THE GIST OF IT...
WITH THE SKILLS I JUST TAUGHT YOU...
...FOCUS ON BREAKING DOWN THE OPPONENT'S DEFENSES.

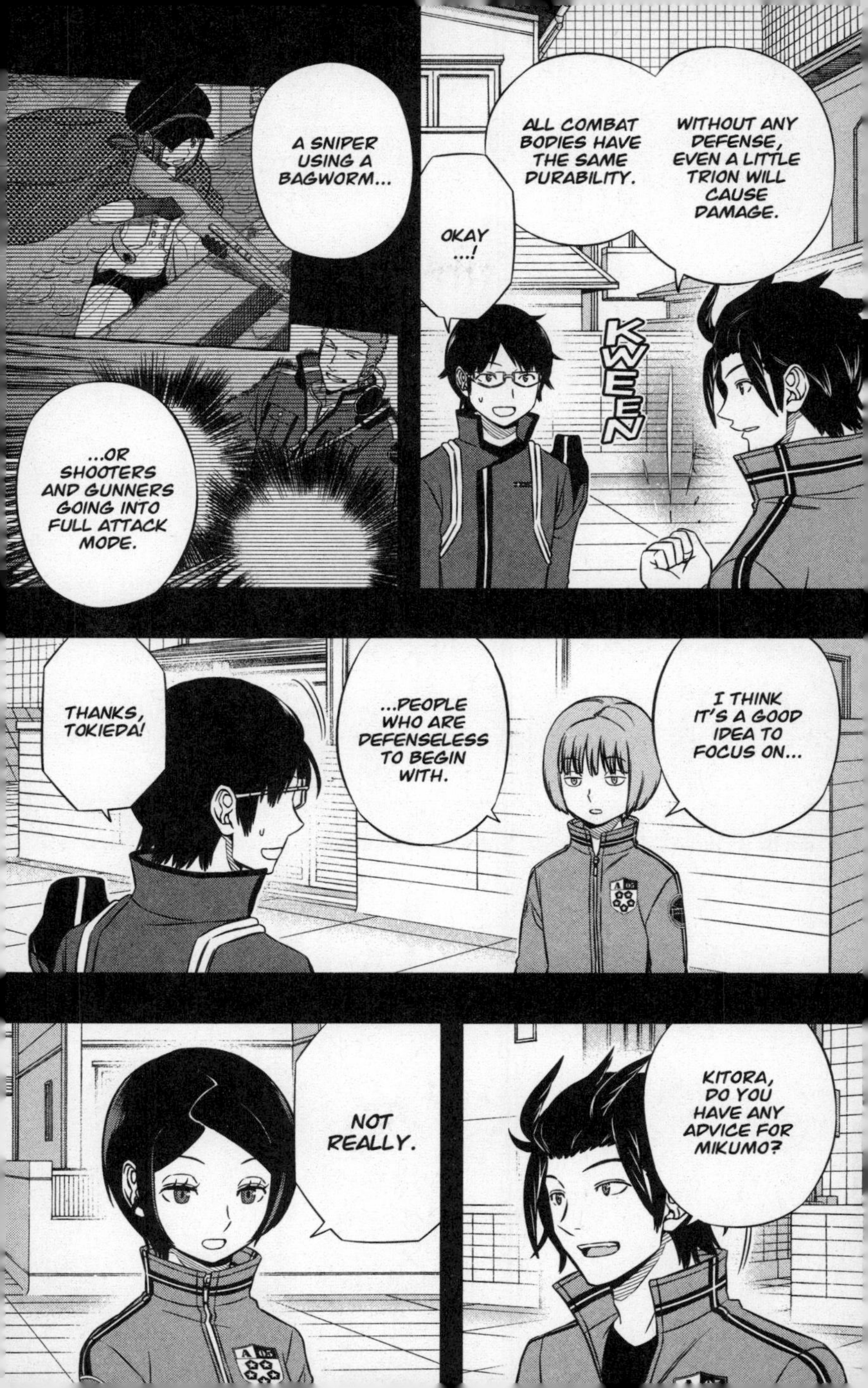
WITHOUT ANY DEFENSE, EVEN A LITTLE TRION WILL CAUSE DAMAGE.
ALL COMBAT BODIES HAVE THE SAME DURABILITY.
OKAY ...!
KWEEN
A SNIPER USING A BAGWORM...
...OR SHOOTERS AND GUNNERS GOING INTO FULL ATTACK MODE.
I THINK IT'S A GOOD IDEA TO FOCUS ON...
...PEOPLE WHO ARE DEFENSELESS TO BEGIN WITH.
THANKS, TOKIEDA!
KITORA, DO YOU HAVE ANY ADVICE FOR MIKUMO?
NOT REALLY.

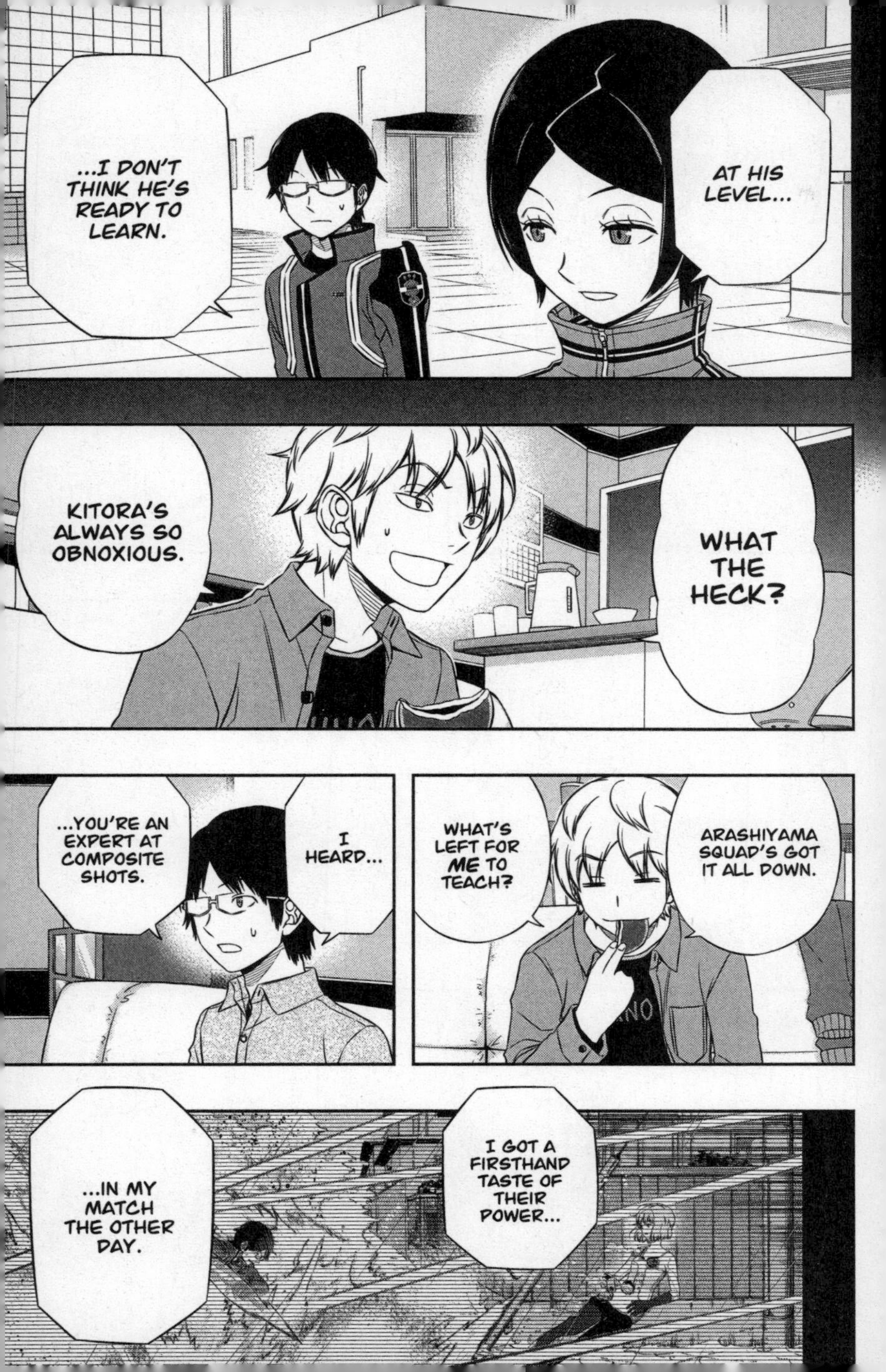
AT HIS LEVEL...
...I DON'T THINK HE'S READY TO LEARN.
WHAT THE HECK?
KITORA'S ALWAYS SO OBNOXIOUS.
ARASHIYAMA SQUAD'S GOT IT ALL DOWN.
WHAT'S LEFT FOR ME TO TEACH?
I HEARD...
...YOU'RE AN EXPERT AT COMPOSITE SHOTS.
I GOT A FIRSTHAND TASTE OF THEIR POWER...
...IN MY MATCH THE OTHER DAY.

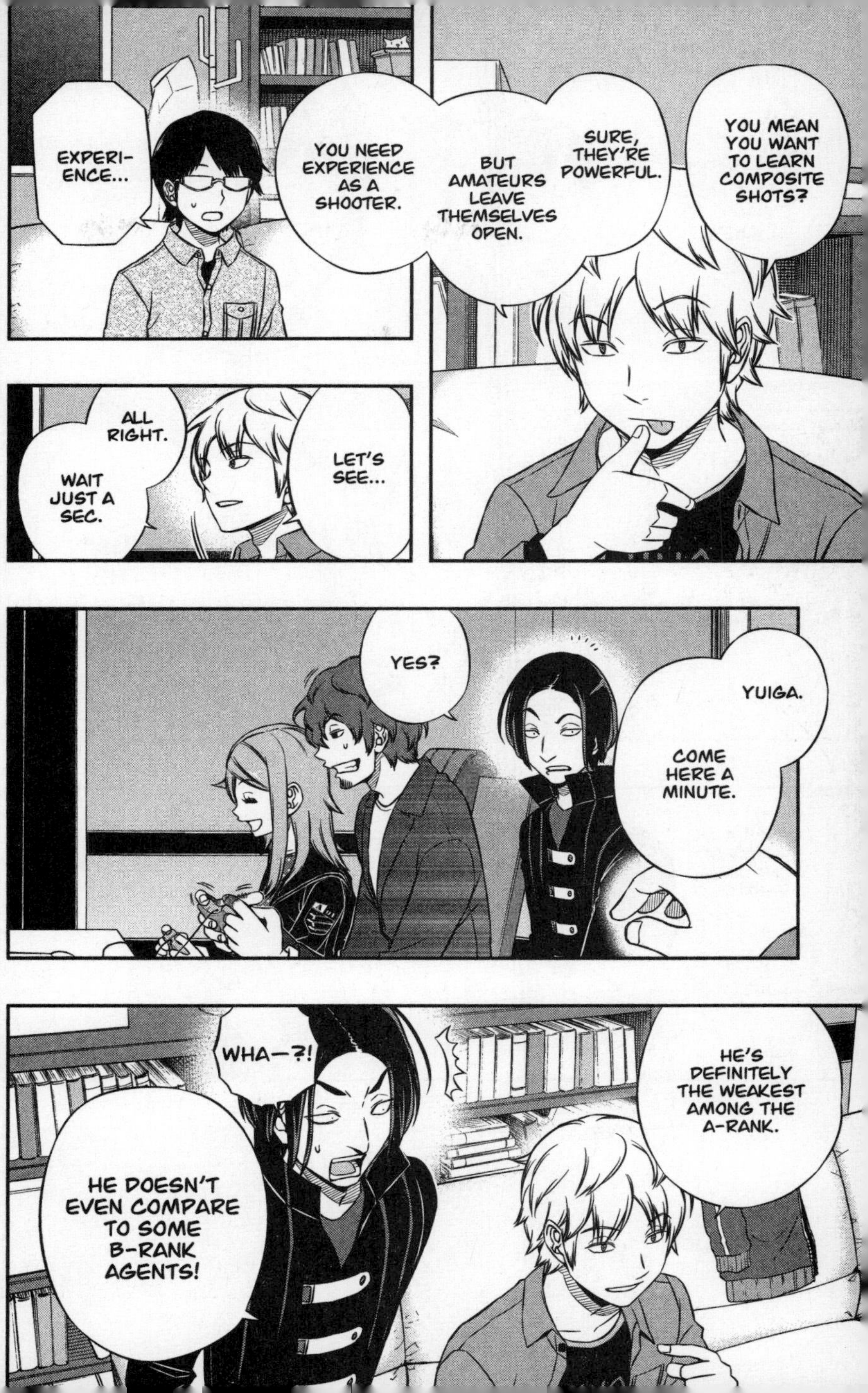
YOU MEAN YOU WANT TO LEARN COMPOSITE SHOTS?
SURE, THEY'RE POWERFUL.
BUT AMATEURS LEAVE THEMSELVES OPEN.
YOU NEED EXPERIENCE AS A SHOOTER.
EXPERI-ENCE...
LET'S SEE...
ALL RIGHT.
WAIT JUST A SEC.
YUIGA.
COME HERE A MINUTE.
YES?
HE'S DEFINITELY THE WEAKEST AMONG THE A-RANK.
WHA—?!
HE DOESN'T EVEN COMPARE TO SOME B-RANK AGENTS!

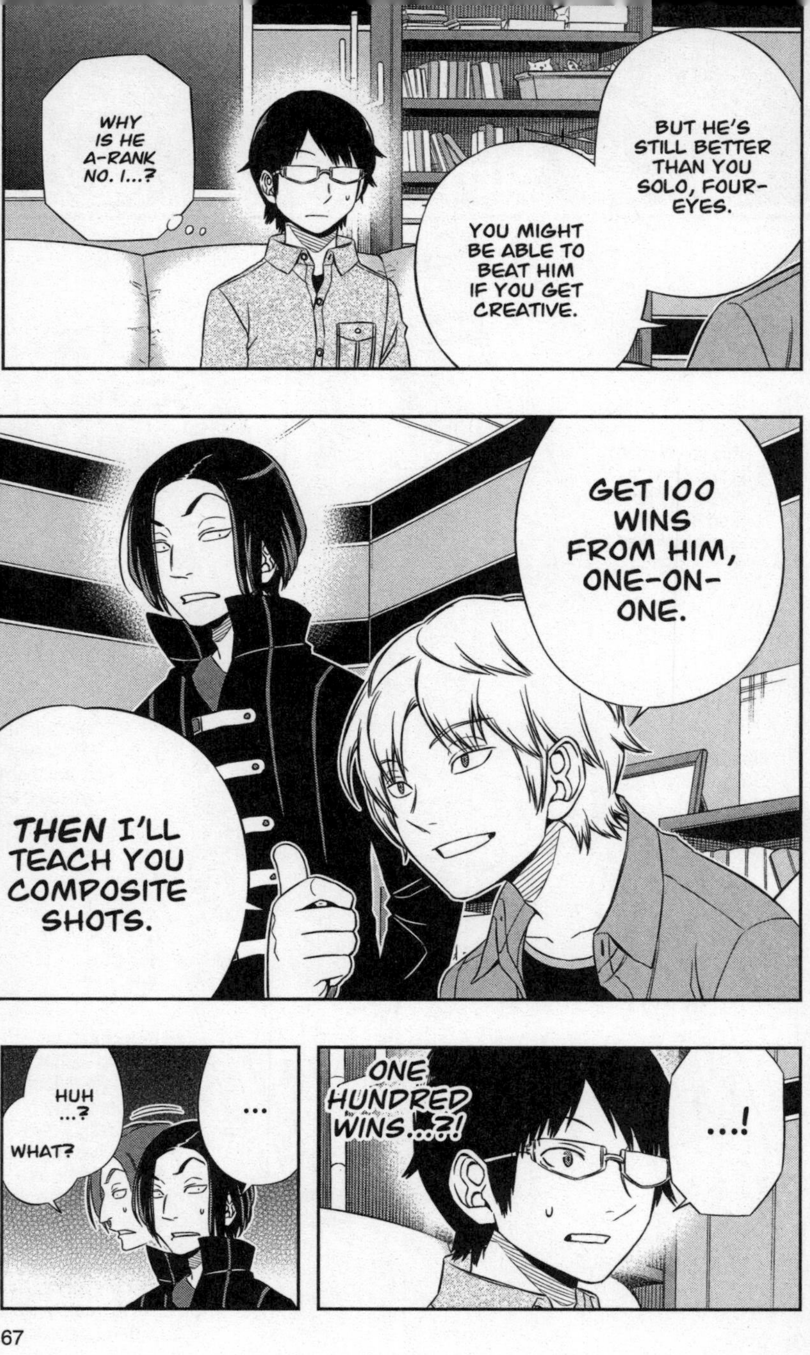
BUT HE'S STILL BETTER THAN YOU SOLO, FOUR-EYES.
YOU MIGHT BE ABLE TO BEAT HIM IF YOU GET CREATIVE.
WHY IS HE A-RANK NO. 1...?
GET 100 WINS FROM HIM, ONE-ON-ONE.
THEN I'LL TEACH YOU COMPOSITE SHOTS.
...!
ONE HUNDRED WINS...?!
...
HUH...?
WHAT?

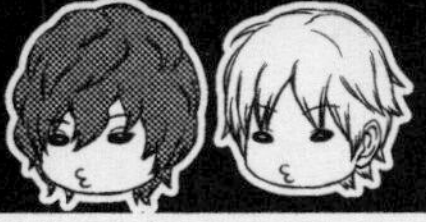

Tachikawa Squad Strategy Room

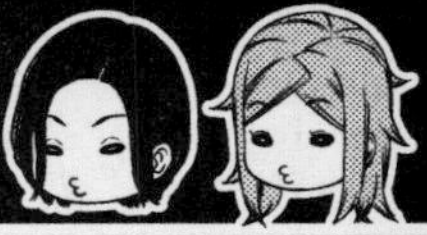

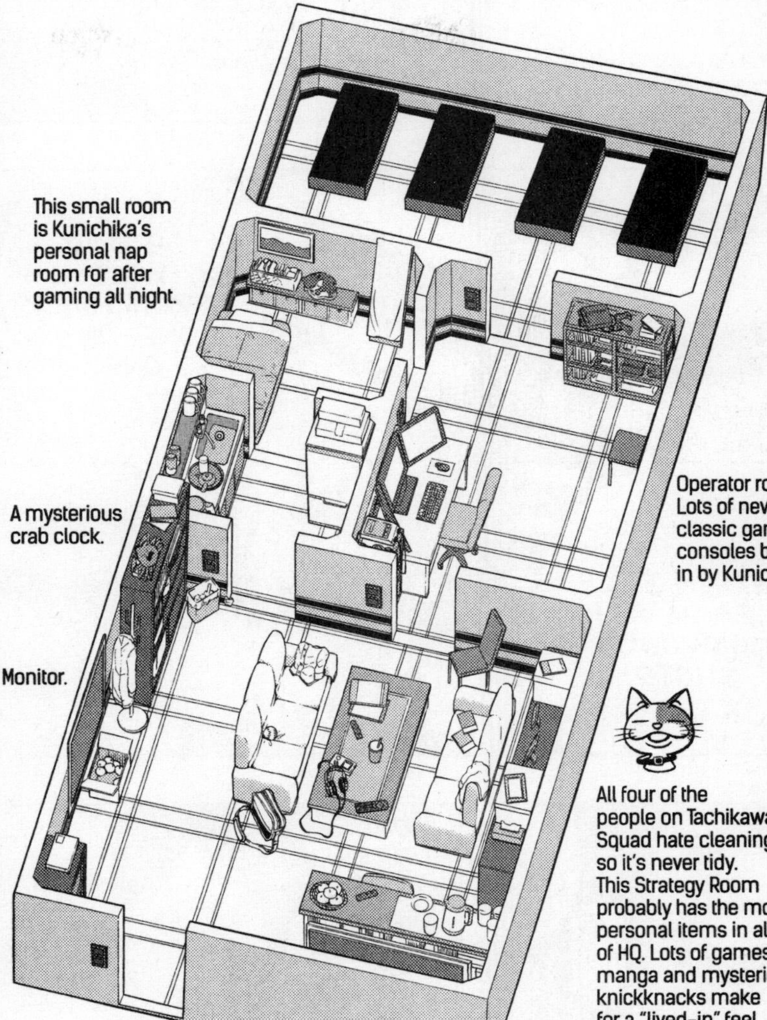

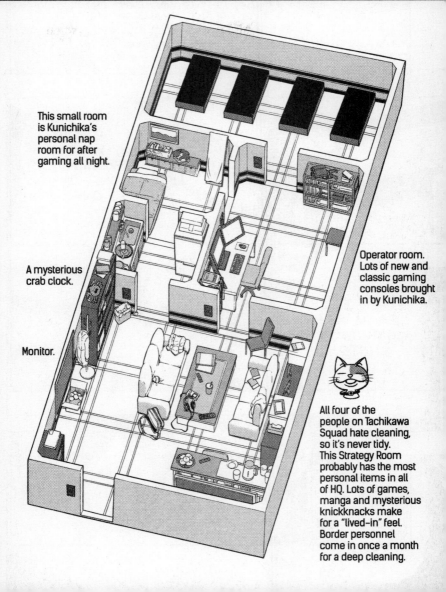

This small room is Kunichika's personal nap room for after gaming all night.

A mysterious crab clock.

Monitor.

Operator room. Lots of new and classic gaming consoles brought in by Kunichika.

All four of the people on Tachikawa Squad hate cleaning, so it's never tidy. This Strategy Room probably has the most personal items in all of HQ. Lots of games, manga and mysterious knickknacks make for a "lived-in" feel. Border personnel come in once a month for a deep cleaning.

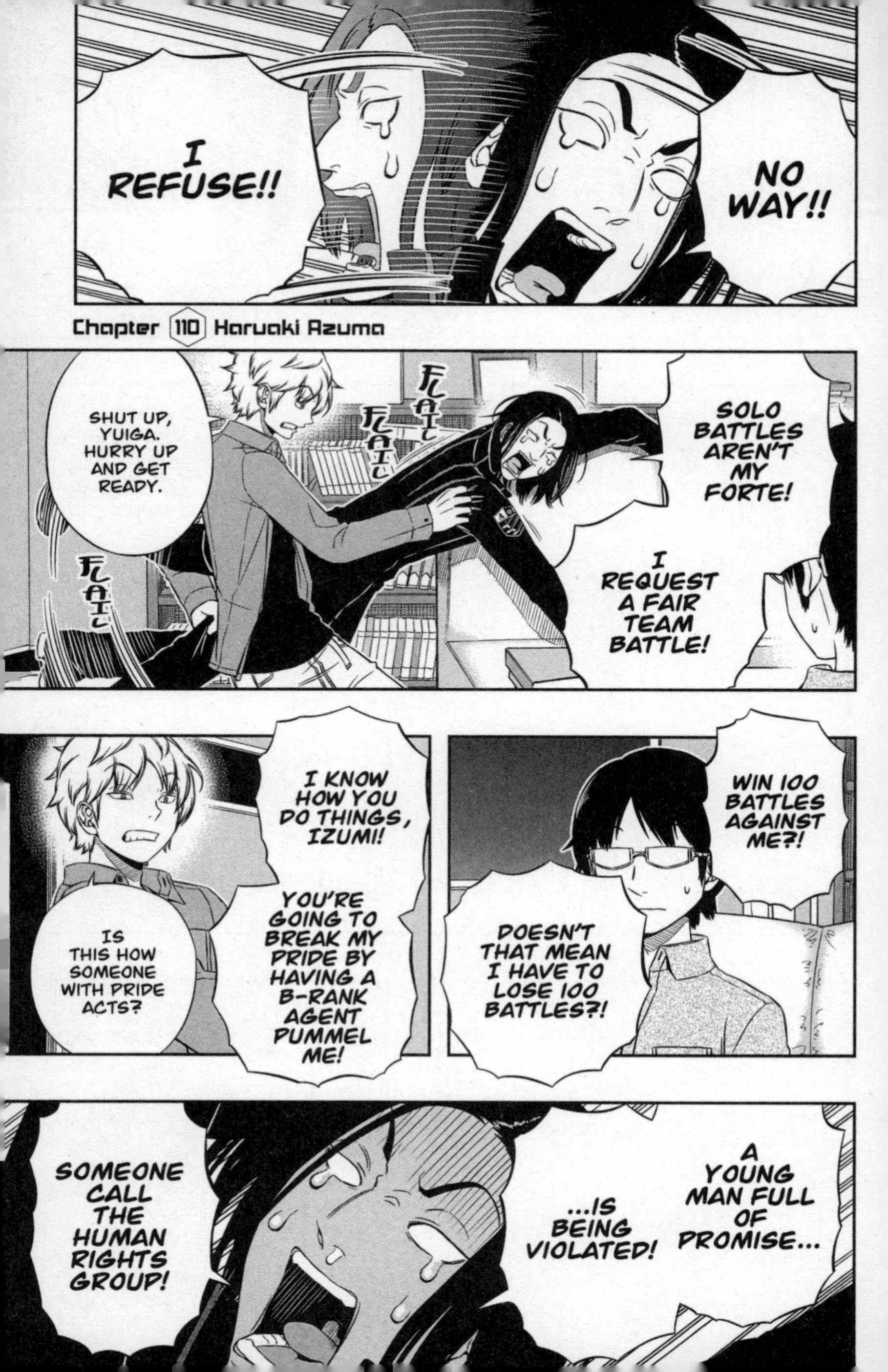
NO WAY!!
I REFUSE!!
Chapter 110 Haruaki Azuma
SOLO BATTLES AREN'T MY FORTE!
I REQUEST A FAIR TEAM BATTLE!
FLAIL
FLAIL
SHUT UP, YUIGA. HURRY UP AND GET READY.
FLAIL
WIN 100 BATTLES AGAINST ME?!
DOESN'T THAT MEAN I HAVE TO LOSE 100 BATTLES?!
I KNOW HOW YOU DO THINGS, IZUMI!
YOU'RE GOING TO BREAK MY PRIDE BY HAVING A B-RANK AGENT PUMMEL ME!
IS THIS HOW SOMEONE WITH PRIDE ACTS?
A YOUNG MAN FULL OF PROMISE...
...IS BEING VIOLATED!
SOMEONE CALL THE HUMAN RIGHTS GROUP!

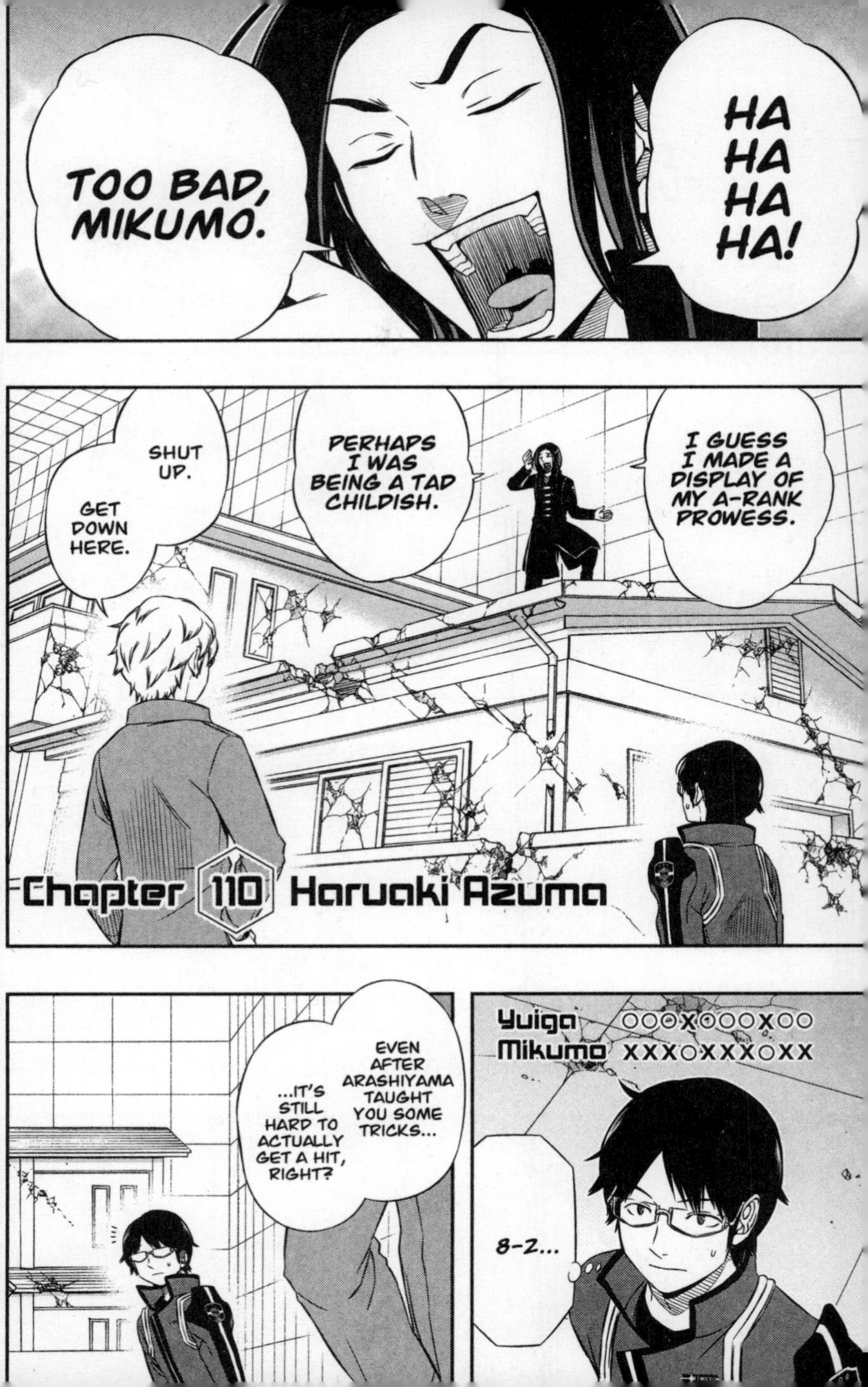
HA HA HA HA!
TOO BAD, MIKUMO.
I GUESS I MADE A DISPLAY OF MY A-RANK PROWESS.
PERHAPS I WAS BEING A TAD CHILDISH.
SHUT UP.
GET DOWN HERE.
Chapter 110 Haruaki Azuma
Yuiga ○○○X○○○X○○
Mikumo XXX○XXX○XX
8-2...
EVEN AFTER ARASHIYAMA TAUGHT YOU SOME TRICKS...
...IT'S STILL HARD TO ACTUALLY GET A HIT, RIGHT?

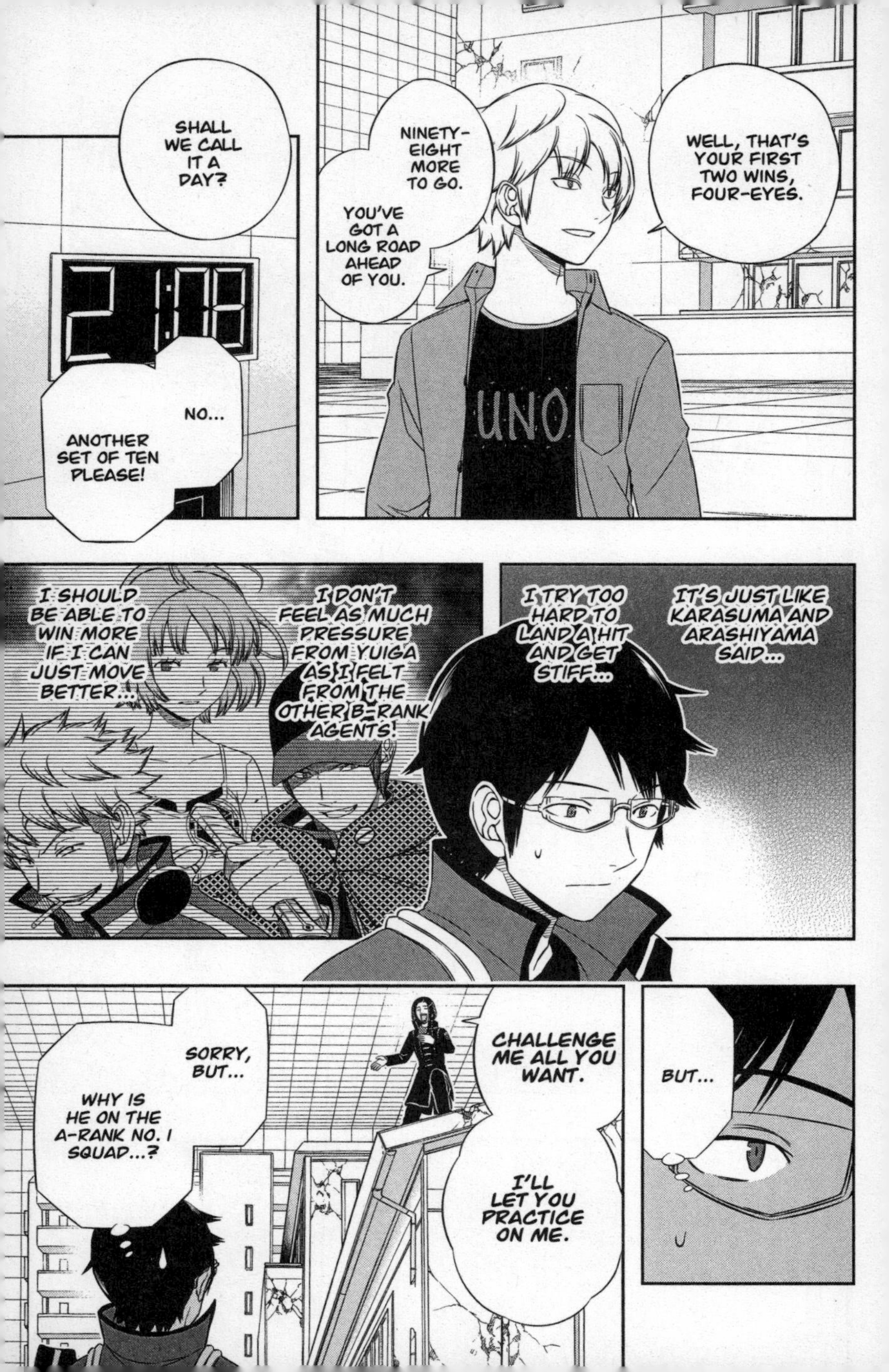
WELL, THAT'S YOUR FIRST TWO WINS, FOUR-EYES.
NINETY-EIGHT MORE TO GO.
YOU'VE GOT A LONG ROAD AHEAD OF YOU.
SHALL WE CALL IT A DAY?
NO...
ANOTHER SET OF TEN PLEASE!
IT'S JUST LIKE KARASUMA AND ARASHIYAMA SAID...
I TRY TOO HARD TO LAND A HIT AND GET STIFF...
I DON'T FEEL AS MUCH PRESSURE FROM YUIGA AS I FELT FROM THE OTHER B-RANK AGENTS!
I SHOULD BE ABLE TO WIN MORE IF I CAN JUST MOVE BETTER...
BUT...
CHALLENGE ME ALL YOU WANT.
I'LL LET YOU PRACTICE ON ME.
SORRY, BUT...
WHY IS HE ON THE A-RANK NO. 1 SQUAD...?

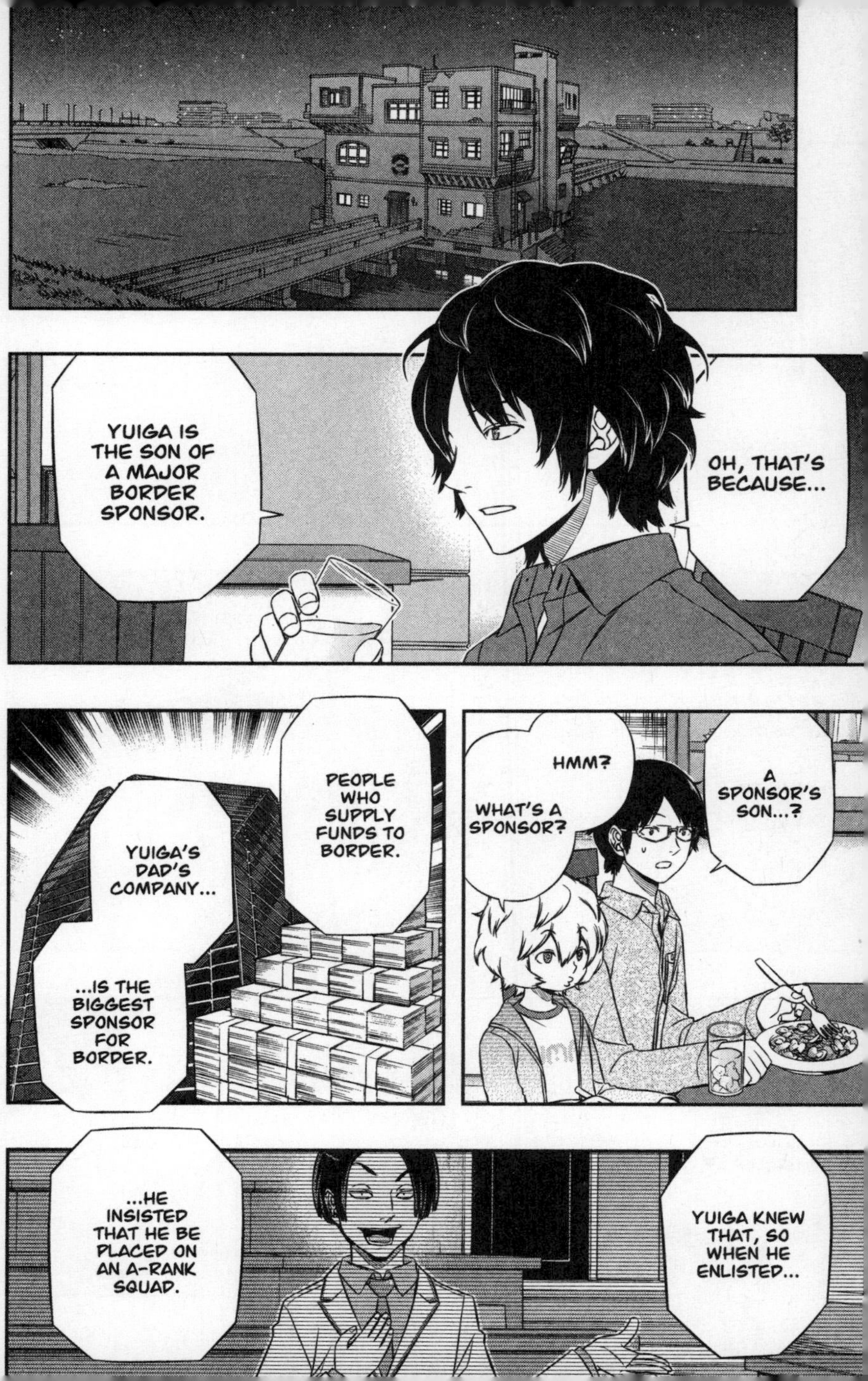
OH, THAT'S BECAUSE...
YUIGA IS THE SON OF A MAJOR BORDER SPONSOR.
A SPONSOR'S SON...?
HMM?
WHAT'S A SPONSOR?
PEOPLE WHO SUPPLY FUNDS TO BORDER.
YUIGA'S DAD'S COMPANY...
...IS THE BIGGEST SPONSOR FOR BORDER.
YUIGA KNEW THAT, SO WHEN HE ENLISTED...
...HE INSISTED THAT HE BE PLACED ON AN A-RANK SQUAD.

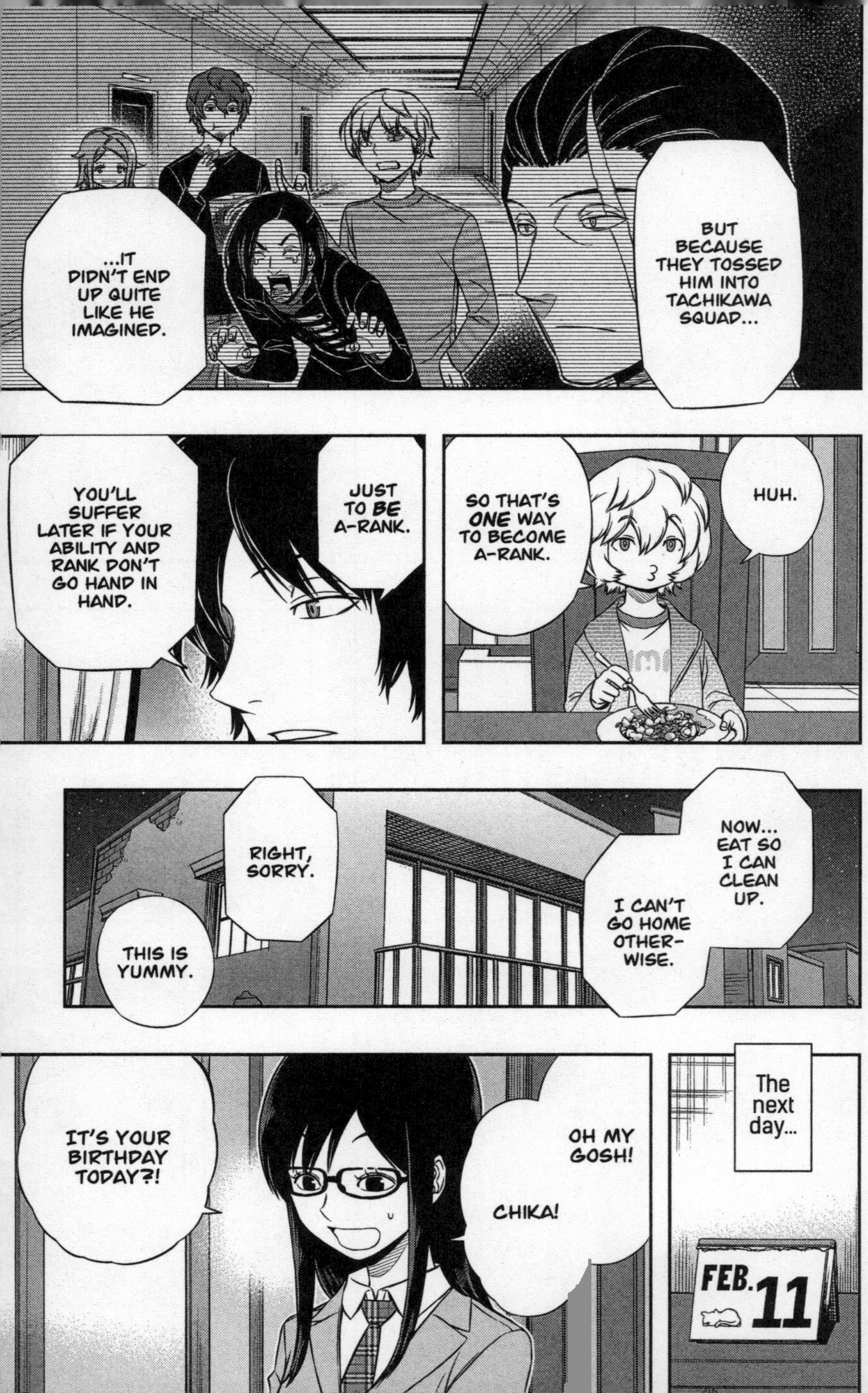
BUT BECAUSE THEY TOSSED HIM INTO TACHIKAWA SQUAD...
...IT DIDN'T END UP QUITE LIKE HE IMAGINED.
HUH.
SO THAT'S ONE WAY TO BECOME A-RANK.
JUST TO BE A-RANK.
YOU'LL SUFFER LATER IF YOUR ABILITY AND RANK DON'T GO HAND IN HAND.
NOW... EAT SO I CAN CLEAN UP.
I CAN'T GO HOME OTHER-WISE.
RIGHT, SORRY.
THIS IS YUMMY.
The next day...
FEB. 11
OH MY GOSH!
CHIKA!
IT'S YOUR BIRTHDAY TODAY?!

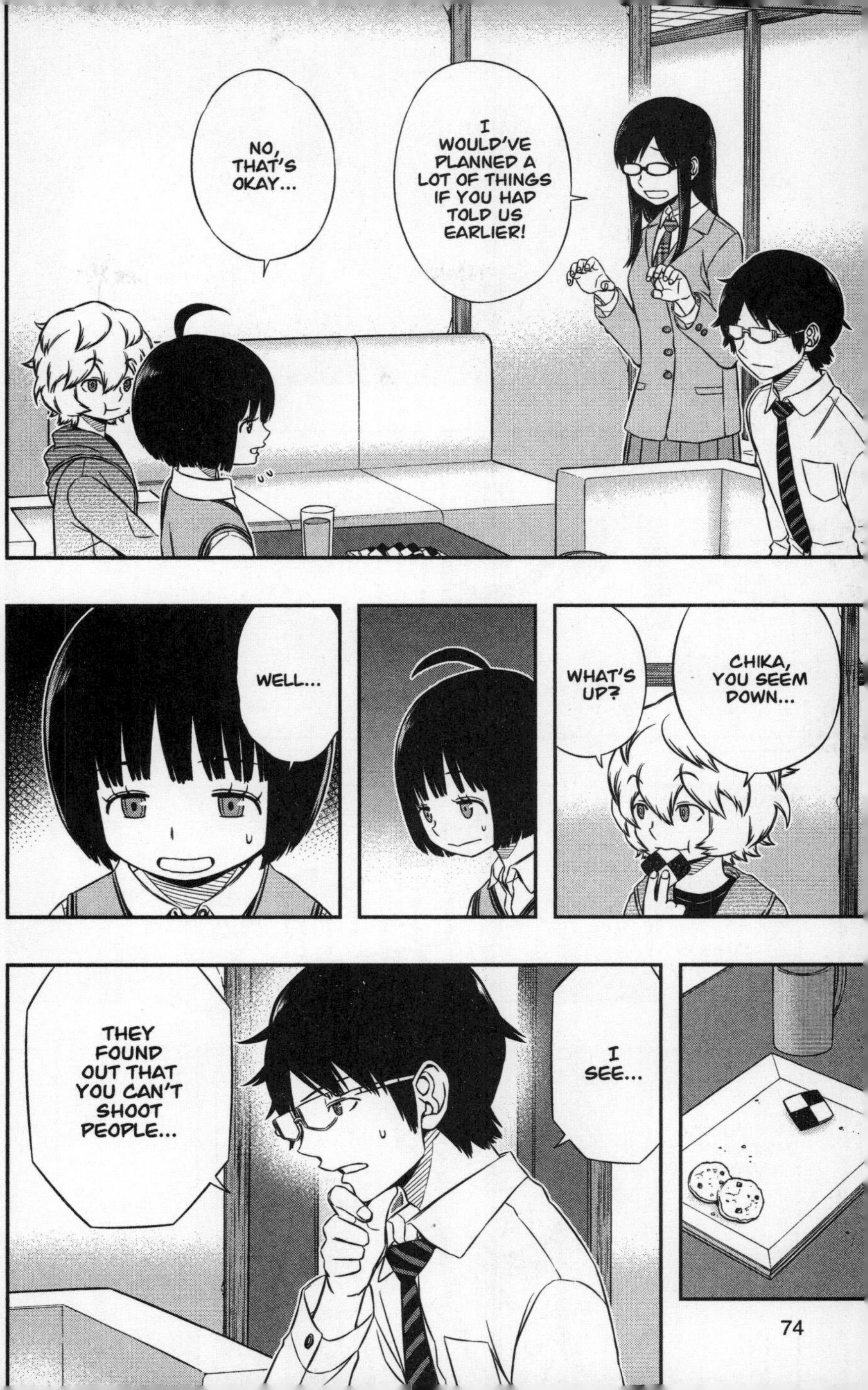
I WOULD'VE PLANNED A LOT OF THINGS IF YOU HAD TOLD US EARLIER!
NO, THAT'S OKAY...
CHIKA, YOU SEEM DOWN...
WHAT'S UP?
WELL...
I SEE...
THEY FOUND OUT THAT YOU CAN'T SHOOT PEOPLE...

I'M SORRY...

YOU SHOULDN'T HAVE TOLD HIM THOUGH.

PEOPLE WOULD'VE FIGURED IT OUT EVENTUALLY BY WATCHING OUR MATCHES...

I'M SORRY IT SLIPPED OUT...

IF HATOHARA WAS SIMILAR TO YOU, THEN...

...NINOMIYA MIGHT'VE REALIZED YOUR WEAKNESS ALREADY.

WE'LL HAVE TO TAKE EXTRA PRECAUTIONS TO MAKE SURE SHE STAYS HIDDEN...

IF THEY KNOW CHIKA WON'T SHOOT BACK...

...THE OTHER SQUADS WILL COME AFTER HER.

AS WELL AS AZUMA, HATOHARA'S MENTOR.

		NOMIYA SQUAD
B-R		KAGEURA SQUAD
B-RANK NO. 6		TAMAKOMA-2
B-RANK NO. 7	AZUMA SQUAD	

YEAH...

WOULDN'T *THAT* BE INTEREST-ING?

THEY MIGHT *THINK* YOU CAN'T SHOOT, BUT THEN YOU *WILL*!

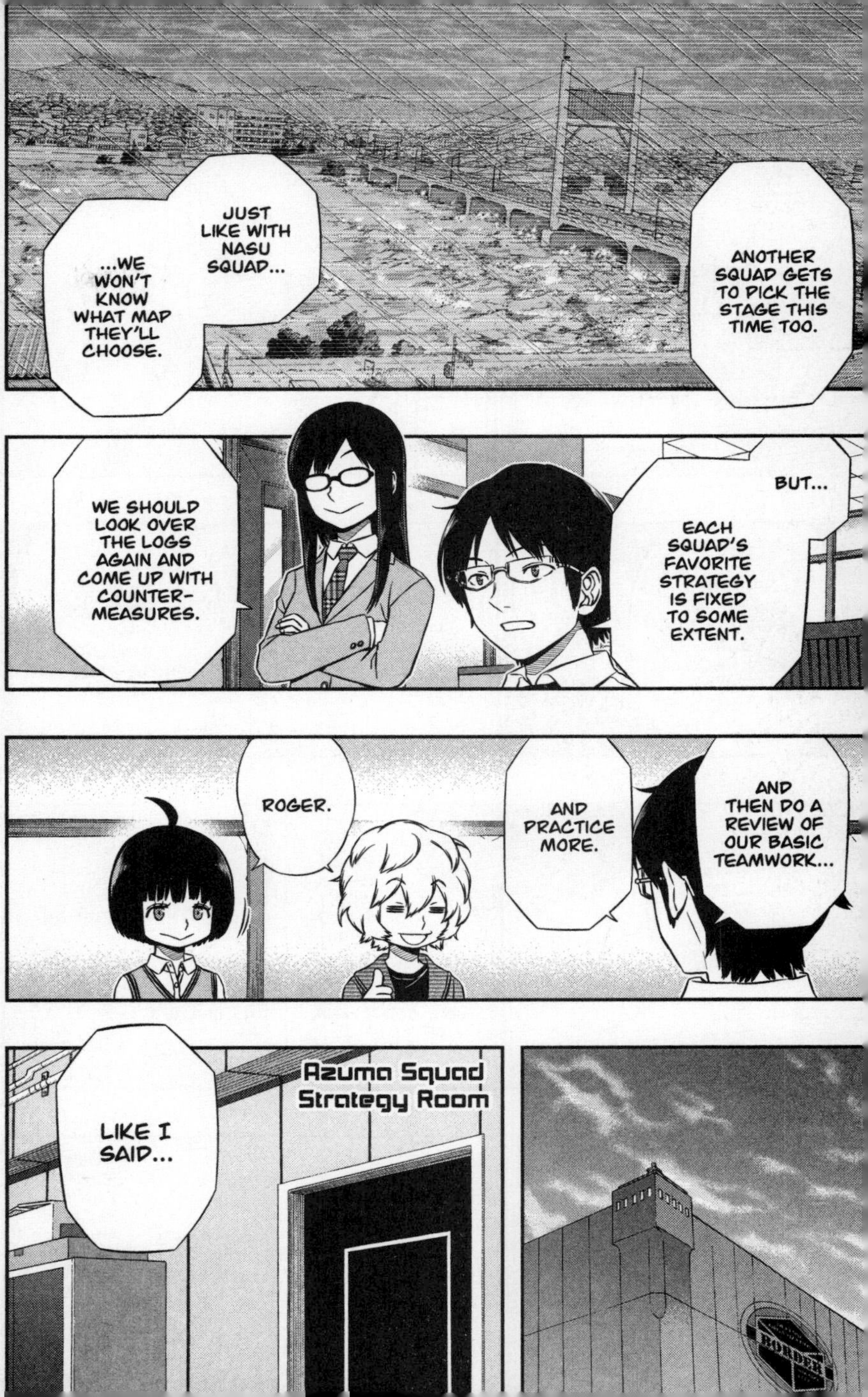
ANOTHER SQUAD GETS TO PICK THE STAGE THIS TIME TOO.
JUST LIKE WITH NASU SQUAD...
...WE WON'T KNOW WHAT MAP THEY'LL CHOOSE.
BUT...
EACH SQUAD'S FAVORITE STRATEGY IS FIXED TO SOME EXTENT.
WE SHOULD LOOK OVER THE LOGS AGAIN AND COME UP WITH COUNTER-MEASURES.
AND THEN DO A REVIEW OF OUR BASIC TEAMWORK...
AND PRACTICE MORE.
ROGER.
Azuma Squad Strategy Room
LIKE I SAID...

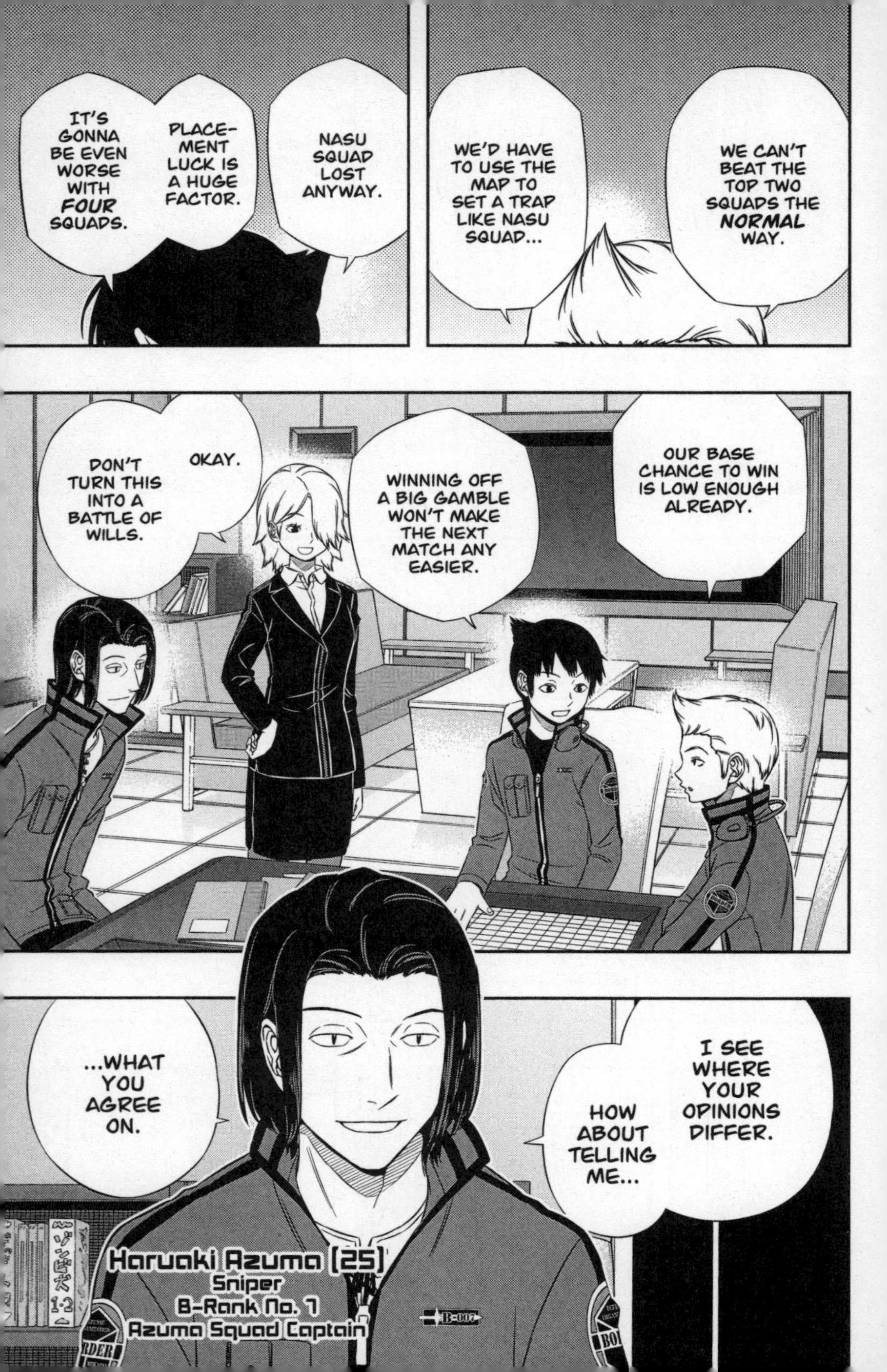
WE CAN'T BEAT THE TOP TWO SQUADS THE NORMAL WAY.
WE'D HAVE TO USE THE MAP TO SET A TRAP LIKE NASU SQUAD...
NASU SQUAD LOST ANYWAY.
PLACE-MENT LUCK IS A HUGE FACTOR.
IT'S GONNA BE EVEN WORSE WITH FOUR SQUADS.
OUR BASE CHANCE TO WIN IS LOW ENOUGH ALREADY.
WINNING OFF A BIG GAMBLE WON'T MAKE THE NEXT MATCH ANY EASIER.
OKAY.
DON'T TURN THIS INTO A BATTLE OF WILLS.
I SEE WHERE YOUR OPINIONS DIFFER.
HOW ABOUT TELLING ME...
...WHAT YOU AGREE ON.
Haruaki Azuma (25)
Sniper
B-Rank No. 1
Azuma Squad Captain

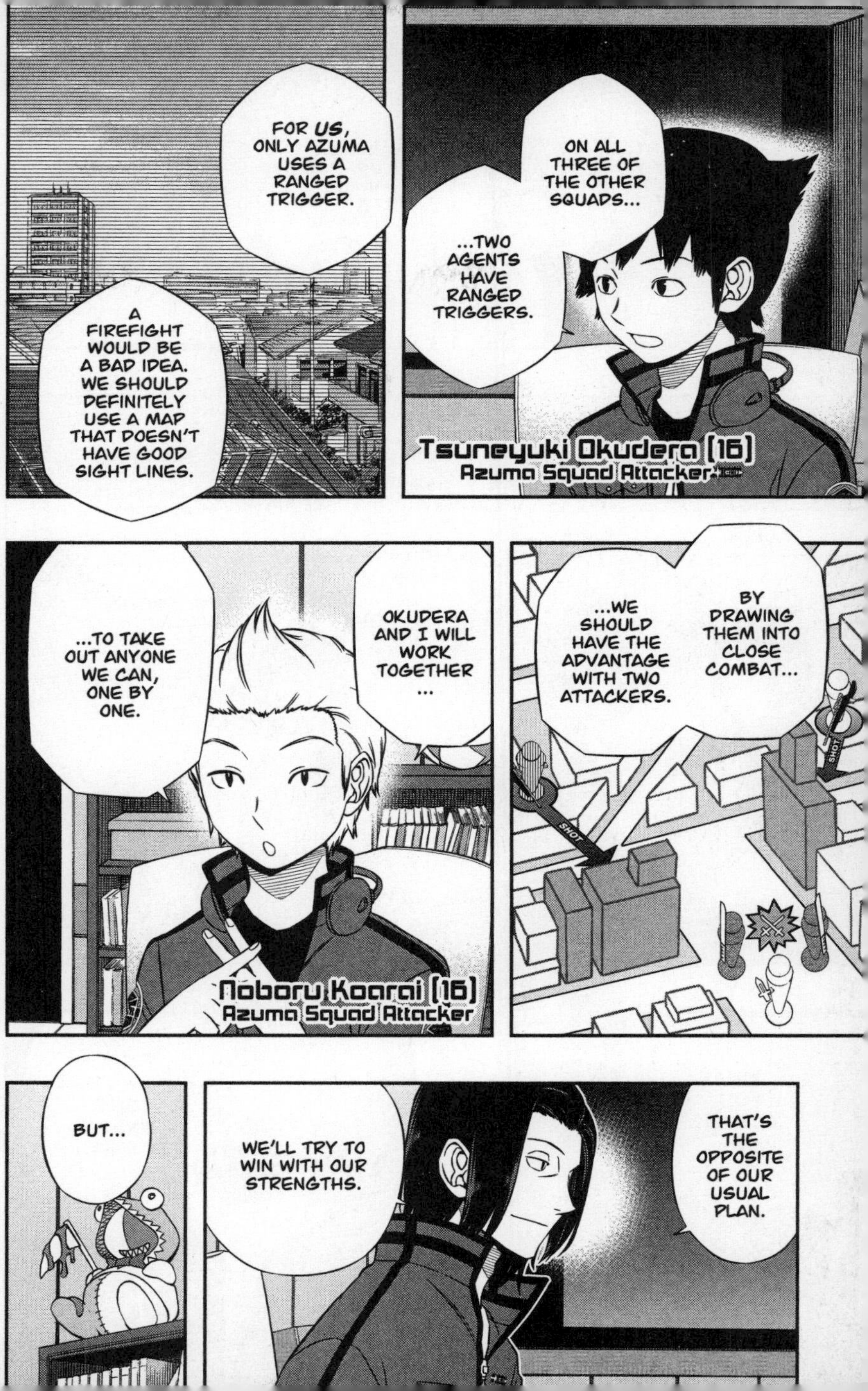
ON ALL THREE OF THE OTHER SQUADS...
...TWO AGENTS HAVE RANGED TRIGGERS.
Tsuneyuki Okudera (16)
Azuma Squad Attacker
FOR US, ONLY AZUMA USES A RANGED TRIGGER.
A FIREFIGHT WOULD BE A BAD IDEA. WE SHOULD DEFINITELY USE A MAP THAT DOESN'T HAVE GOOD SIGHT LINES.
BY DRAWING THEM INTO CLOSE COMBAT...
...WE SHOULD HAVE THE ADVANTAGE WITH TWO ATTACKERS.
SHOT
SHOT
OKUDERA AND I WILL WORK TOGETHER ...
...TO TAKE OUT ANYONE WE CAN, ONE BY ONE.
Noboru Koarai (16)
Azuma Squad Attacker
THAT'S THE OPPOSITE OF OUR USUAL PLAN.
WE'LL TRY TO WIN WITH OUR STRENGTHS.
BUT...

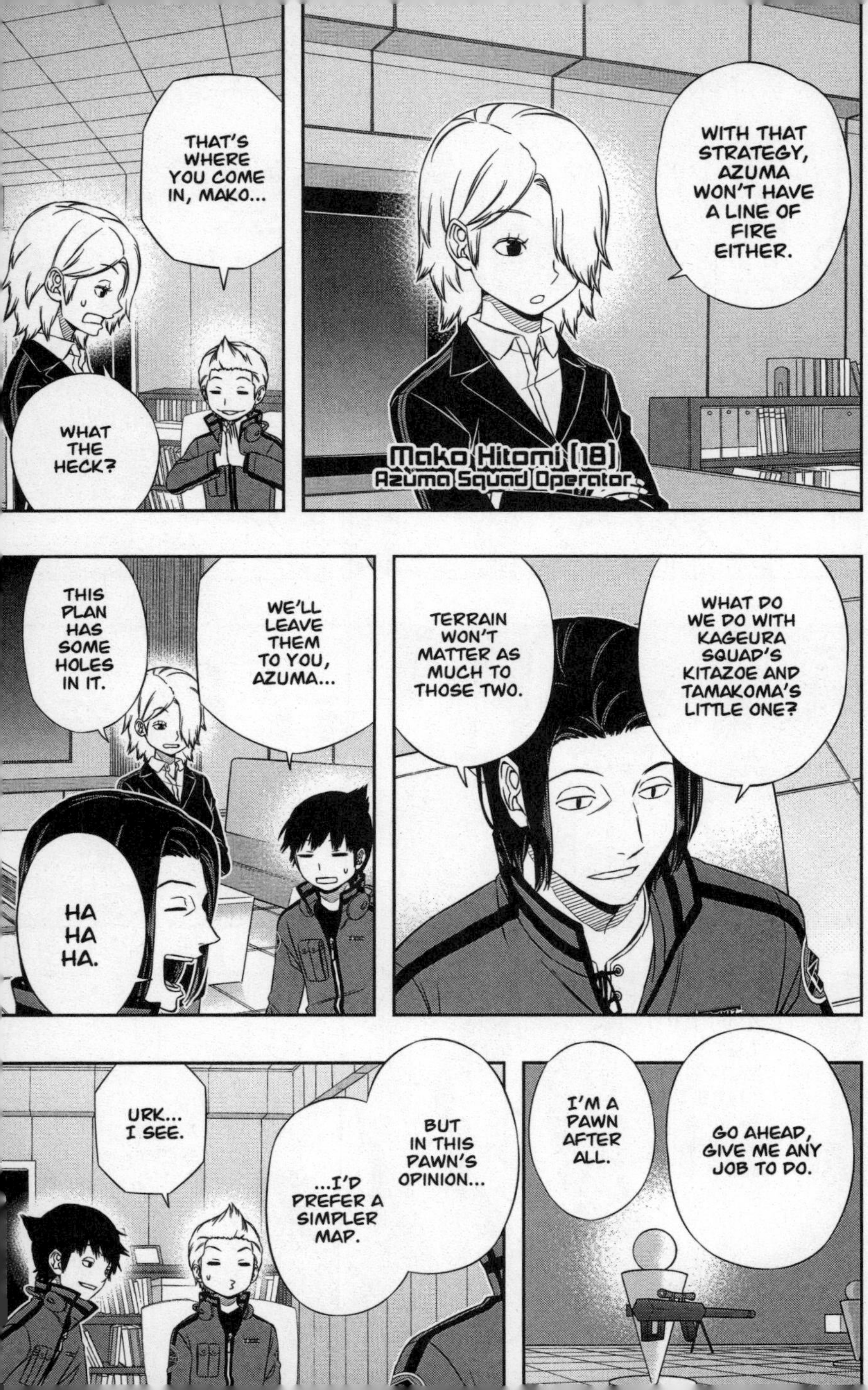
WITH THAT STRATEGY, AZUMA WON'T HAVE A LINE OF FIRE EITHER.
Mako Hitomi (18)
Azuma Squad Operator
THAT'S WHERE YOU COME IN, MAKO...
WHAT THE HECK?
WHAT DO WE DO WITH KAGEURA SQUAD'S KITAZOE AND TAMAKOMA'S LITTLE ONE?
TERRAIN WON'T MATTER AS MUCH TO THOSE TWO.
WE'LL LEAVE THEM TO YOU, AZUMA...
THIS PLAN HAS SOME HOLES IN IT.
HA HA HA.
GO AHEAD, GIVE ME ANY JOB TO DO.
I'M A PAWN AFTER ALL.
BUT IN THIS PAWN'S OPINION...
...I'D PREFER A SIMPLER MAP.
URK... I SEE.

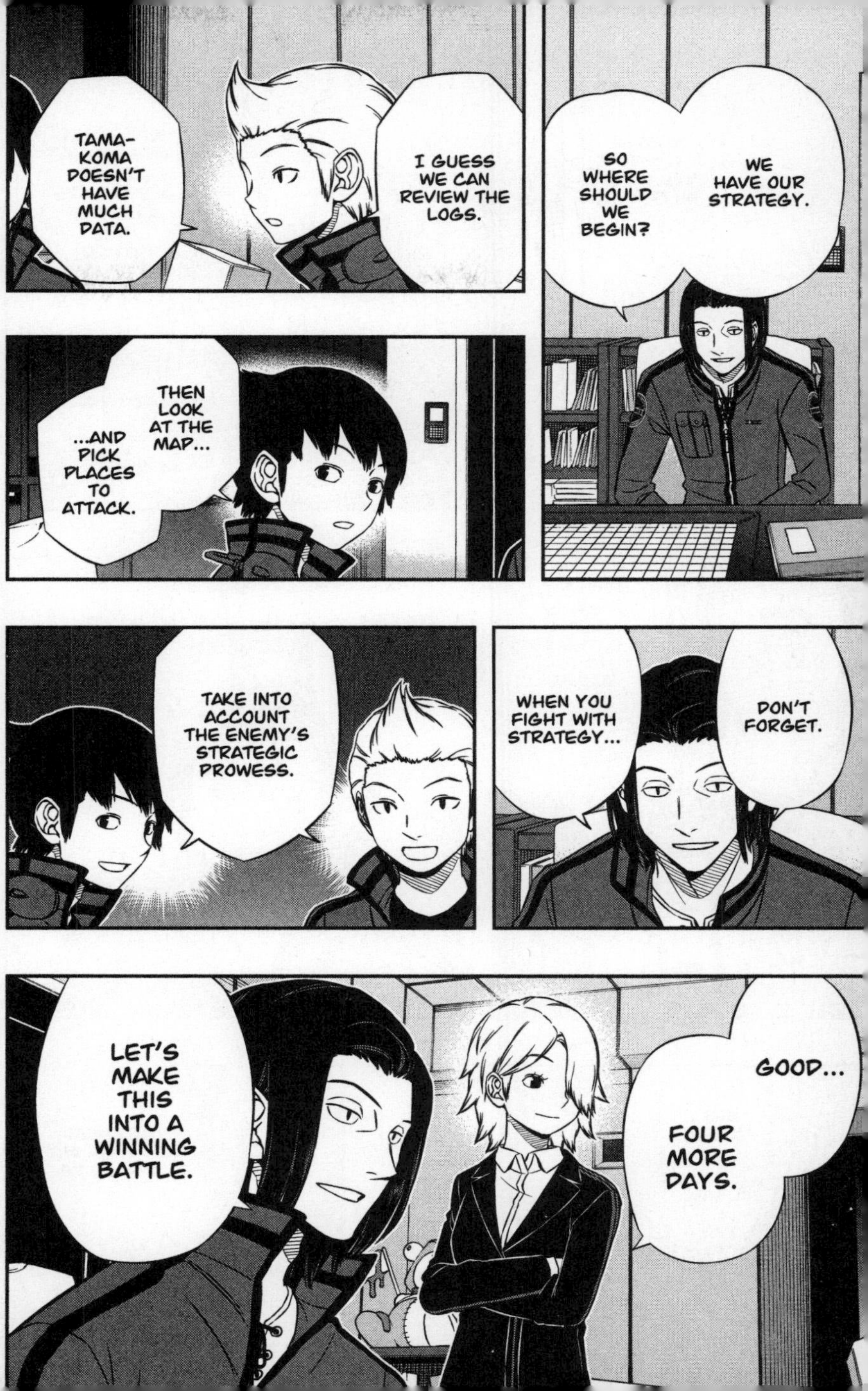
WE HAVE OUR STRATEGY.
SO WHERE SHOULD WE BEGIN?
I GUESS WE CAN REVIEW THE LOGS.
TAMA-KOMA DOESN'T HAVE MUCH DATA.
THEN LOOK AT THE MAP...
...AND PICK PLACES TO ATTACK.
DON'T FORGET.
WHEN YOU FIGHT WITH STRATEGY...
TAKE INTO ACCOUNT THE ENEMY'S STRATEGIC PROWESS.
GOOD...
FOUR MORE DAYS.
LET'S MAKE THIS INTO A WINNING BATTLE.

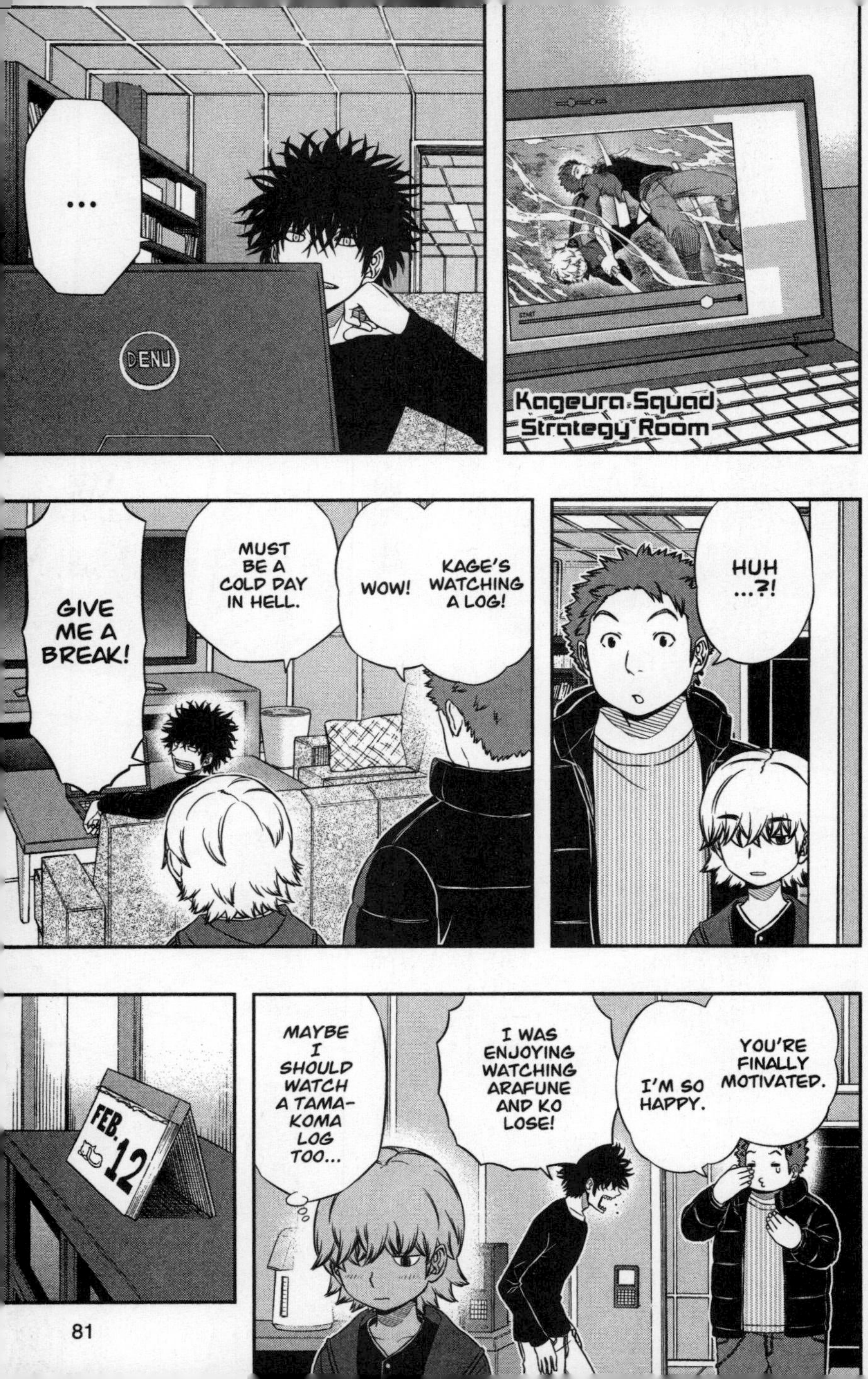
Kageura Squad Strategy Room
...
HUH ...?!
WOW! KAGE'S WATCHING A LOG!
MUST BE A COLD DAY IN HELL.
GIVE ME A BREAK!
YOU'RE FINALLY MOTIVATED. I'M SO HAPPY.
I WAS ENJOYING WATCHING ARAFUNE AND KO LOSE!
MAYBE I SHOULD WATCH A TAMA-KOMA LOG TOO...
FEB. 12

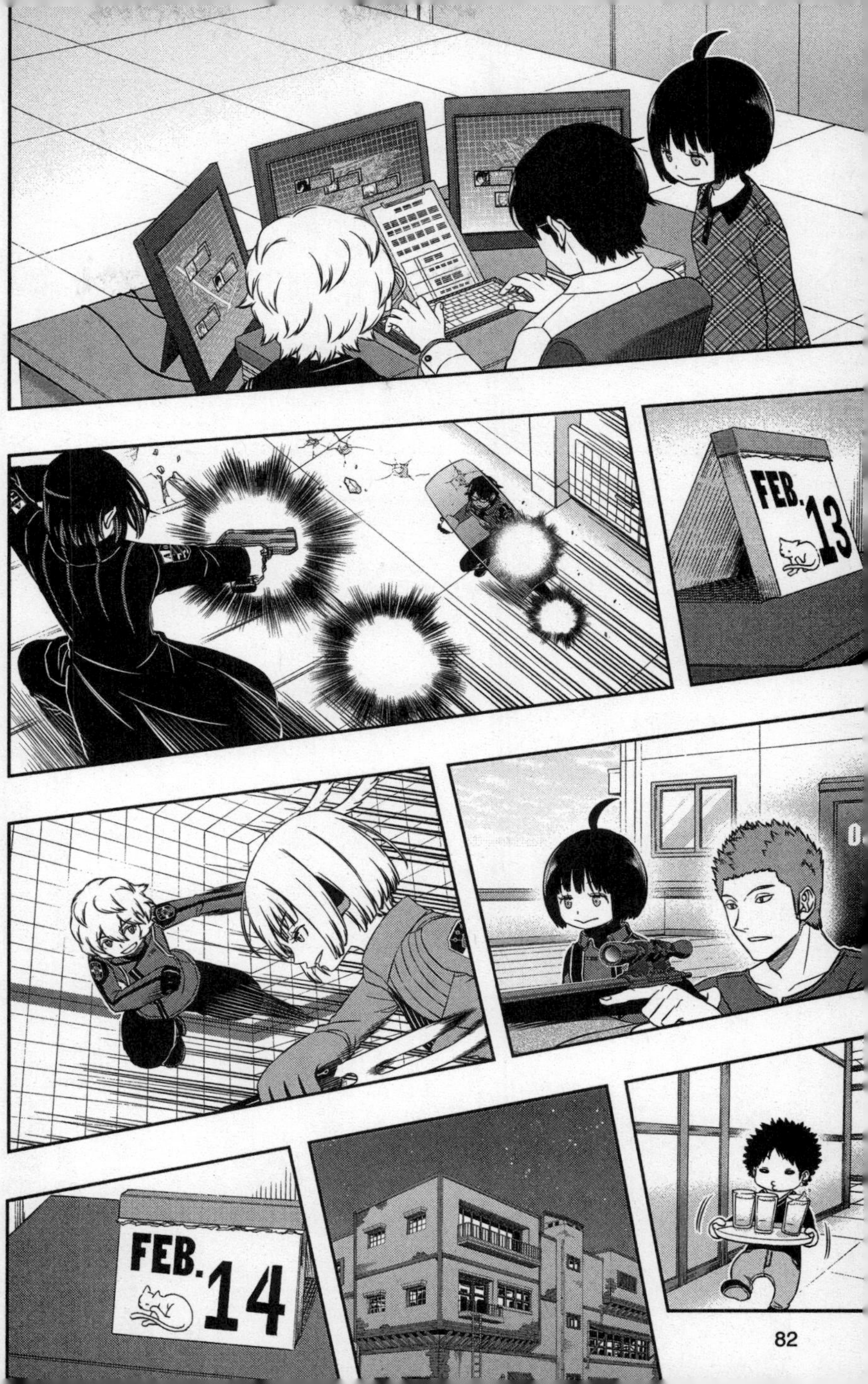
FEB. 13
FEB. 14

...SEEMS TO HAVE BEEN TOO HIGH OF A HURDLE.

I DIGRESS, MIKUMO...

WINNING 100 BATTLES AGAINST ME...

I UNDERSTAND NOW THAT I WON'T BE ABLE TO MASTER THEM...

...EVEN IF YOU TEACH ME COMPOSITE SHOTS NOW.

NO...

SHOULD I MAKE IT FIFTY?

MIKUMO	YUIGA
48	152

...TO HELP THE TEAM MORE THAN BEFORE...!

I SHOULD BE ABLE...

I'M STARTING TO LEARN HOW TO GET MORE HITS.

BY FIGHTING SOMEONE NOT TOO STRONG...

BUT...

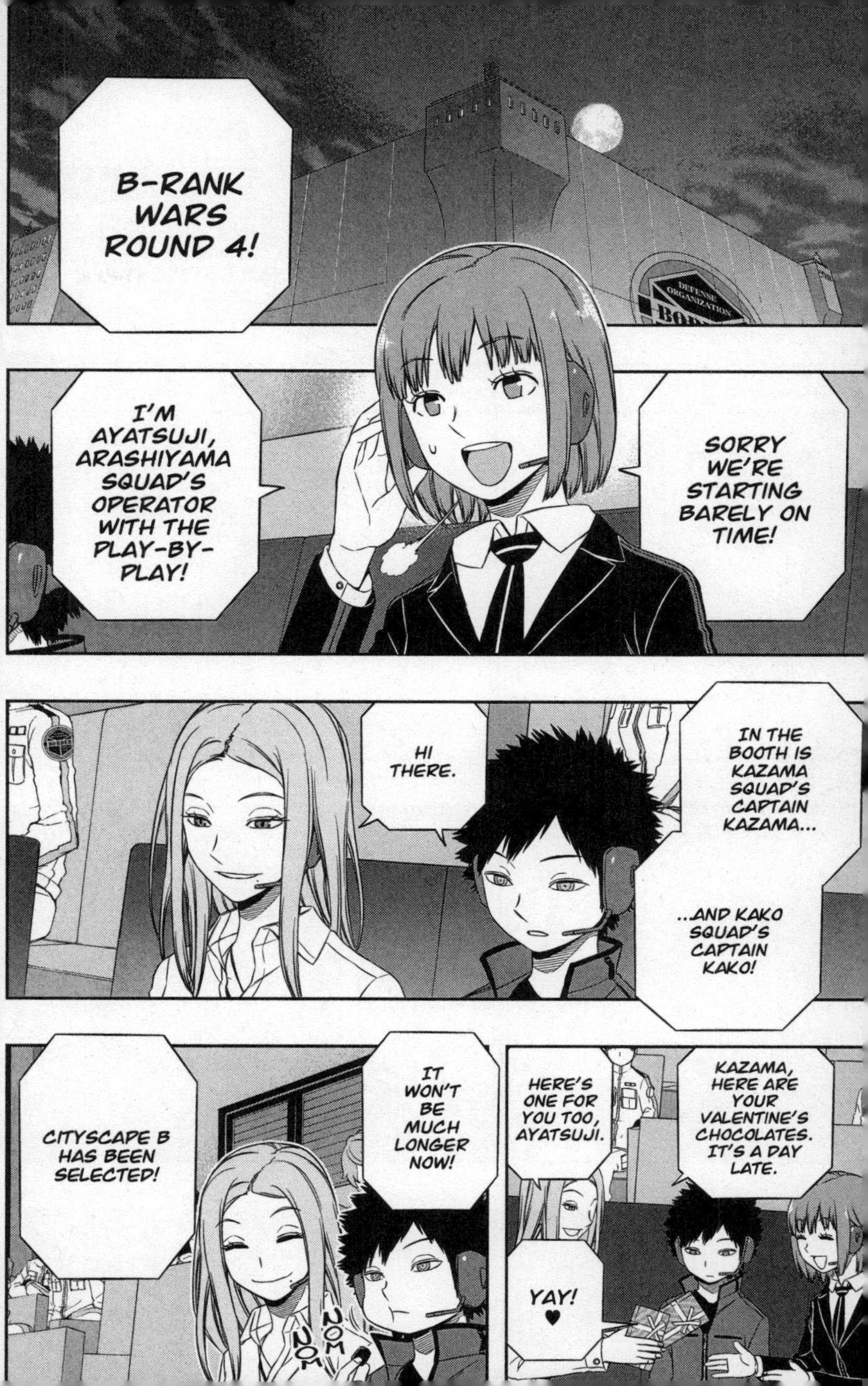
B-RANK WARS ROUND 4!
DEFENSE ORGANIZATION
SORRY WE'RE STARTING BARELY ON TIME!
I'M AYATSUJI, ARASHIYAMA SQUAD'S OPERATOR WITH THE PLAY-BY-PLAY!
IN THE BOOTH IS KAZAMA SQUAD'S CAPTAIN KAZAMA...
...AND KAKO SQUAD'S CAPTAIN KAKO!
HI THERE.
KAZAMA, HERE ARE YOUR VALENTINE'S CHOCOLATES. IT'S A DAY LATE.
HERE'S ONE FOR YOU TOO, AYATSUJI.
YAY! ♥
IT WON'T BE MUCH LONGER NOW!
CITYSCAPE B HAS BEEN SELECTED!
NOM NOM NOM

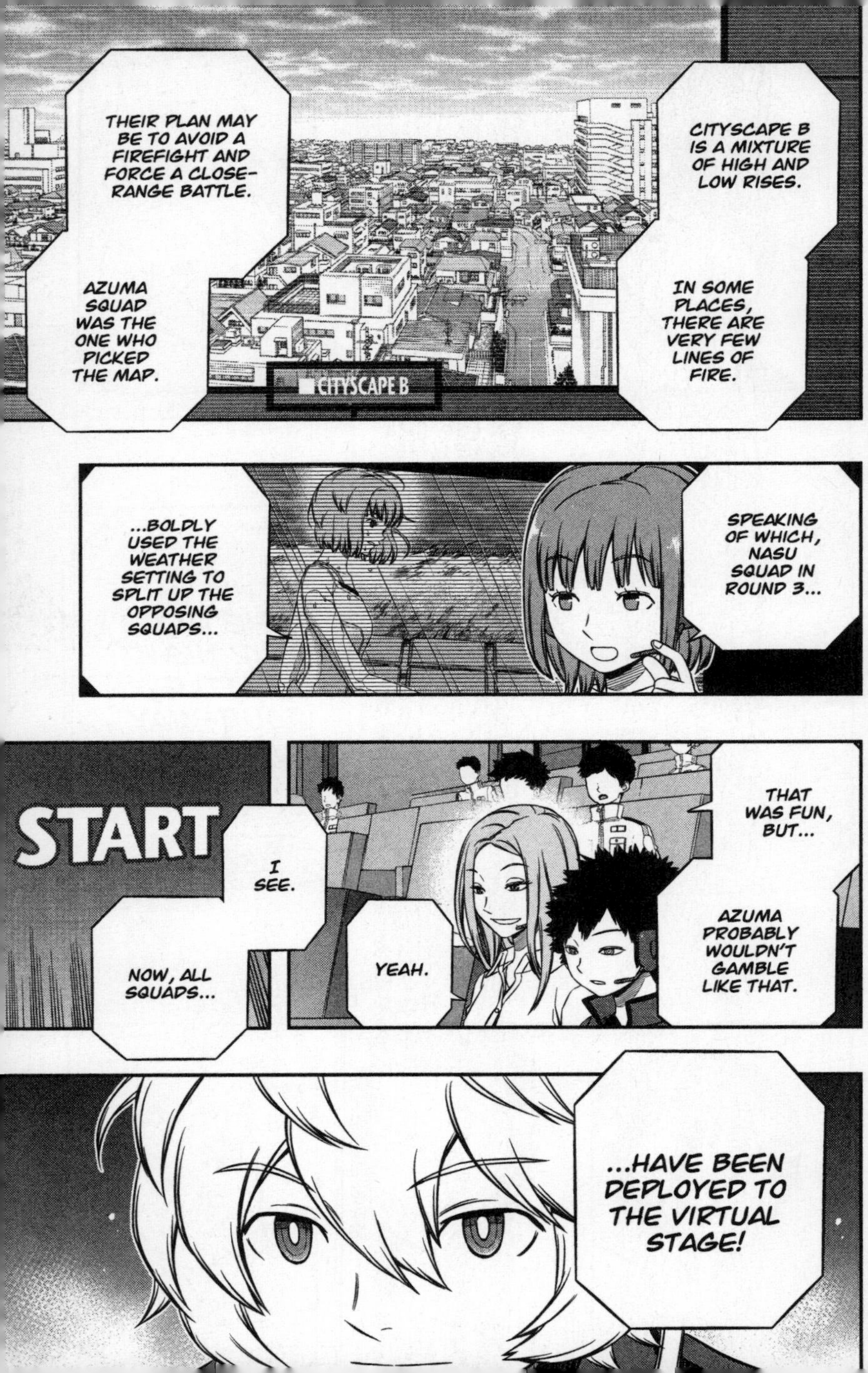
CITYSCAPE B
CITYSCAPE B IS A MIXTURE OF HIGH AND LOW RISES.
IN SOME PLACES, THERE ARE VERY FEW LINES OF FIRE.
THEIR PLAN MAY BE TO AVOID A FIREFIGHT AND FORCE A CLOSE-RANGE BATTLE.
AZUMA SQUAD WAS THE ONE WHO PICKED THE MAP.
SPEAKING OF WHICH, NASU SQUAD IN ROUND 3...
...BOLDLY USED THE WEATHER SETTING TO SPLIT UP THE OPPOSING SQUADS...
THAT WAS FUN, BUT...
AZUMA PROBABLY WOULDN'T GAMBLE LIKE THAT.
I SEE.
YEAH.
START
NOW, ALL SQUADS...
...HAVE BEEN DEPLOYED TO THE VIRTUAL STAGE!

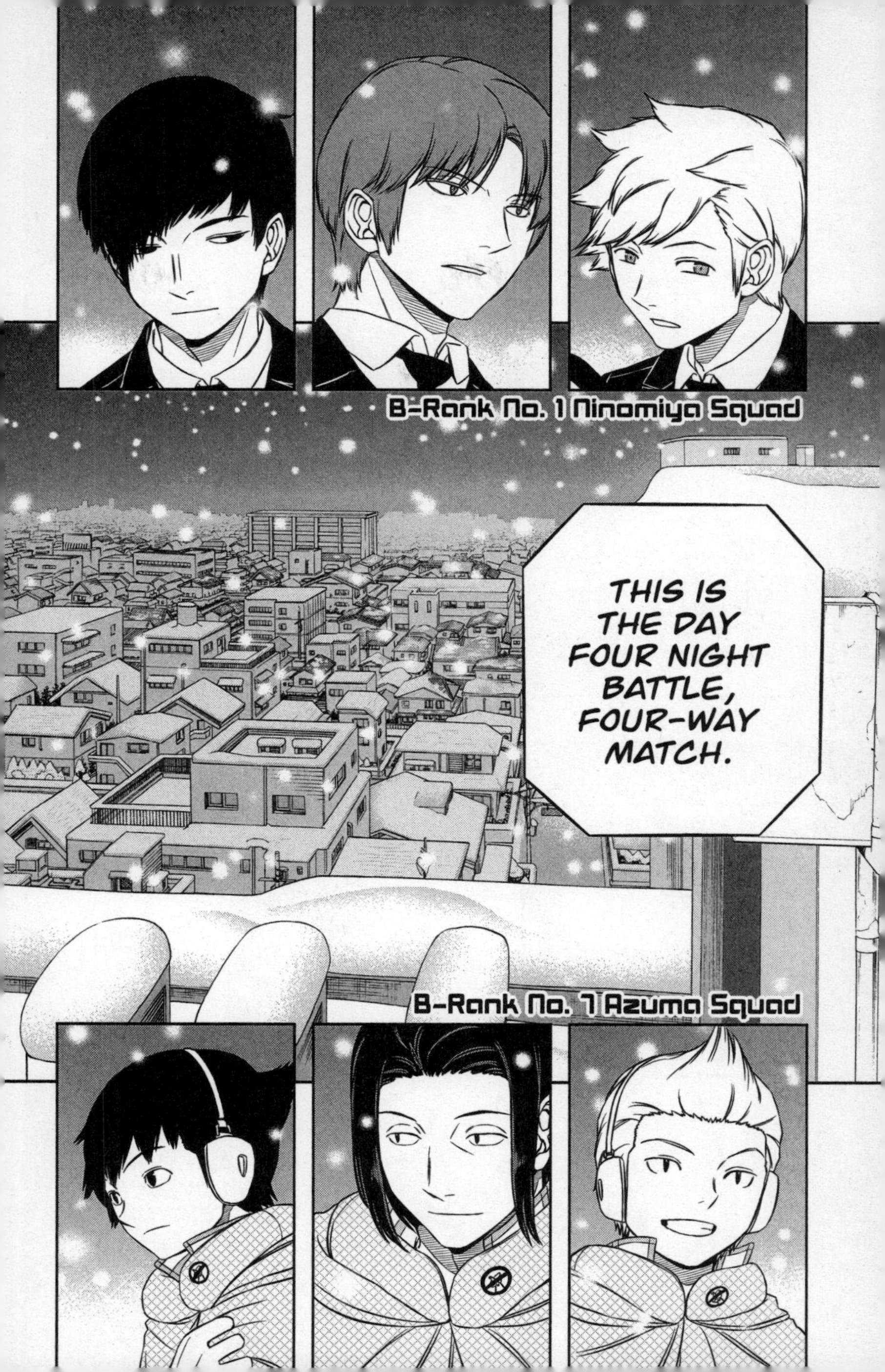
B-Rank No. 1 Ninomiya Squad
THIS IS THE DAY FOUR NIGHT BATTLE, FOUR-WAY MATCH.
B-Rank No. 7 Azuma Squad

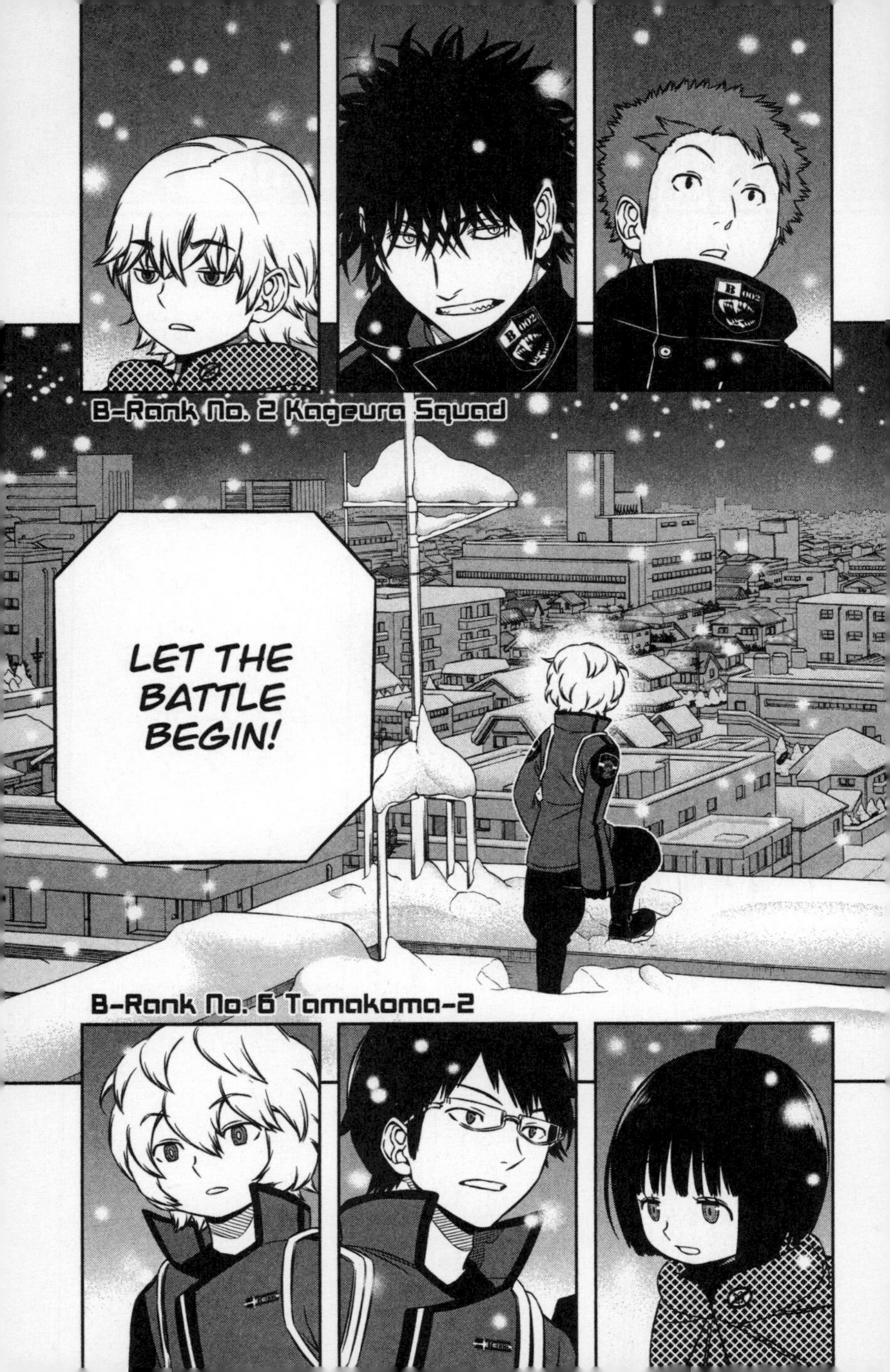
B-Rank No. 2 Kageura Squad
LET THE BATTLE BEGIN!
B-Rank No. 6 Tamakoma-2

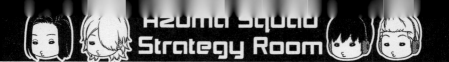

Azuma Squad Strategy Room

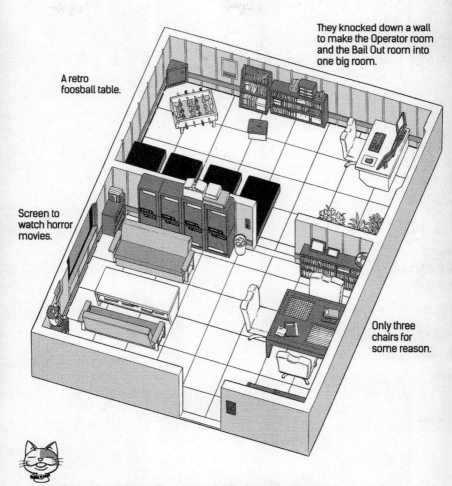

They knocked down a wall to make the Operator room and the Bail Out room into one big room.

A retro foosball table.

Screen to watch horror movies.

Only three chairs for some reason.

Kept clean through Hitomi's competence. The living room furniture is for Azuma's guests. When Koarai and Okudera return, they often find Hitomi alone in the dark giggling while watching horror movies. The two have become used to it. Azuma gets freaked out every time.

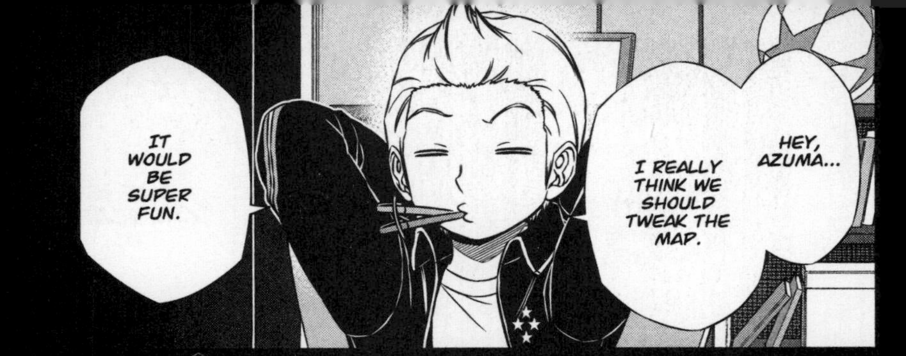
HEY, AZUMA...
I REALLY THINK WE SHOULD TWEAK THE MAP.
IT WOULD BE SUPER FUN.

Chapter 111 Yuichi Jin: Part 8

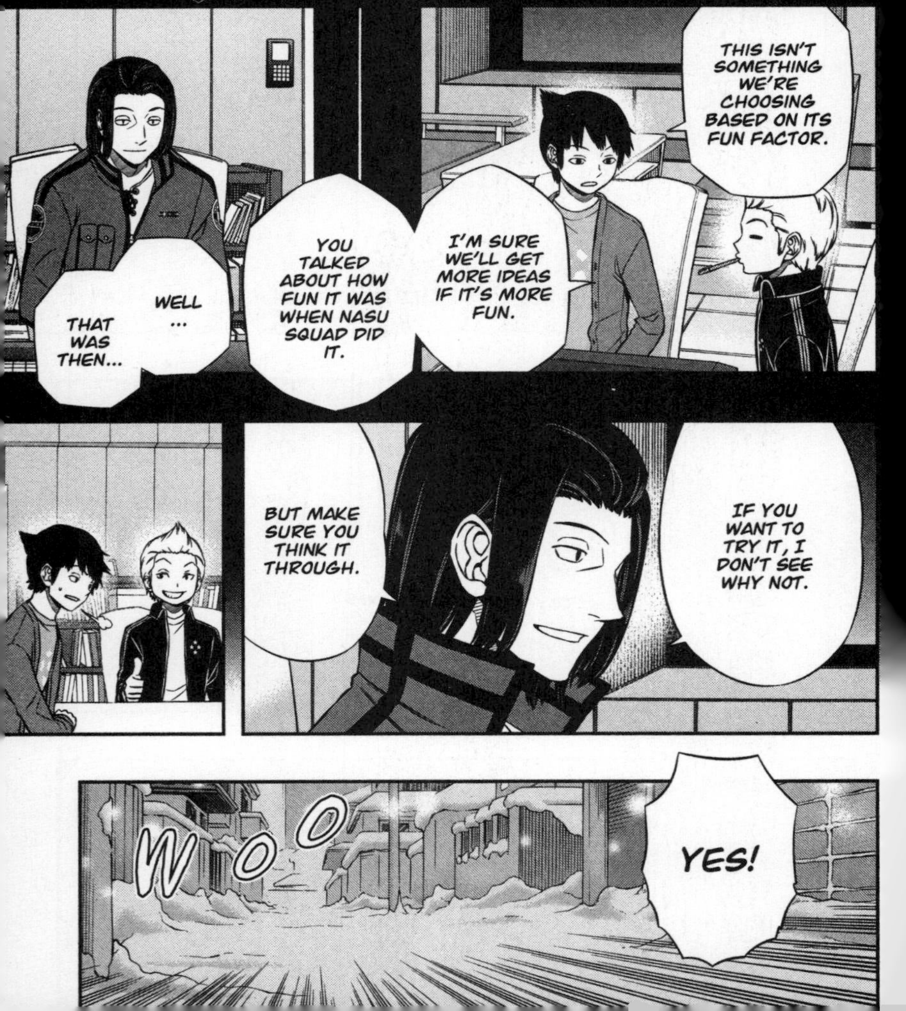
THIS ISN'T SOMETHING WE'RE CHOOSING BASED ON ITS FUN FACTOR.
I'M SURE WE'LL GET MORE IDEAS IF IT'S MORE FUN.
YOU TALKED ABOUT HOW FUN IT WAS WHEN NASU SQUAD DID IT.
WELL...
THAT WAS THEN...
IF YOU WANT TO TRY IT, I DON'T SEE WHY NOT.
BUT MAKE SURE YOU THINK IT THROUGH.
YES!
WOOO

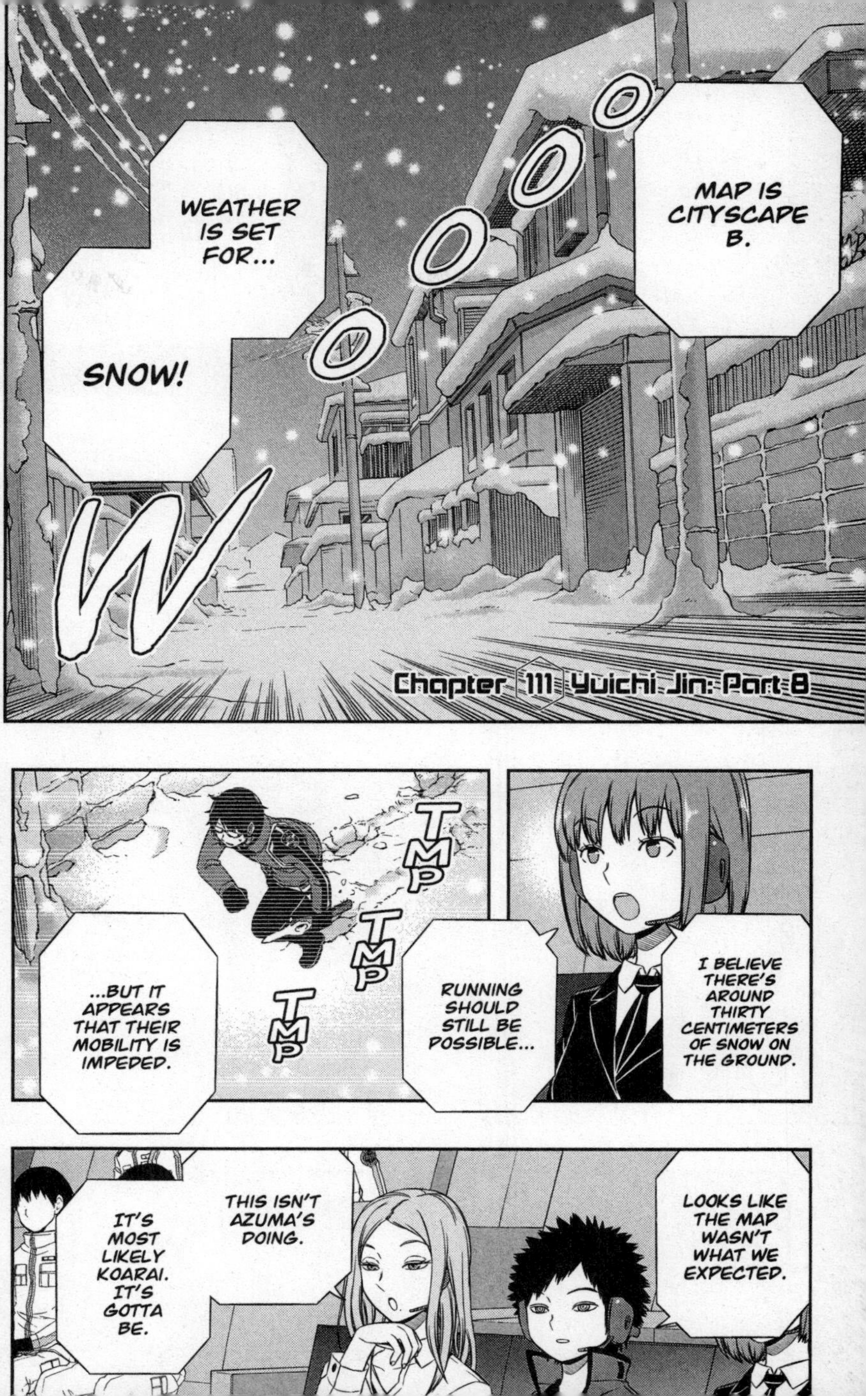
MAP IS CITYSCAPE B.
WEATHER IS SET FOR...
SNOW!
WOOOOOO
Chapter 111 Yuichi Jin: Part 8
I BELIEVE THERE'S AROUND THIRTY CENTIMETERS OF SNOW ON THE GROUND.
RUNNING SHOULD STILL BE POSSIBLE...
TMP
TMP
TMP
...BUT IT APPEARS THAT THEIR MOBILITY IS IMPEDED.
LOOKS LIKE THE MAP WASN'T WHAT WE EXPECTED.
THIS ISN'T AZUMA'S DOING.
IT'S MOST LIKELY KOARAI. IT'S GOTTA BE.

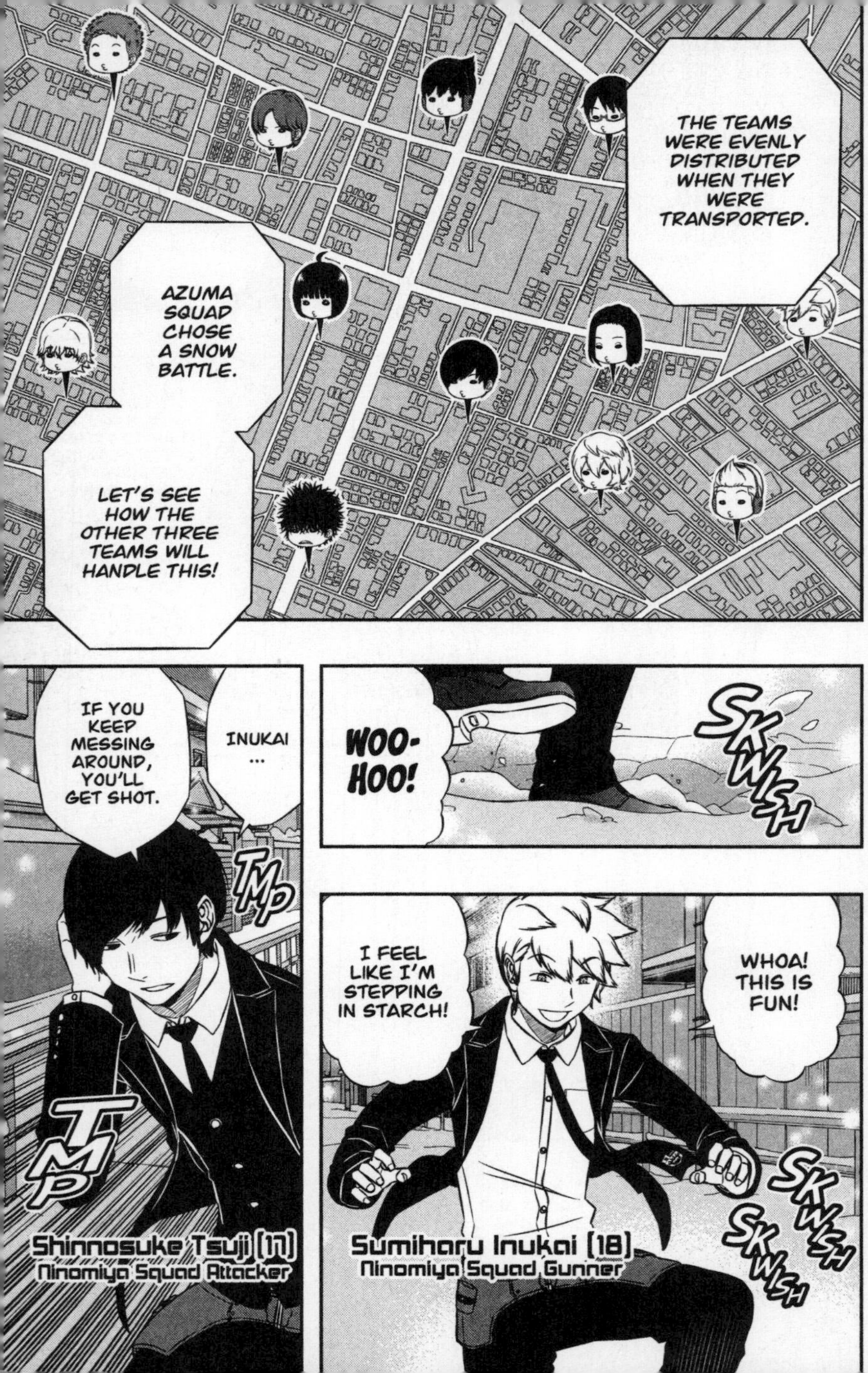
THE TEAMS WERE EVENLY DISTRIBUTED WHEN THEY WERE TRANSPORTED.
AZUMA SQUAD CHOSE A SNOW BATTLE.
LET'S SEE HOW THE OTHER THREE TEAMS WILL HANDLE THIS!
SKWISH
WOO-HOO!
WHOA! THIS IS FUN!
I FEEL LIKE I'M STEPPING IN STARCH!
SKWISH SKWISH
Sumiharu Inukai (18)
Ninomiya Squad Gunner
INUKAI...
IF YOU KEEP MESSING AROUND, YOU'LL GET SHOT.
TMP
TMP
Shinnosuke Tsuji (17)
Ninomiya Squad Attacker

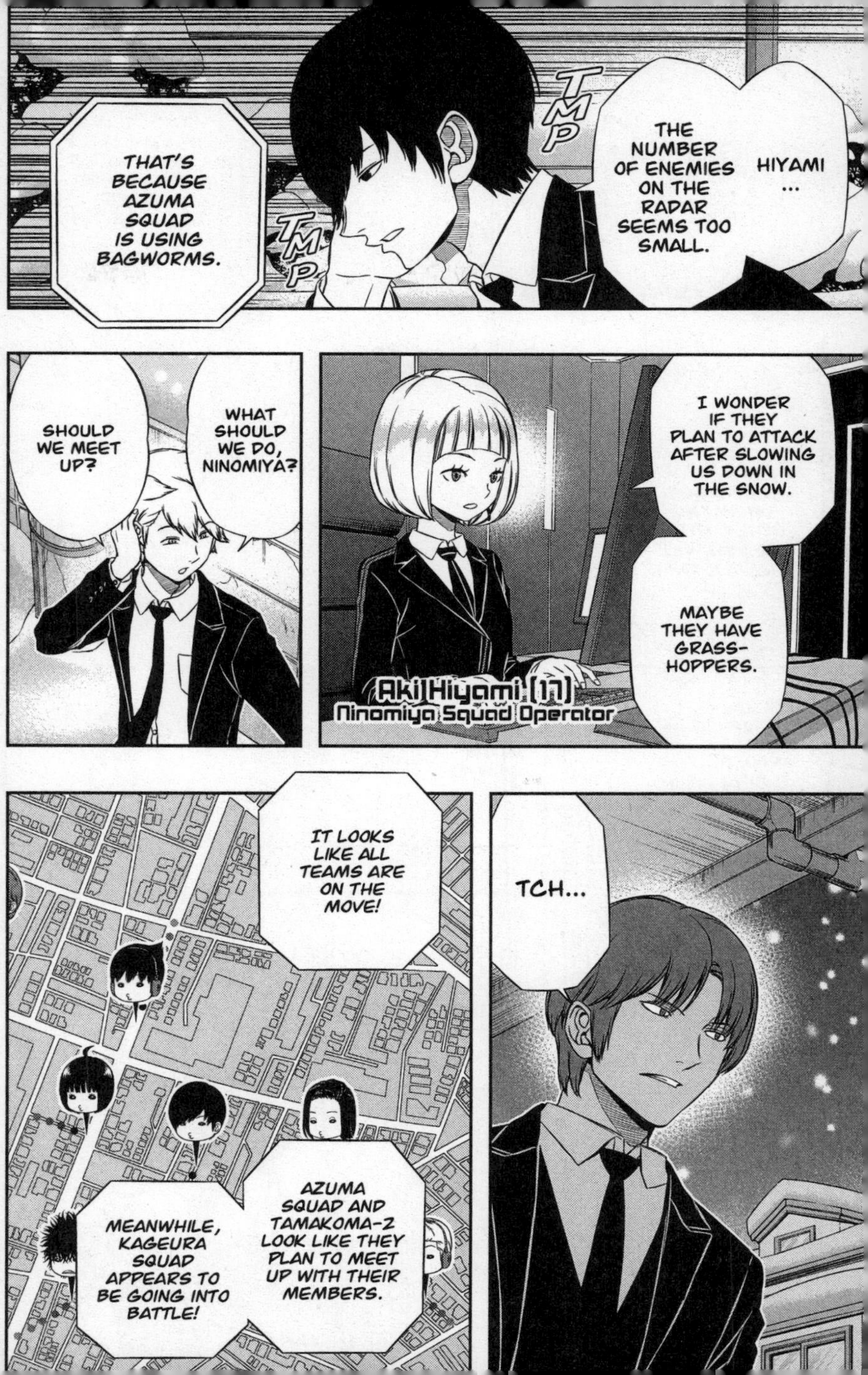
HIYAMI ...
THE NUMBER OF ENEMIES ON THE RADAR SEEMS TOO SMALL.
TMP
TMP
THAT'S BECAUSE AZUMA SQUAD IS USING BAGWORMS.
I WONDER IF THEY PLAN TO ATTACK AFTER SLOWING US DOWN IN THE SNOW.
MAYBE THEY HAVE GRASS-HOPPERS.
Aki Hiyami (17)
Ninomiya Squad Operator
WHAT SHOULD WE DO, NINOMIYA?
SHOULD WE MEET UP?
TCH...
IT LOOKS LIKE ALL TEAMS ARE ON THE MOVE!
AZUMA SQUAD AND TAMAKOMA-2 LOOK LIKE THEY PLAN TO MEET UP WITH THEIR MEMBERS.
MEANWHILE, KAGEURA SQUAD APPEARS TO BE GOING INTO BATTLE!

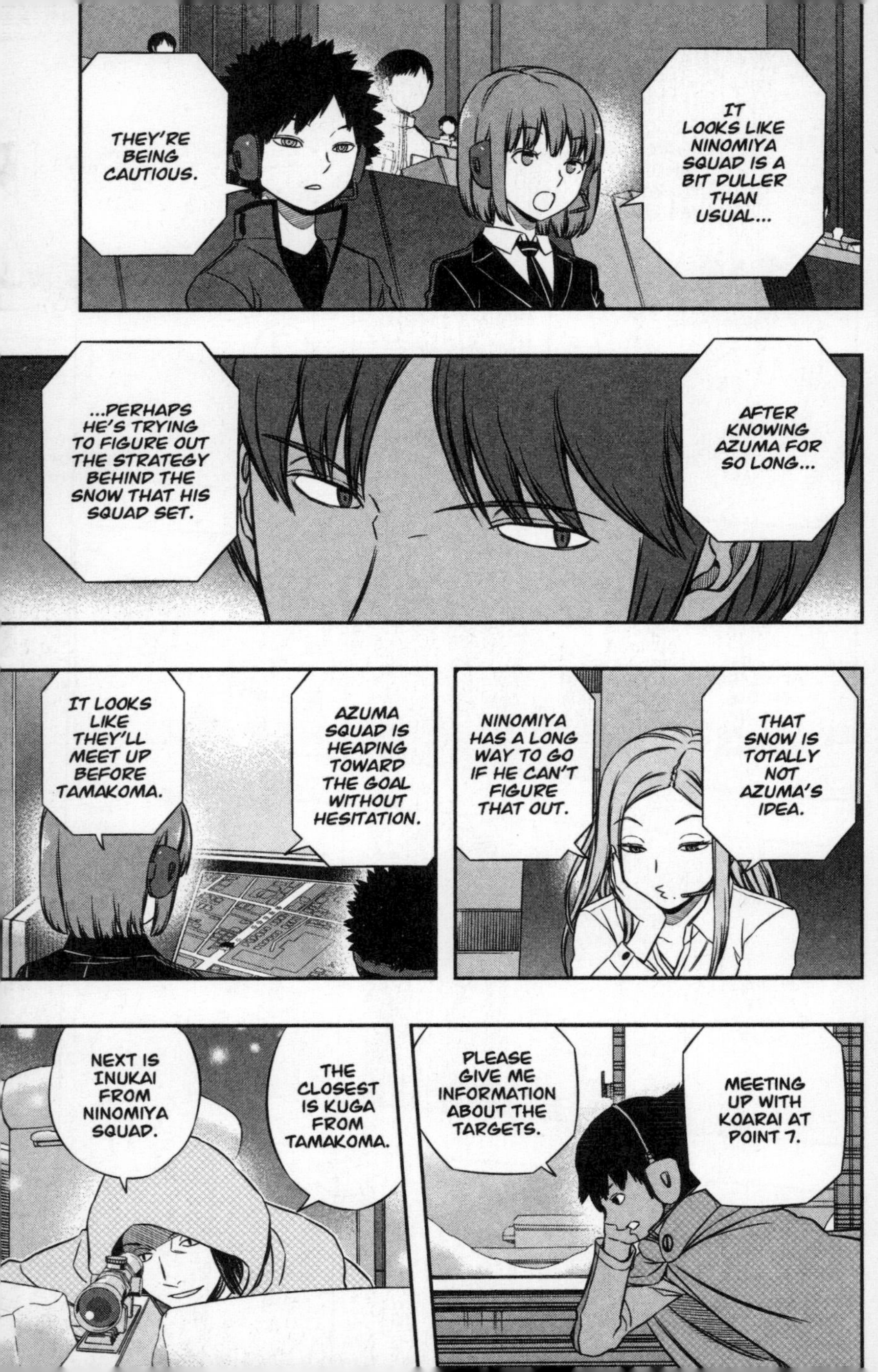
IT LOOKS LIKE NINOMIYA SQUAD IS A BIT DULLER THAN USUAL...
THEY'RE BEING CAUTIOUS.
AFTER KNOWING AZUMA FOR SO LONG...
...PERHAPS HE'S TRYING TO FIGURE OUT THE STRATEGY BEHIND THE SNOW THAT HIS SQUAD SET.
THAT SNOW IS TOTALLY NOT AZUMA'S IDEA.
NINOMIYA HAS A LONG WAY TO GO IF HE CAN'T FIGURE THAT OUT.
AZUMA SQUAD IS HEADING TOWARD THE GOAL WITHOUT HESITATION.
IT LOOKS LIKE THEY'LL MEET UP BEFORE TAMAKOMA.
MEETING UP WITH KOARAI AT POINT 7.
PLEASE GIVE ME INFORMATION ABOUT THE TARGETS.
THE CLOSEST IS KUGA FROM TAMAKOMA.
NEXT IS INUKAI FROM NINOMIYA SQUAD.

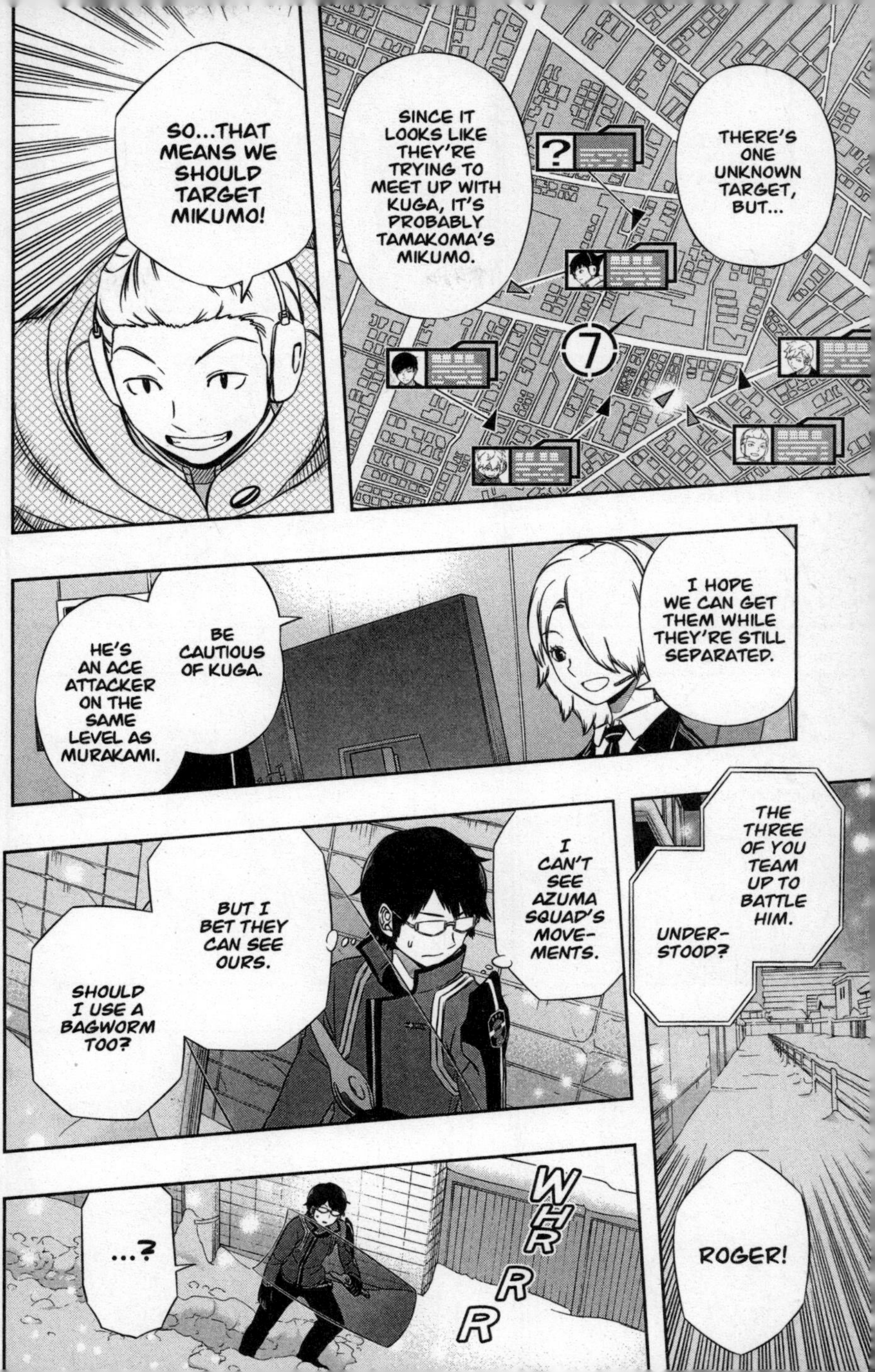
THERE'S ONE UNKNOWN TARGET, BUT...
SINCE IT LOOKS LIKE THEY'RE TRYING TO MEET UP WITH KUGA, IT'S PROBABLY TAMAKOMA'S MIKUMO.
?
7
SO...THAT MEANS WE SHOULD TARGET MIKUMO!
I HOPE WE CAN GET THEM WHILE THEY'RE STILL SEPARATED.
BE CAUTIOUS OF KUGA.
HE'S AN ACE ATTACKER ON THE SAME LEVEL AS MURAKAMI.
THE THREE OF YOU TEAM UP TO BATTLE HIM.
UNDER-STOOD?
ROGER!
I CAN'T SEE AZUMA SQUAD'S MOVE-MENTS.
BUT I BET THEY CAN SEE OURS.
SHOULD I USE A BAGWORM TOO?
WHRRR
...?

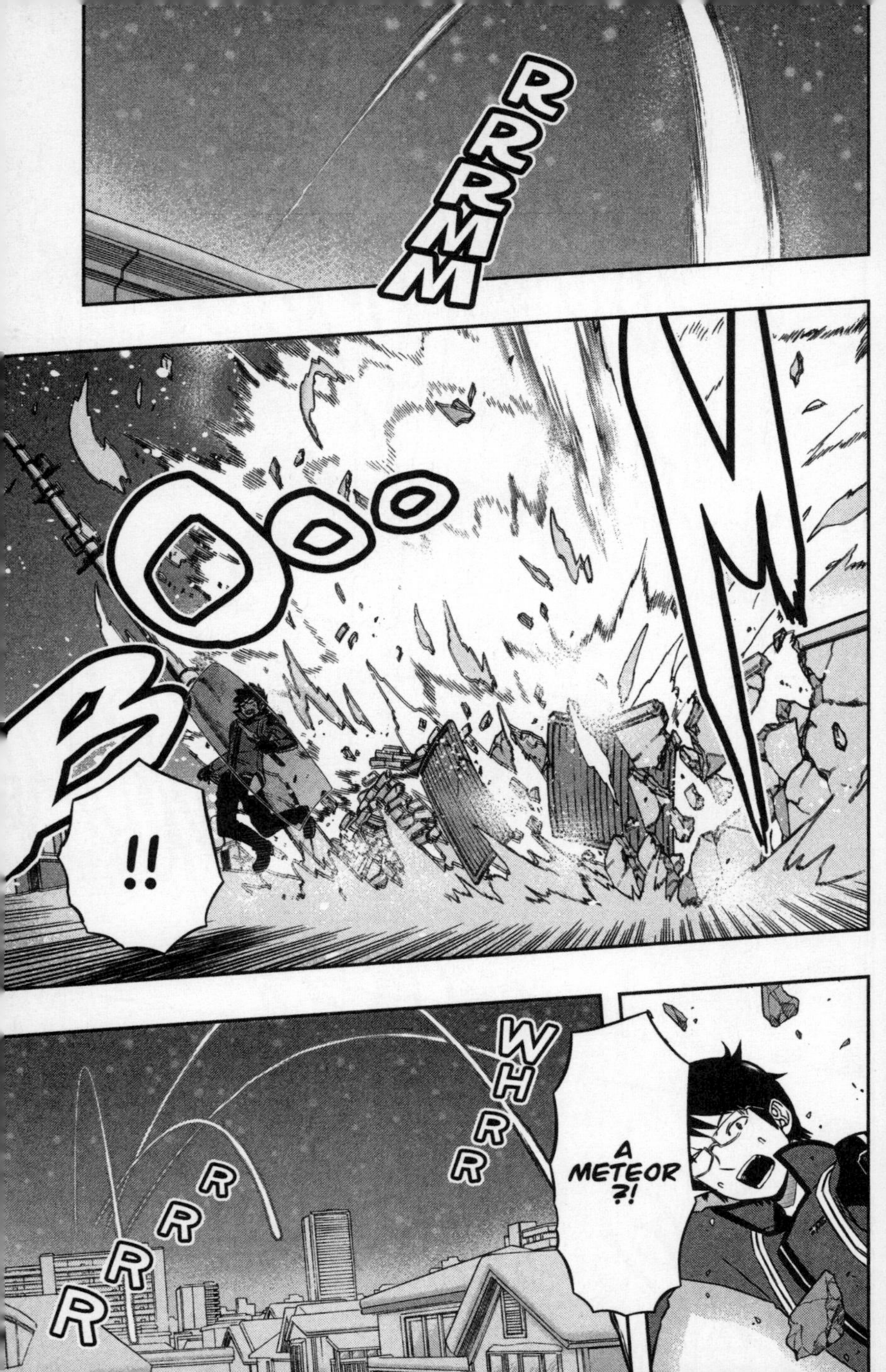
RRRMM
BOOOM
!!
WHRR
A METEOR?!
RRRR

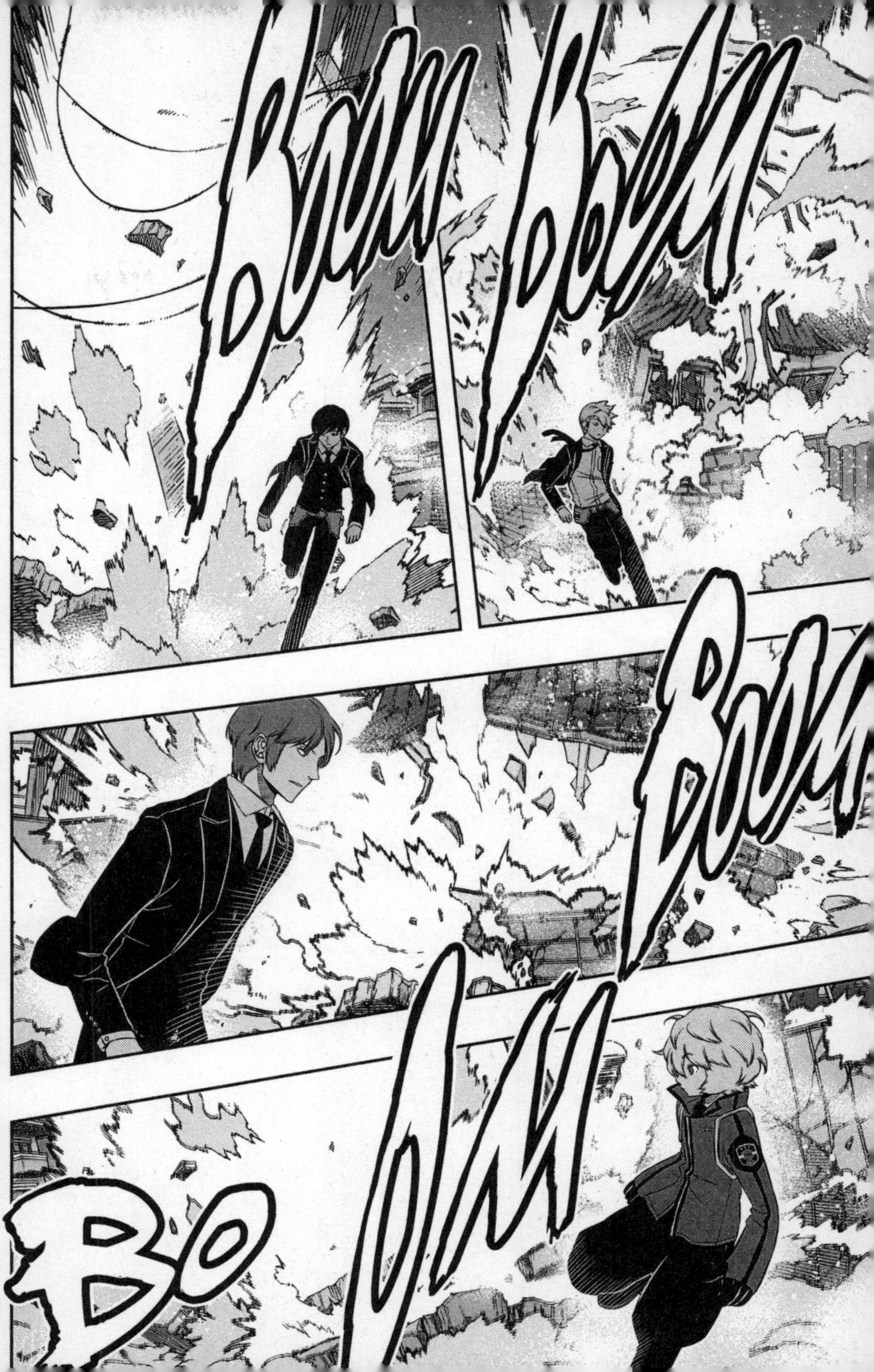
BOOM
BOOM
BOOM

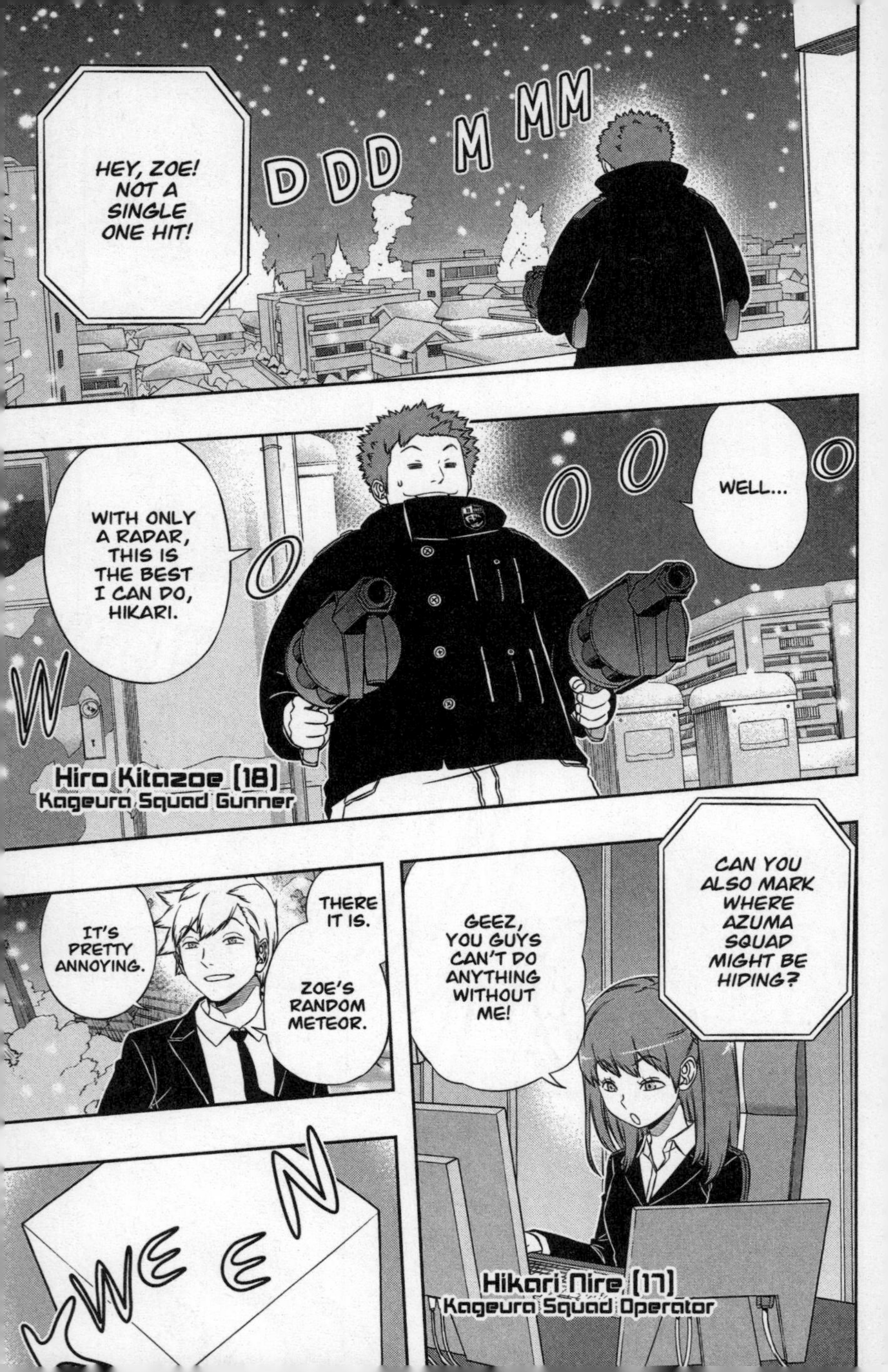
DDD M MM
HEY, ZOE! NOT A SINGLE ONE HIT!
WELL...
OOOOOO
WITH ONLY A RADAR, THIS IS THE BEST I CAN DO, HIKARI.
W
Hiro Kitazoe (18)
Kageura Squad Gunner
CAN YOU ALSO MARK WHERE AZUMA SQUAD MIGHT BE HIDING?
GEEZ, YOU GUYS CAN'T DO ANYTHING WITHOUT ME!
Hikari Nire (17)
Kageura Squad Operator
THERE IT IS.
ZOE'S RANDOM METEOR.
IT'S PRETTY ANNOYING.
WEEN

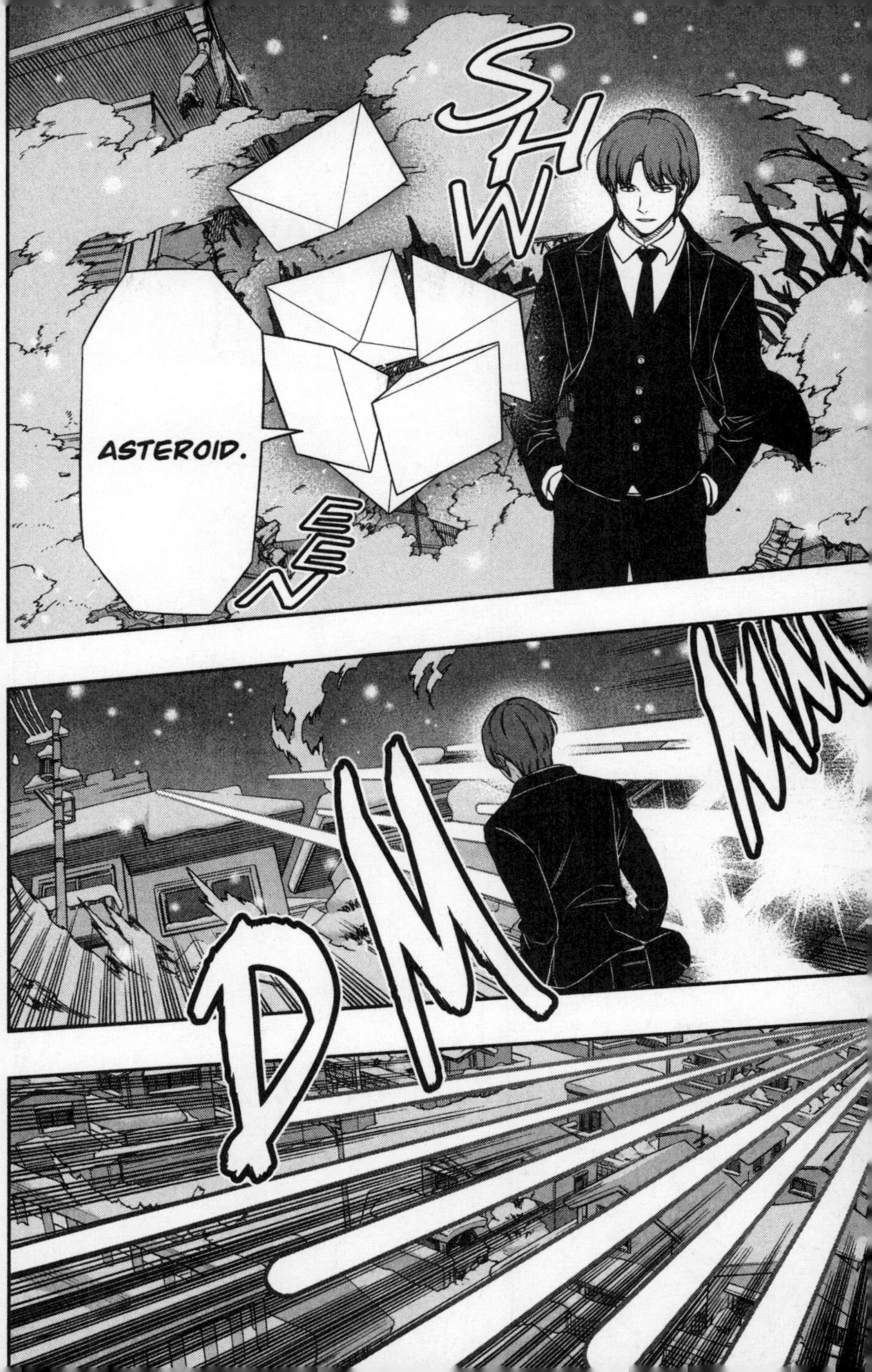
SHW
ASTEROID.
EEEN
MMM
DM

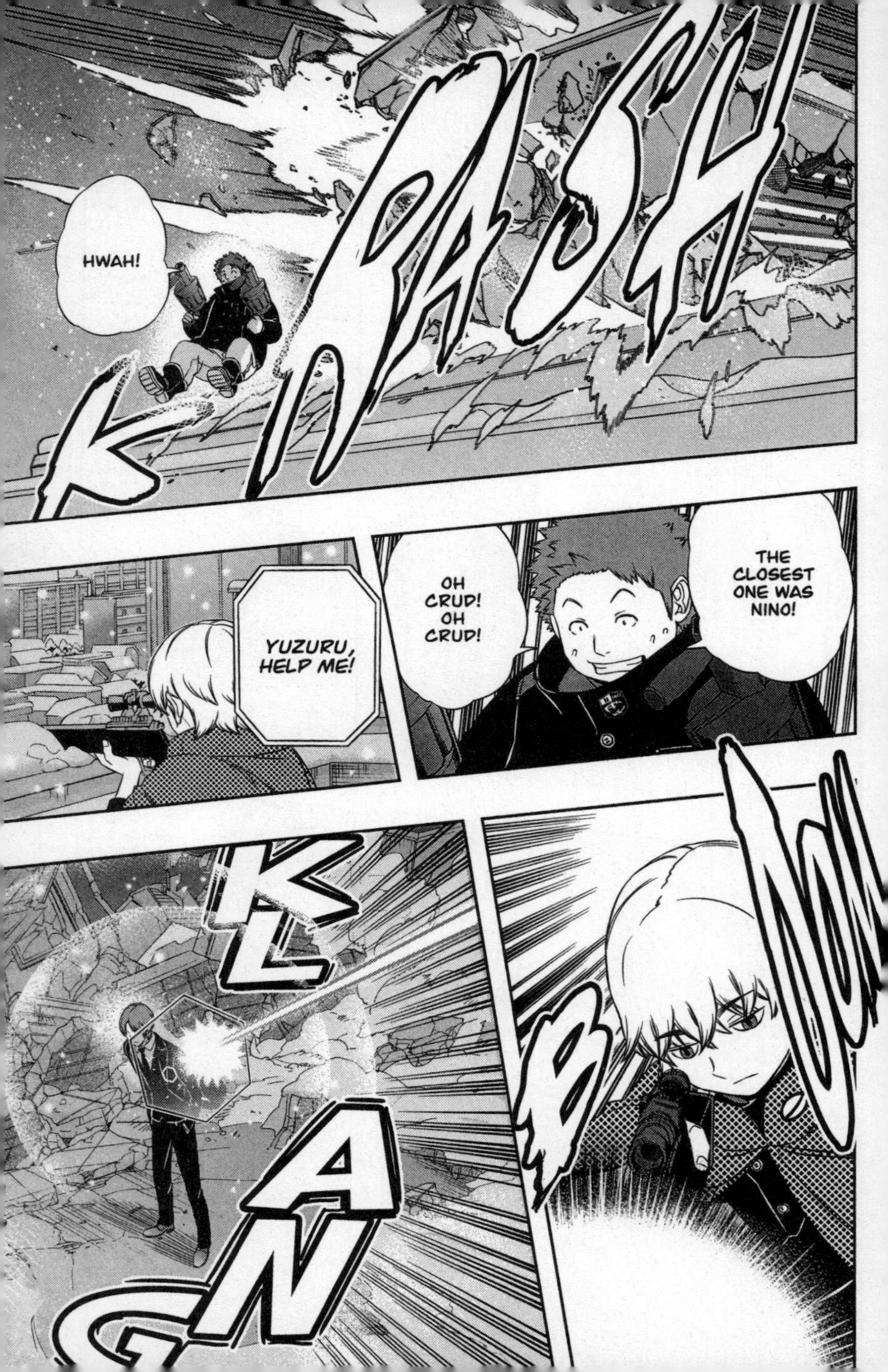
KRASH
HWAH!
THE CLOSEST ONE WAS NINO!
OH CRUD! OH CRUD!
YUZURU, HELP ME!
KLANG

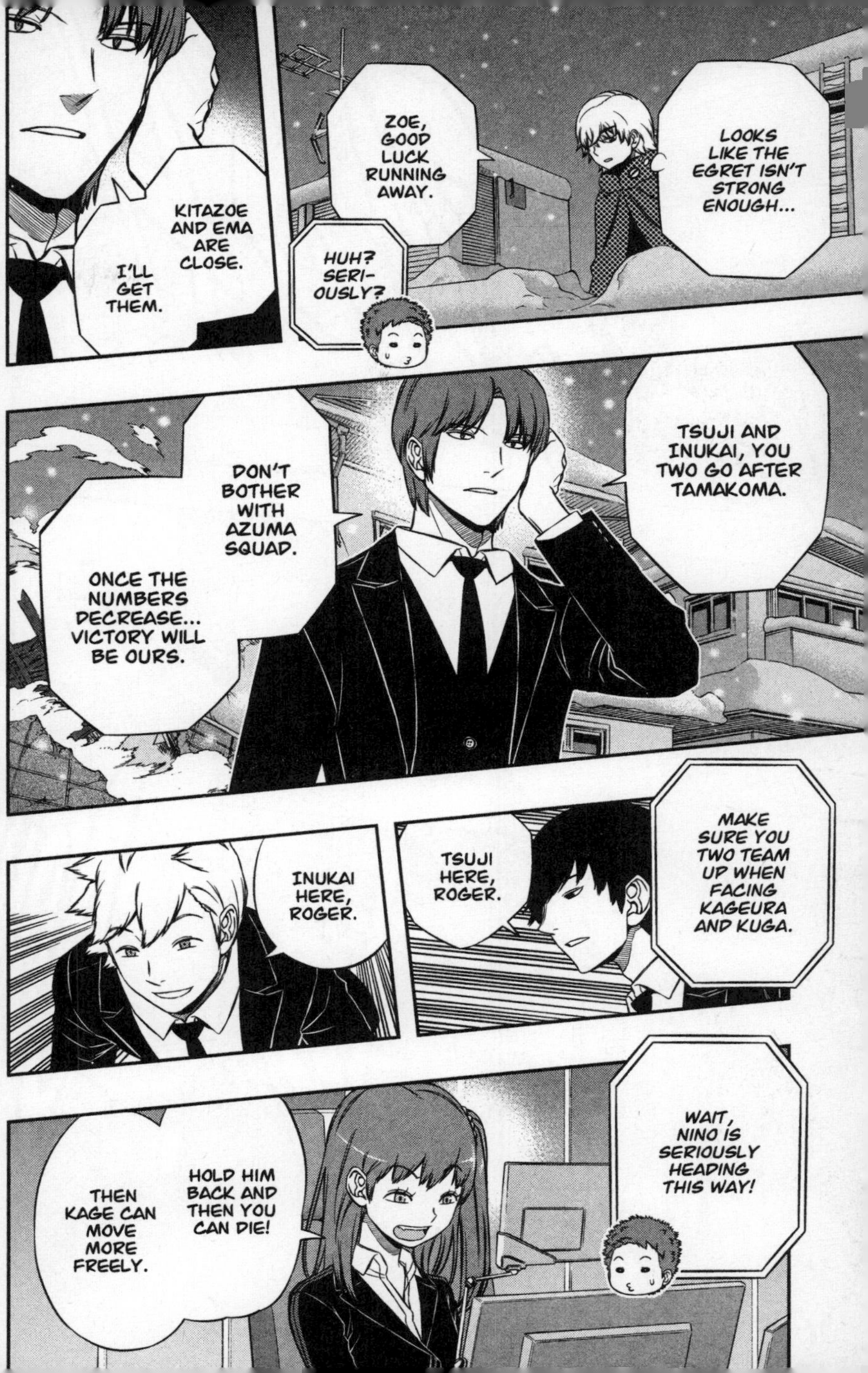
LOOKS LIKE THE EGRET ISN'T STRONG ENOUGH...
ZOE, GOOD LUCK RUNNING AWAY.
HUH? SERI-OUSLY?
KITAZOE AND EMA ARE CLOSE.
I'LL GET THEM.
TSUJI AND INUKAI, YOU TWO GO AFTER TAMAKOMA.
DON'T BOTHER WITH AZUMA SQUAD.
ONCE THE NUMBERS DECREASE... VICTORY WILL BE OURS.
MAKE SURE YOU TWO TEAM UP WHEN FACING KAGEURA AND KUGA.
TSUJI HERE, ROGER.
INUKAI HERE, ROGER.
WAIT, NINO IS SERIOUSLY HEADING THIS WAY!
HOLD HIM BACK AND THEN YOU CAN DIE!
THEN KAGE CAN MOVE MORE FREELY.

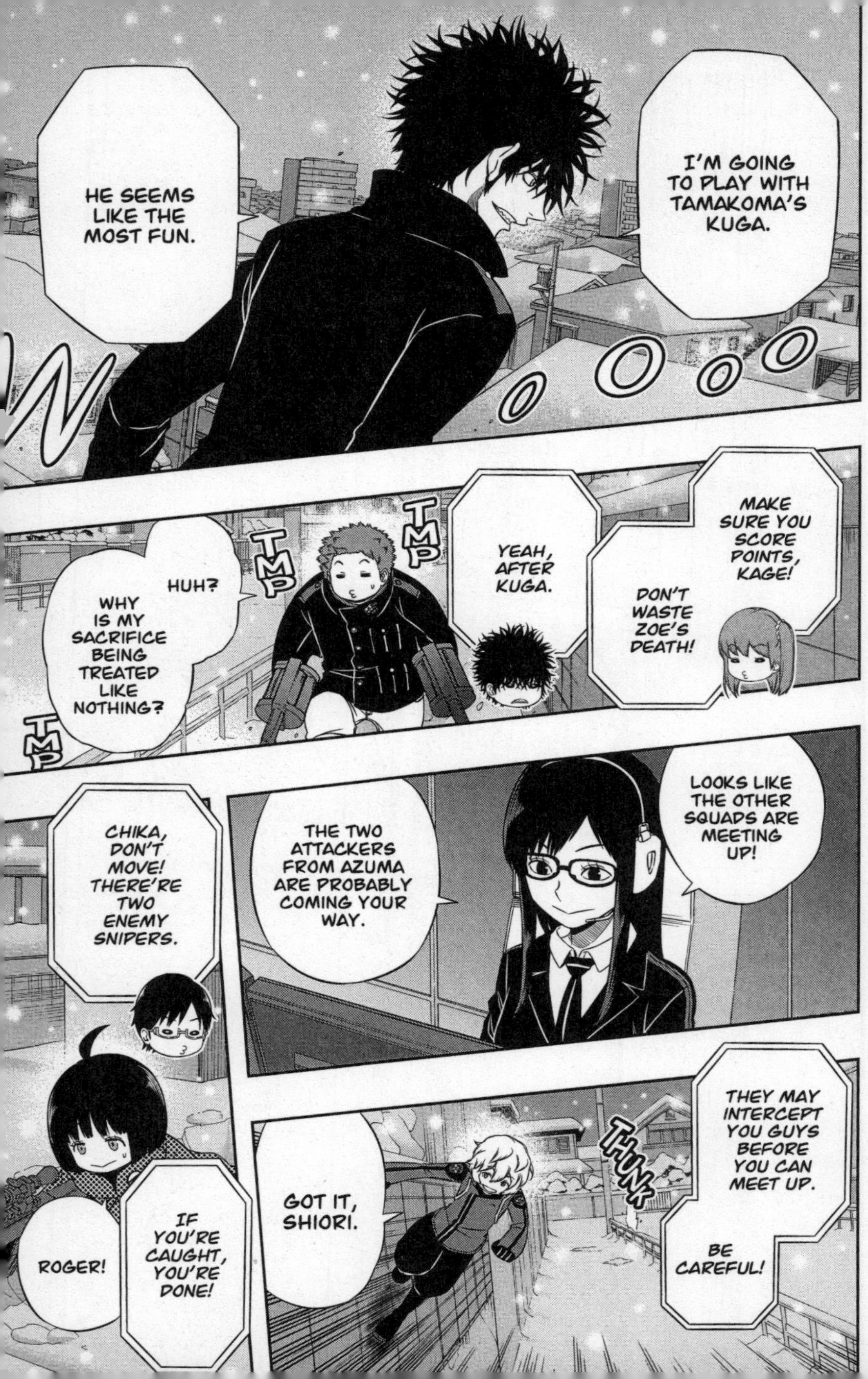
I'M GOING TO PLAY WITH TAMAKOMA'S KUGA.
HE SEEMS LIKE THE MOST FUN.
NOOOO
MAKE SURE YOU SCORE POINTS, KAGE!
DON'T WASTE ZOE'S DEATH!
YEAH, AFTER KUGA.
TMP
TMP
HUH?
WHY IS MY SACRIFICE BEING TREATED LIKE NOTHING?
TMP
LOOKS LIKE THE OTHER SQUADS ARE MEETING UP!
THE TWO ATTACKERS FROM AZUMA ARE PROBABLY COMING YOUR WAY.
THUNK
THEY MAY INTERCEPT YOU GUYS BEFORE YOU CAN MEET UP.
BE CAREFUL!
GOT IT, SHIORI.
CHIKA, DON'T MOVE! THERE'RE TWO ENEMY SNIPERS.
IF YOU'RE CAUGHT, YOU'RE DONE!
ROGER!

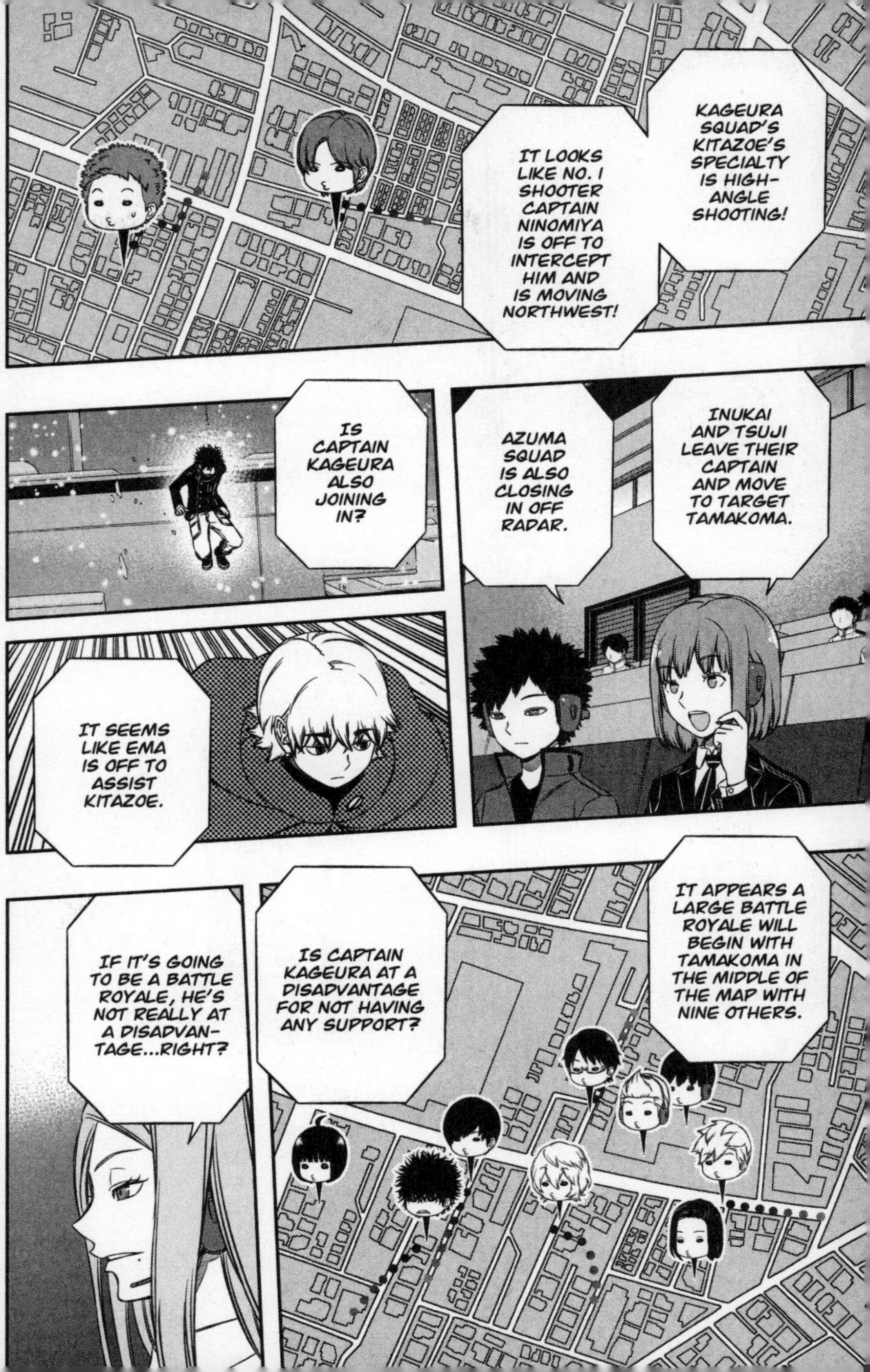
KAGEURA SQUAD'S KITAZOE'S SPECIALTY IS HIGH-ANGLE SHOOTING!
IT LOOKS LIKE NO. 1 SHOOTER CAPTAIN NINOMIYA IS OFF TO INTERCEPT HIM AND IS MOVING NORTHWEST!
INUKAI AND TSUJI LEAVE THEIR CAPTAIN AND MOVE TO TARGET TAMAKOMA.
AZUMA SQUAD IS ALSO CLOSING IN OFF RADAR.
IS CAPTAIN KAGEURA ALSO JOINING IN?
IT SEEMS LIKE EMA IS OFF TO ASSIST KITAZOE.
IT APPEARS A LARGE BATTLE ROYALE WILL BEGIN WITH TAMAKOMA IN THE MIDDLE OF THE MAP WITH NINE OTHERS.
IS CAPTAIN KAGEURA AT A DISADVANTAGE FOR NOT HAVING ANY SUPPORT?
IF IT'S GOING TO BE A BATTLE ROYALE, HE'S NOT REALLY AT A DISADVANTAGE...RIGHT?

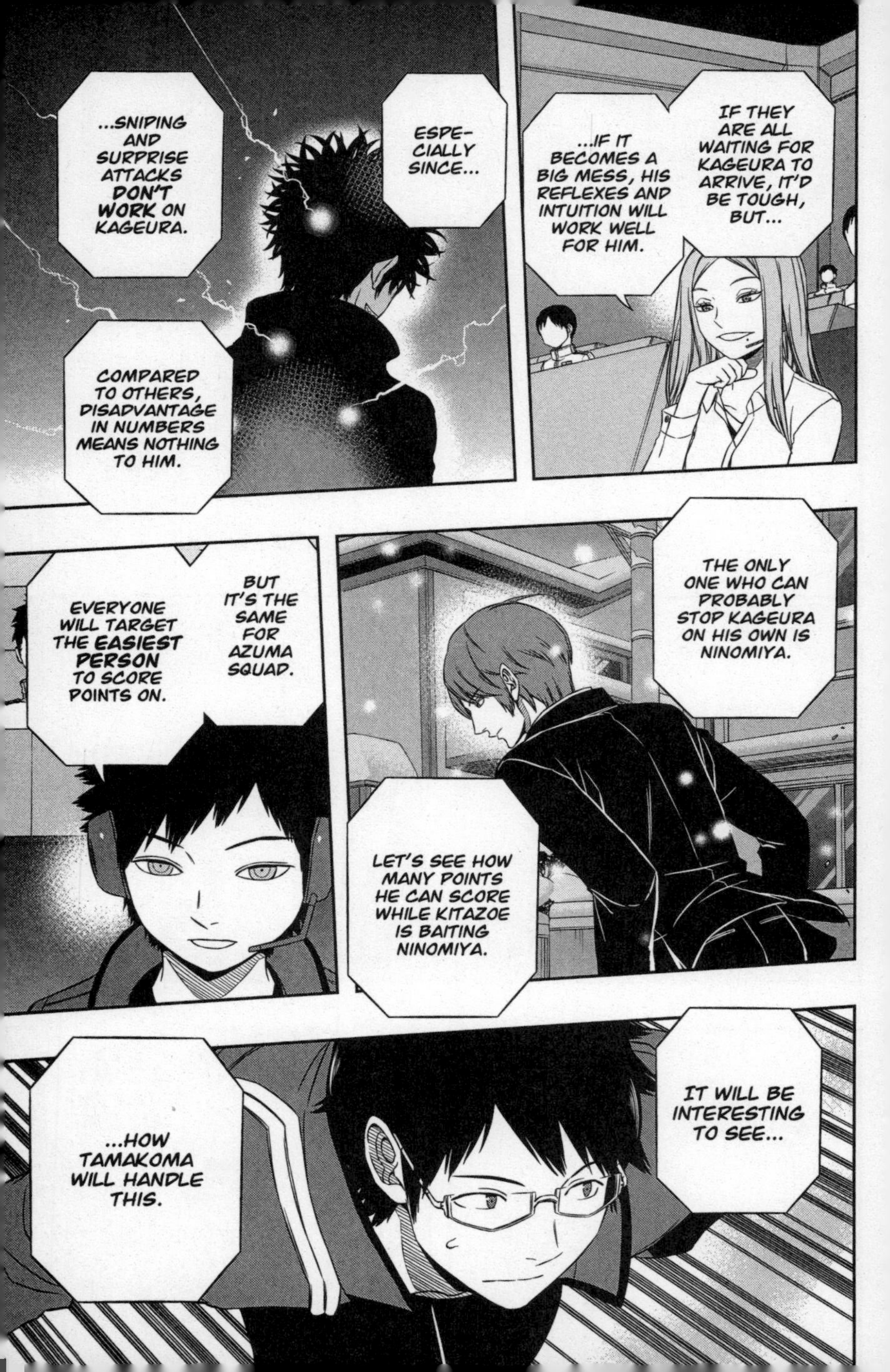
IF THEY ARE ALL WAITING FOR KAGEURA TO ARRIVE, IT'D BE TOUGH, BUT...
...IF IT BECOMES A BIG MESS, HIS REFLEXES AND INTUITION WILL WORK WELL FOR HIM.
ESPE-CIALLY SINCE...
...SNIPING AND SURPRISE ATTACKS DON'T WORK ON KAGEURA.
COMPARED TO OTHERS, DISADVANTAGE IN NUMBERS MEANS NOTHING TO HIM.
THE ONLY ONE WHO CAN PROBABLY STOP KAGEURA ON HIS OWN IS NINOMIYA.
LET'S SEE HOW MANY POINTS HE CAN SCORE WHILE KITAZOE IS BAITING NINOMIYA.
BUT IT'S THE SAME FOR AZUMA SQUAD.
EVERYONE WILL TARGET THE EASIEST PERSON TO SCORE POINTS ON.
IT WILL BE INTERESTING TO SEE...
...HOW TAMAKOMA WILL HANDLE THIS.

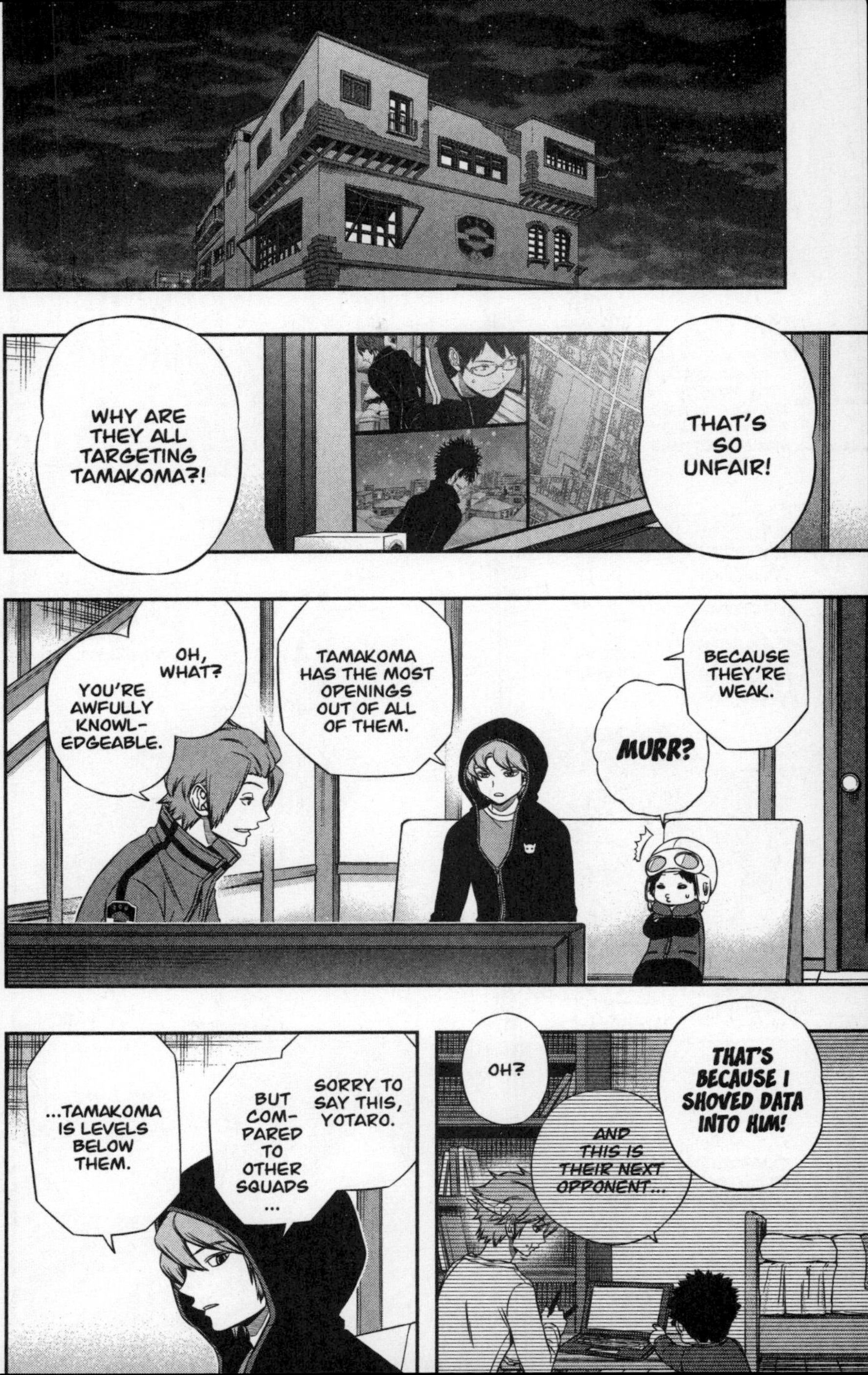
THAT'S SO UNFAIR!
WHY ARE THEY ALL TARGETING TAMAKOMA?!
BECAUSE THEY'RE WEAK.
MURR?
TAMAKOMA HAS THE MOST OPENINGS OUT OF ALL OF THEM.
OH, WHAT? YOU'RE AWFULLY KNOWL-EDGEABLE.
THAT'S BECAUSE I SHOVED DATA INTO HIM!
OH?
AND THIS IS THEIR NEXT OPPONENT...
SORRY TO SAY THIS, YOTARO.
BUT COM-PARED TO OTHER SQUADS...
...TAMAKOMA IS LEVELS BELOW THEM.

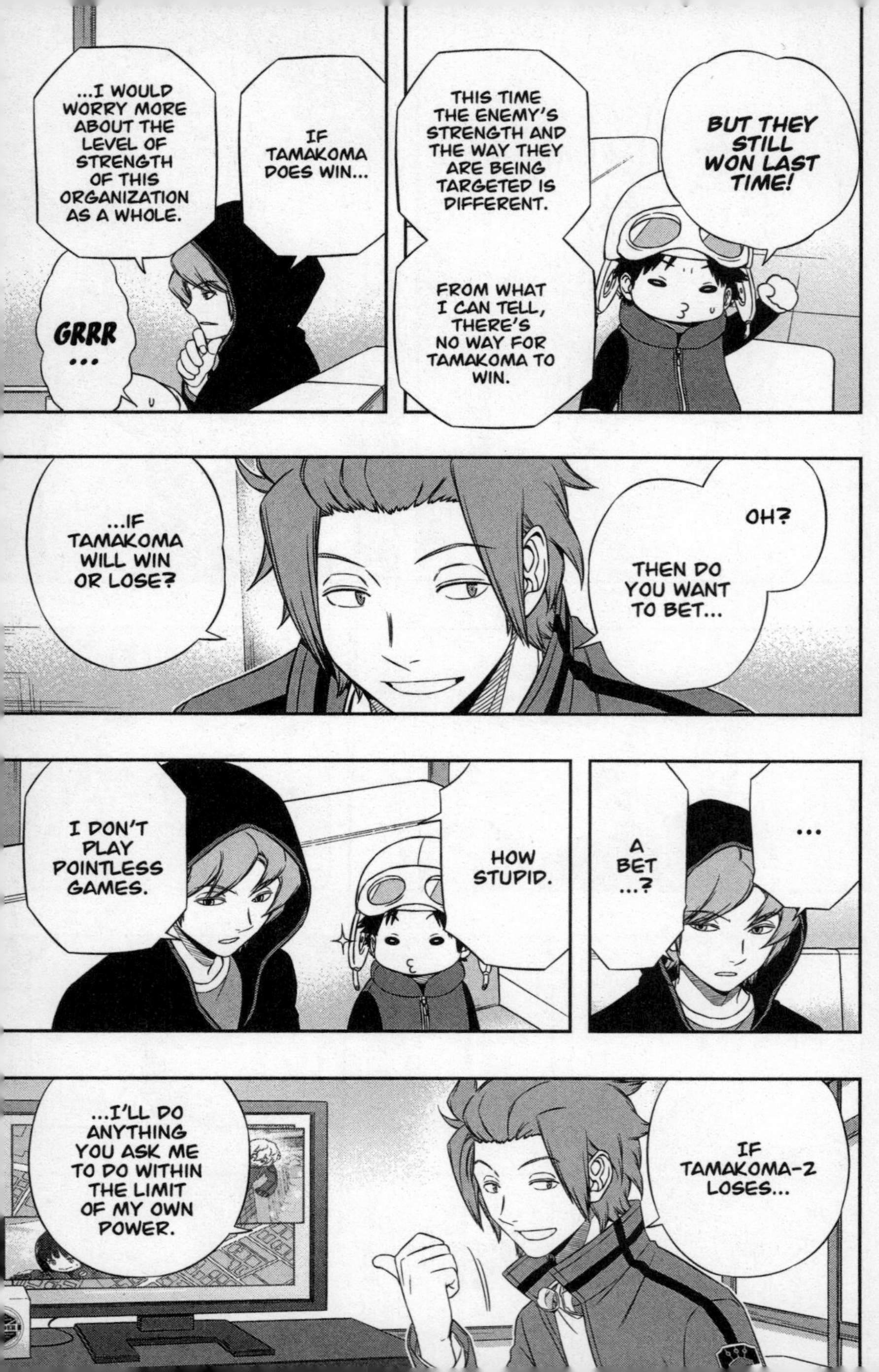
BUT THEY STILL WON LAST TIME!
THIS TIME THE ENEMY'S STRENGTH AND THE WAY THEY ARE BEING TARGETED IS DIFFERENT.
FROM WHAT I CAN TELL, THERE'S NO WAY FOR TAMAKOMA TO WIN.
IF TAMAKOMA DOES WIN...
...I WOULD WORRY MORE ABOUT THE LEVEL OF STRENGTH OF THIS ORGANIZATION AS A WHOLE.
GRRR...
OH?
THEN DO YOU WANT TO BET...
...IF TAMAKOMA WILL WIN OR LOSE?
...
A BET...?
HOW STUPID.
I DON'T PLAY POINTLESS GAMES.
IF TAMAKOMA-2 LOSES...
...I'LL DO ANYTHING YOU ASK ME TO DO WITHIN THE LIMIT OF MY OWN POWER.

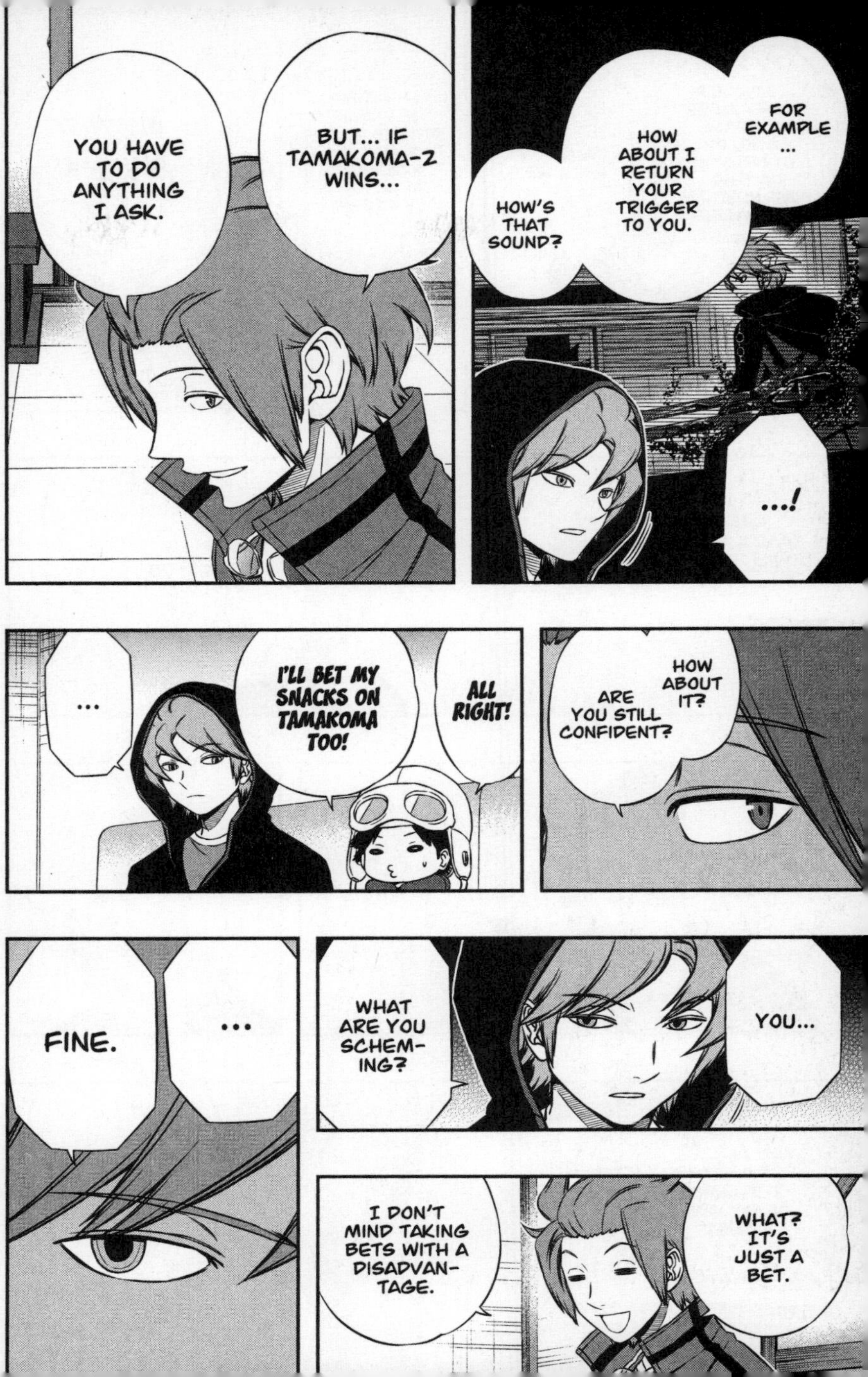
FOR EXAMPLE...
HOW ABOUT I RETURN YOUR TRIGGER TO YOU.
HOW'S THAT SOUND?
...!
BUT... IF TAMAKOMA-2 WINS...
YOU HAVE TO DO ANYTHING I ASK.
HOW ABOUT IT? ARE YOU STILL CONFIDENT?
ALL RIGHT!
I'LL BET MY SNACKS ON TAMAKOMA TOO!
...
YOU...
WHAT ARE YOU SCHEMING?
WHAT? IT'S JUST A BET.
I DON'T MIND TAKING BETS WITH A DISADVANTAGE.
...
FINE.

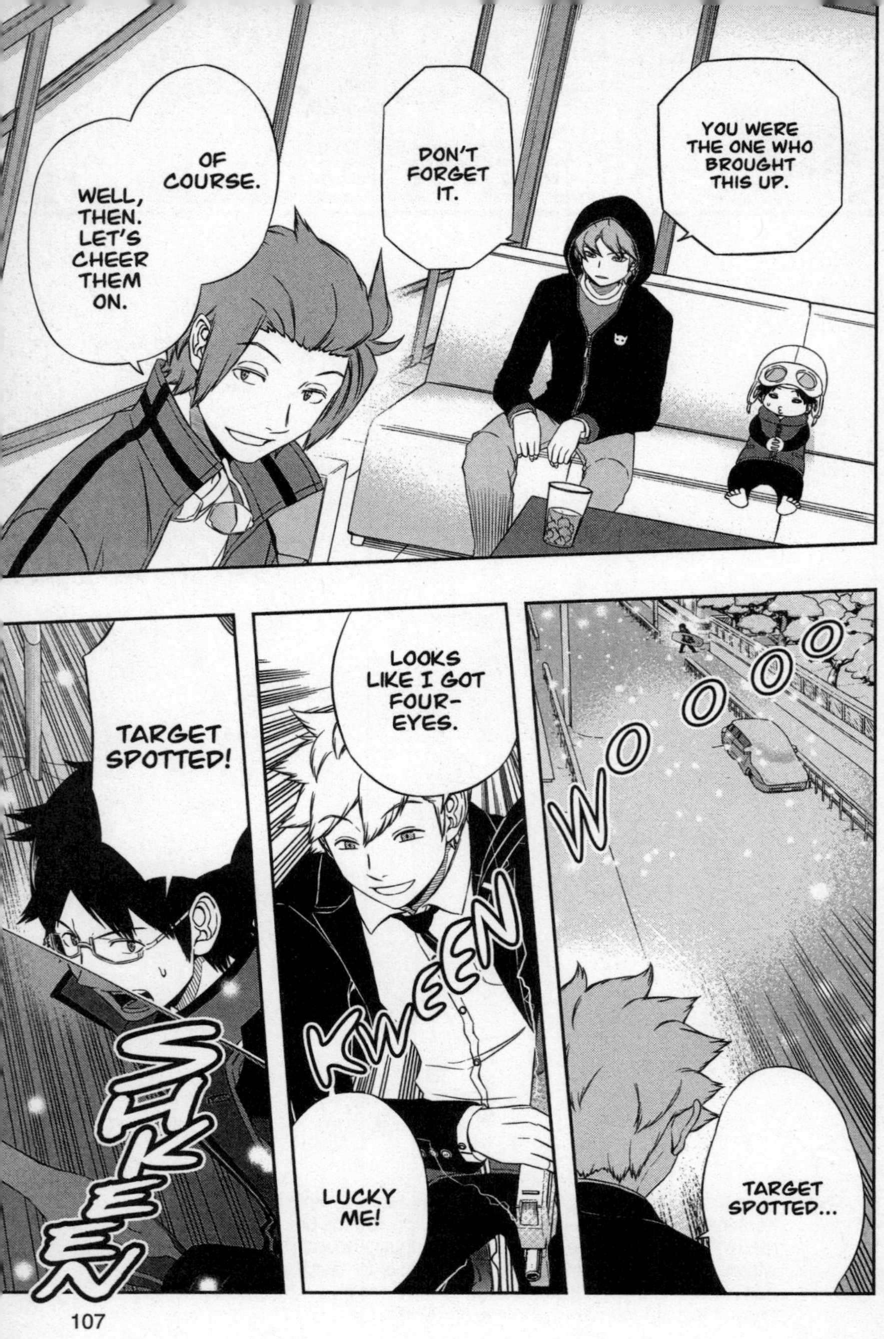
YOU WERE THE ONE WHO BROUGHT THIS UP.
DON'T FORGET IT.
OF COURSE.
WELL, THEN. LET'S CHEER THEM ON.
WOOOOOO
TARGET SPOTTED...
LOOKS LIKE I GOT FOUR-EYES.
KWEEN
LUCKY ME!
TARGET SPOTTED!
SHKEEN

[redacted] Strategy Room

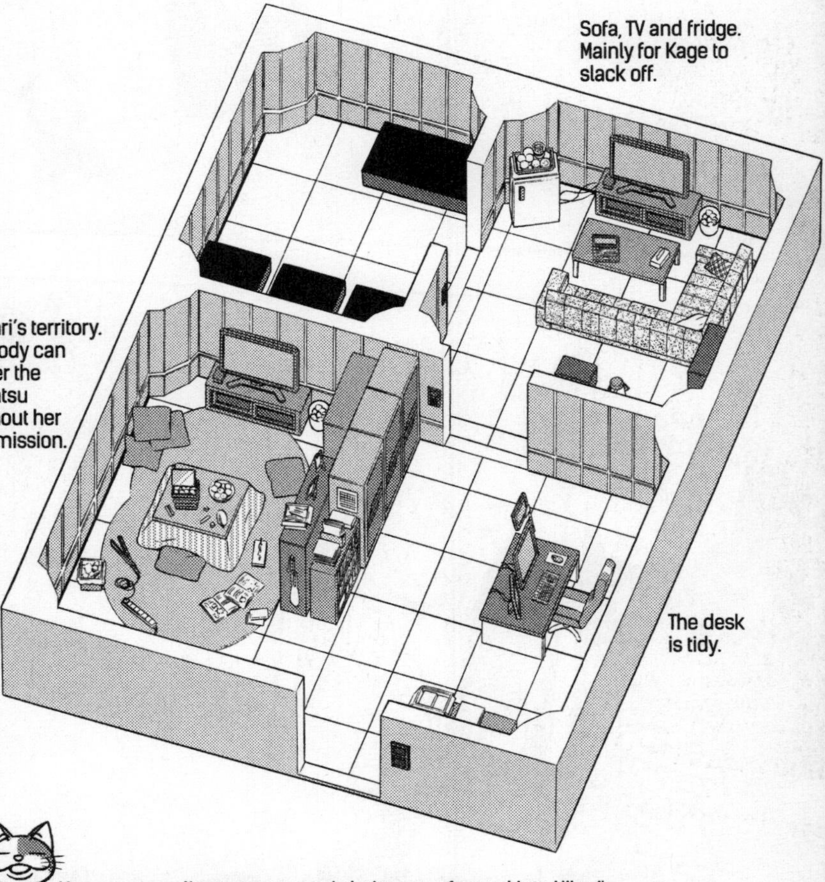

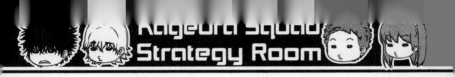

Sofa, TV and fridge. Mainly for Kage to slack off.
Hikari's territory. Nobody can enter the kotatsu without her permission.
The desk is tidy.

Kageura squad's strategy room is being transformed into Hikari's personal room and barely maintains the appearance of a strategy room. People sadly expect Border's first kotatsu-bound Operator next winter. The three guys don't make too much of a mess (because they don't have any personal items) so it's possible to give it the appearance of a clean room by curtaining off Hikari's nest.

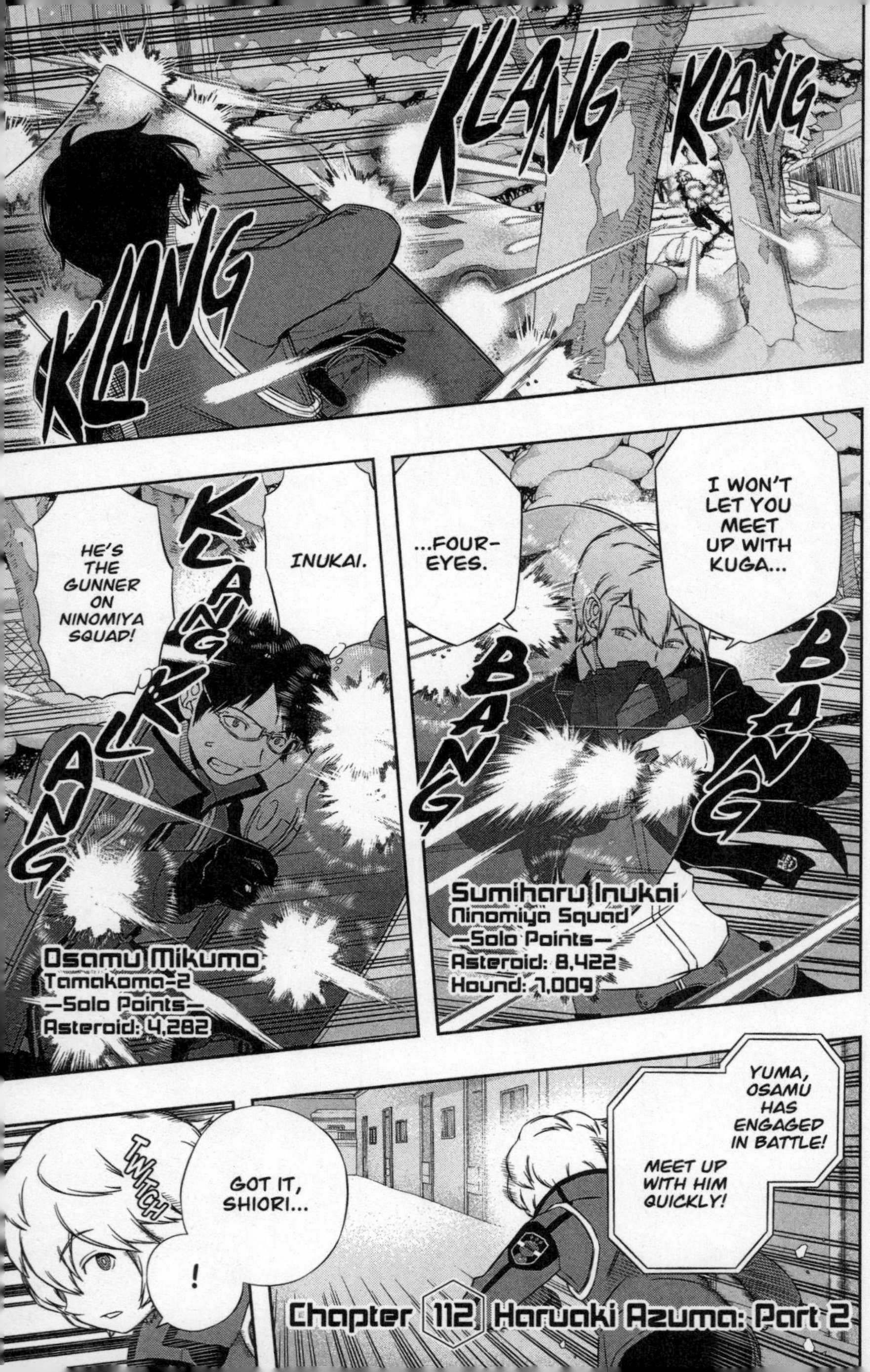
KLANG KLANG
KLANG
I WON'T LET YOU MEET UP WITH KUGA...
...FOUR-EYES.
BANG
BANG
Sumiharu Inukai
Ninomiya Squad
—Solo Points—
Asteroid: 8,422
Hound: 7,009
INUKAI.
HE'S THE GUNNER ON NINOMIYA SQUAD!
KLANG
KLANG
Osamu Mikumo
Tamakoma-2
—Solo Points—
Asteroid: 4,282
YUMA, OSAMU HAS ENGAGED IN BATTLE!
MEET UP WITH HIM QUICKLY!
GOT IT, SHIORI...
TWITCH
!
Chapter 112 Haruaki Azuma: Part 2

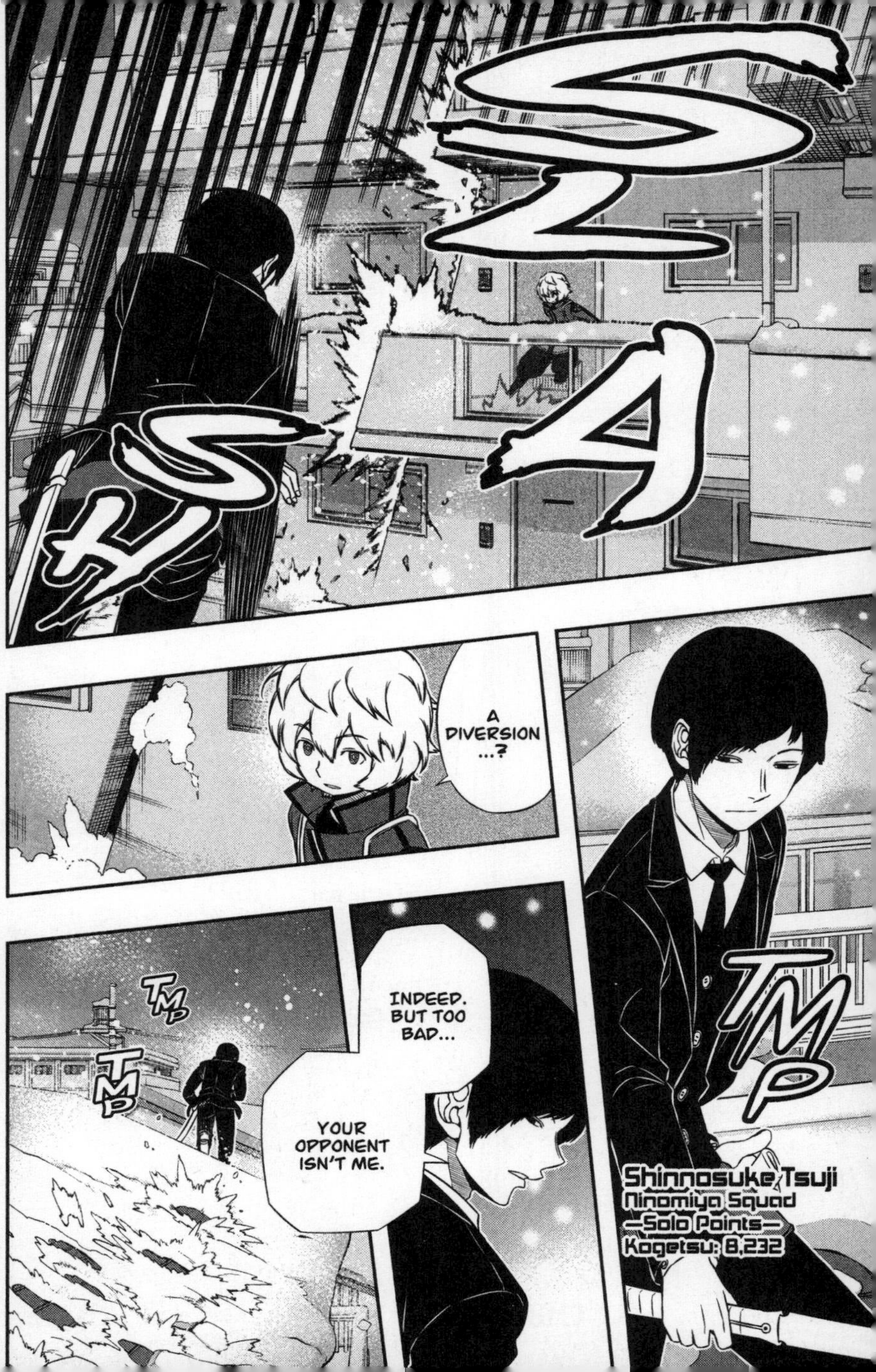
SHA
TMP
Shinnosuke Tsuji
Ninomiya Squad
—Solo Points—
Kogetsu: 8,232
A DIVERSION ...?
INDEED. BUT TOO BAD...
YOUR OPPONENT ISN'T ME.
TMP
TMP

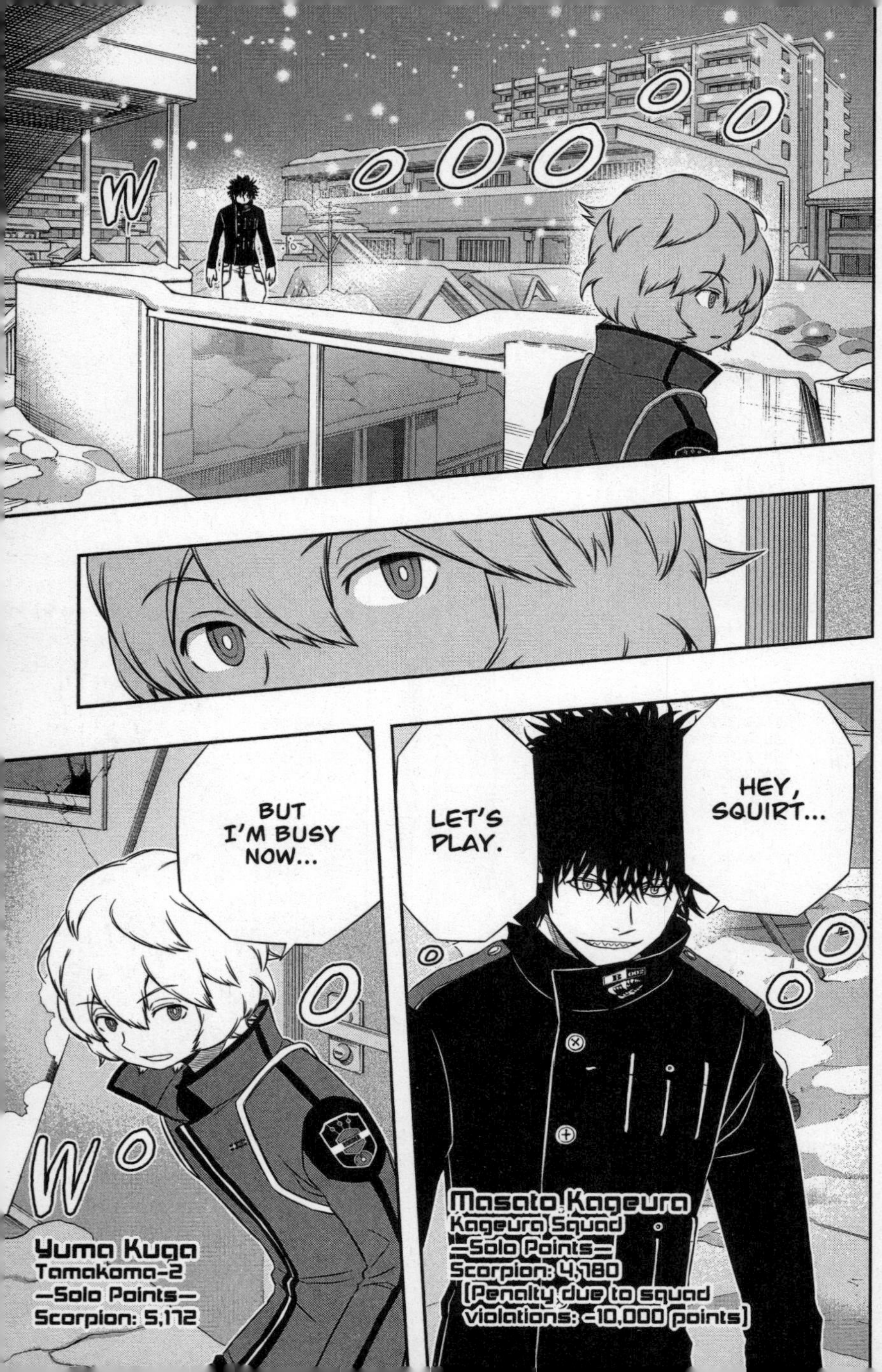
WOOOOOOOO
HEY, SQUIRT...
LET'S PLAY.
OOO
Masato Kageura
Kageura Squad
—Solo Points—
Scorpion: 4,780
[Penalty due to squad violations: -10,000 points]
BUT I'M BUSY NOW...
WOO
Yuma Kuga
Tamakoma-2
—Solo Points—
Scorpion: 5,172

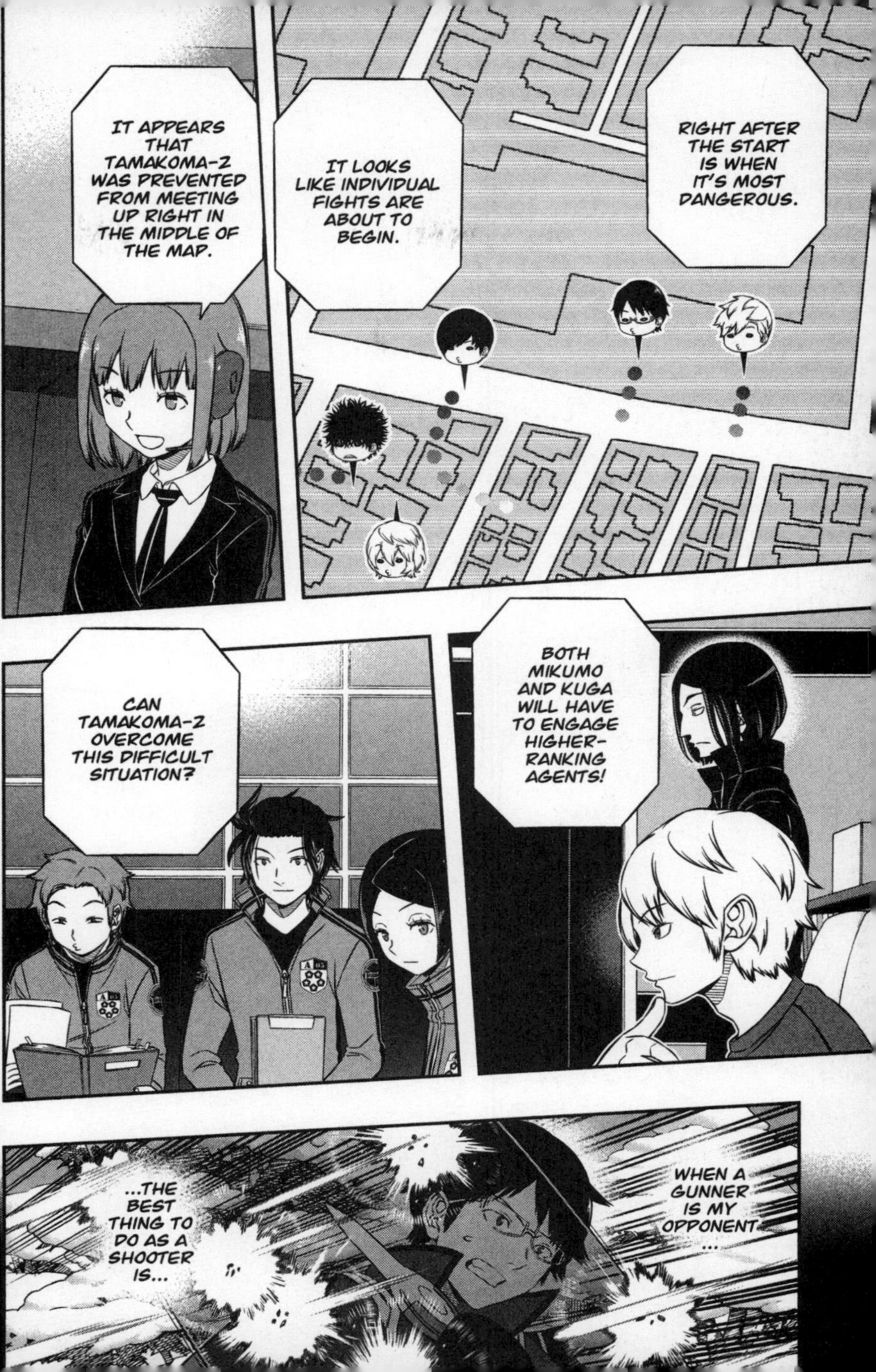
RIGHT AFTER THE START IS WHEN IT'S MOST DANGEROUS.
IT LOOKS LIKE INDIVIDUAL FIGHTS ARE ABOUT TO BEGIN.
IT APPEARS THAT TAMAKOMA-2 WAS PREVENTED FROM MEETING UP RIGHT IN THE MIDDLE OF THE MAP.
BOTH MIKUMO AND KUGA WILL HAVE TO ENGAGE HIGHER-RANKING AGENTS!
CAN TAMAKOMA-2 OVERCOME THIS DIFFICULT SITUATION?
WHEN A GUNNER IS MY OPPONENT...
...THE BEST THING TO DO AS A SHOOTER IS...

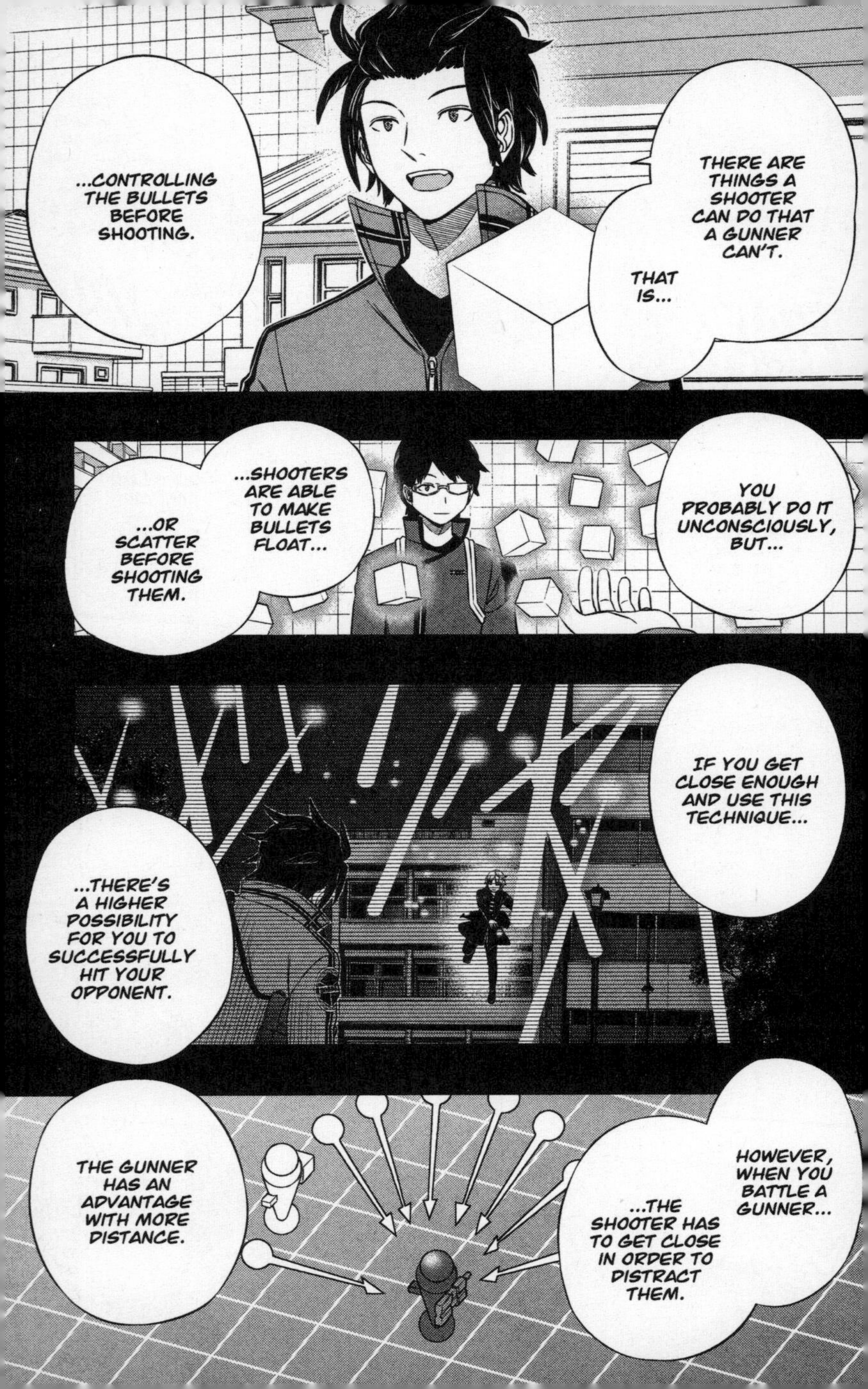
THERE ARE THINGS A SHOOTER CAN DO THAT A GUNNER CAN'T.
THAT IS...
...CONTROLLING THE BULLETS BEFORE SHOOTING.
YOU PROBABLY DO IT UNCONSCIOUSLY, BUT...
...SHOOTERS ARE ABLE TO MAKE BULLETS FLOAT...
...OR SCATTER BEFORE SHOOTING THEM.
IF YOU GET CLOSE ENOUGH AND USE THIS TECHNIQUE...
...THERE'S A HIGHER POSSIBILITY FOR YOU TO SUCCESSFULLY HIT YOUR OPPONENT.
HOWEVER, WHEN YOU BATTLE A GUNNER...
...THE SHOOTER HAS TO GET CLOSE IN ORDER TO DISTRACT THEM.
THE GUNNER HAS AN ADVANTAGE WITH MORE DISTANCE.

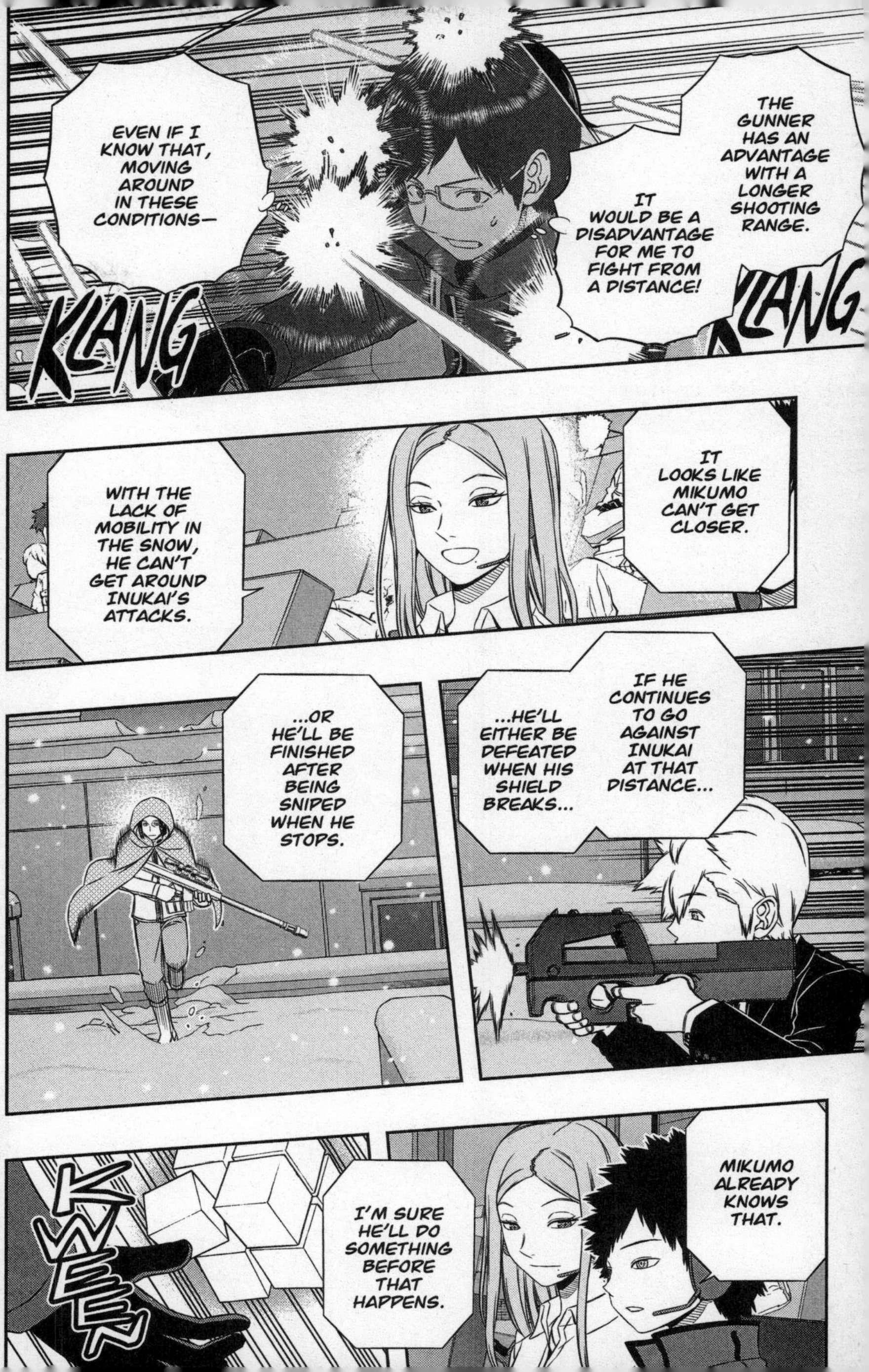
THE GUNNER HAS AN ADVANTAGE WITH A LONGER SHOOTING RANGE.
IT WOULD BE A DISADVANTAGE FOR ME TO FIGHT FROM A DISTANCE!
KLANG
EVEN IF I KNOW THAT, MOVING AROUND IN THESE CONDITIONS—
KLANG
IT LOOKS LIKE MIKUMO CAN'T GET CLOSER.
WITH THE LACK OF MOBILITY IN THE SNOW, HE CAN'T GET AROUND INUKAI'S ATTACKS.
IF HE CONTINUES TO GO AGAINST INUKAI AT THAT DISTANCE...
...HE'LL EITHER BE DEFEATED WHEN HIS SHIELD BREAKS...
...OR HE'LL BE FINISHED AFTER BEING SNIPED WHEN HE STOPS.
MIKUMO ALREADY KNOWS THAT.
I'M SURE HE'LL DO SOMETHING BEFORE THAT HAPPENS.
KWEEN

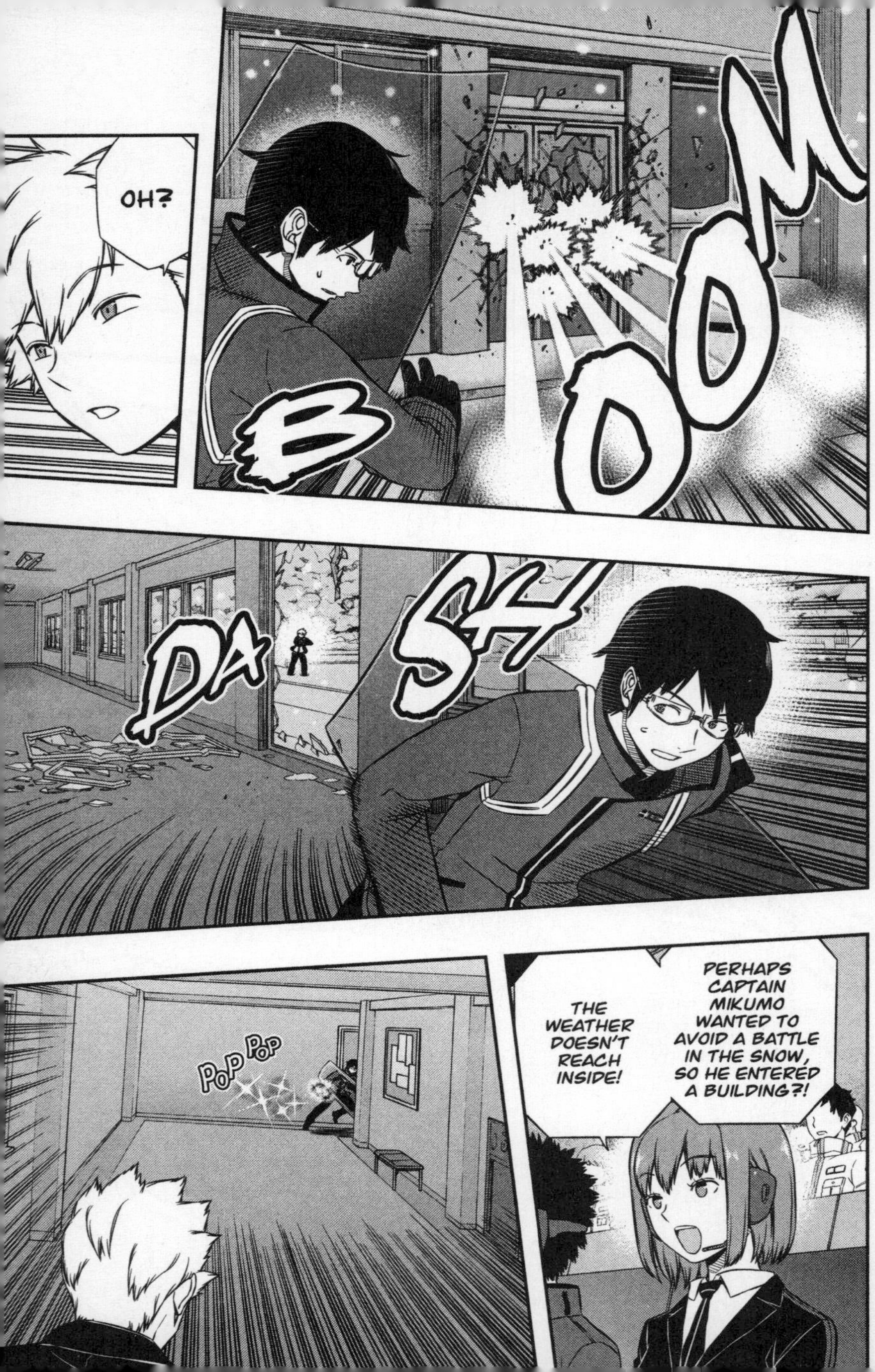
BOOM
OH?
DASH
PERHAPS CAPTAIN MIKUMO WANTED TO AVOID A BATTLE IN THE SNOW, SO HE ENTERED A BUILDING?!
THE WEATHER DOESN'T REACH INSIDE!
POP POP

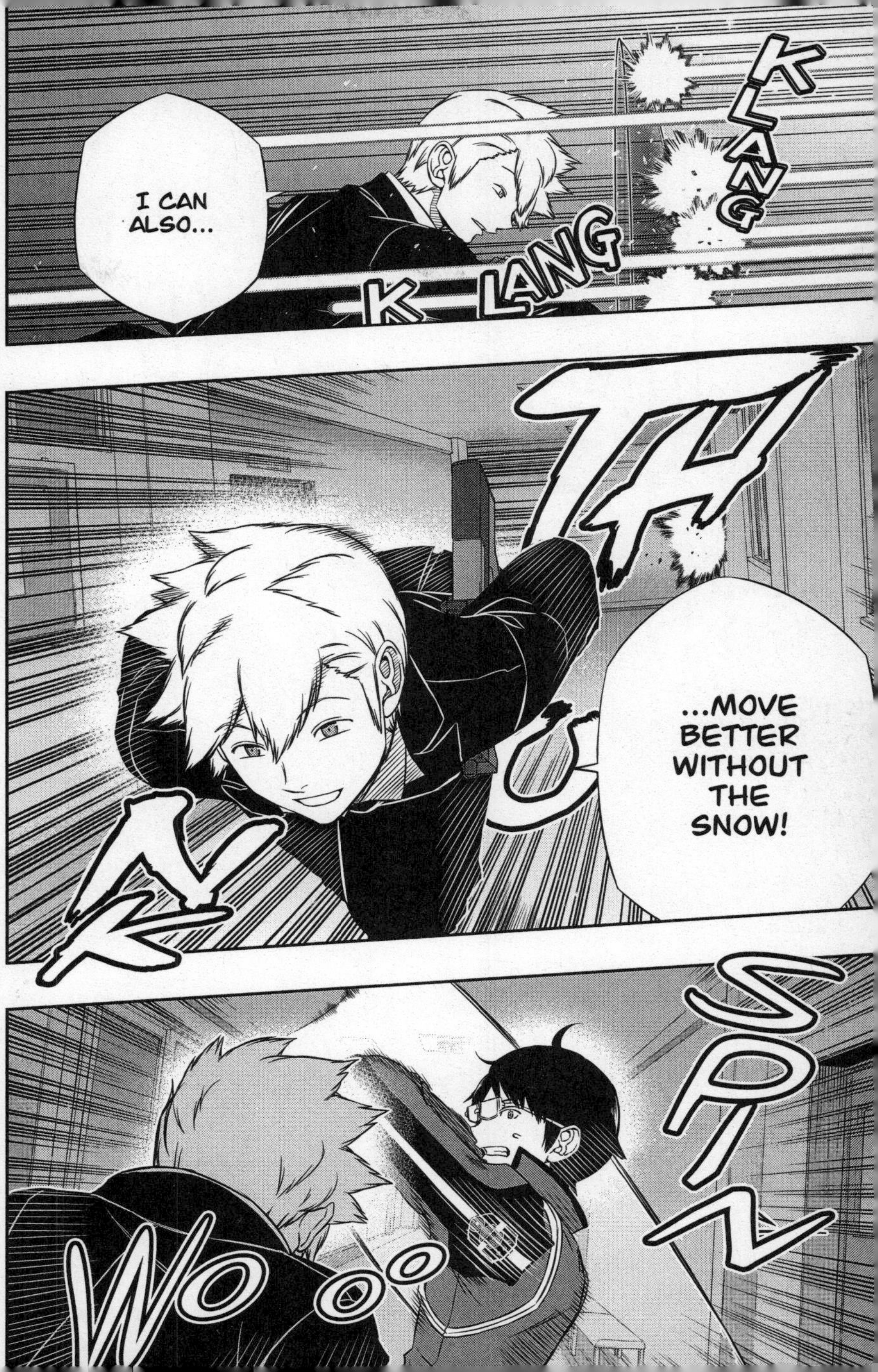
KLANG
K LANG
I CAN ALSO...
...MOVE BETTER WITHOUT THE SNOW!

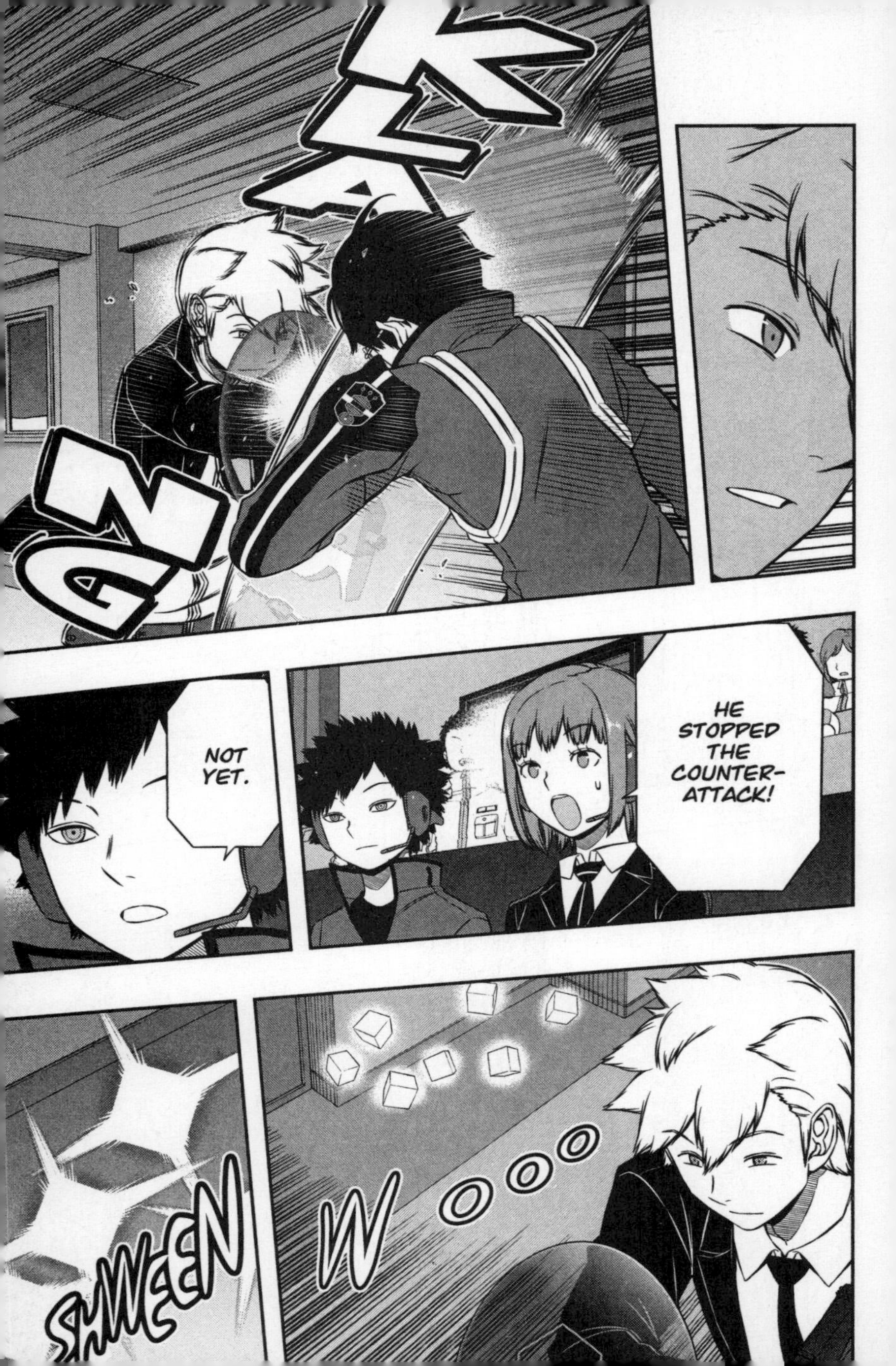
HE STOPPED THE COUNTER-ATTACK!
NOT YET.
WOOOO
SHWEEN

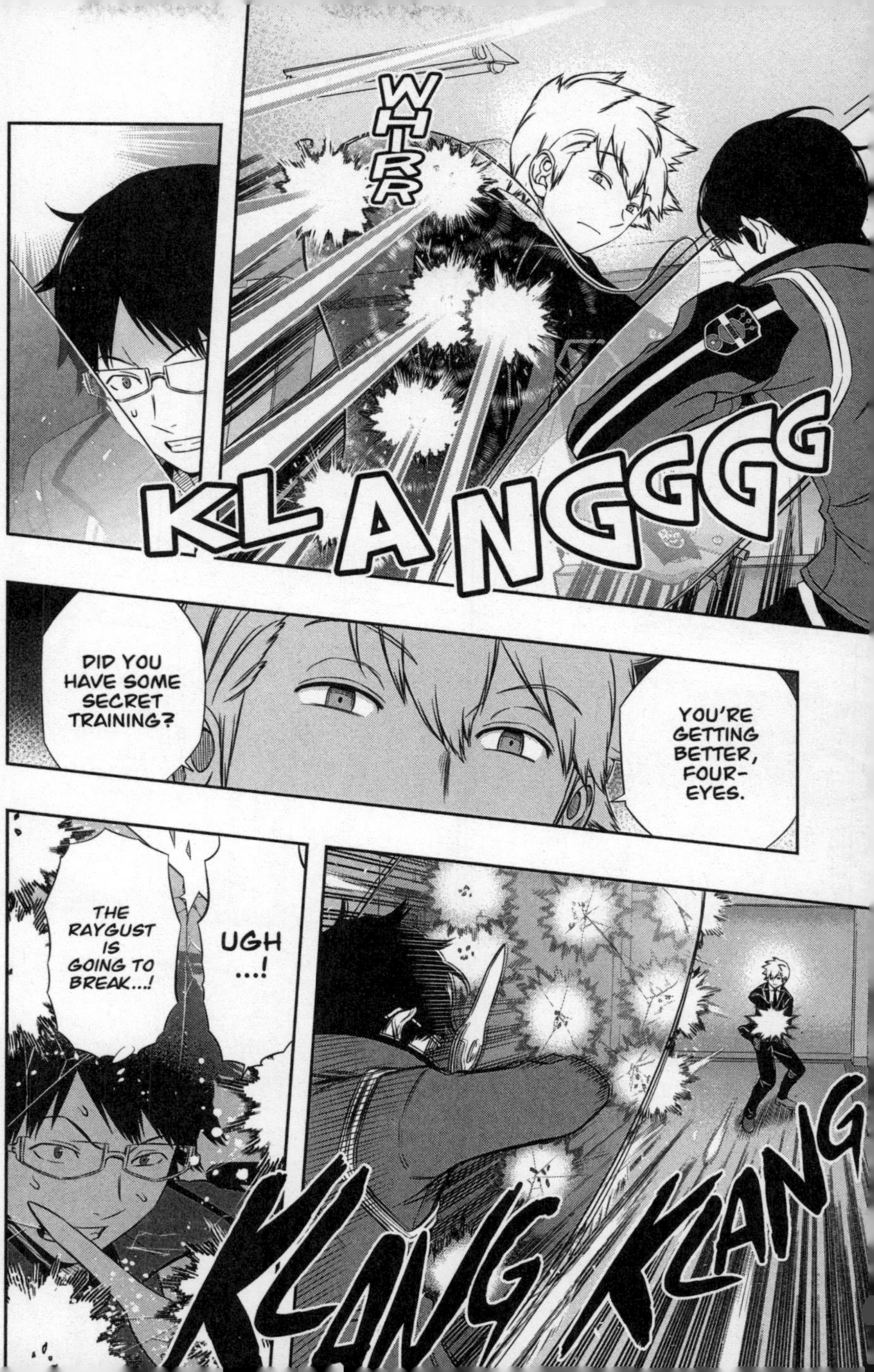
WHIRR
KLANGGGG
YOU'RE GETTING BETTER, FOUR-EYES.
DID YOU HAVE SOME SECRET TRAINING?
KLANG KLANG
UGH ...!
THE RAYGUST IS GOING TO BREAK...!

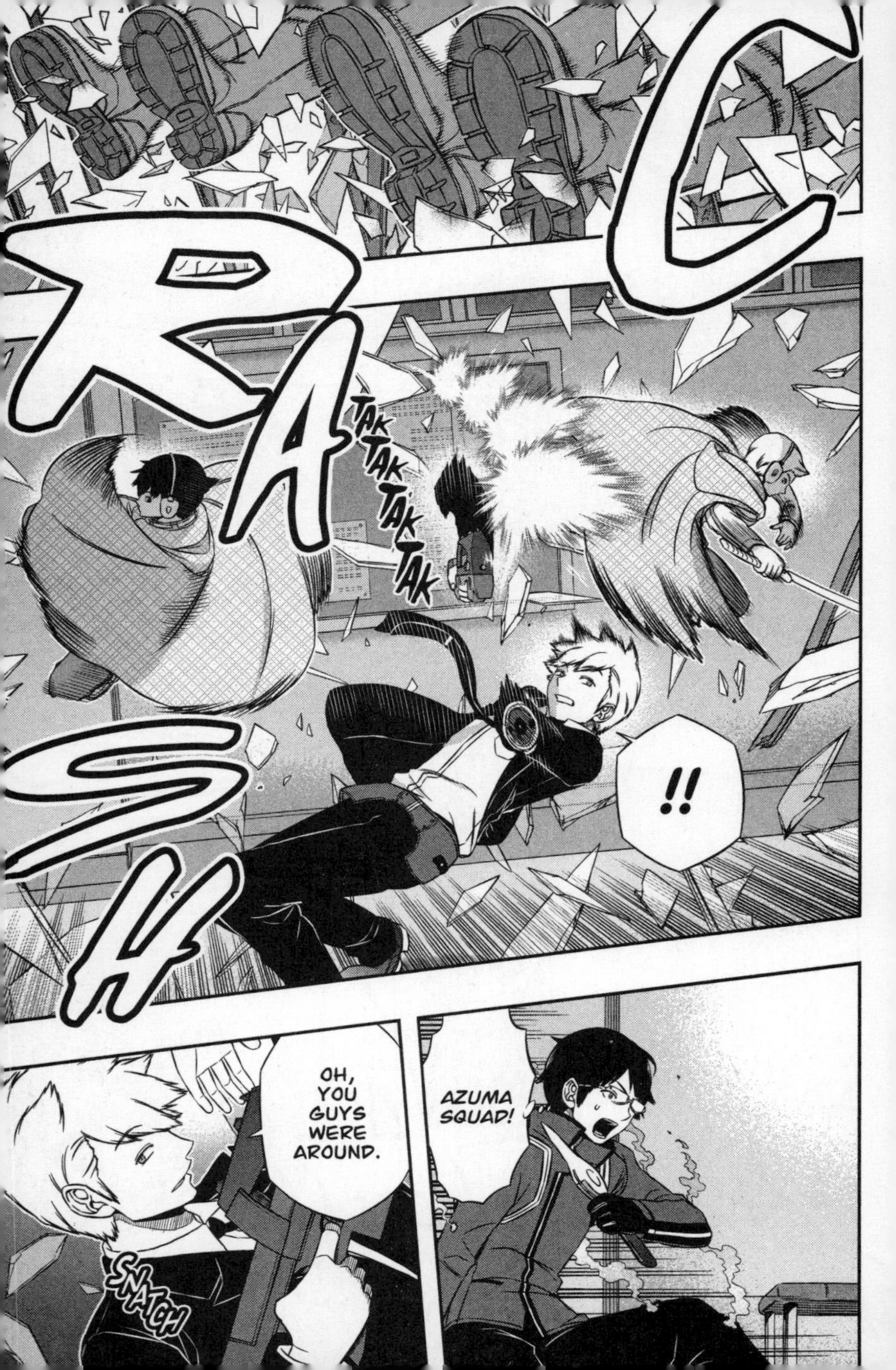
CRASH
TAK TAK TAK TAK TAK
!!
AZUMA SQUAD!
OH, YOU GUYS WERE AROUND.
SNATCH

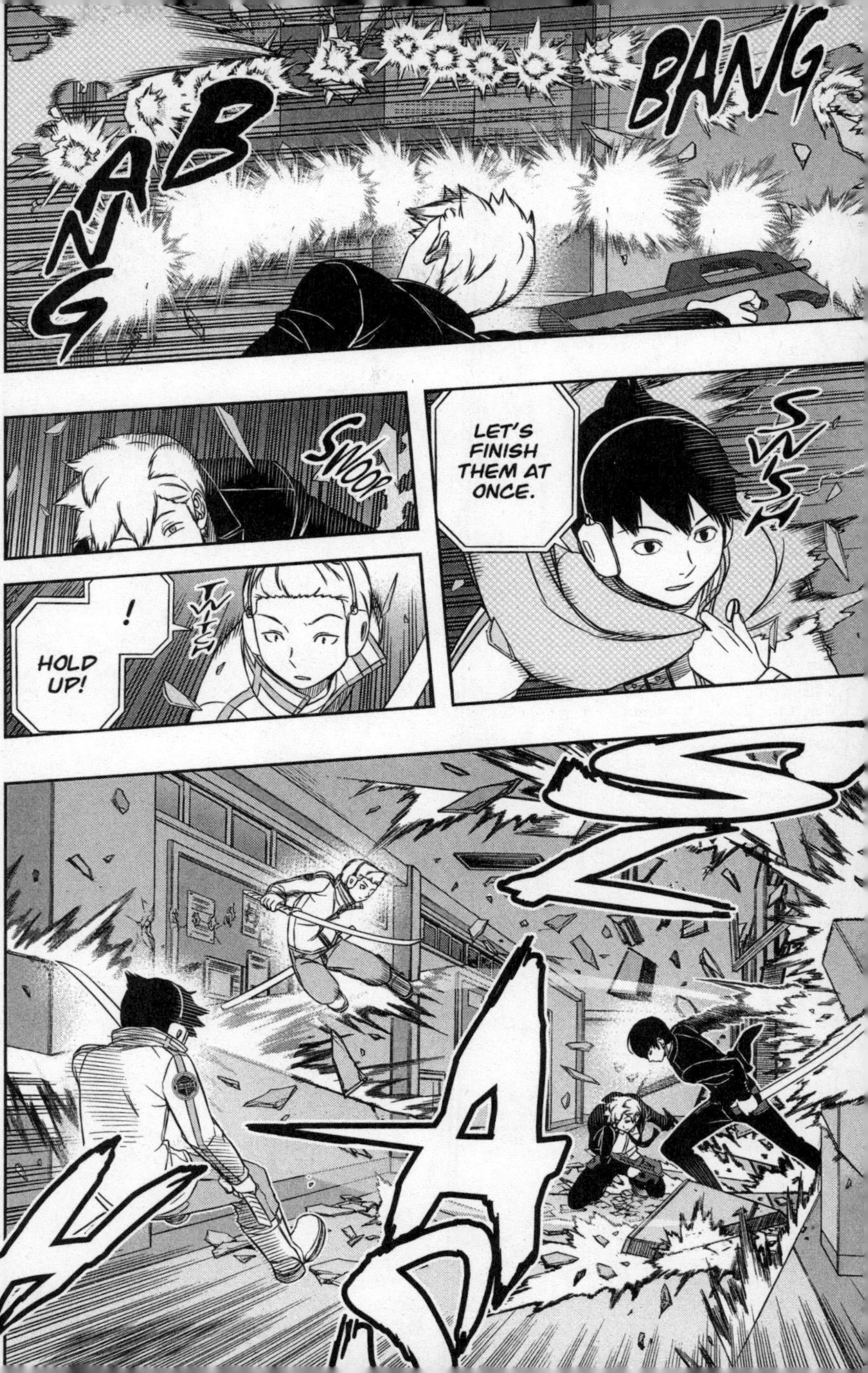
BANG
BANG
LET'S FINISH THEM AT ONCE.
SWISH
!
HOLD UP!

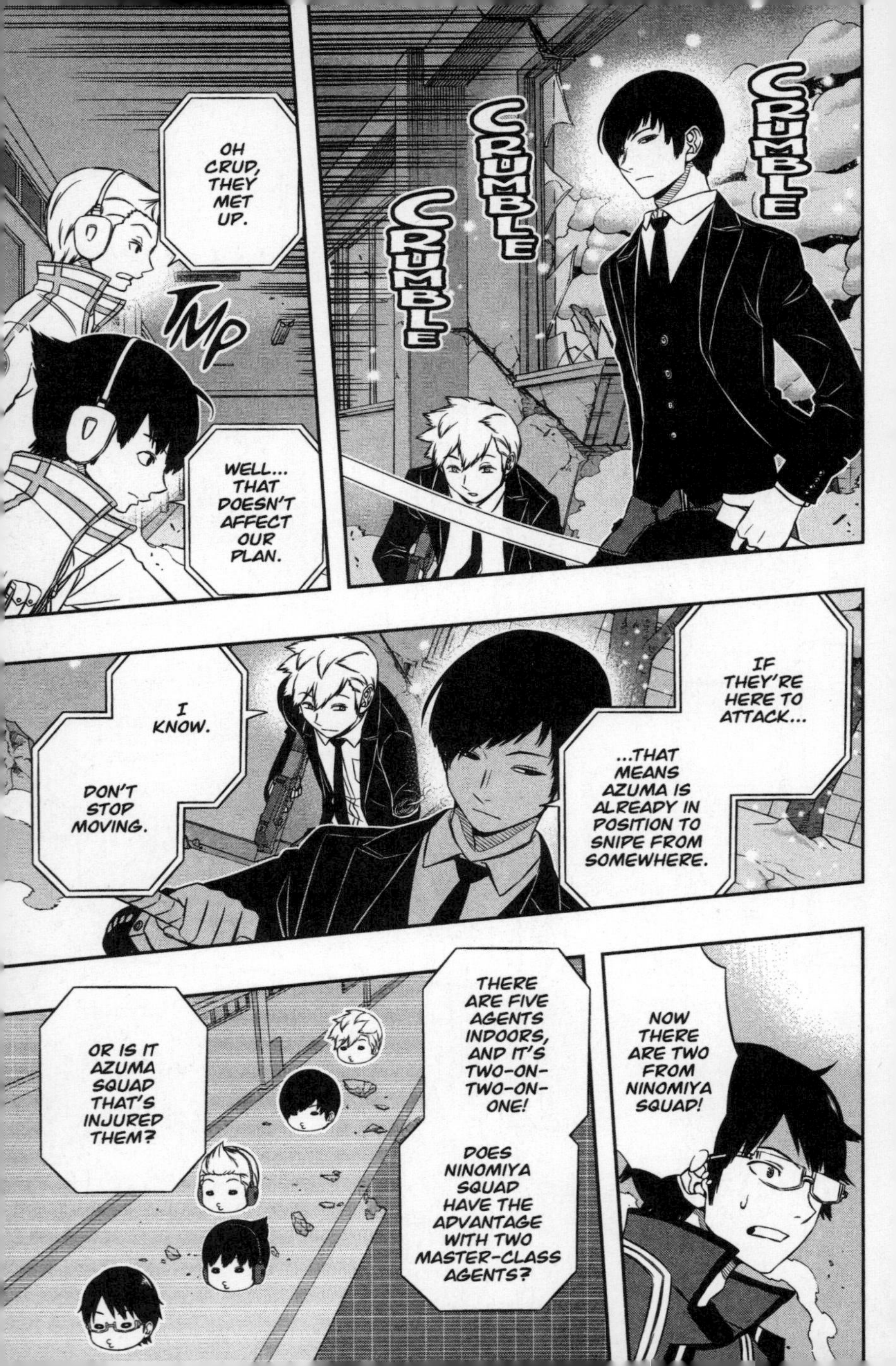
CRUMBLE
CRUMBLE
CRUMBLE
OH CRUD, THEY MET UP.
TMP
WELL... THAT DOESN'T AFFECT OUR PLAN.
IF THEY'RE HERE TO ATTACK...
...THAT MEANS AZUMA IS ALREADY IN POSITION TO SNIPE FROM SOMEWHERE.
I KNOW.
DON'T STOP MOVING.
NOW THERE ARE TWO FROM NINOMIYA SQUAD!
THERE ARE FIVE AGENTS INDOORS, AND IT'S TWO-ON-TWO-ON-ONE!
DOES NINOMIYA SQUAD HAVE THE ADVANTAGE WITH TWO MASTER-CLASS AGENTS?
OR IS IT AZUMA SQUAD THAT'S INJURED THEM?

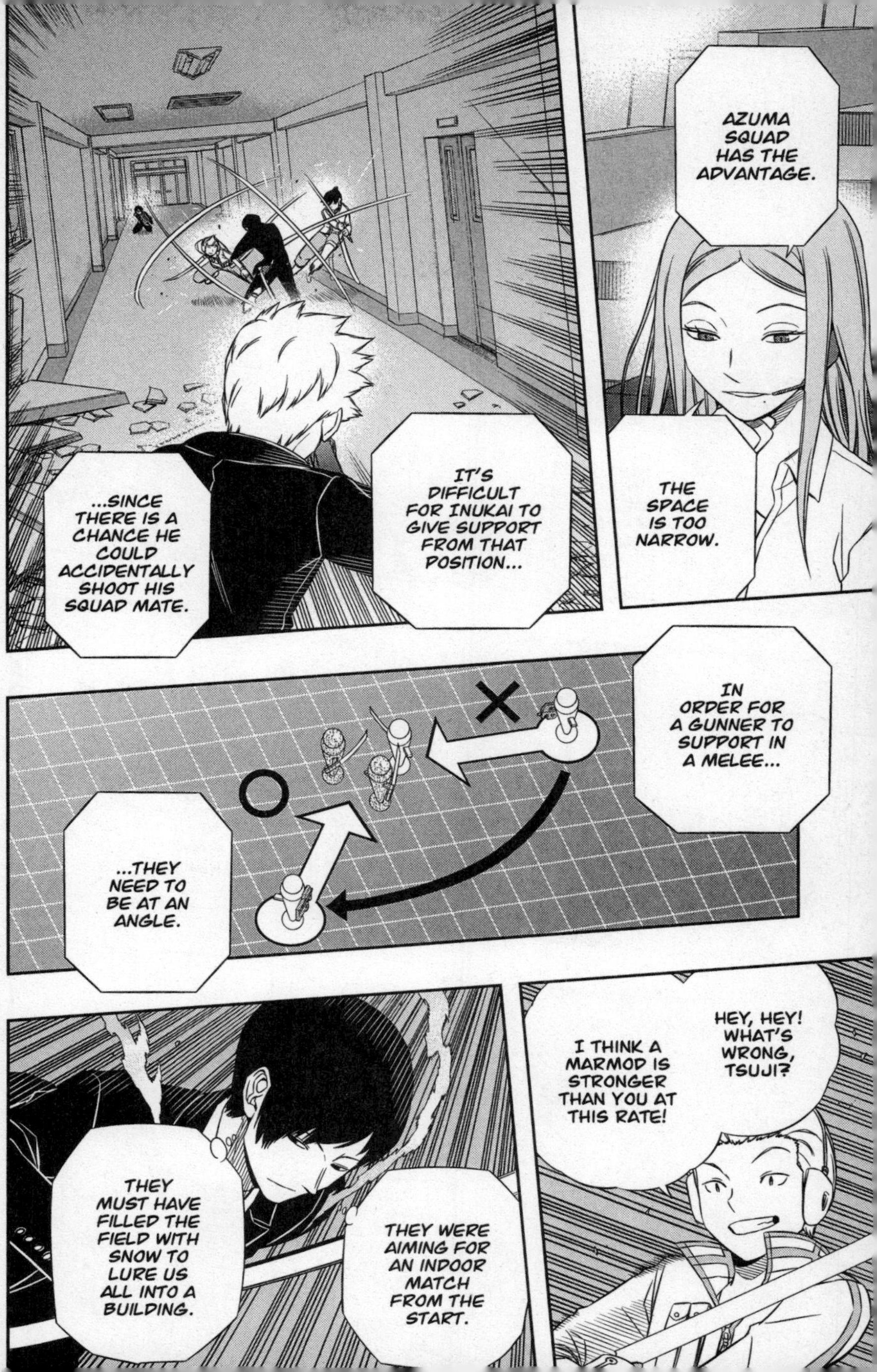
AZUMA SQUAD HAS THE ADVANTAGE.
THE SPACE IS TOO NARROW.
IT'S DIFFICULT FOR INUKAI TO GIVE SUPPORT FROM THAT POSITION...
...SINCE THERE IS A CHANCE HE COULD ACCIDENTALLY SHOOT HIS SQUAD MATE.
IN ORDER FOR A GUNNER TO SUPPORT IN A MELEE...
...THEY NEED TO BE AT AN ANGLE.
HEY, HEY! WHAT'S WRONG, TSUJI?
I THINK A MARMOD IS STRONGER THAN YOU AT THIS RATE!
THEY WERE AIMING FOR AN INDOOR MATCH FROM THE START.
THEY MUST HAVE FILLED THE FIELD WITH SNOW TO LURE US ALL INTO A BUILDING.

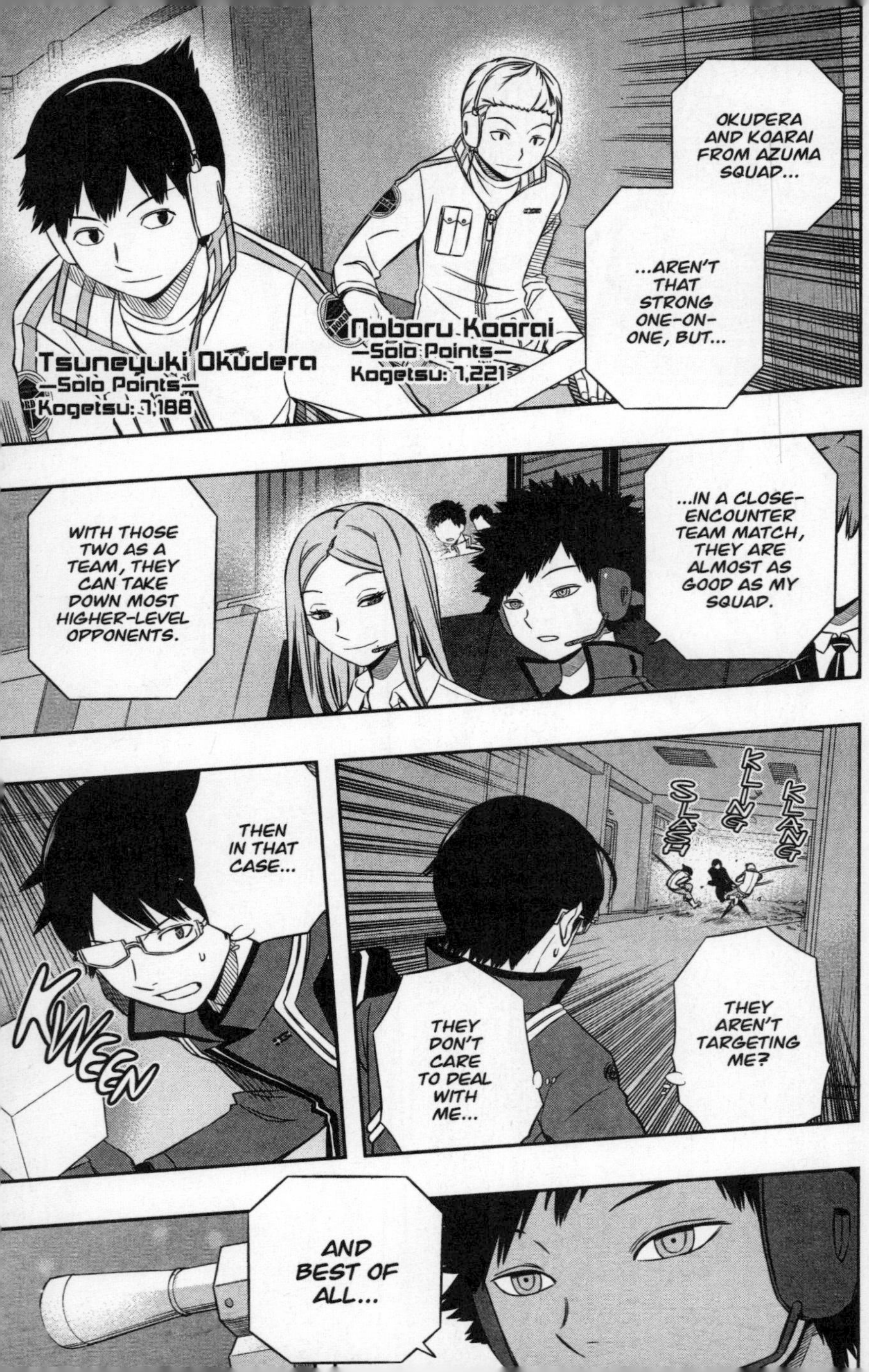
OKUDERA AND KOARAI FROM AZUMA SQUAD...
...AREN'T THAT STRONG ONE-ON-ONE, BUT...
Noboru Koarai —Solo Points— Kogetsu: 7,221
Tsuneyuki Okudera —Solo Points— Kogetsu: 7,188
...IN A CLOSE-ENCOUNTER TEAM MATCH, THEY ARE ALMOST AS GOOD AS MY SQUAD.
WITH THOSE TWO AS A TEAM, THEY CAN TAKE DOWN MOST HIGHER-LEVEL OPPONENTS.
KLANG
KLING
SLASH
THEY AREN'T TARGETING ME?
THEY DON'T CARE TO DEAL WITH ME...
THEN IN THAT CASE...
KWEEN
AND BEST OF ALL...

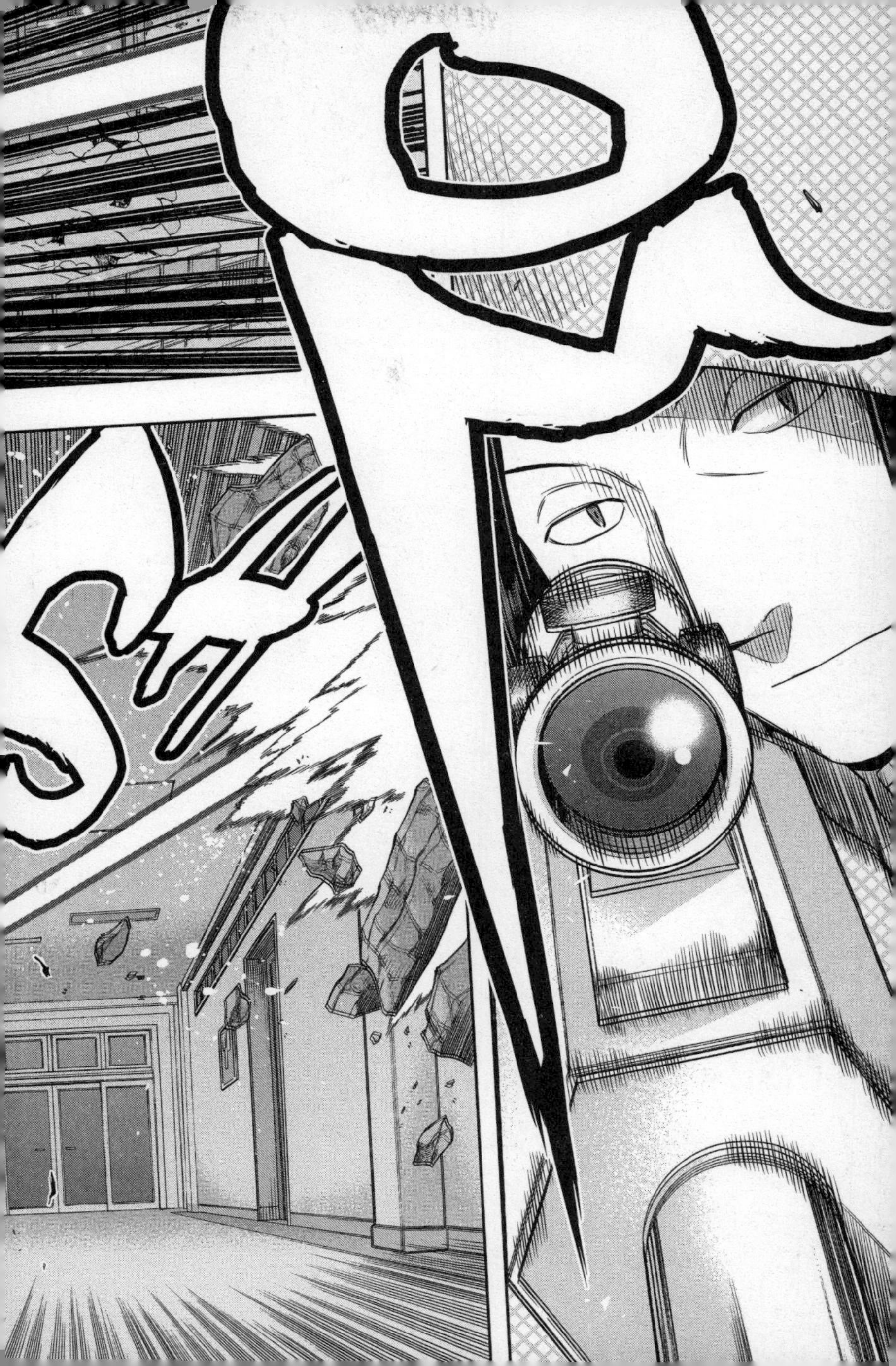

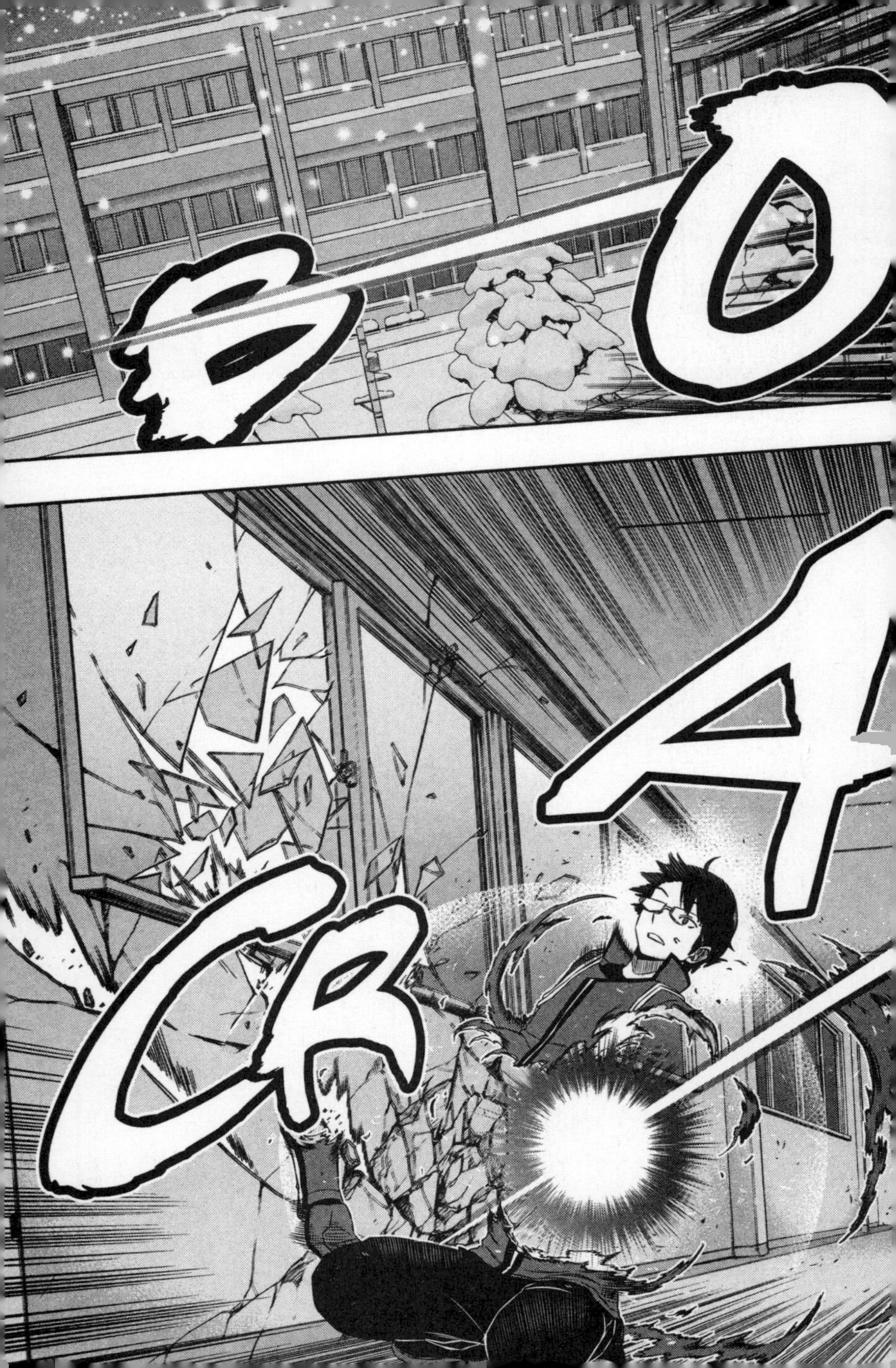
BO
CRA

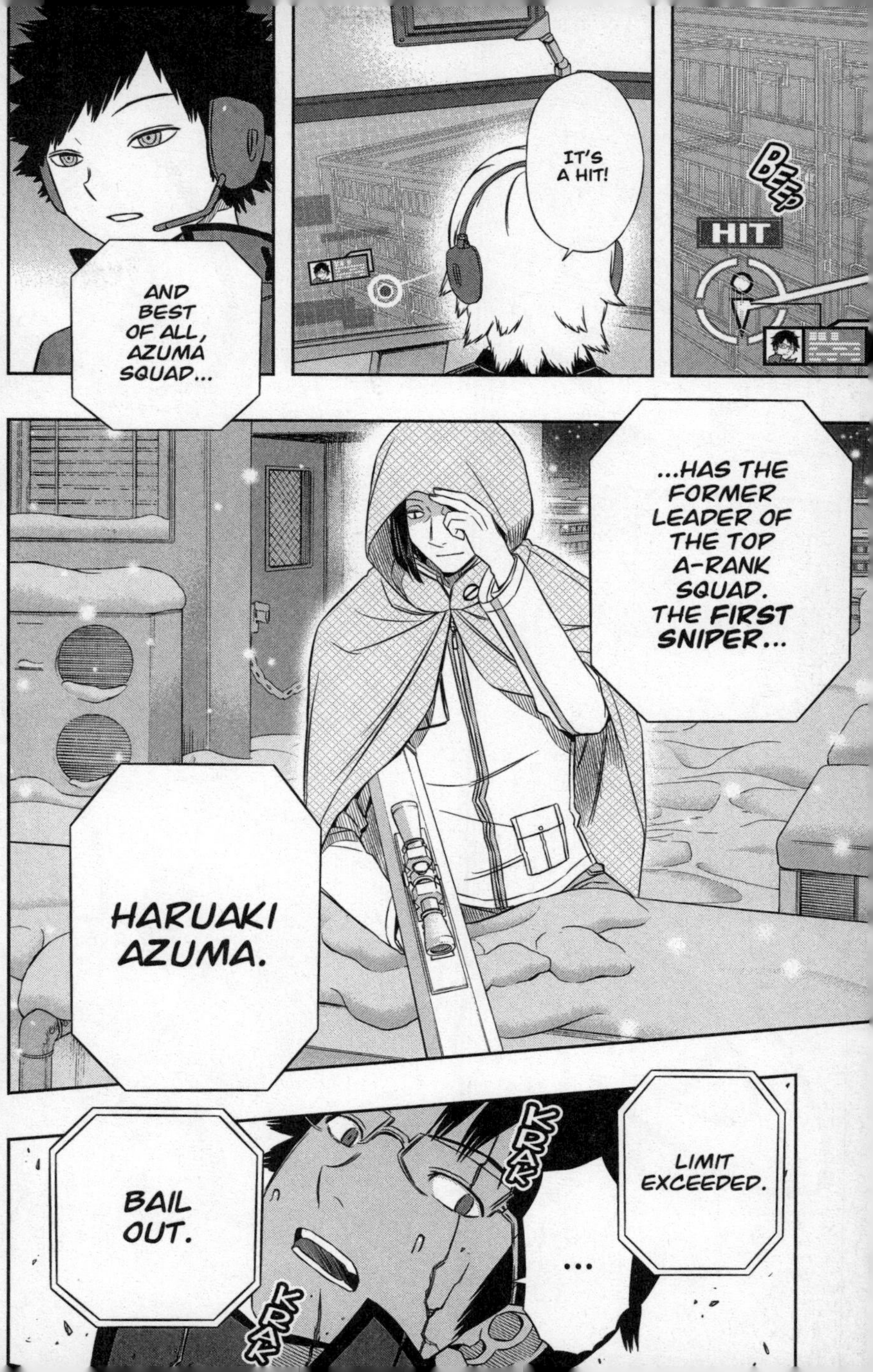
BEEP
HIT
IT'S A HIT!
AND BEST OF ALL, AZUMA SQUAD...
...HAS THE FORMER LEADER OF THE TOP A-RANK SQUAD. THE FIRST SNIPER...
HARUAKI AZUMA.
LIMIT EXCEEDED.
KRAK
...
BAIL OUT.
KRAK

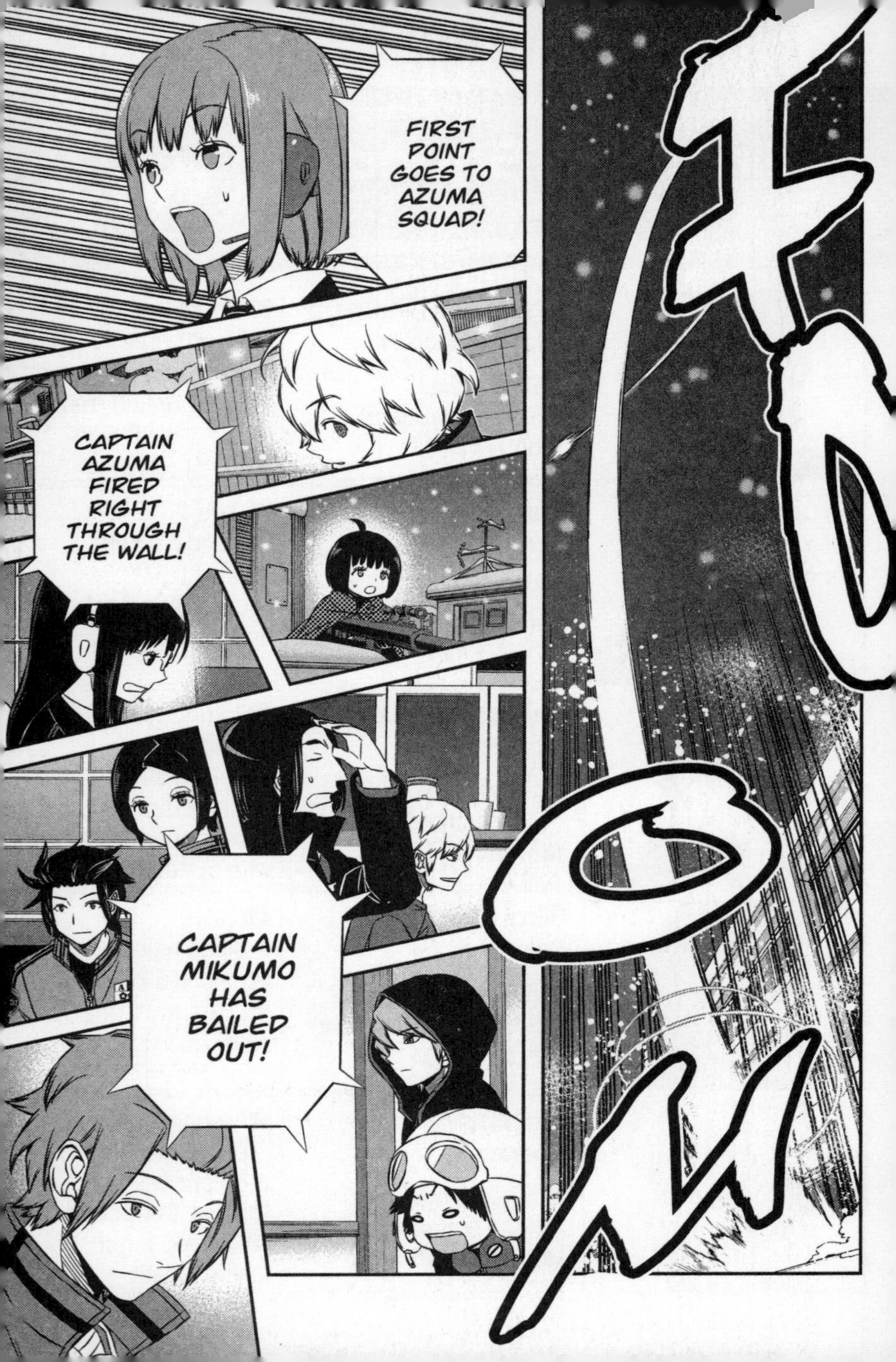
FIRST POINT GOES TO AZUMA SQUAD!
CAPTAIN AZUMA FIRED RIGHT THROUGH THE WALL!
CAPTAIN MIKUMO HAS BAILED OUT!

Ninomiya Squad

Border HQ B-Rank No. 1

Masataka Ninomiya
Captain, Shooter

- ■20 years old
  (College student)
- ■Born Oct. 27

- ■Chronos,
  Blood type A
- ■Height: 6′
- ■Likes: Grilled meat, ginger ale, talented people

Sumiharu Inukai
Gunner

- ■18 years old
  (High school student)
- ■Born May 1

- ■Felis,
  Blood type AB
- ■Height: 5′9″
- ■Likes: Airplanes, hot dogs, grapes

Shinnosuke Tsuji
Attacker

- ■17 years old
  (High school student)
- ■Born Aug. 16

- ■Aptenodytes,
  Blood type B
- ■Height: 5′10″
- ■Likes: Dinosaurs, cream puffs, dorayaki with buttercream

Mirai Hatohara
Sniper

- ■18 years old
  (High school student)
- ■Born Jan. 14

- ■Clavis,
  Blood type O
- ■Height: 5′2″
- ■Likes: Kids, pears, clam miso soup

Aki Hiyami
Operator

- ■17 years old
  (High school student)
- ■Born Jan. 25

- ■Amphibious,
  Blood type B
- ■Height: 5′1″
- ■Likes: Sweet and sour pork, yogurt, taking a bath

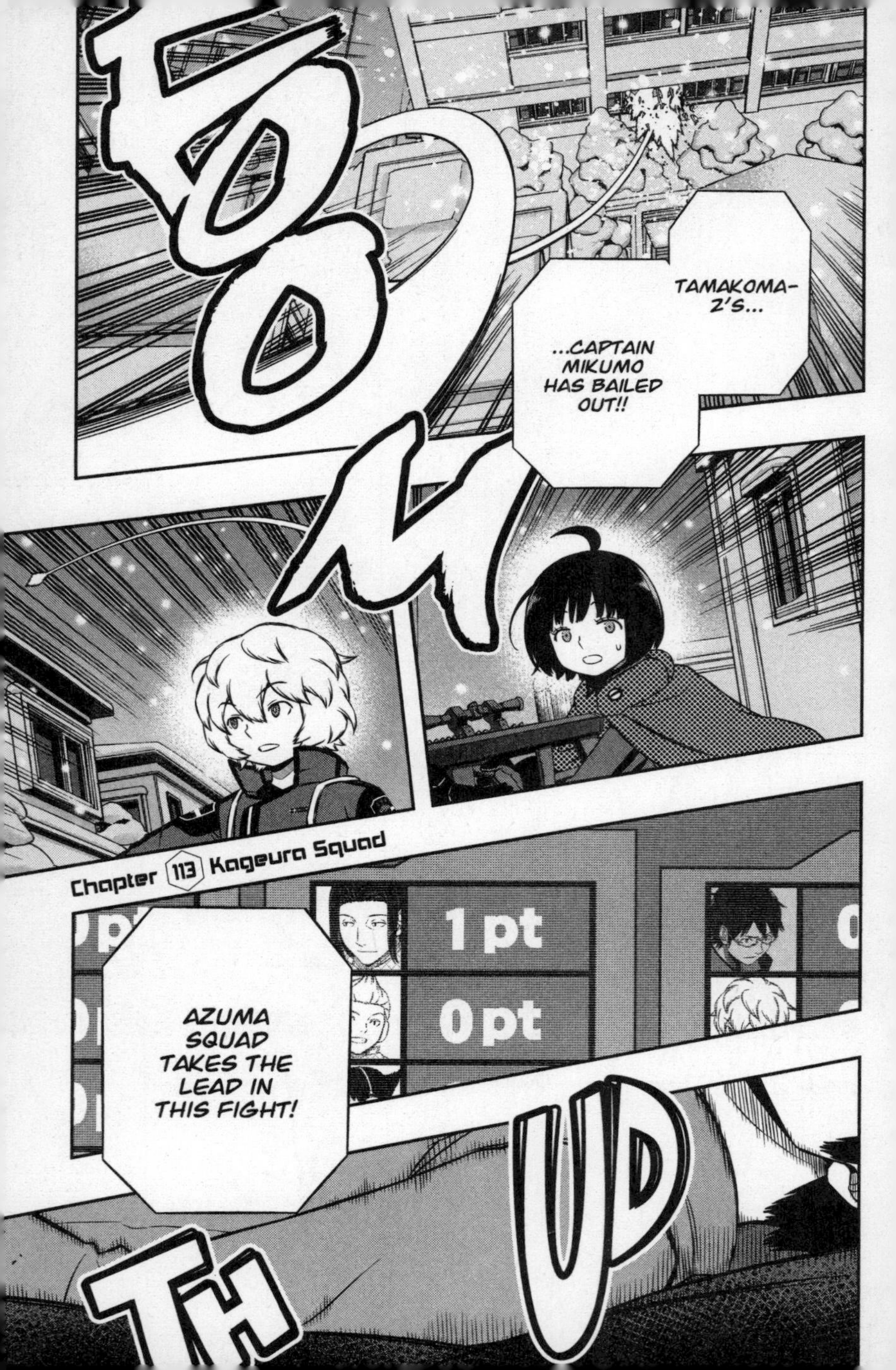
BOOM
TAMAKOMA-2'S...
...CAPTAIN MIKUMO HAS BAILED OUT!!
Chapter 113 Kageura Squad
1 pt
0 pt
AZUMA SQUAD TAKES THE LEAD IN THIS FIGHT!
THUD

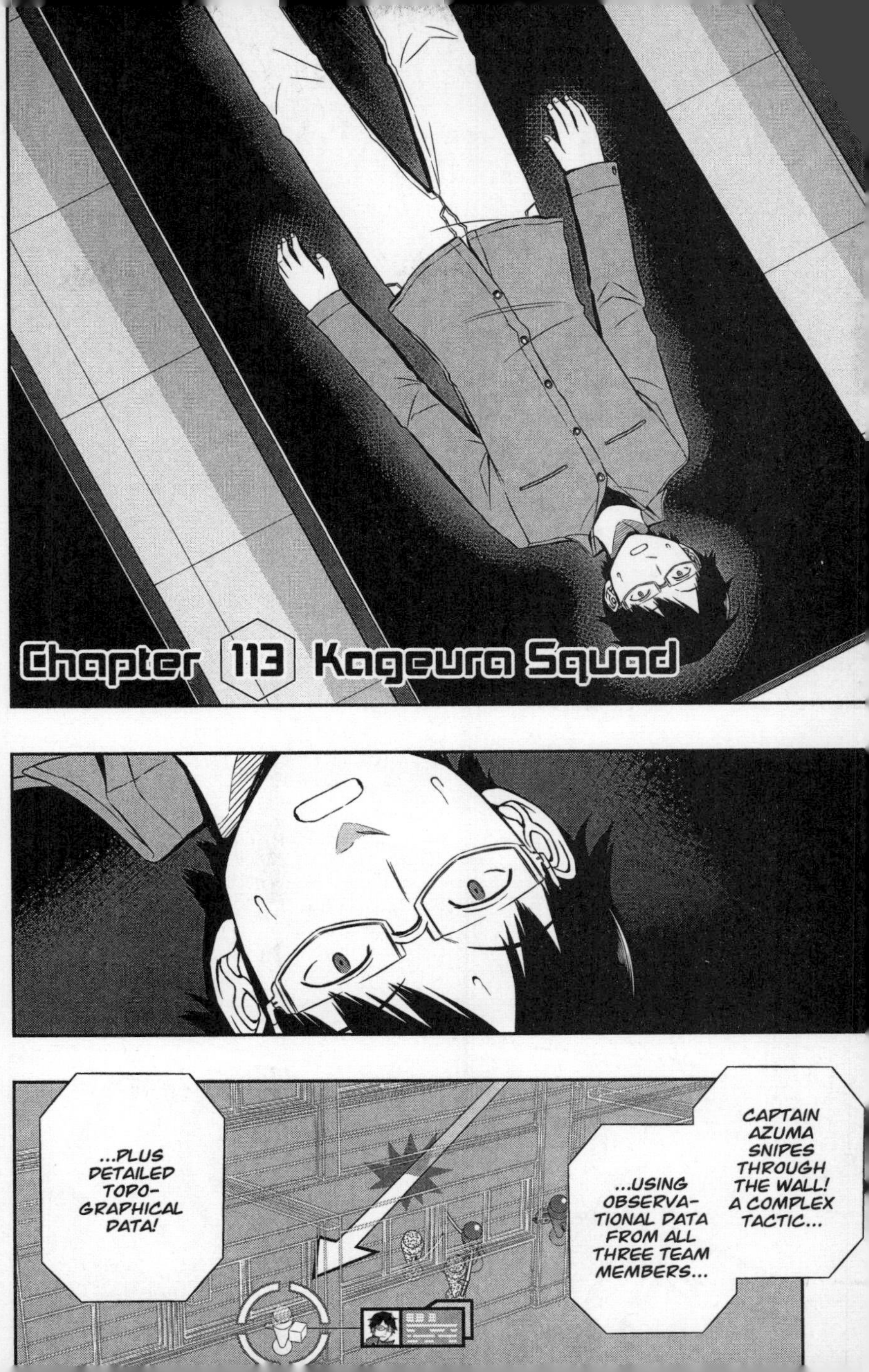
Chapter 113 Kageura Squad
CAPTAIN AZUMA SNIPES THROUGH THE WALL! A COMPLEX TACTIC...
...USING OBSERVATIONAL DATA FROM ALL THREE TEAM MEMBERS...
...PLUS DETAILED TOPOGRAPHICAL DATA!

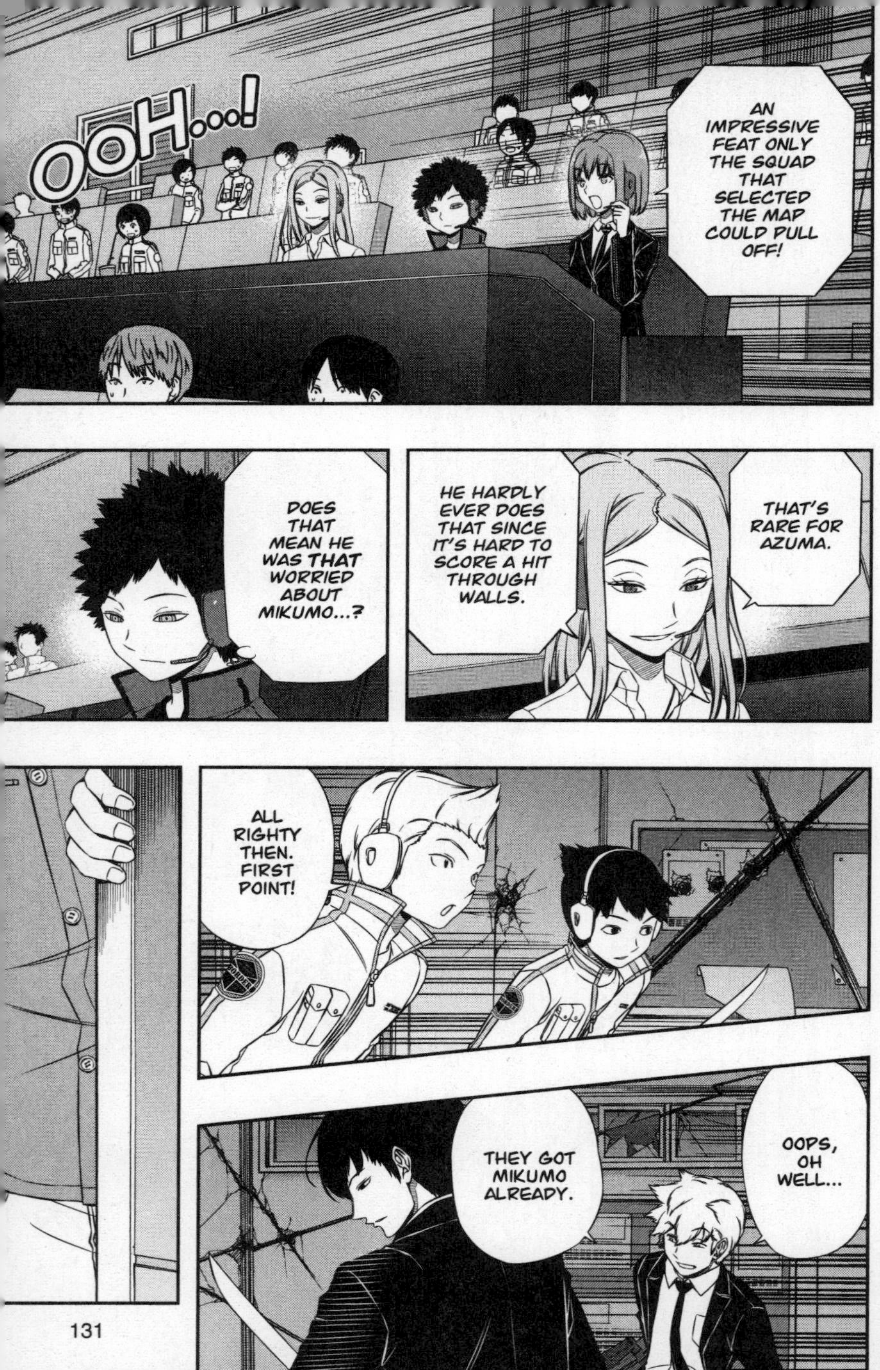
AN IMPRESSIVE FEAT ONLY THE SQUAD THAT SELECTED THE MAP COULD PULL OFF!
OOH...!
THAT'S RARE FOR AZUMA.
HE HARDLY EVER DOES THAT SINCE IT'S HARD TO SCORE A HIT THROUGH WALLS.
DOES THAT MEAN HE WAS THAT WORRIED ABOUT MIKUMO...?
ALL RIGHTY THEN. FIRST POINT!
OOPS, OH WELL...
THEY GOT MIKUMO ALREADY.

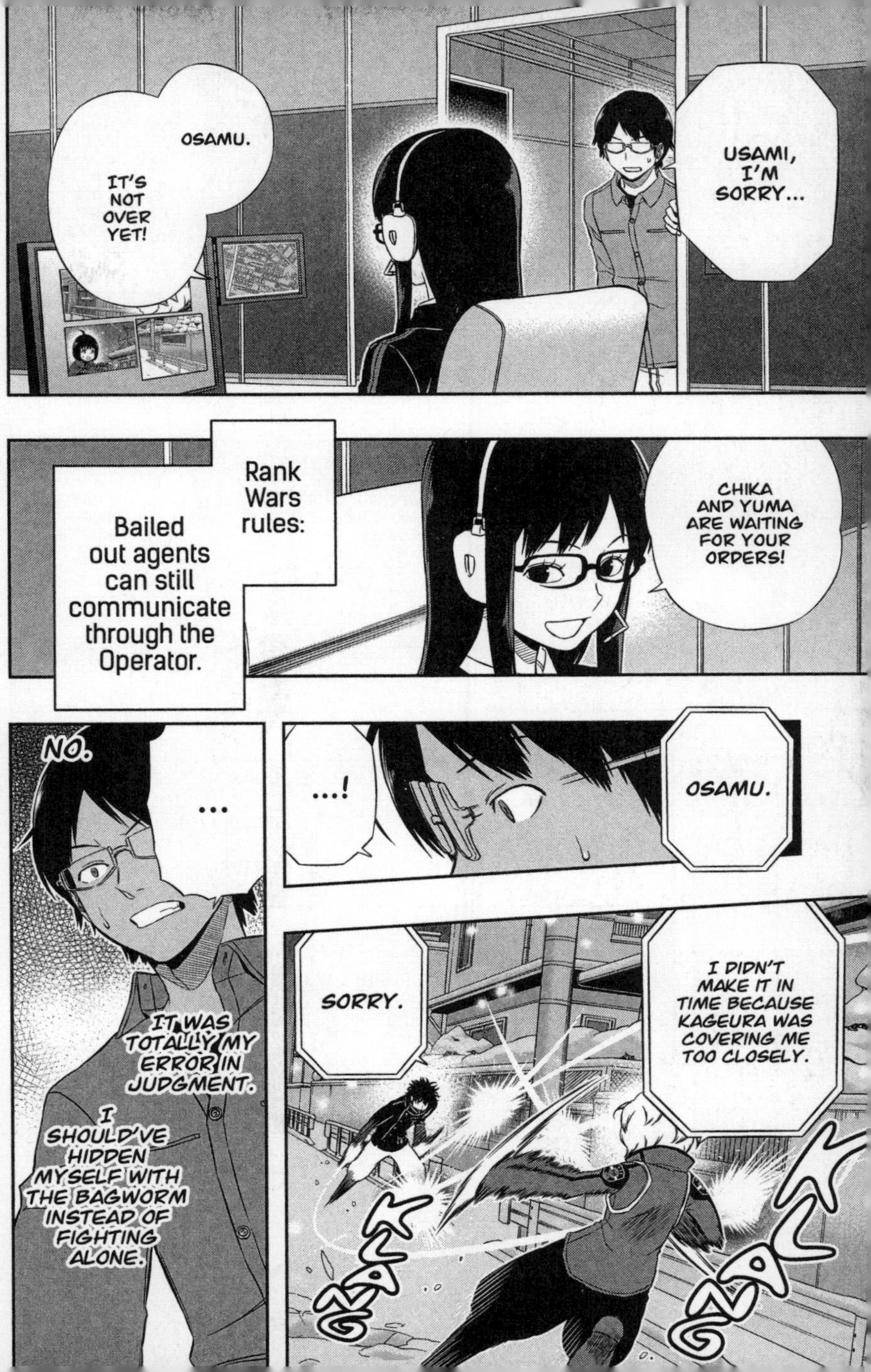
USAMI, I'M SORRY...
OSAMU.
IT'S NOT OVER YET!
CHIKA AND YUMA ARE WAITING FOR YOUR ORDERS!
Rank Wars rules:
Bailed out agents can still communicate through the Operator.
OSAMU.
...!
I DIDN'T MAKE IT IN TIME BECAUSE KAGEURA WAS COVERING ME TOO CLOSELY.
SORRY.
KLANG
KLANG
NO.
...
IT WAS TOTALLY MY ERROR IN JUDGMENT.
I SHOULD'VE HIDDEN MYSELF WITH THE BAGWORM INSTEAD OF FIGHTING ALONE.

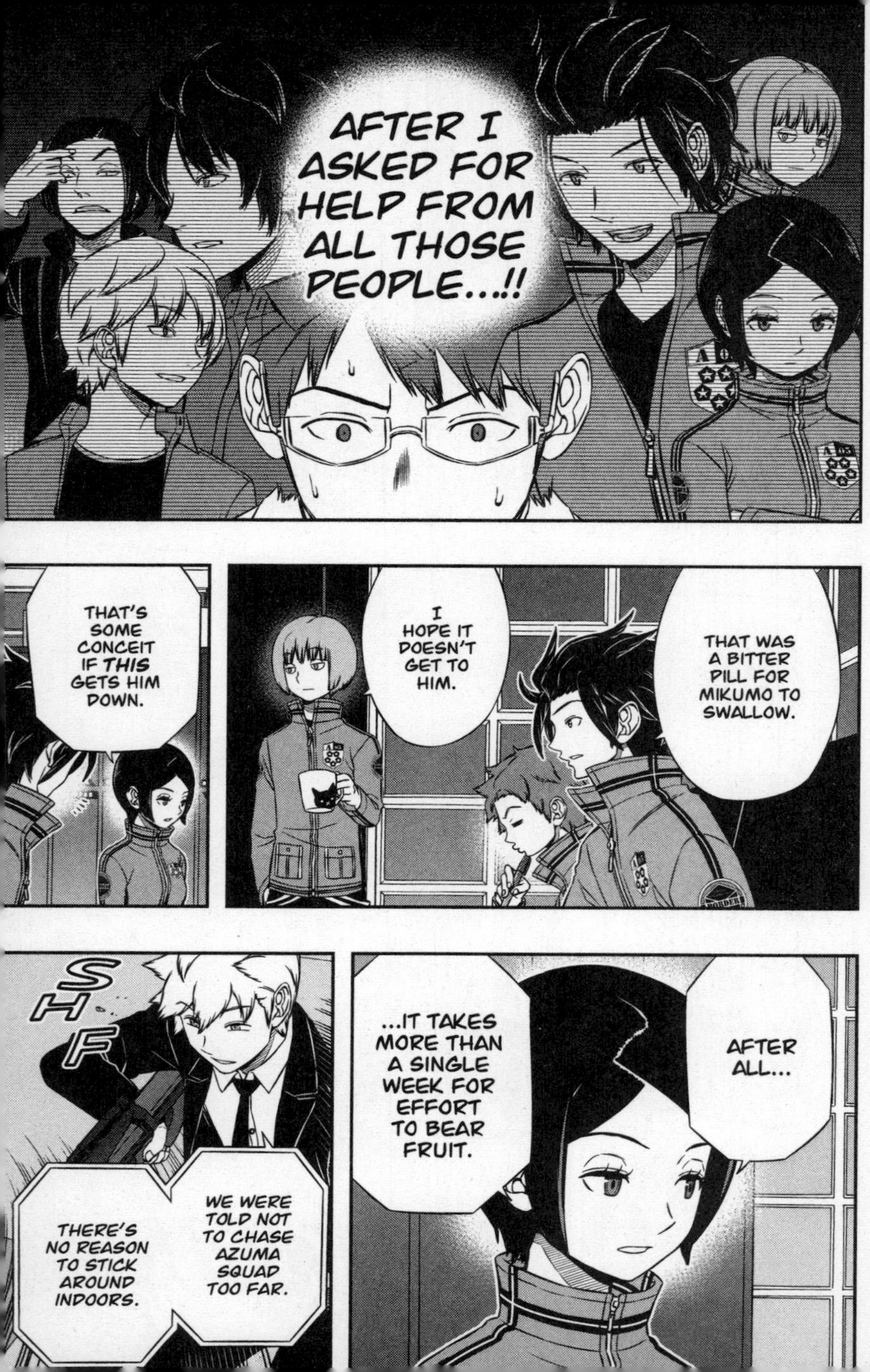
AFTER I ASKED FOR HELP FROM ALL THOSE PEOPLE...!!
THAT WAS A BITTER PILL FOR MIKUMO TO SWALLOW.
I HOPE IT DOESN'T GET TO HIM.
THAT'S SOME CONCEIT IF THIS GETS HIM DOWN.
AFTER ALL...
...IT TAKES MORE THAN A SINGLE WEEK FOR EFFORT TO BEAR FRUIT.
SHF
WE WERE TOLD NOT TO CHASE AZUMA SQUAD TOO FAR.
THERE'S NO REASON TO STICK AROUND INDOORS.

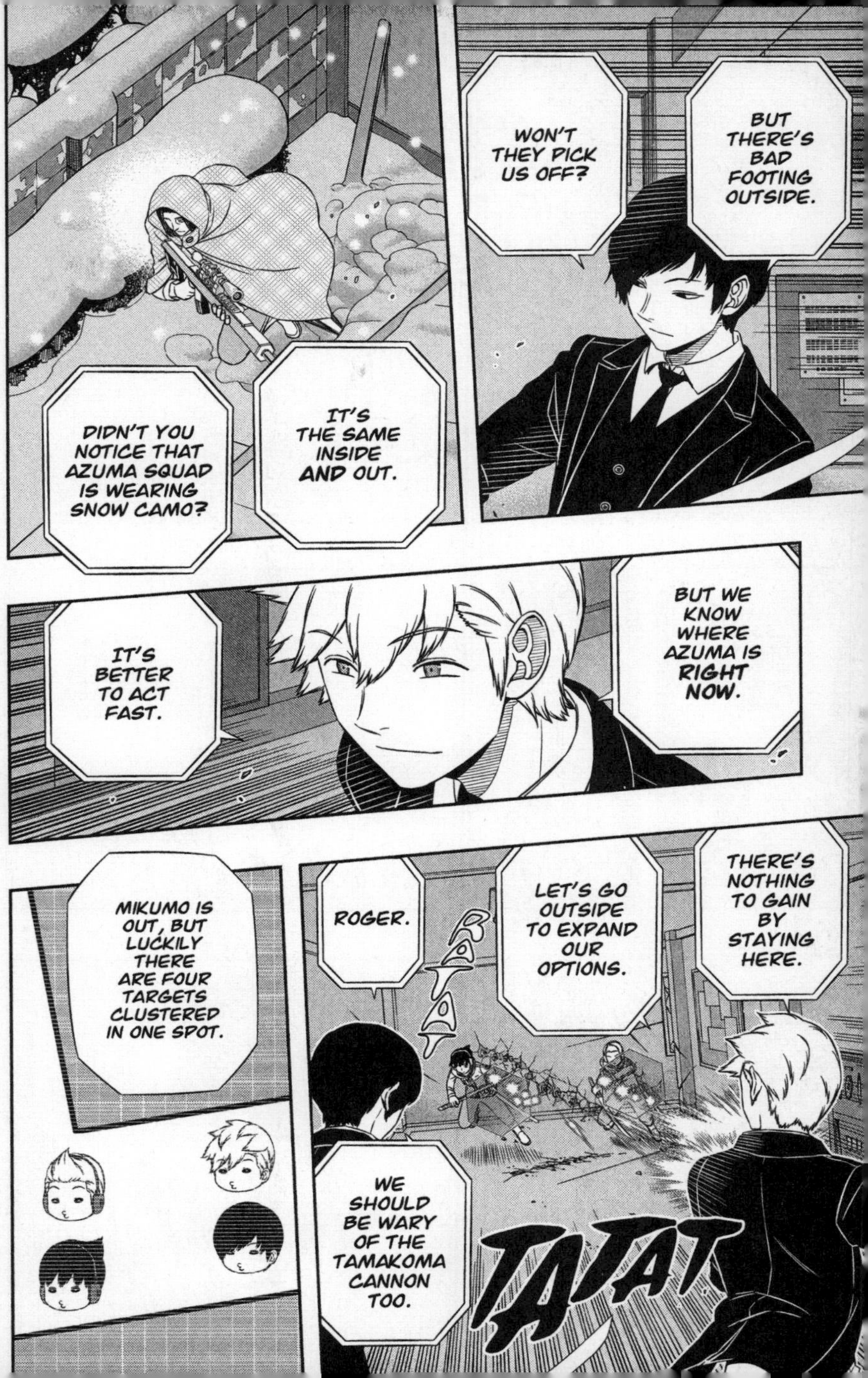
BUT THERE'S BAD FOOTING OUTSIDE.
WON'T THEY PICK US OFF?
IT'S THE SAME INSIDE AND OUT.
DIDN'T YOU NOTICE THAT AZUMA SQUAD IS WEARING SNOW CAMO?
BUT WE KNOW WHERE AZUMA IS RIGHT NOW.
IT'S BETTER TO ACT FAST.
THERE'S NOTHING TO GAIN BY STAYING HERE.
LET'S GO OUTSIDE TO EXPAND OUR OPTIONS.
ROGER.
WE SHOULD BE WARY OF THE TAMAKOMA CANNON TOO.
TATAT
MIKUMO IS OUT, BUT LUCKILY THERE ARE FOUR TARGETS CLUSTERED IN ONE SPOT.

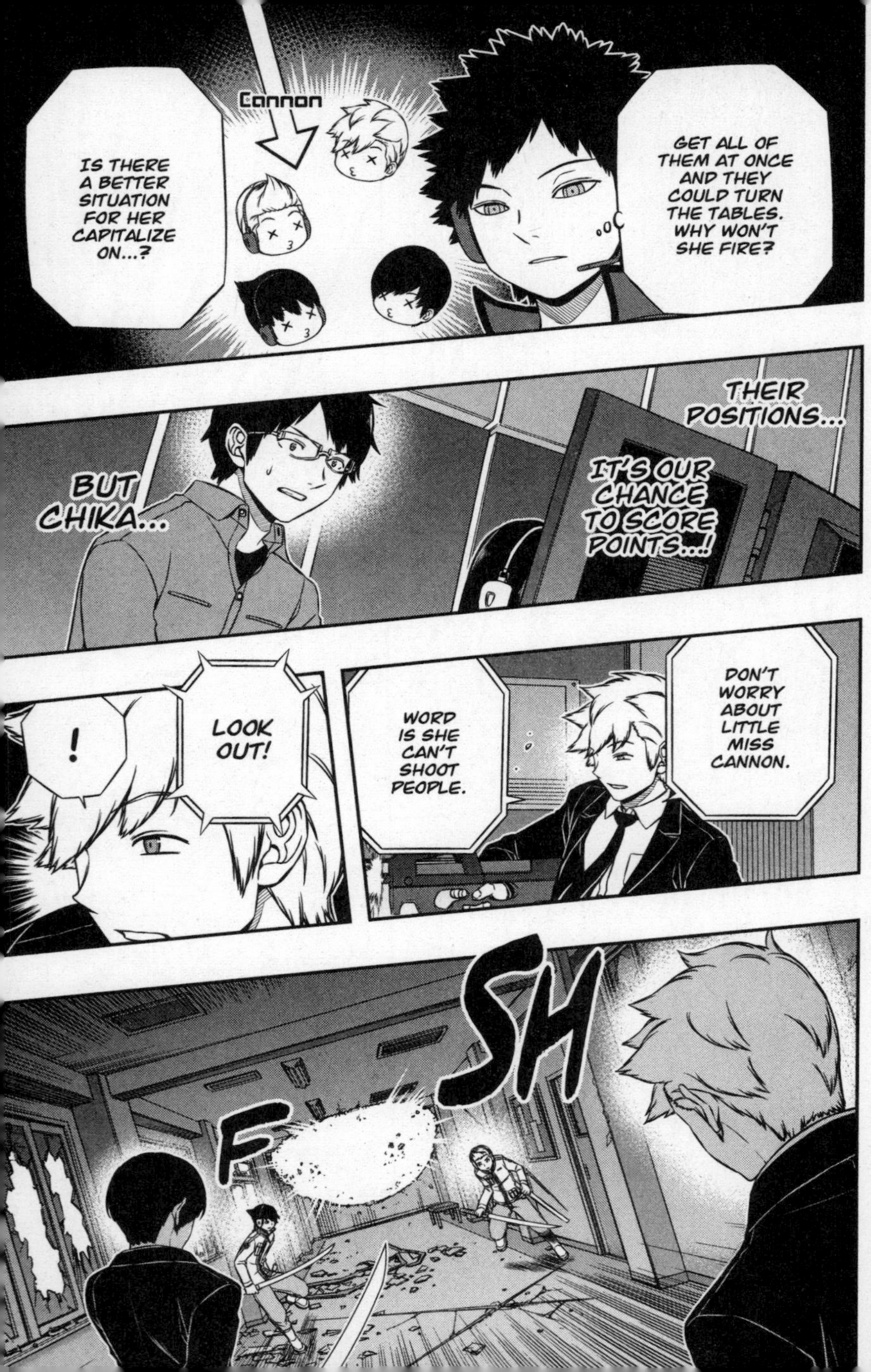
GET ALL OF THEM AT ONCE AND THEY COULD TURN THE TABLES. WHY WON'T SHE FIRE?
Cannon
IS THERE A BETTER SITUATION FOR HER CAPITALIZE ON...?
THEIR POSITIONS...
IT'S OUR CHANCE TO SCORE POINTS...!
BUT CHIKA...
DON'T WORRY ABOUT LITTLE MISS CANNON.
WORD IS SHE CAN'T SHOOT PEOPLE.
LOOK OUT!
!
SH
F

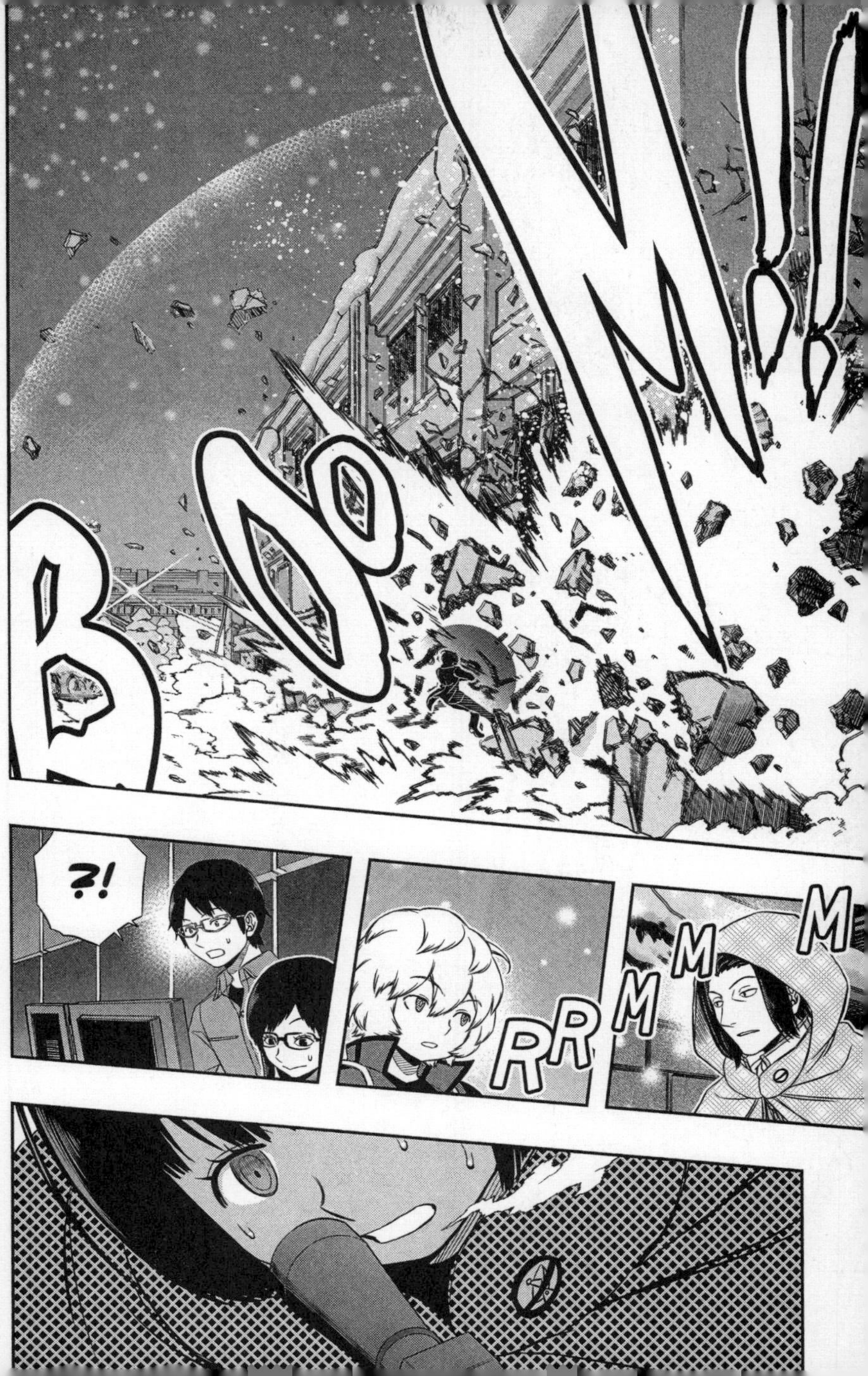
BOOM!!
RRMMMM
?!

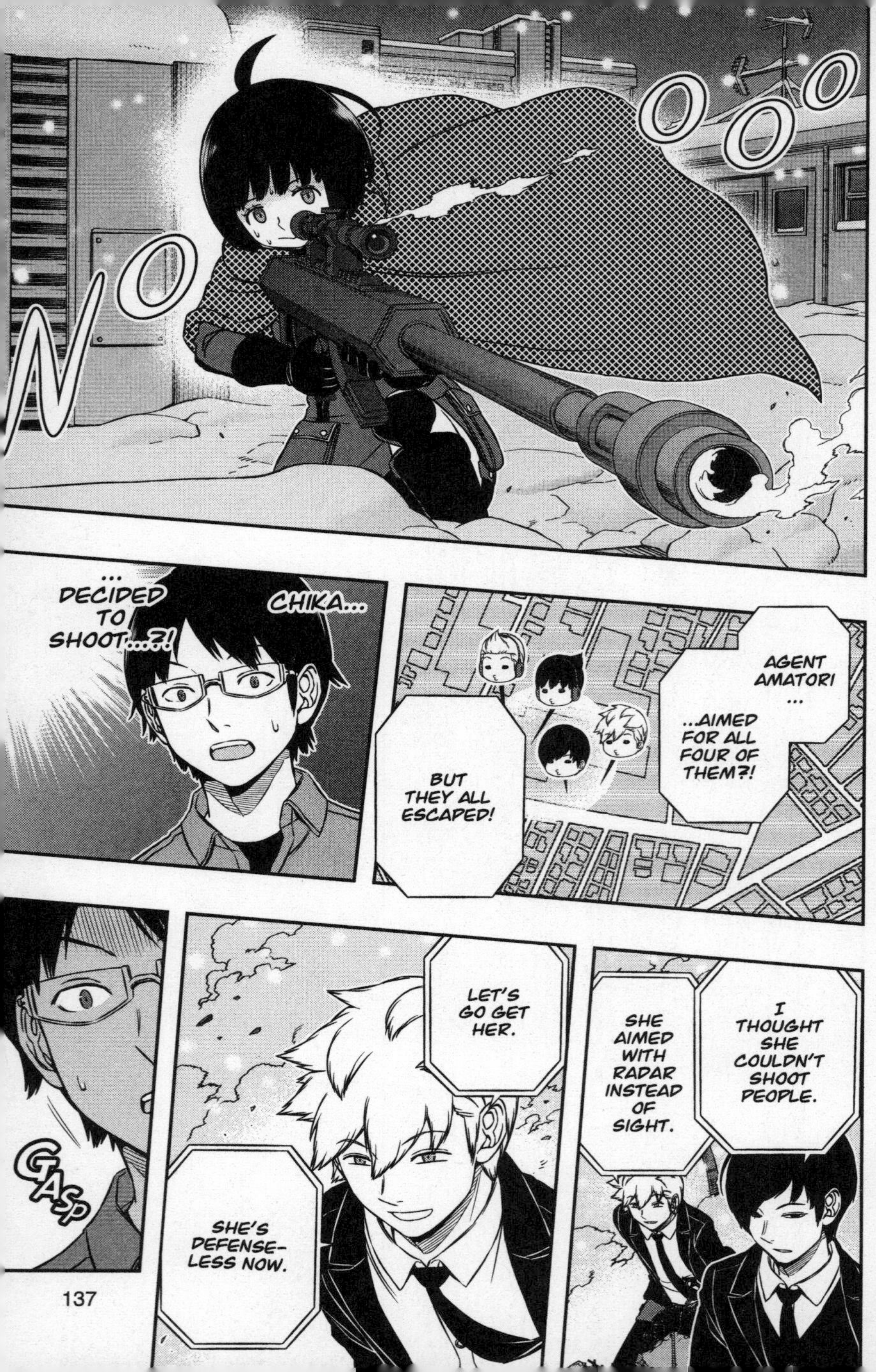
WOOOOOO
AGENT AMATORI ...
...AIMED FOR ALL FOUR OF THEM?!
BUT THEY ALL ESCAPED!
CHIKA...
...DECIDED TO SHOOT...?!
I THOUGHT SHE COULDN'T SHOOT PEOPLE.
SHE AIMED WITH RADAR INSTEAD OF SIGHT.
LET'S GO GET HER.
SHE'S DEFENSE-LESS NOW.
GASP

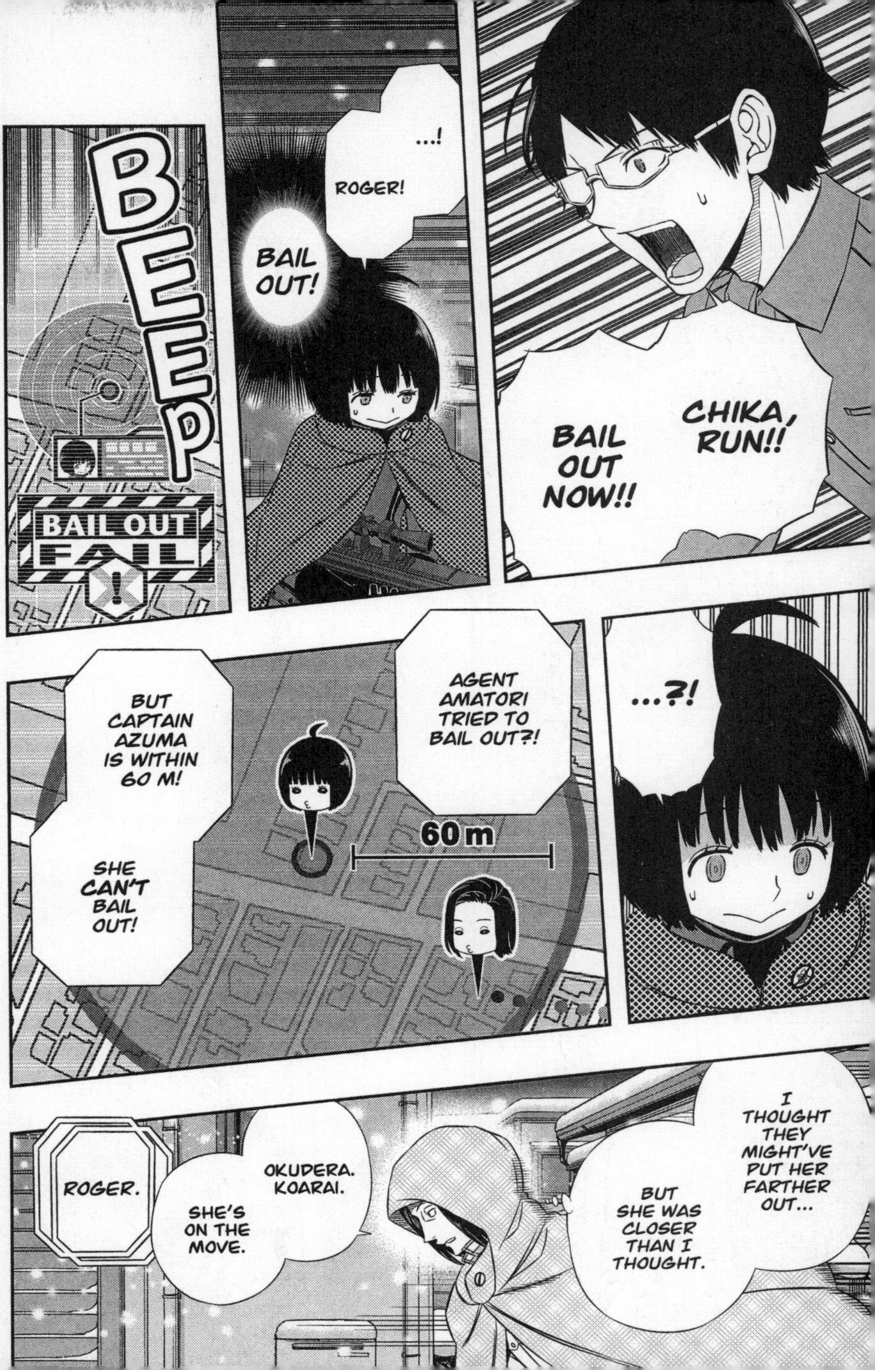
CHIKA, RUN!!
BAIL OUT NOW!!
...!
ROGER!
BAIL OUT!
BEEP
BAIL OUT FAIL
!
...?!
AGENT AMATORI TRIED TO BAIL OUT?!
BUT CAPTAIN AZUMA IS WITHIN 60 M!
60 m
SHE CAN'T BAIL OUT!
I THOUGHT THEY MIGHT'VE PUT HER FARTHER OUT...
BUT SHE WAS CLOSER THAN I THOUGHT.
OKUDERA. KOARAI.
SHE'S ON THE MOVE.
ROGER.

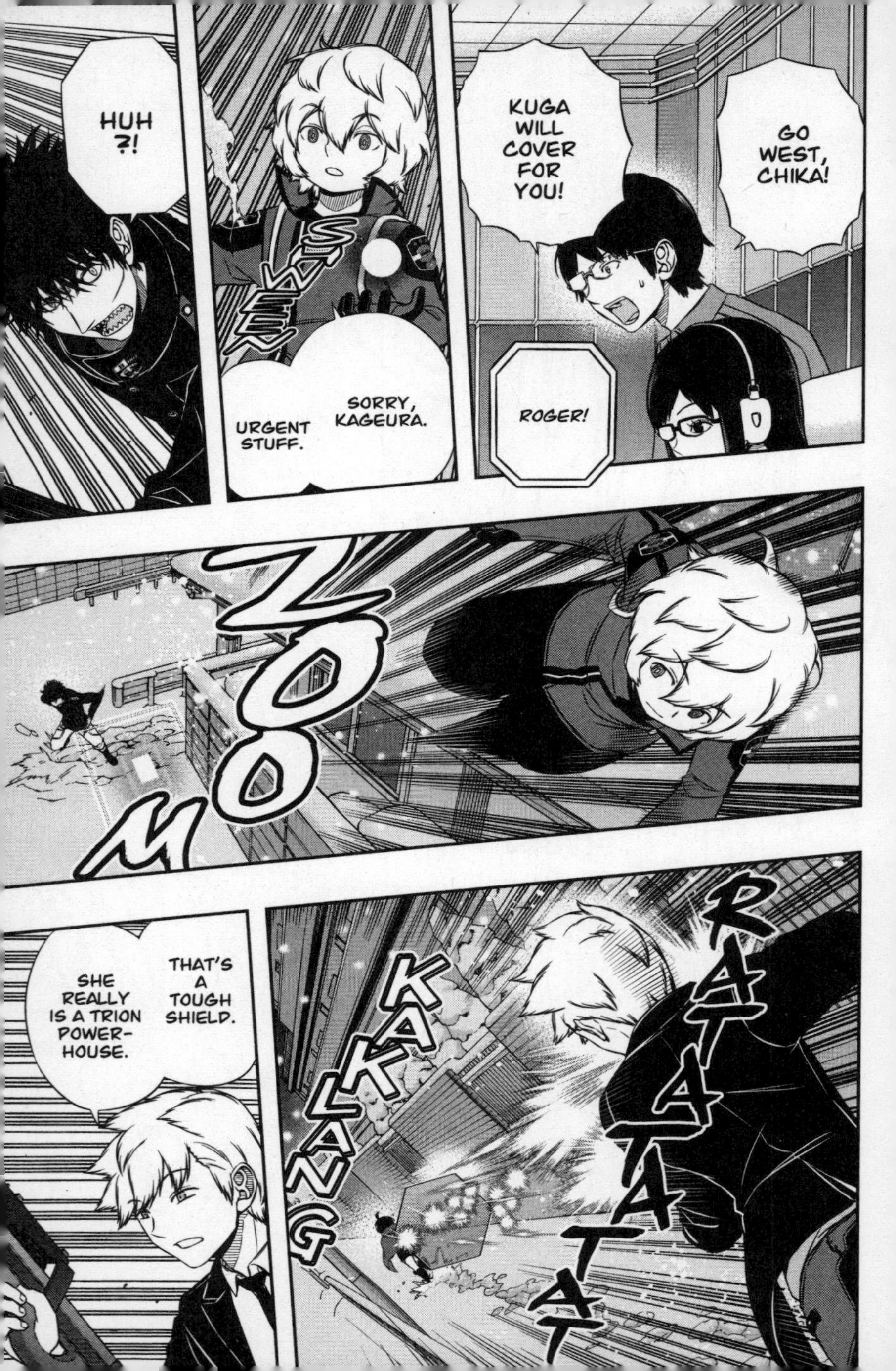
GO WEST, CHIKA!
KUGA WILL COVER FOR YOU!
ROGER!
SWEEE
SORRY, KAGEURA.
URGENT STUFF.
HUH ?!
ZOOM
RATATATAT
KAKAKLANG
THAT'S A TOUGH SHIELD.
SHE REALLY IS A TRION POWER-HOUSE.

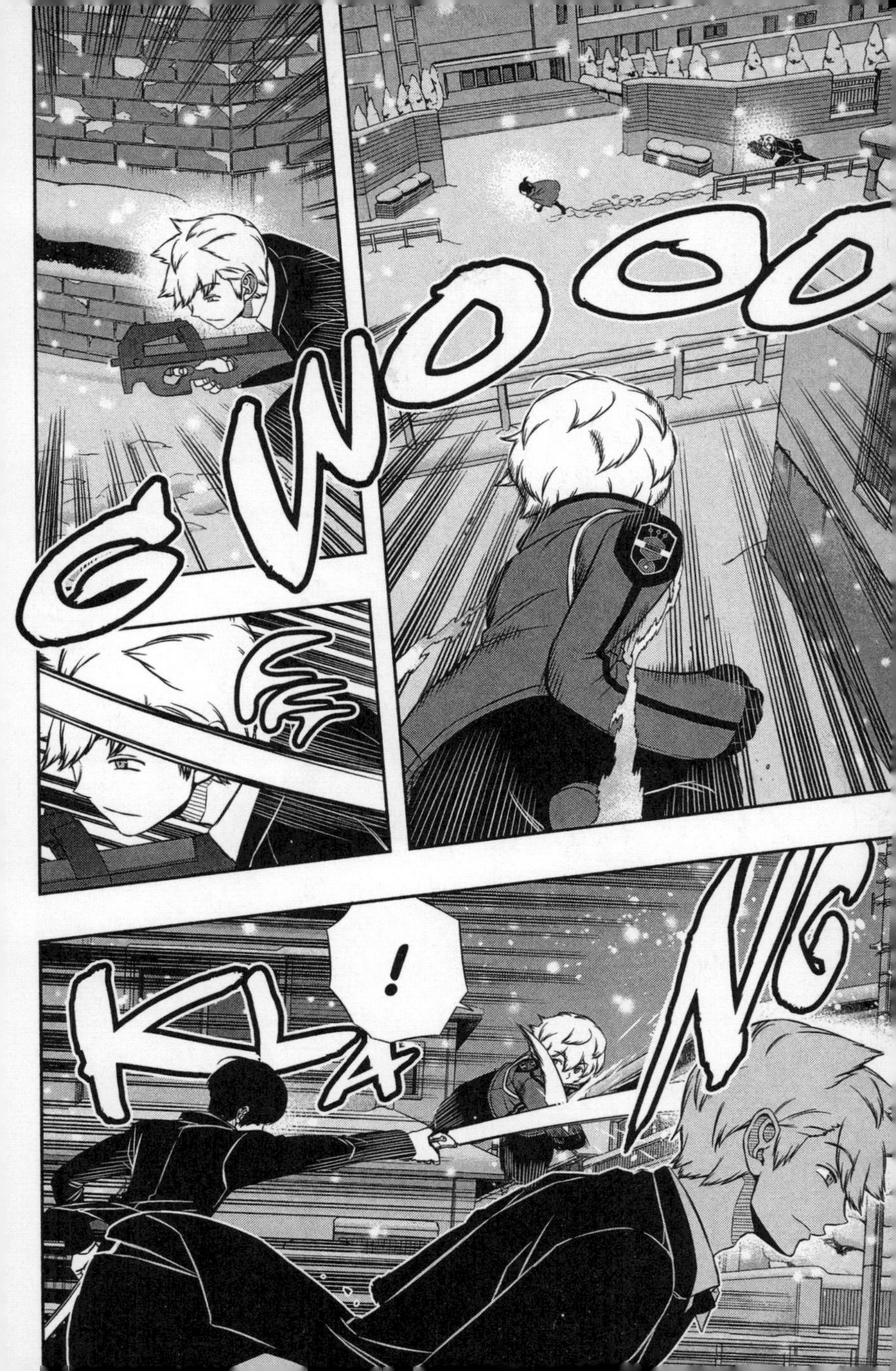
GWOOO
KLANG
!

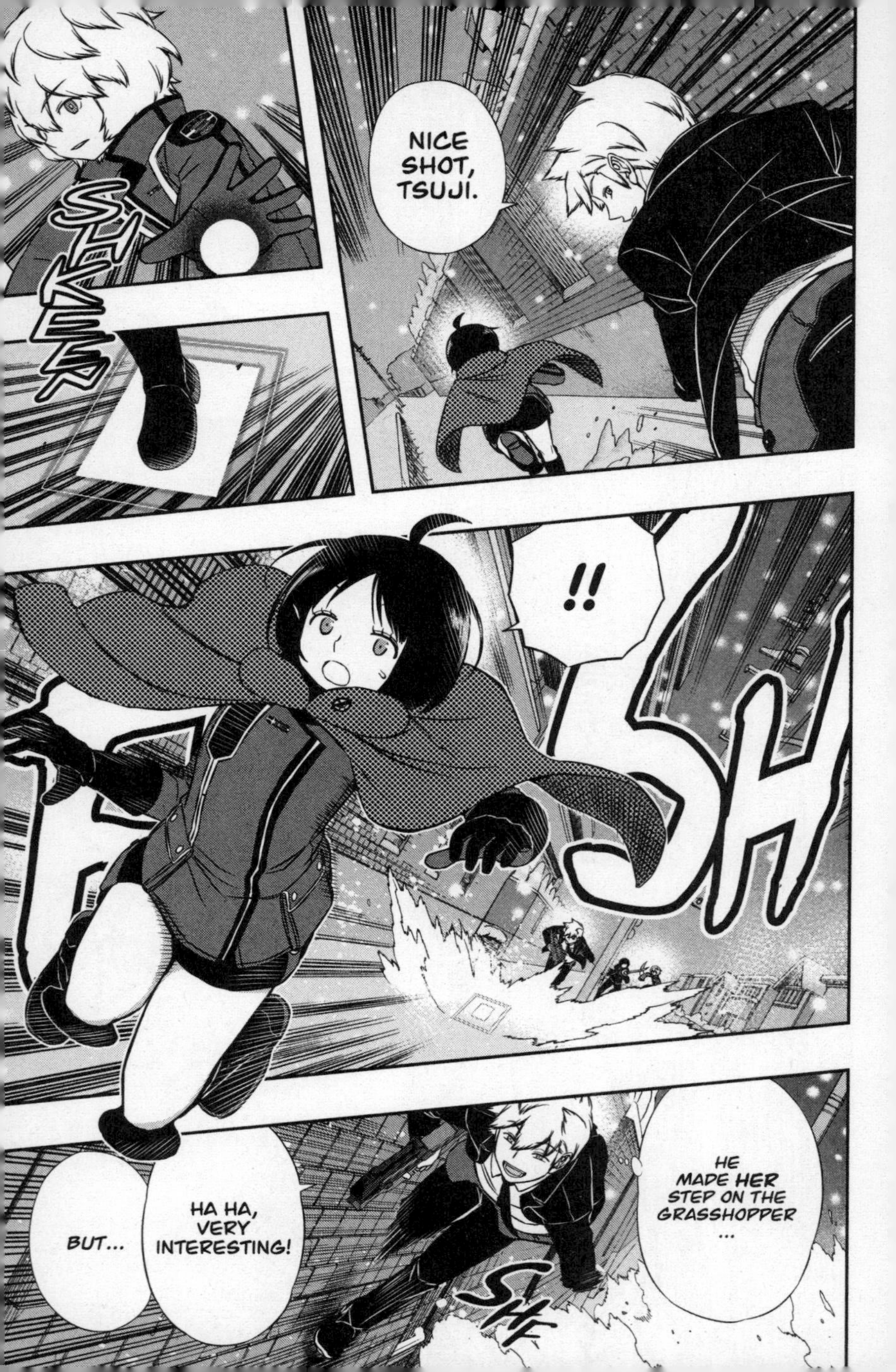
NICE SHOT, TSUJI.
SHIVER
!!
SH
HE MADE HER STEP ON THE GRASSHOPPER ...
SHF
HA HA, VERY INTERESTING!
BUT...

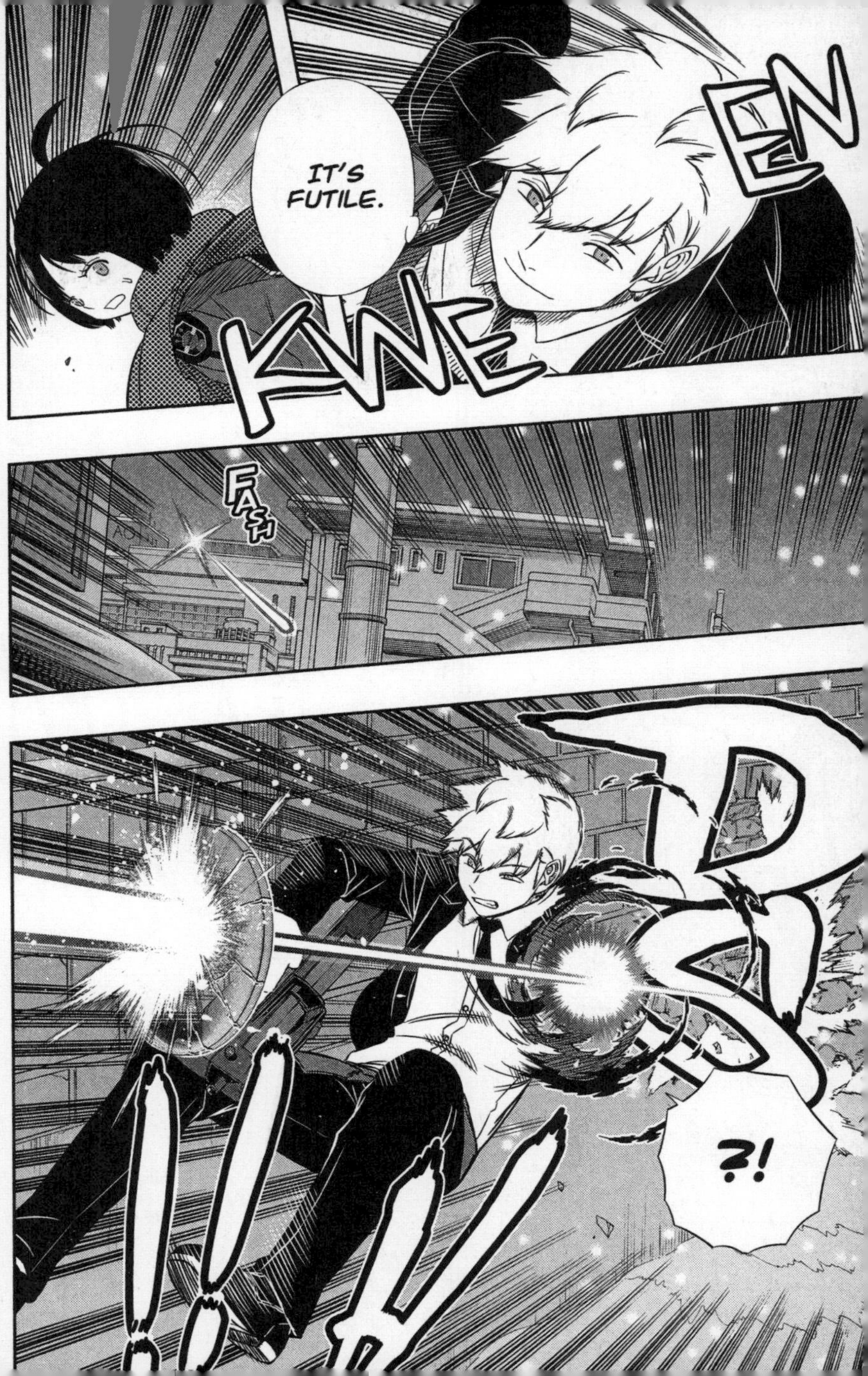
IT'S FUTILE.
KWEEN
FASH
D
?!

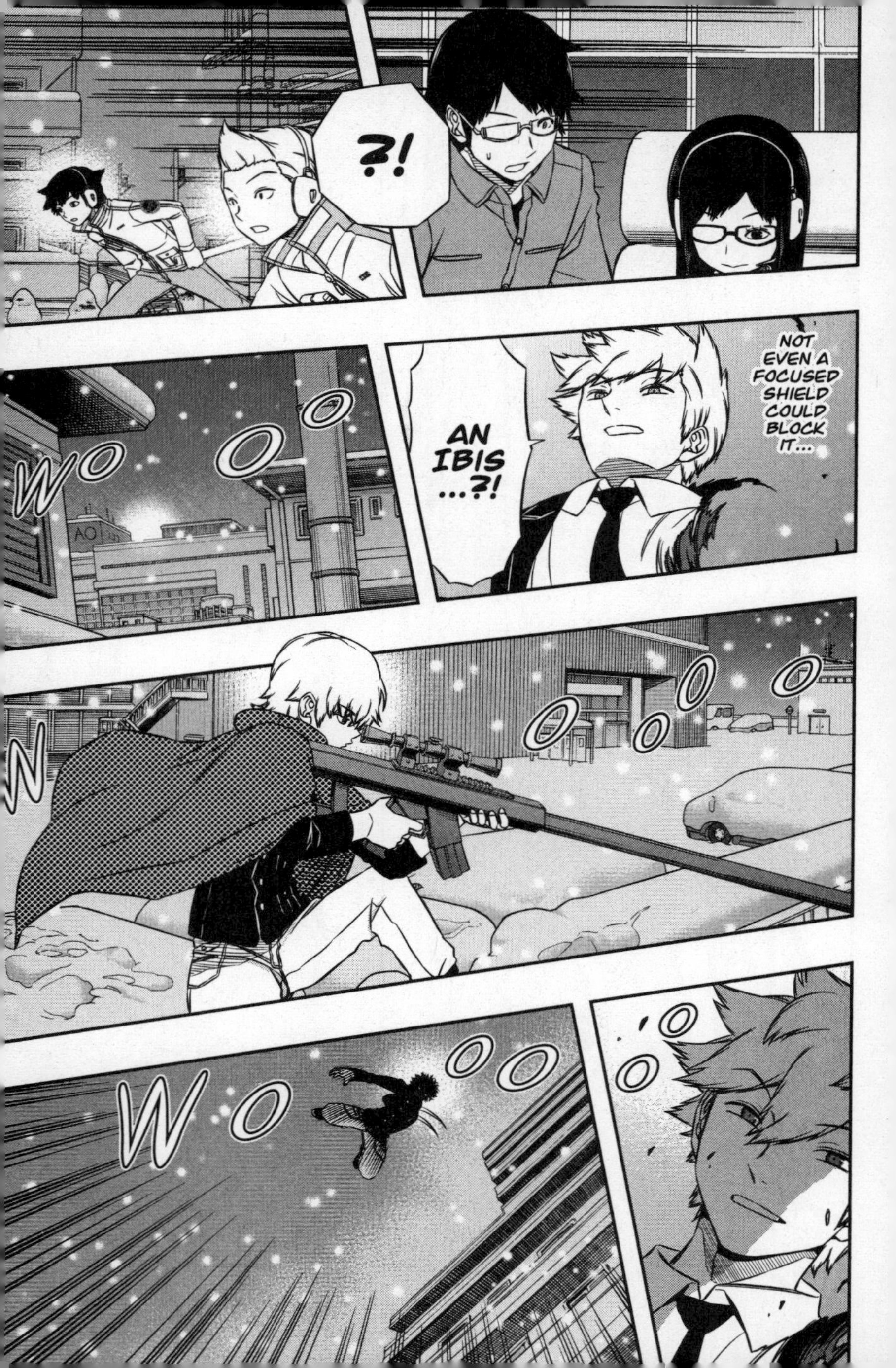
?!
NOT EVEN A FOCUSED SHIELD COULD BLOCK IT...
AN IBIS ...?!
WOOO
WOOOOO
OOO
WOOOO

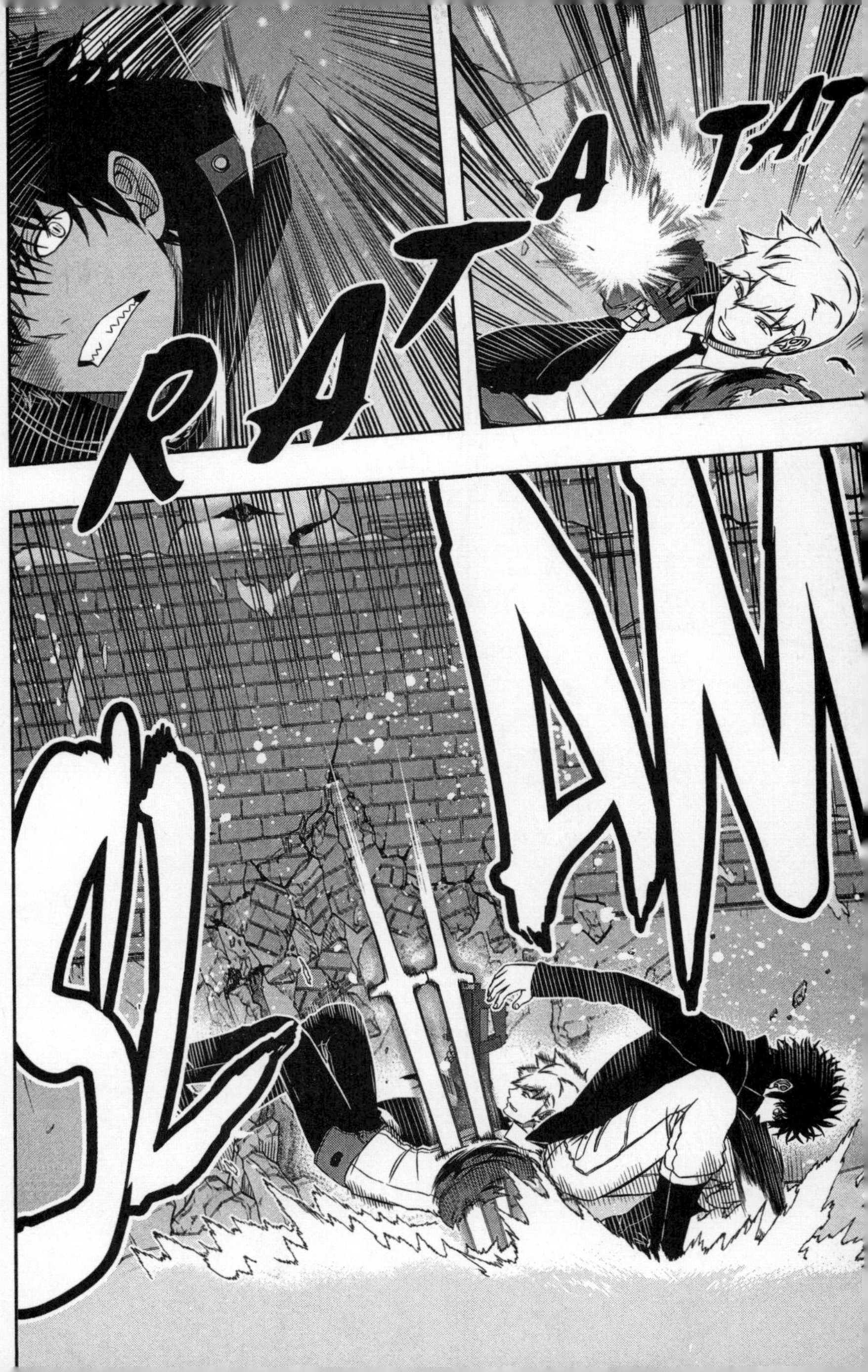
RATATAT

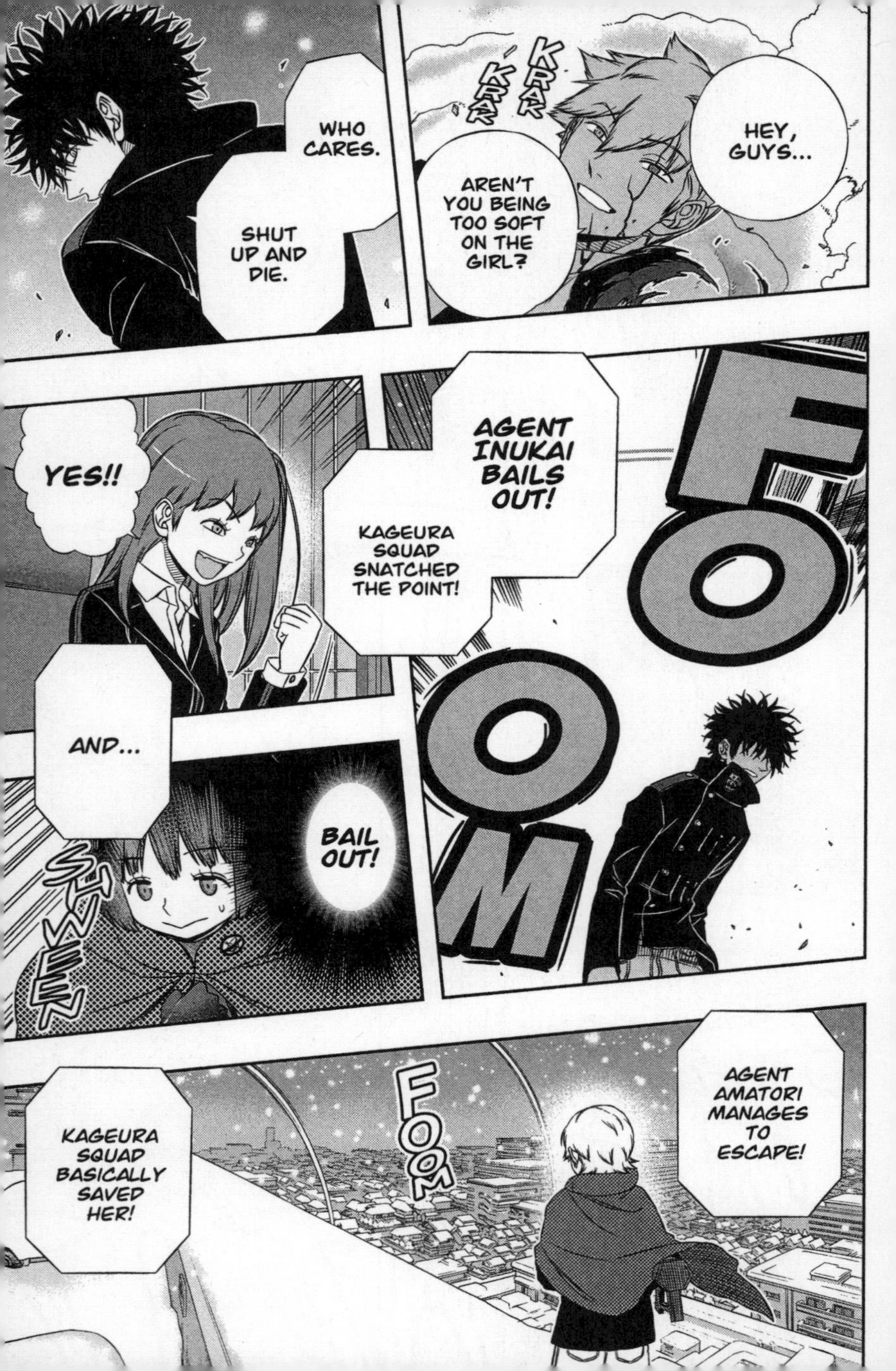
HEY, GUYS...
KRAK KRAK
AREN'T YOU BEING TOO SOFT ON THE GIRL?
WHO CARES.
SHUT UP AND DIE.
FOOM
AGENT INUKAI BAILS OUT!
KAGEURA SQUAD SNATCHED THE POINT!
YES!!
AND...
BAIL OUT!
SHWEEN
AGENT AMATORI MANAGES TO ESCAPE!
FOOM
KAGEURA SQUAD BASICALLY SAVED HER!

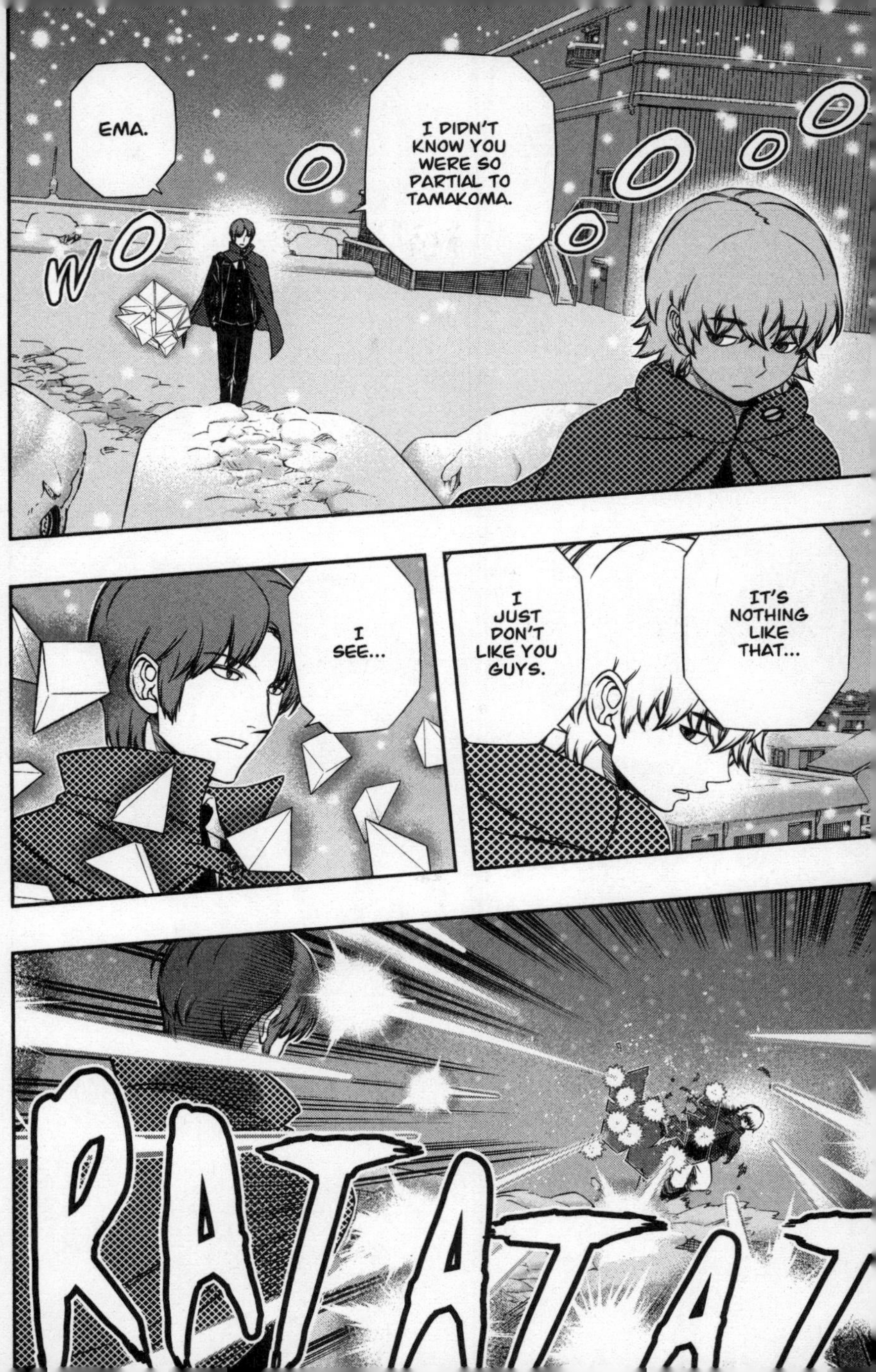
WOOOOOO
I DIDN'T KNOW YOU WERE SO PARTIAL TO TAMAKOMA.
EMA.
IT'S NOTHING LIKE THAT...
I JUST DON'T LIKE YOU GUYS.
I SEE...
RATATAT

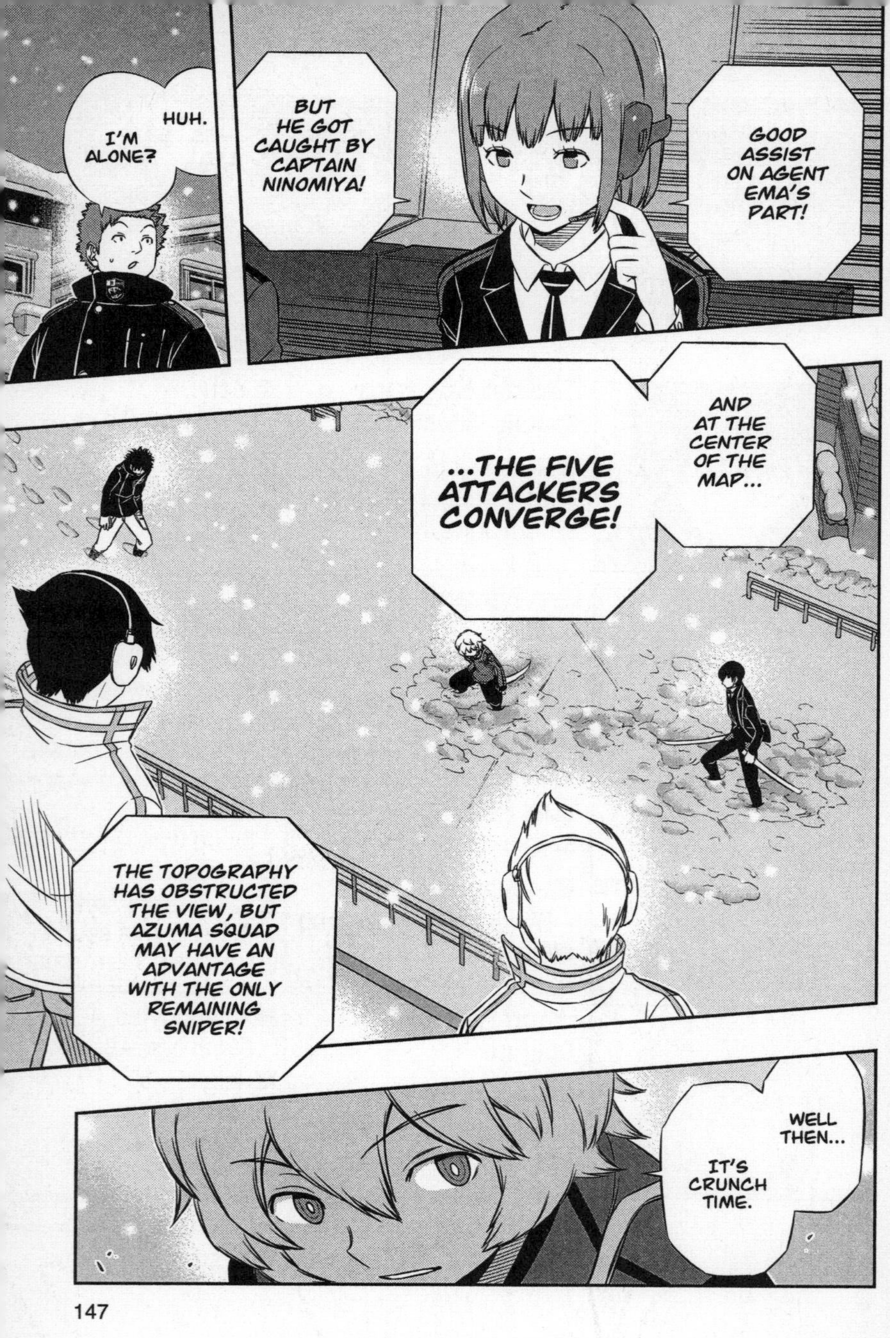
GOOD ASSIST ON AGENT EMA'S PART!
BUT HE GOT CAUGHT BY CAPTAIN NINOMIYA!
HUH.
I'M ALONE?
AND AT THE CENTER OF THE MAP...
...THE FIVE ATTACKERS CONVERGE!
THE TOPOGRAPHY HAS OBSTRUCTED THE VIEW, BUT AZUMA SQUAD MAY HAVE AN ADVANTAGE WITH THE ONLY REMAINING SNIPER!
WELL THEN...
IT'S CRUNCH TIME.

Kageura Squad
Border HQ B-Rank No. 2

Masato Kageura
Captain, Attacker

- 18 years old
  (High school student)
- Born June 4

- Lepus,
  Blood type B
- Height: 5'9"
- Likes: Sushi, yakitori, manga, lazing around in the strategy room

Hiro Kitazoe
Gunner

- 18 years old
  (High school student)
- Born April 15

- Falco,
  Blood type O
- Height: 6'1"
- Likes: Strawberries, spring rolls, meat & rice bowls, mah-jongg

Yuzuru Ema
Sniper

- 14 years old
  (Middle school student)
- Born Dec. 9

- Cetacea,
  Blood type O
- Height: 5'1"
- Likes: Curry, stew with béchamel sauce, teammates, his mentor

Hikari Nire
Operator

- 17 years old
  (High school student)
- Born July 27

- Aptenodytes,
  Blood type AB
- Height: 5'3"
- Likes: Manga, animals, shopping, loafing around

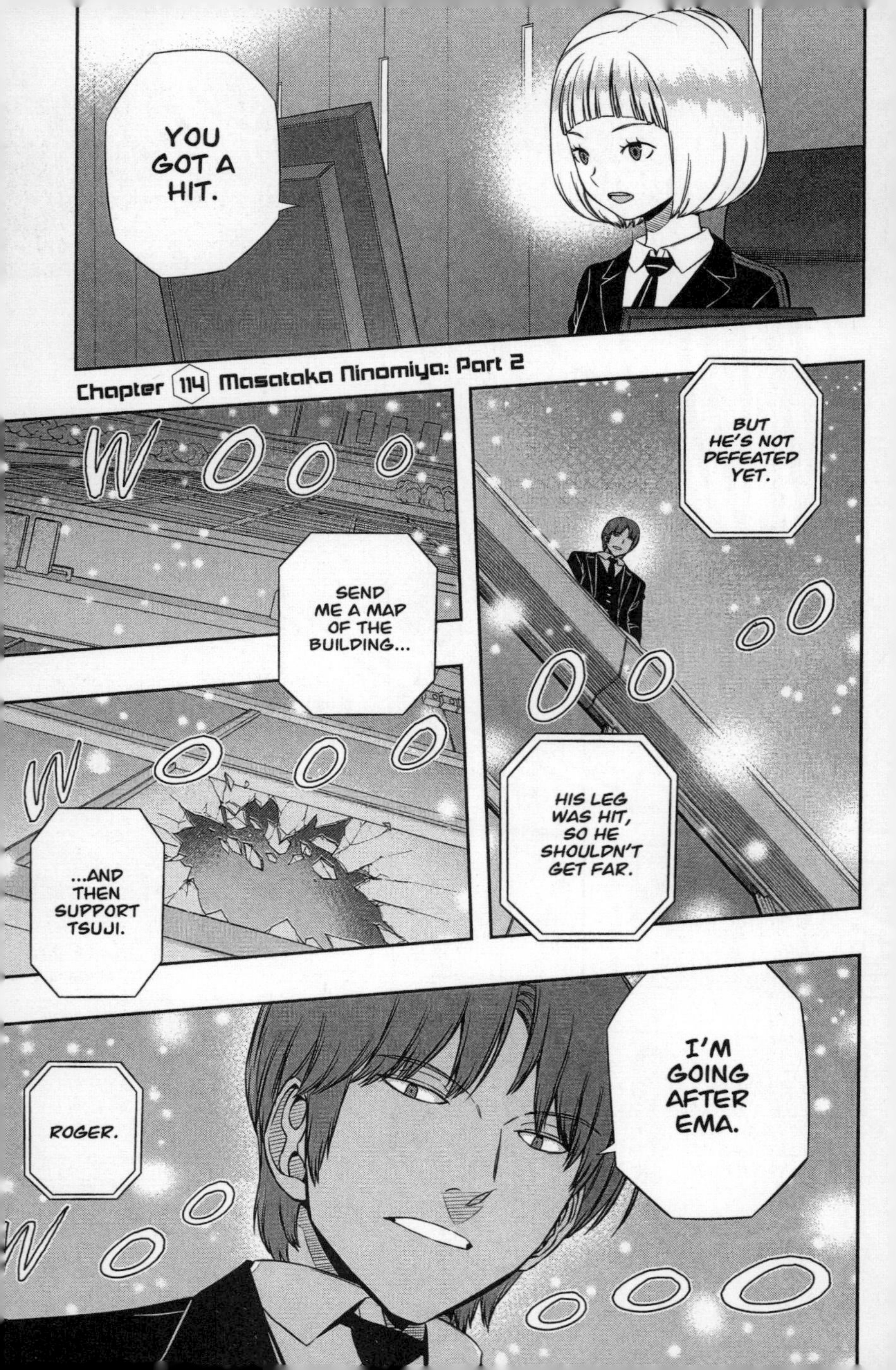
YOU GOT A HIT.
Chapter 114 Masataka Ninomiya: Part 2
BUT HE'S NOT DEFEATED YET.
HIS LEG WAS HIT, SO HE SHOULDN'T GET FAR.
WOOOO
SEND ME A MAP OF THE BUILDING...
WOOOO
...AND THEN SUPPORT TSUJI.
I'M GOING AFTER EMA.
ROGER.
WOOOOO

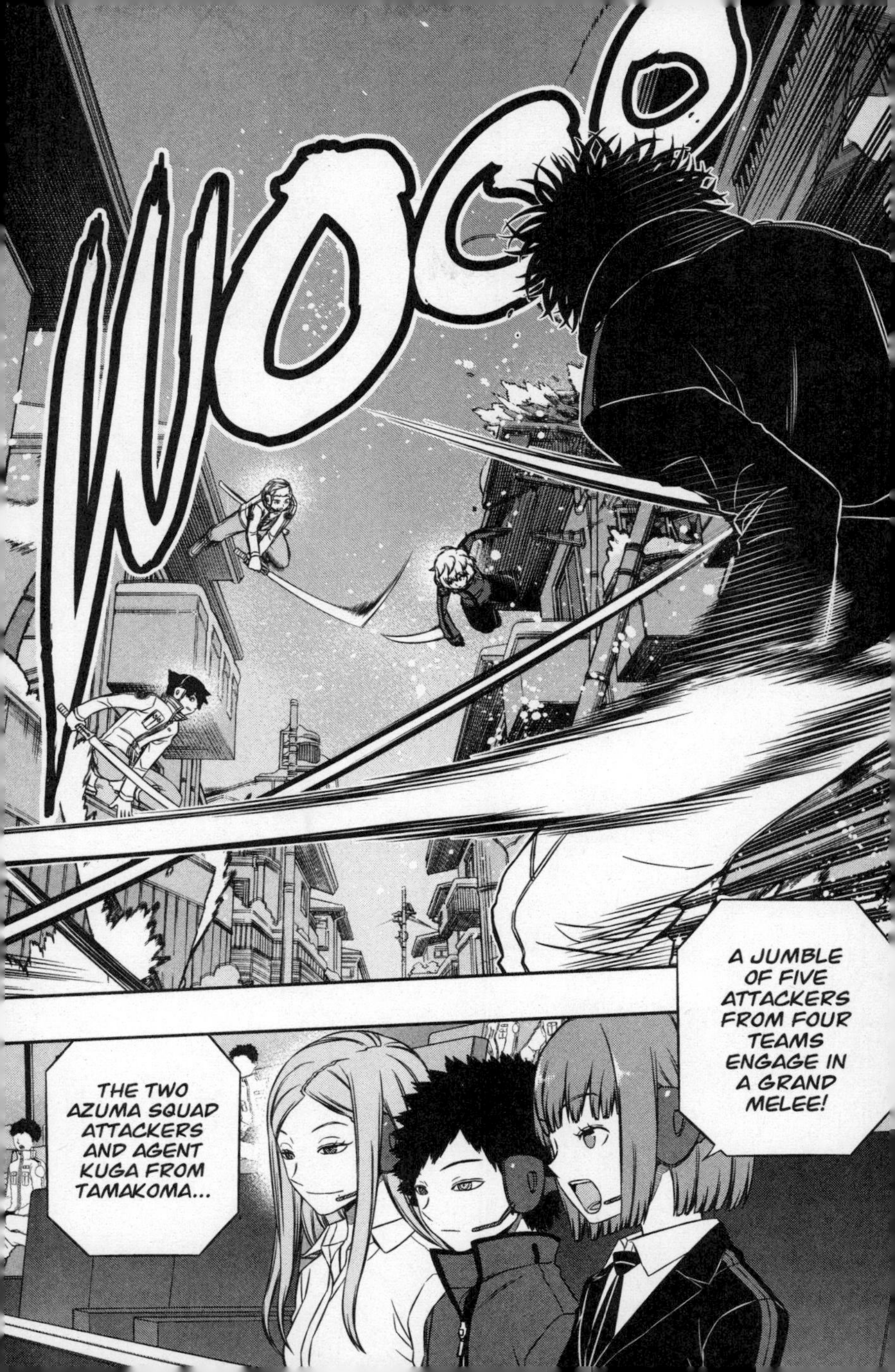
WOOO
A JUMBLE OF FIVE ATTACKERS FROM FOUR TEAMS ENGAGE IN A GRAND MELEE!
THE TWO AZUMA SQUAD ATTACKERS AND AGENT KUGA FROM TAMAKOMA...

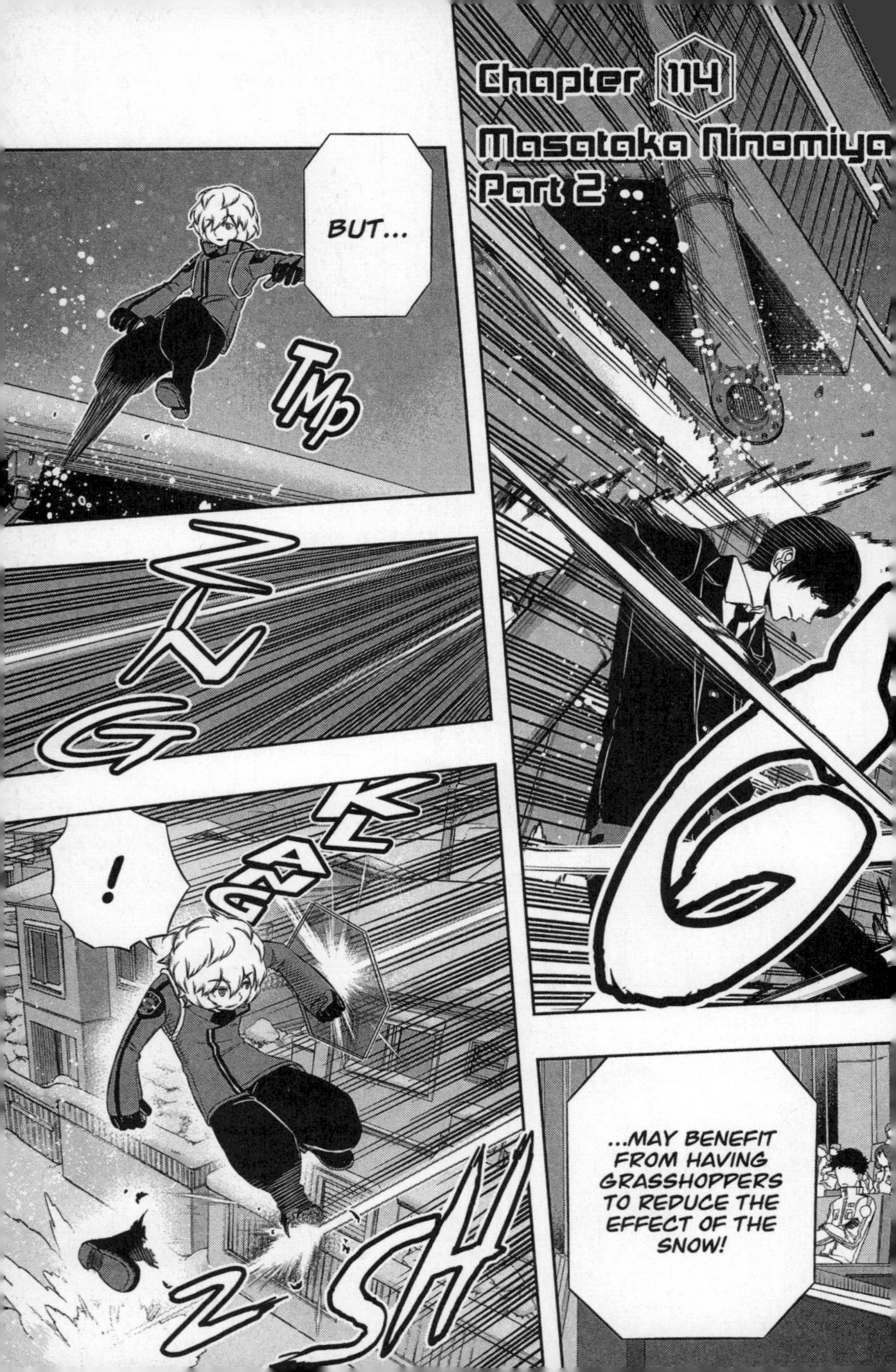
Chapter 114
Masataka Ninomiya Part 2
G
BUT...
TMP
ZING
...MAY BENEFIT FROM HAVING GRASSHOPPERS TO REDUCE THE EFFECT OF THE SNOW!
!
KLANG
ZSH

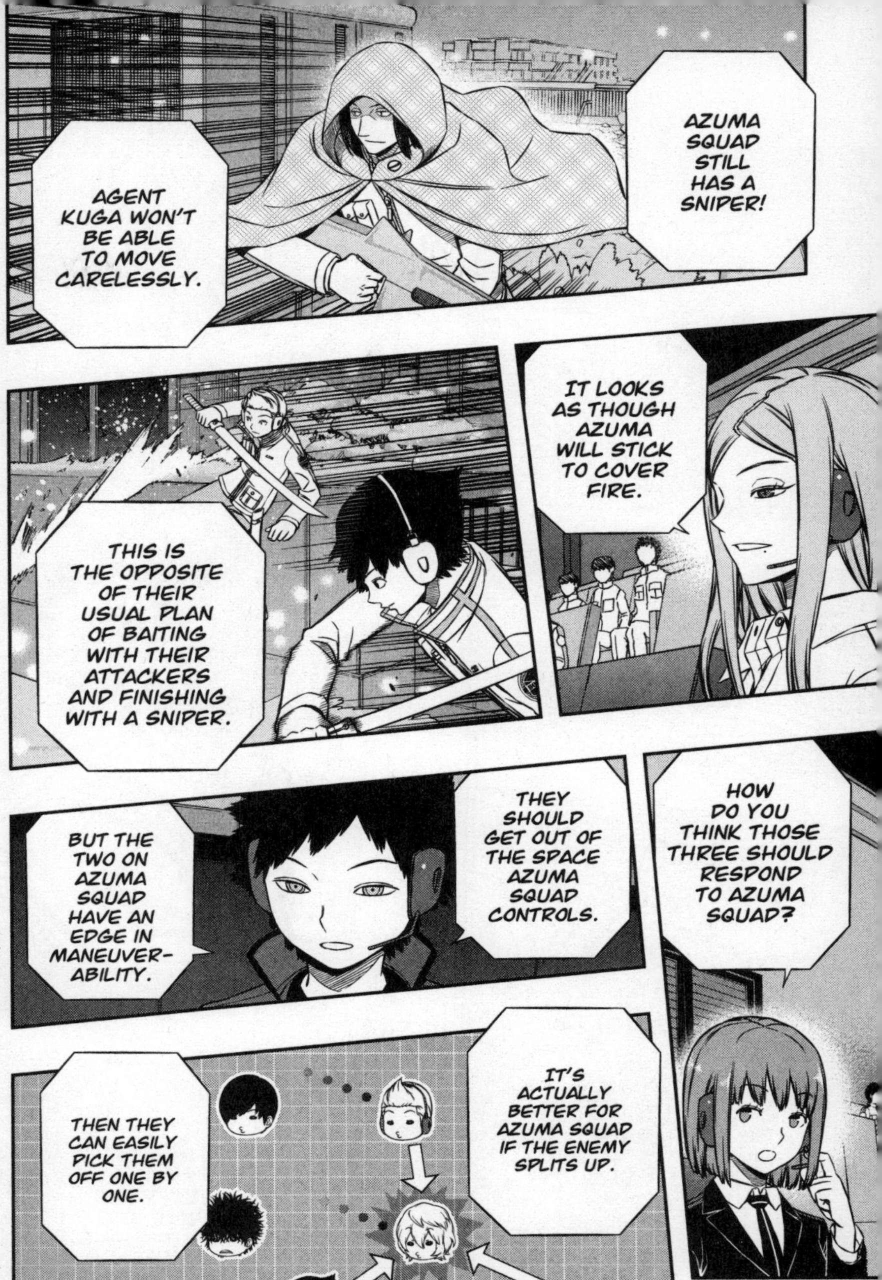
AZUMA SQUAD STILL HAS A SNIPER!
AGENT KUGA WON'T BE ABLE TO MOVE CARELESSLY.
IT LOOKS AS THOUGH AZUMA WILL STICK TO COVER FIRE.
THIS IS THE OPPOSITE OF THEIR USUAL PLAN OF BAITING WITH THEIR ATTACKERS AND FINISHING WITH A SNIPER.
HOW DO YOU THINK THOSE THREE SHOULD RESPOND TO AZUMA SQUAD?
THEY SHOULD GET OUT OF THE SPACE AZUMA SQUAD CONTROLS.
BUT THE TWO ON AZUMA SQUAD HAVE AN EDGE IN MANEUVER-ABILITY.
IT'S ACTUALLY BETTER FOR AZUMA SQUAD IF THE ENEMY SPLITS UP.
THEN THEY CAN EASILY PICK THEM OFF ONE BY ONE.

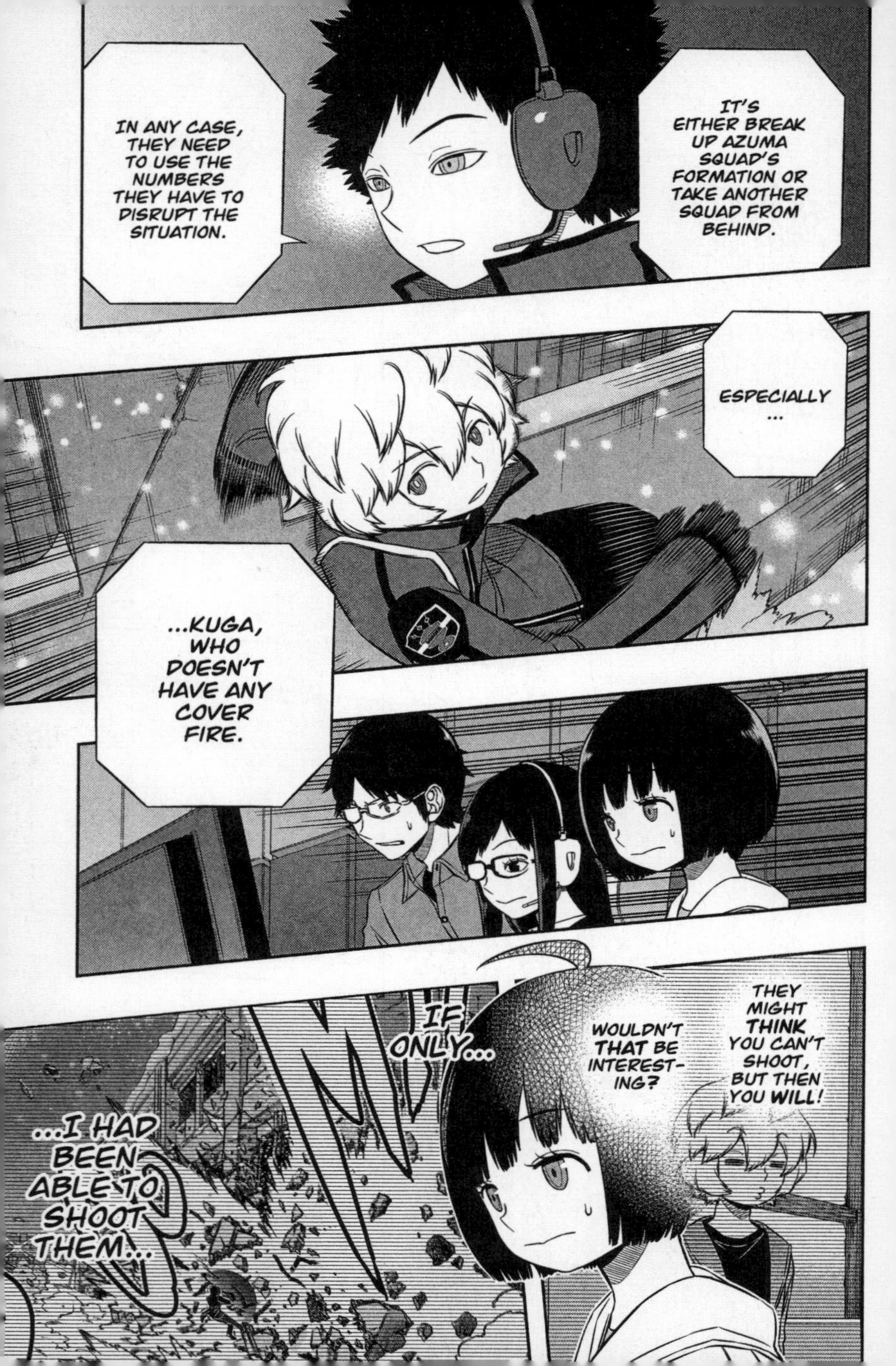
IT'S EITHER BREAK UP AZUMA SQUAD'S FORMATION OR TAKE ANOTHER SQUAD FROM BEHIND.
IN ANY CASE, THEY NEED TO USE THE NUMBERS THEY HAVE TO DISRUPT THE SITUATION.
ESPECIALLY ...
...KUGA, WHO DOESN'T HAVE ANY COVER FIRE.
THEY MIGHT THINK YOU CAN'T SHOOT, BUT THEN YOU WILL!
WOULDN'T THAT BE INTEREST-ING?
IF ONLY...
...I HAD BEEN ABLE TO SHOOT THEM...

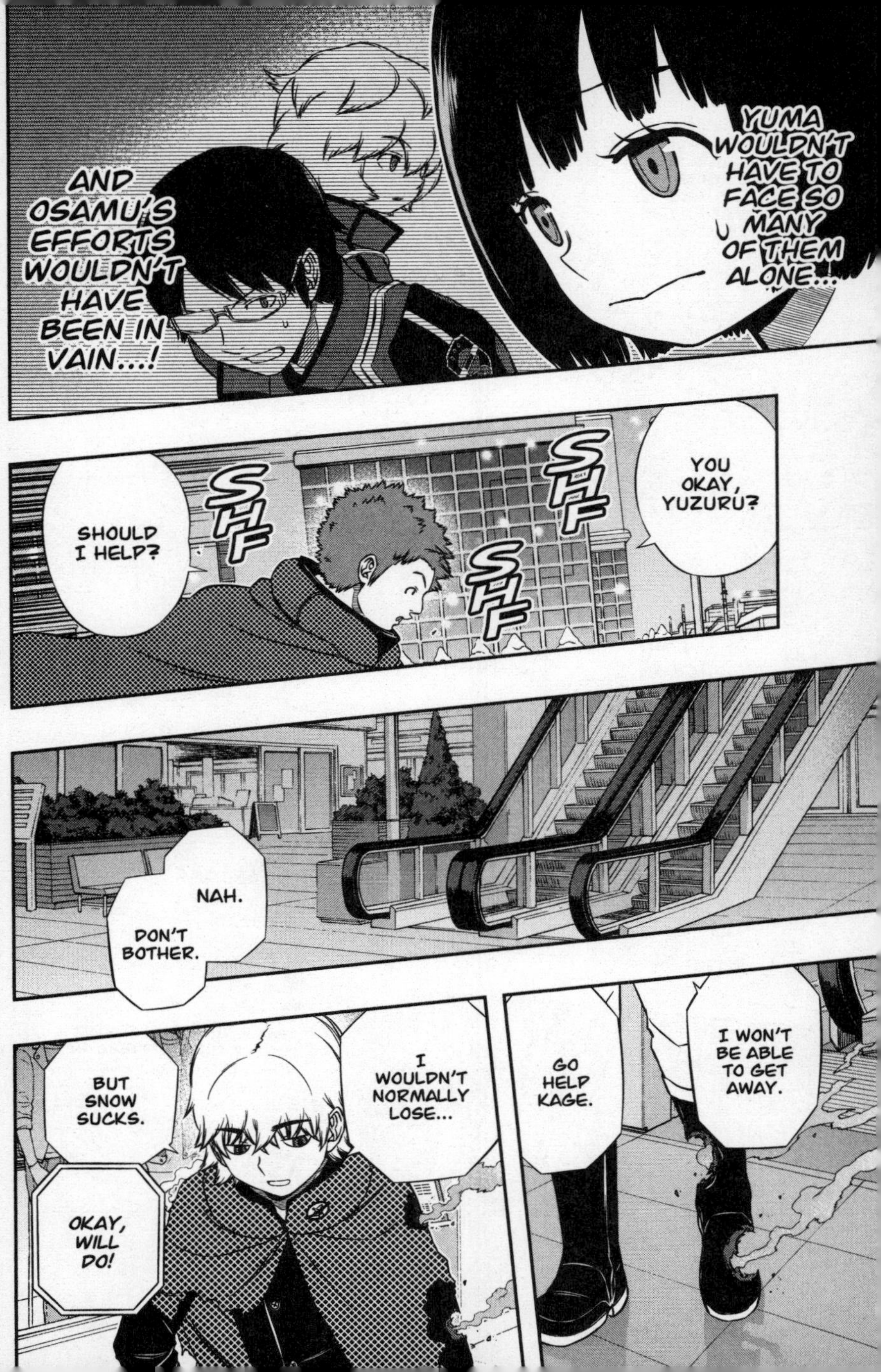
YUMA WOULDN'T HAVE TO FACE SO MANY OF THEM ALONE...
AND OSAMU'S EFFORTS WOULDN'T HAVE BEEN IN VAIN...!
YOU OKAY, YUZURU?
SHF
SHF
SHOULD I HELP?
NAH.
DON'T BOTHER.
I WON'T BE ABLE TO GET AWAY.
GO HELP KAGE.
I WOULDN'T NORMALLY LOSE...
BUT SNOW SUCKS.
OKAY, WILL DO!

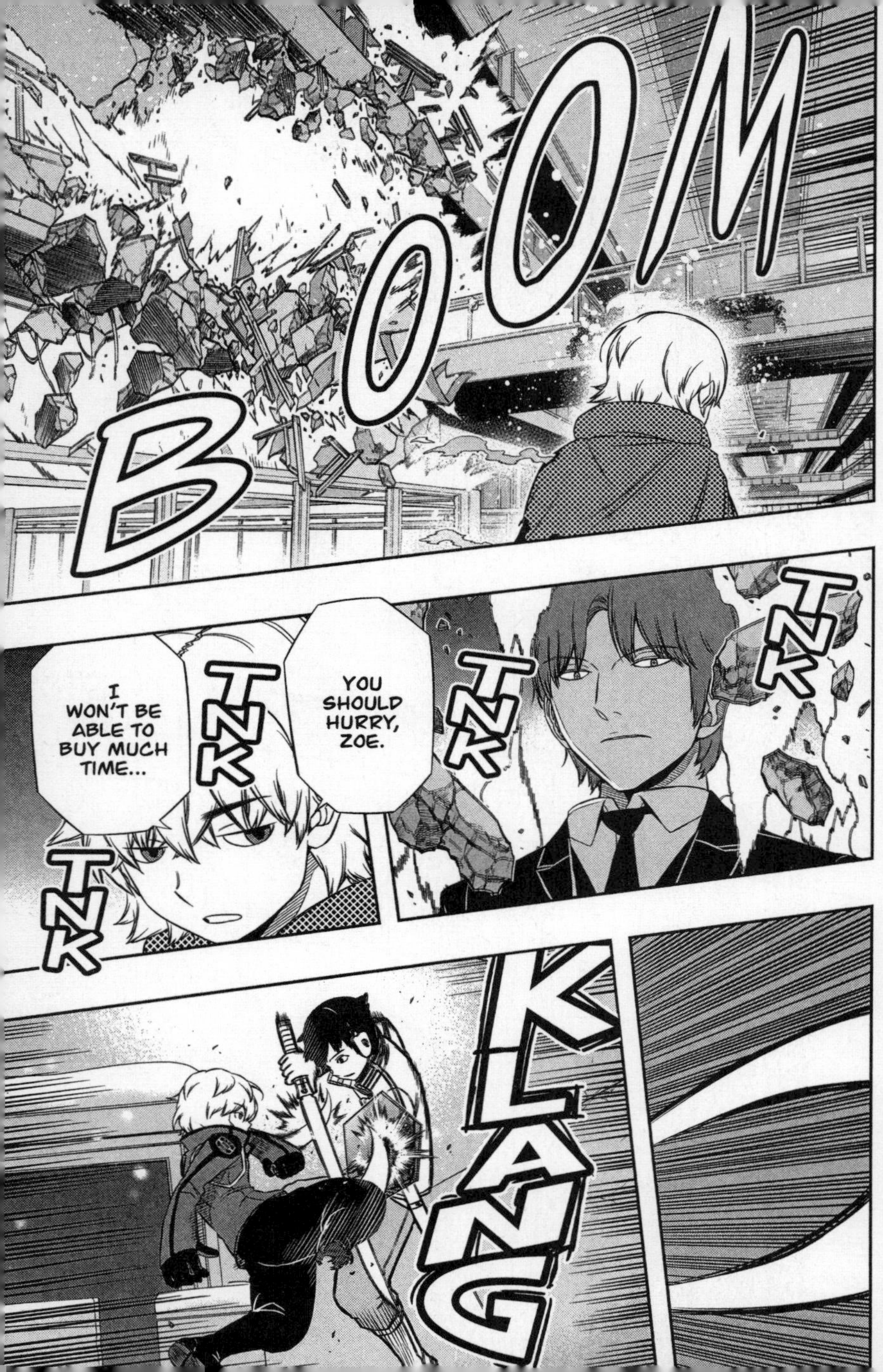
BOOOM
TNK
TNK
YOU SHOULD HURRY, ZOE.
TNK
I WON'T BE ABLE TO BUY MUCH TIME...
TNK
KLANG

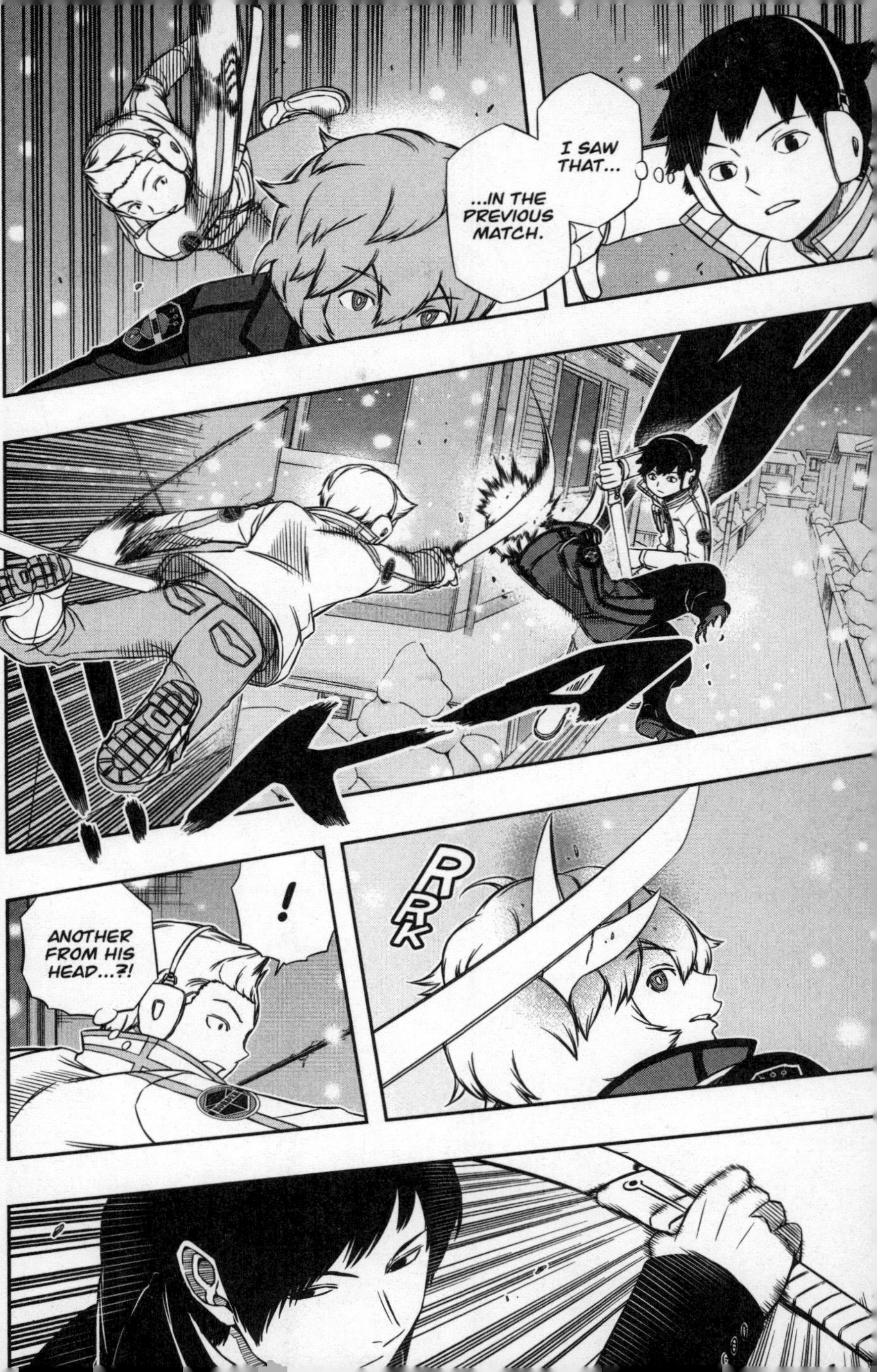
I SAW THAT...
...IN THE PREVIOUS MATCH.
RRK
!
ANOTHER FROM HIS HEAD...?!

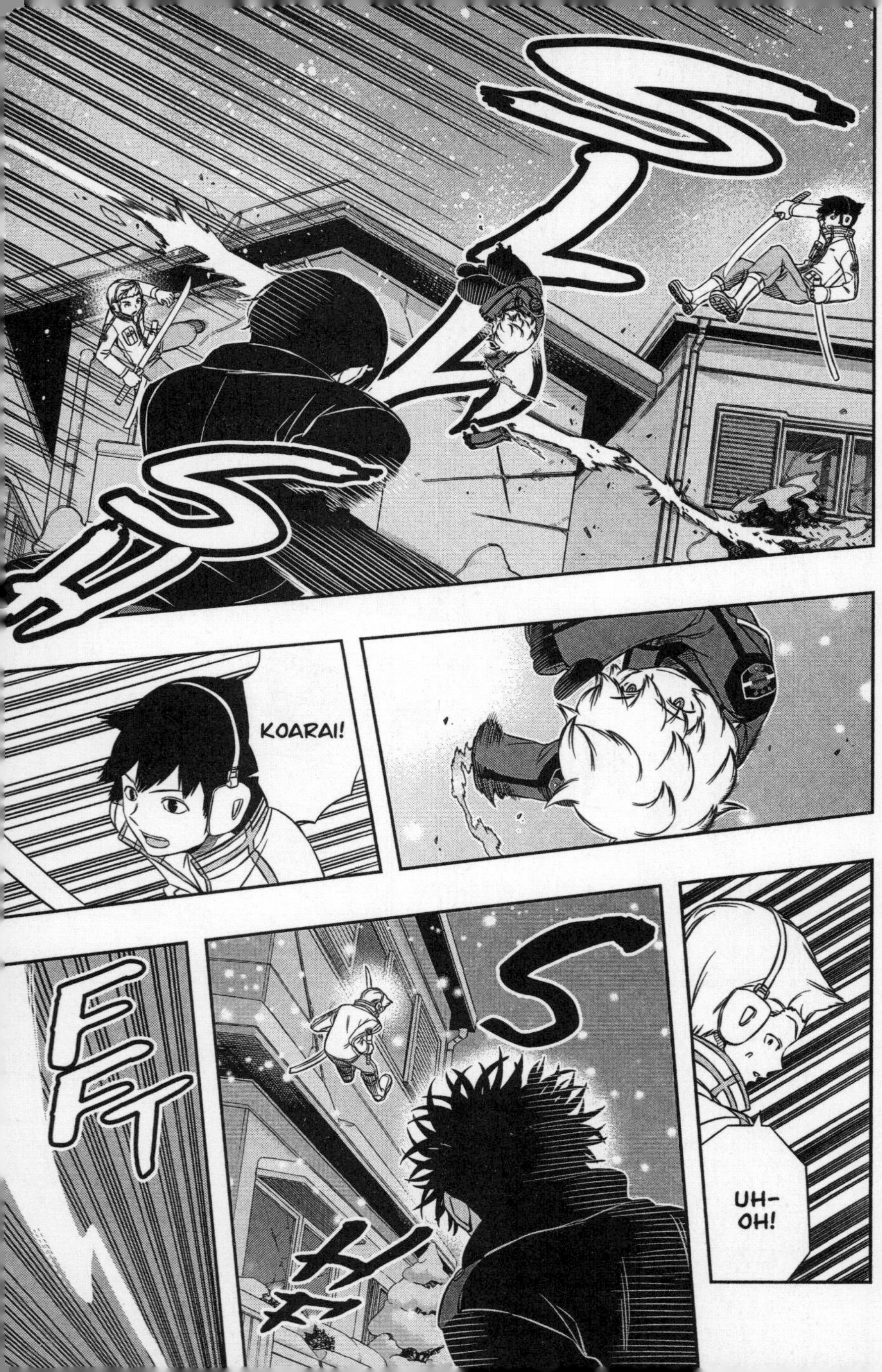
KOARAI!
UH-
OH!
S
FFT

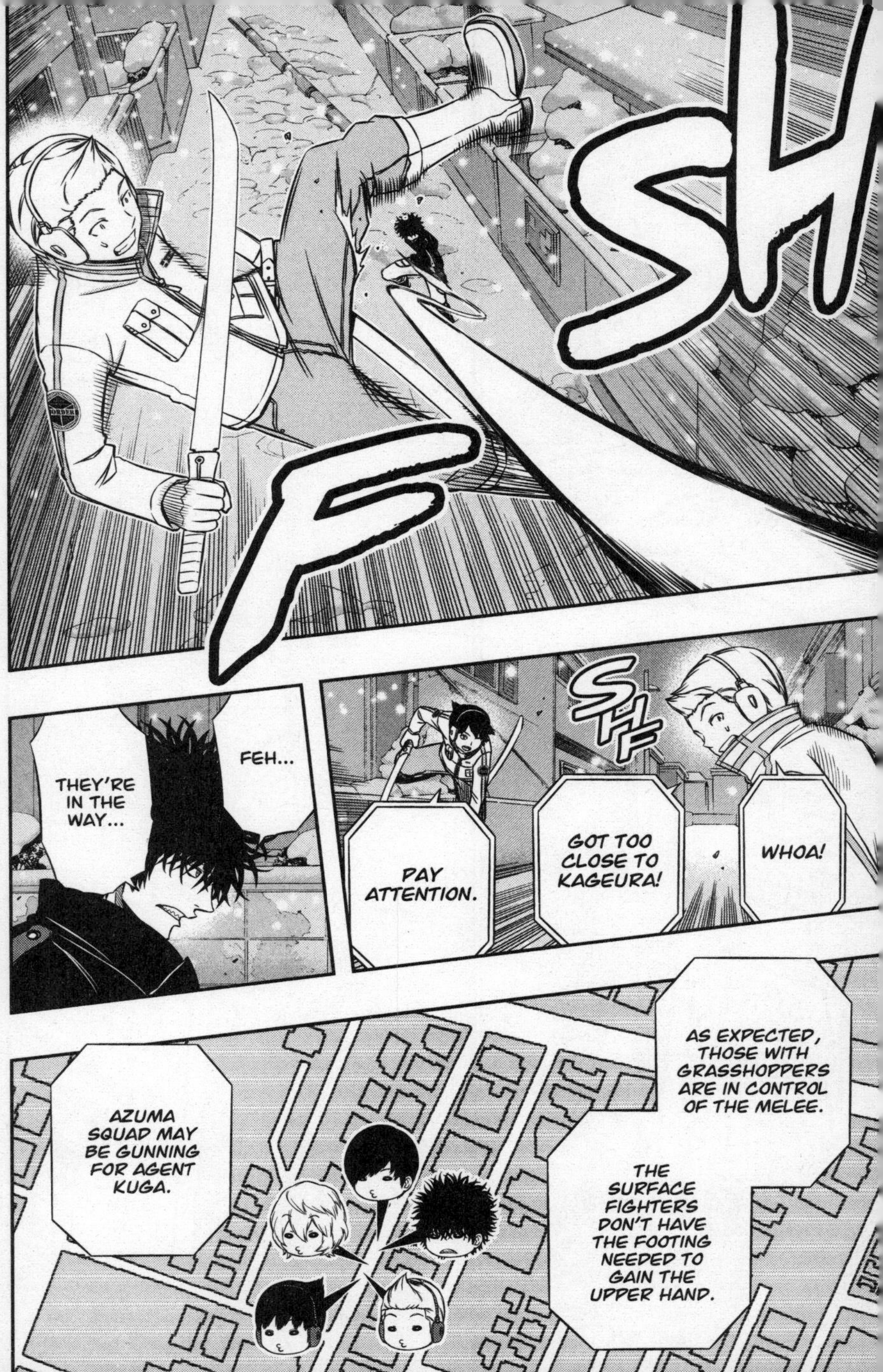
SHF
SHF
WHOA!
GOT TOO CLOSE TO KAGEURA!
PAY ATTENTION.
FEH...
THEY'RE IN THE WAY...
AS EXPECTED, THOSE WITH GRASSHOPPERS ARE IN CONTROL OF THE MELEE.
THE SURFACE FIGHTERS DON'T HAVE THE FOOTING NEEDED TO GAIN THE UPPER HAND.
AZUMA SQUAD MAY BE GUNNING FOR AGENT KUGA.

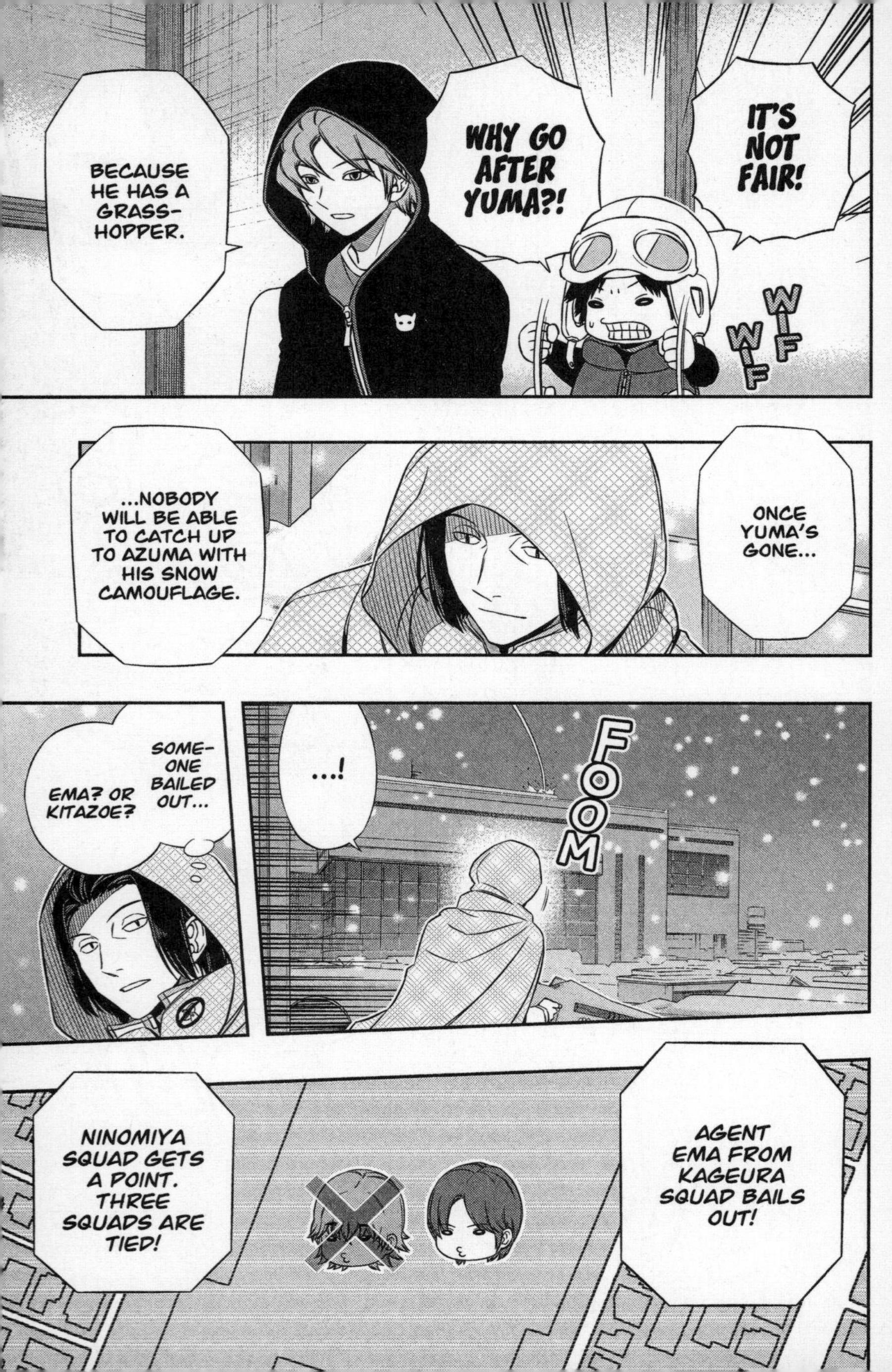
IT'S NOT FAIR!
WHY GO AFTER YUMA?!
WIF WIF
BECAUSE HE HAS A GRASS-HOPPER.
ONCE YUMA'S GONE...
...NOBODY WILL BE ABLE TO CATCH UP TO AZUMA WITH HIS SNOW CAMOUFLAGE.
FOOM
...!
SOME-ONE BAILED OUT...
EMA? OR KITAZOE?
AGENT EMA FROM KAGEURA SQUAD BAILS OUT!
NINOMIYA SQUAD GETS A POINT. THREE SQUADS ARE TIED!

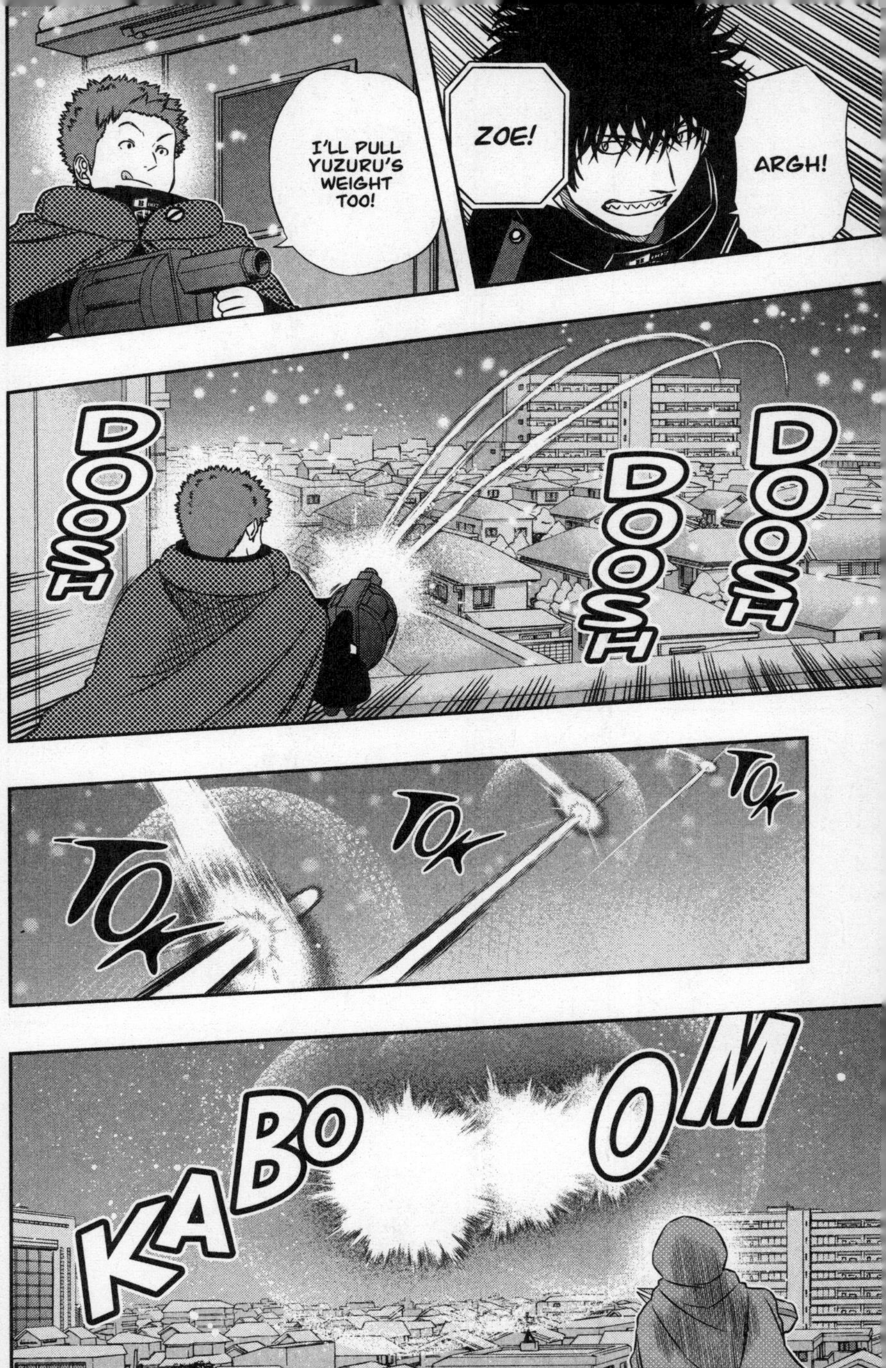
ARGH!
ZOE!
I'LL PULL YUZURU'S WEIGHT TOO!
DOOSH
DOOSH
DOOSH
TOK
TOK
TOK
KABOOM

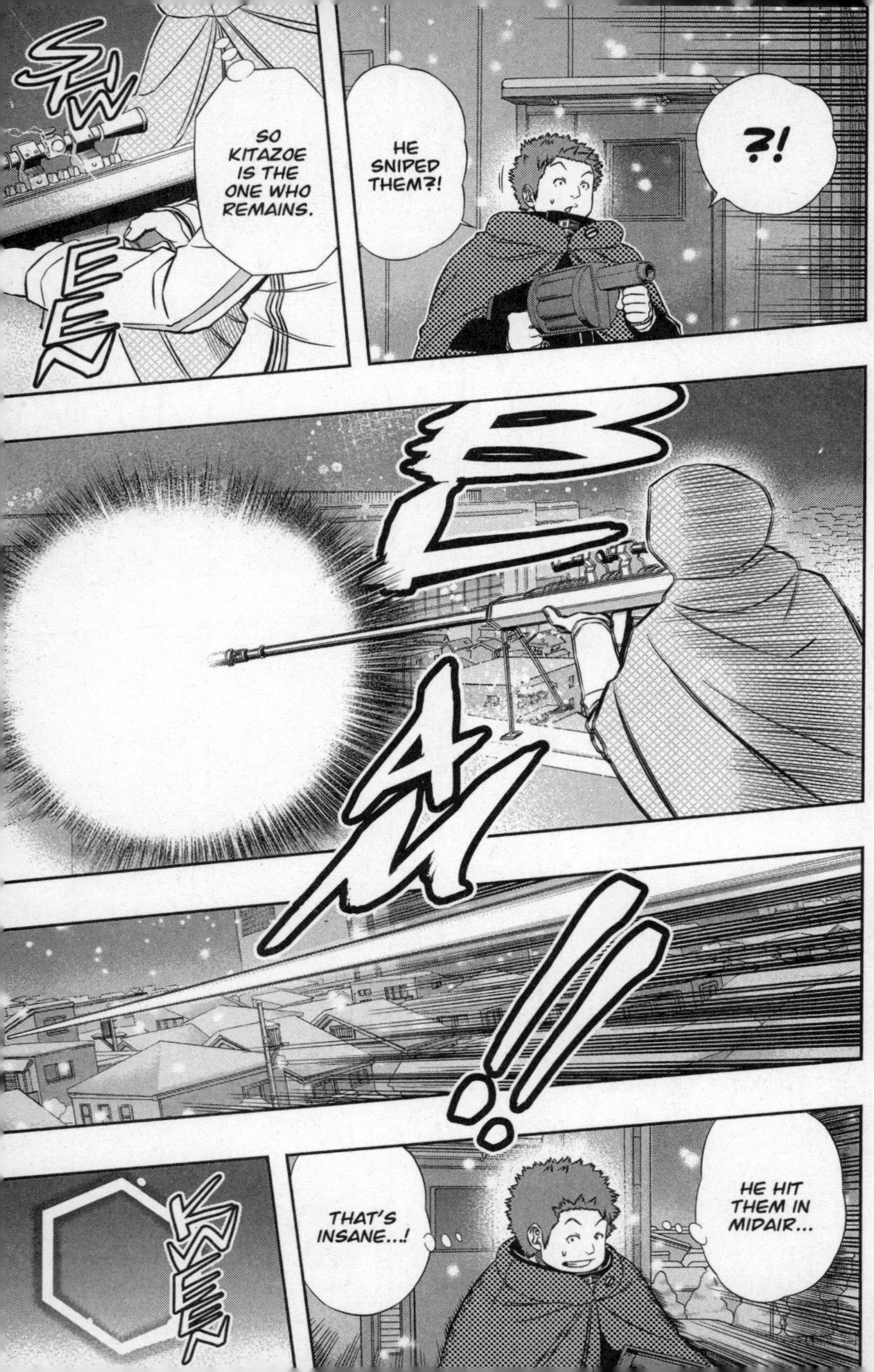
?!
HE SNIPED THEM?!
SO KITAZOE IS THE ONE WHO REMAINS.
SWEEN
BLAM!!
HE HIT THEM IN MIDAIR...
THAT'S INSANE...!
KWEEN

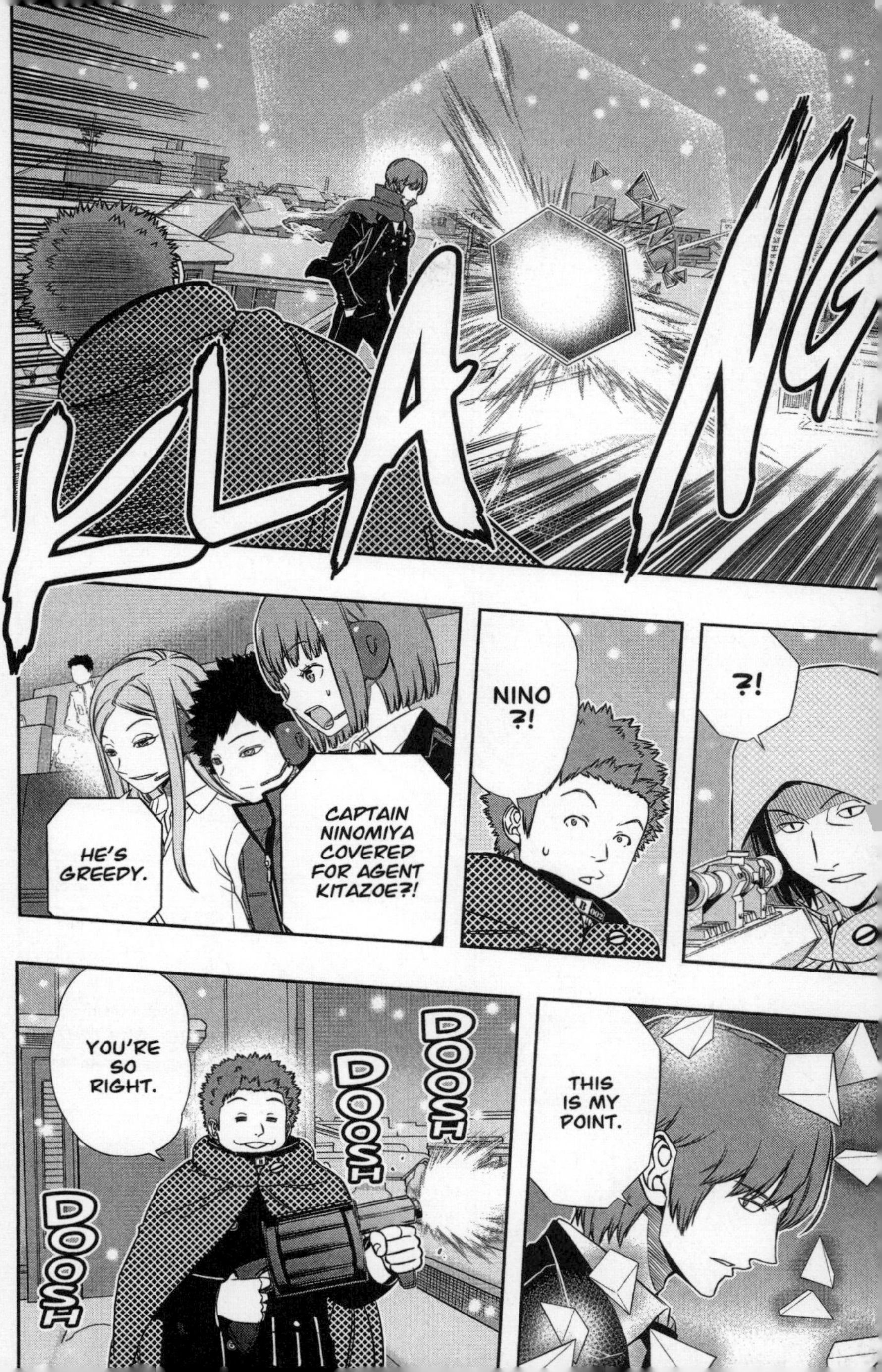
KLANG
?!
NINO ?!
CAPTAIN NINOMIYA COVERED FOR AGENT KITAZOE?!
HE'S GREEDY.
THIS IS MY POINT.
YOU'RE SO RIGHT.
DOOSH
DOOSH
DOOSH

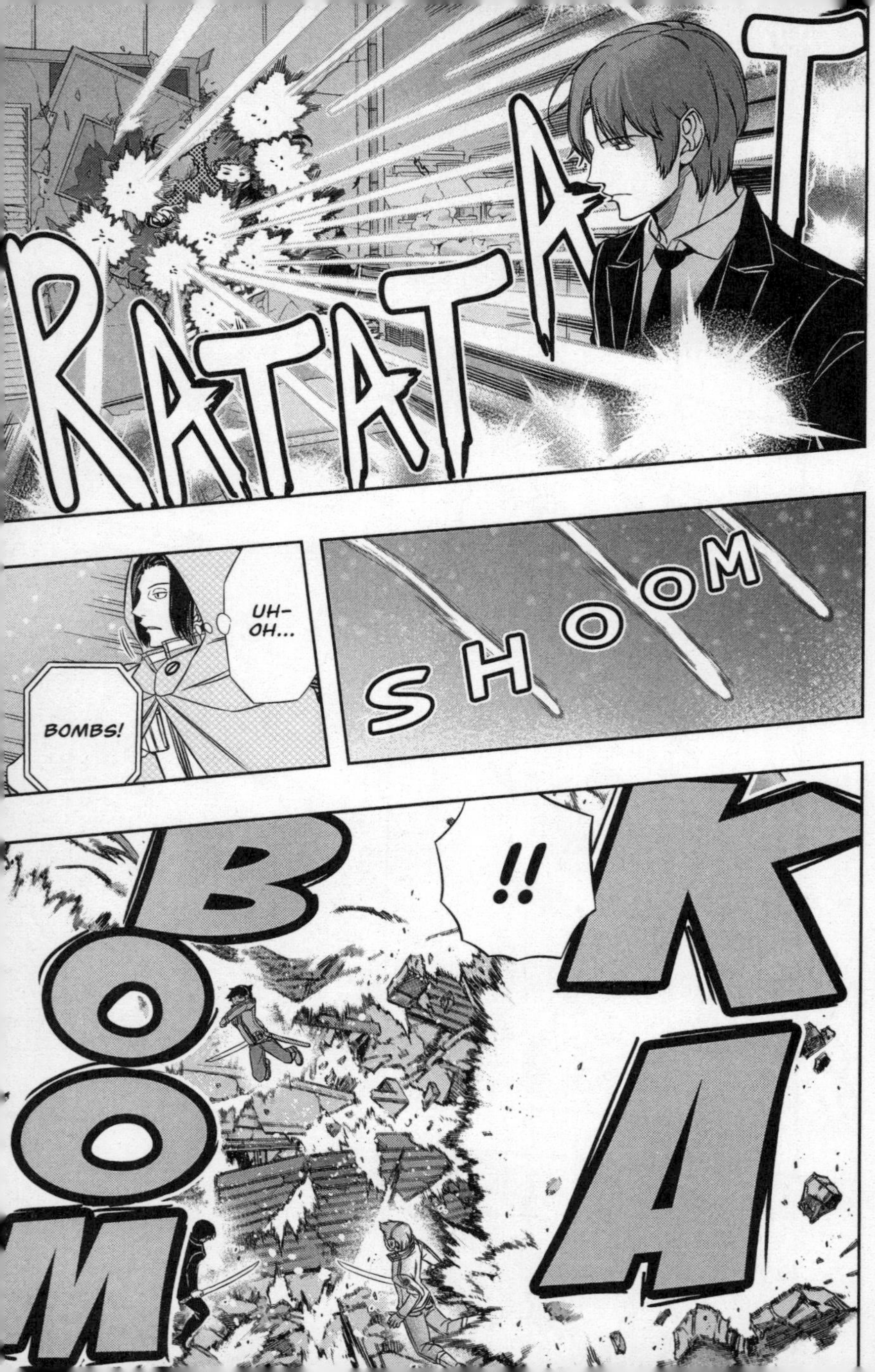
RATATAT
SHOOM
UH-OH...
BOMBS!
!!
KA
BOOM

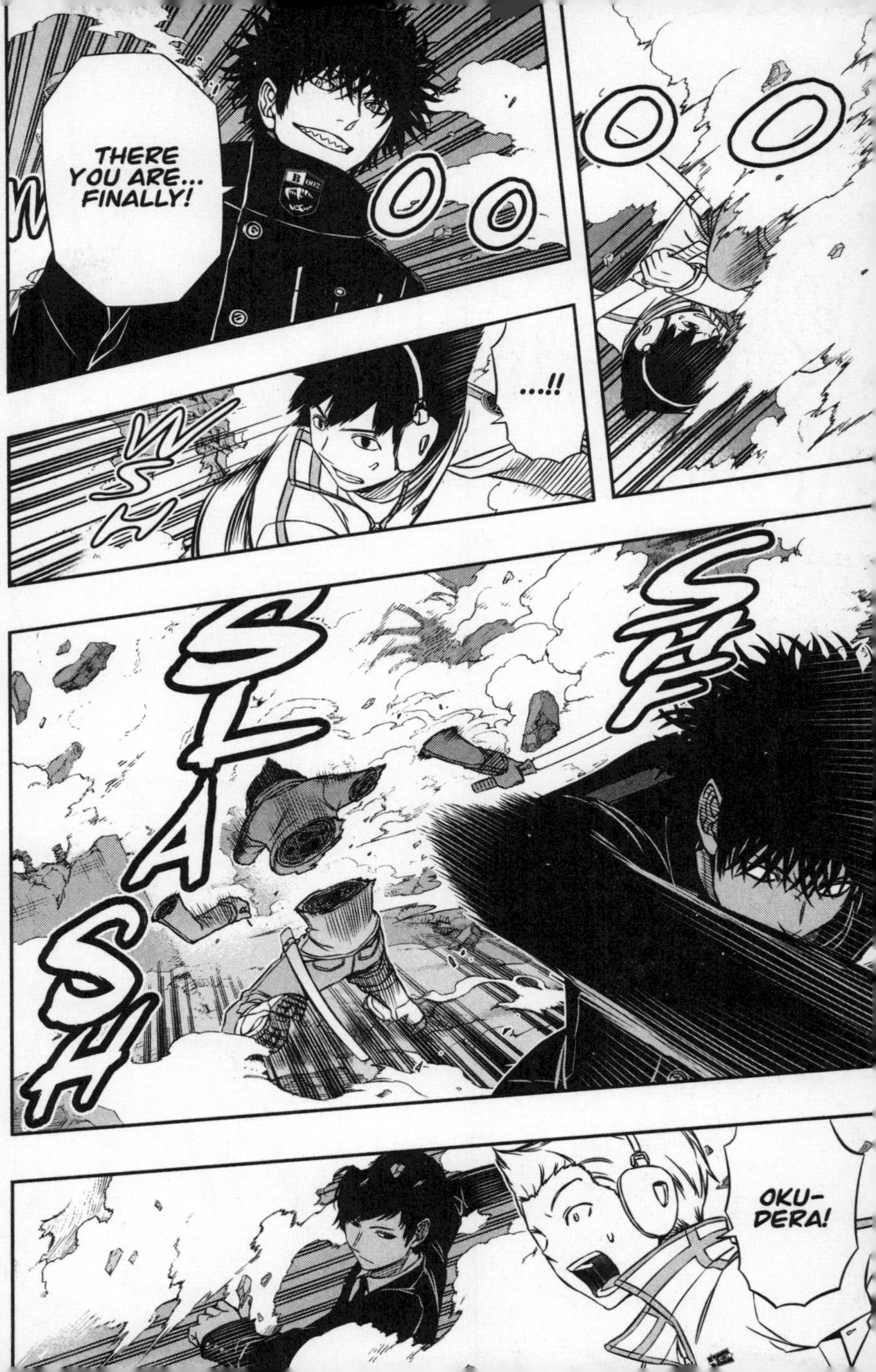

OO
THERE YOU ARE... FINALLY!
OO
...!!
WSSH
SHF
SLASH
OKU-DERA!

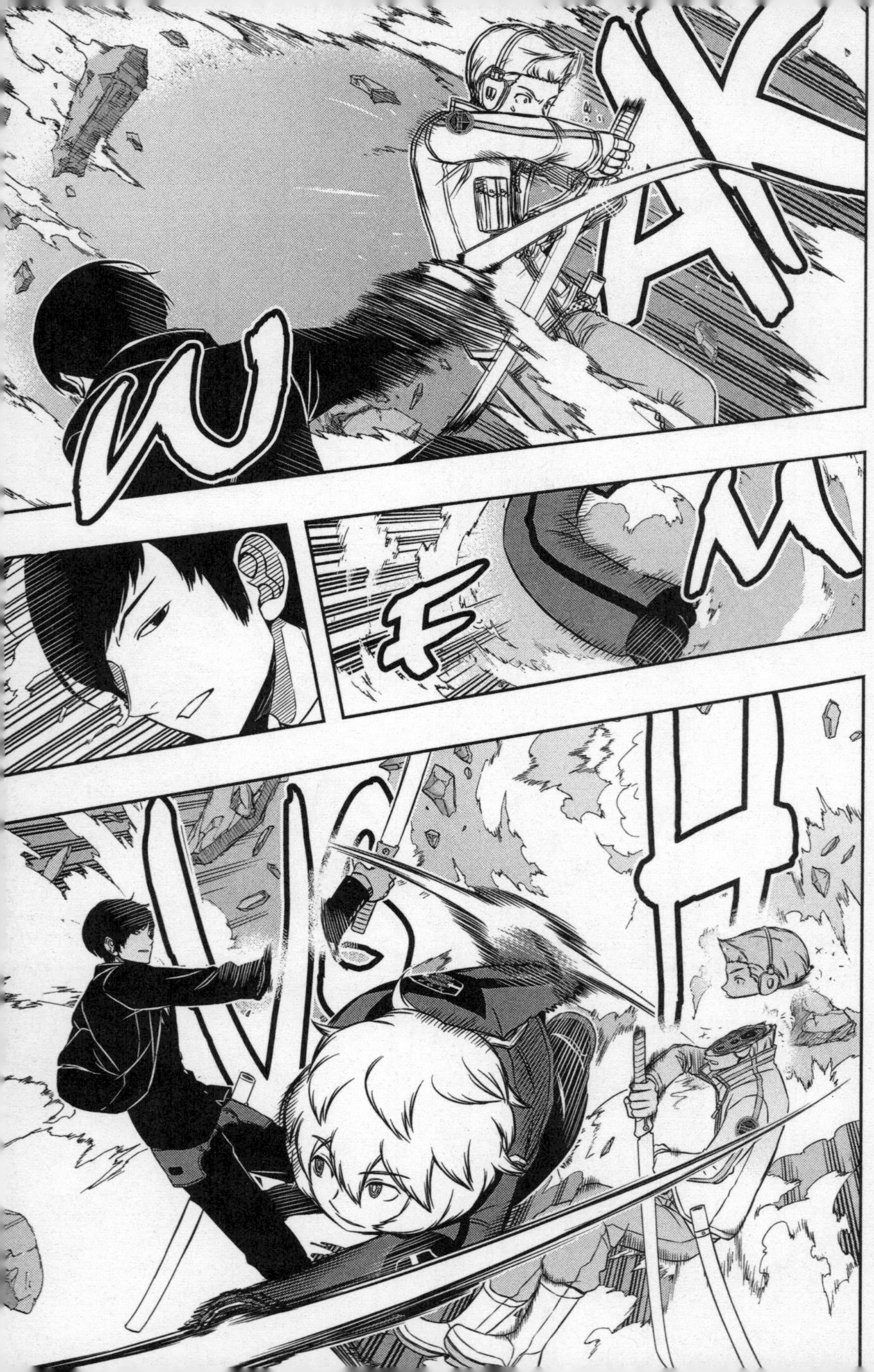

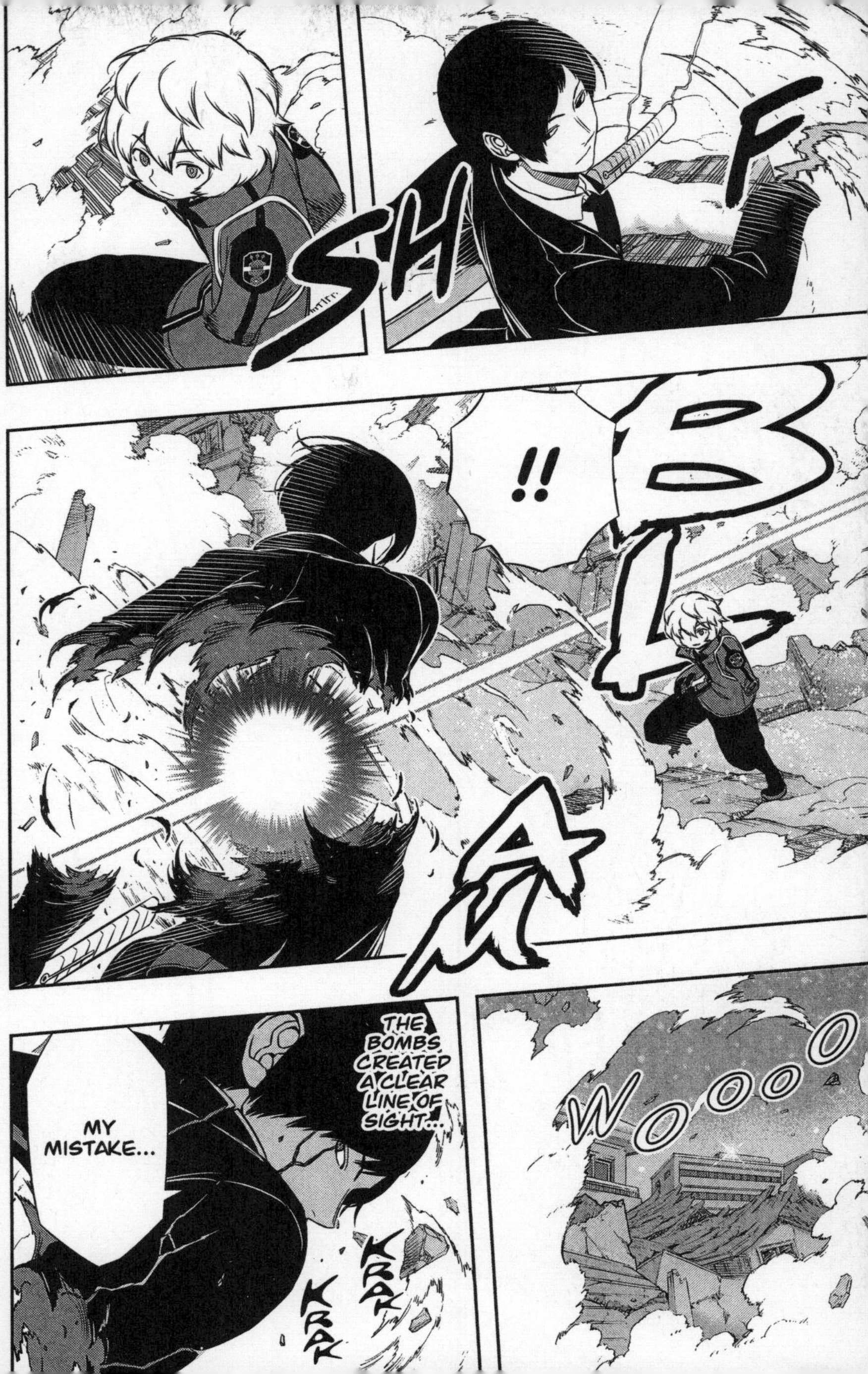
SHF
!!
BLAM
WOOOO
THE BOMBS CREATED A CLEAR LINE OF SIGHT...
MY MISTAKE...
KRAK
KRAK

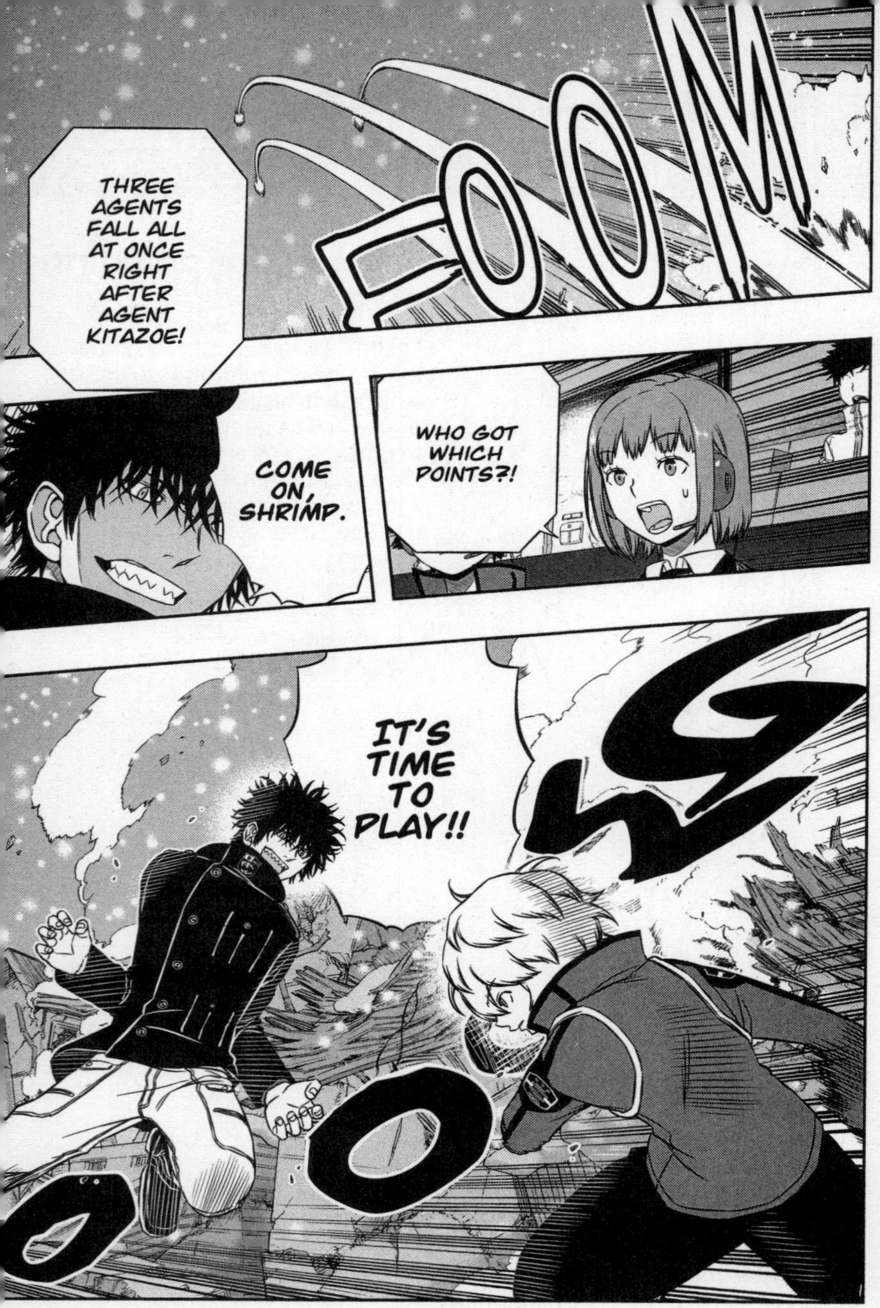
FOOM
THREE AGENTS FALL ALL AT ONCE RIGHT AFTER AGENT KITAZOE!
WHO GOT WHICH POINTS?!
COME ON, SHRIMP.
IT'S TIME TO PLAY!!

The Way They Were: Part 4

They barely look like them now.

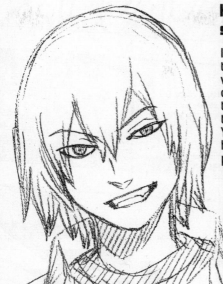

Kage in the planning stages

I used this haircut for one of the three idiots in volume 1, so that's why he has his current cut. This one would've been much easier to draw. He was supposed to be the top Scorpion master and Yuma's rival. He already had his Side Effect at this stage in planning.

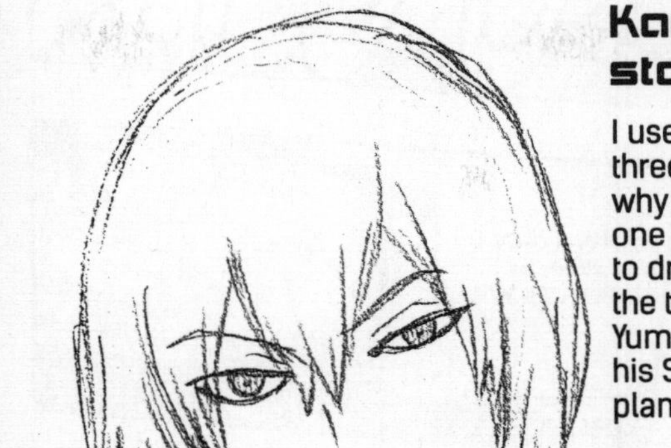

B-Rank No. 1
Kageura (18)
High school senior

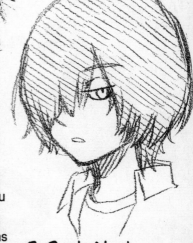

Yuzuru in the planning stages

He looks more like an indoors-only kid. This look was inherited by Sayoko in Nasu Squad and Tokieda. He was going to fall in love with Chika and hate Osamu. He's probably nicer in his current form. He was still Toma's pupil and a genius Sniper, but he ended up one year younger.

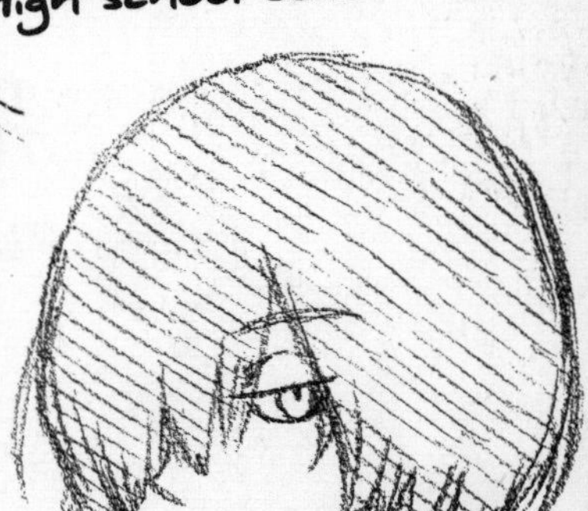

B-Rank No. 1
Yuzuru Ema (15)
Ninth grade

KAGEURA SQUAD'S AND TAMAKOMA-2'S ACES FACE OFF!

THEY'RE CARVING EACH OTHER UP WITH THEIR SCORPIONS!

WITH ONLY ONE LEG AND ONE ARM, AGENT KUGA SEEMS TO BE LOSING GROUND!

THREE SQUADS ARE TIED.

SO, NATU- RALLY...

NINOMIYA	KAGEURA	AZUMA	TA
2	2	2	1

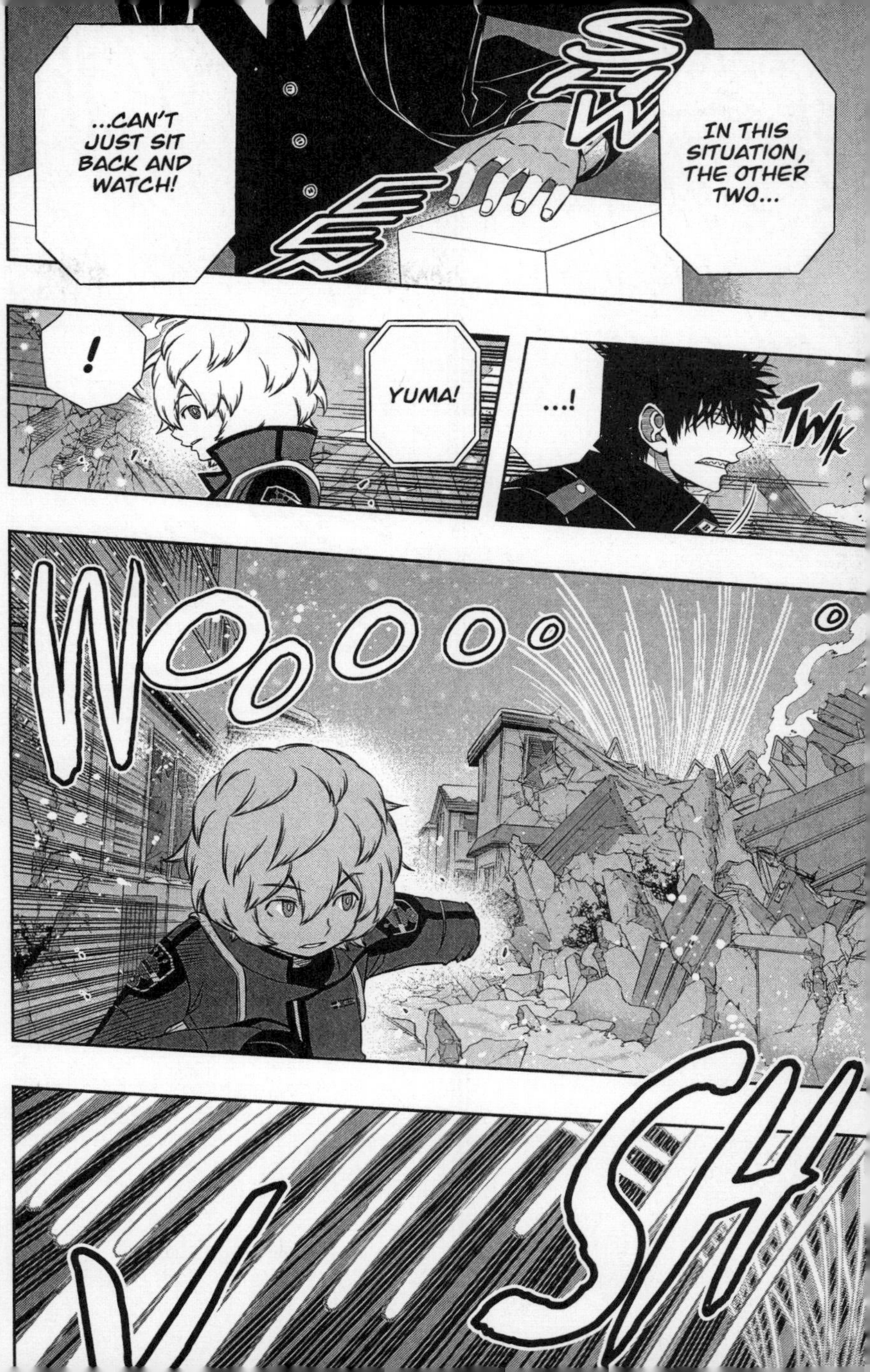
IN THIS SITUATION, THE OTHER TWO...
...CAN'T JUST SIT BACK AND WATCH!
...!
TWK
YUMA!
!
WOOOOOO
SH

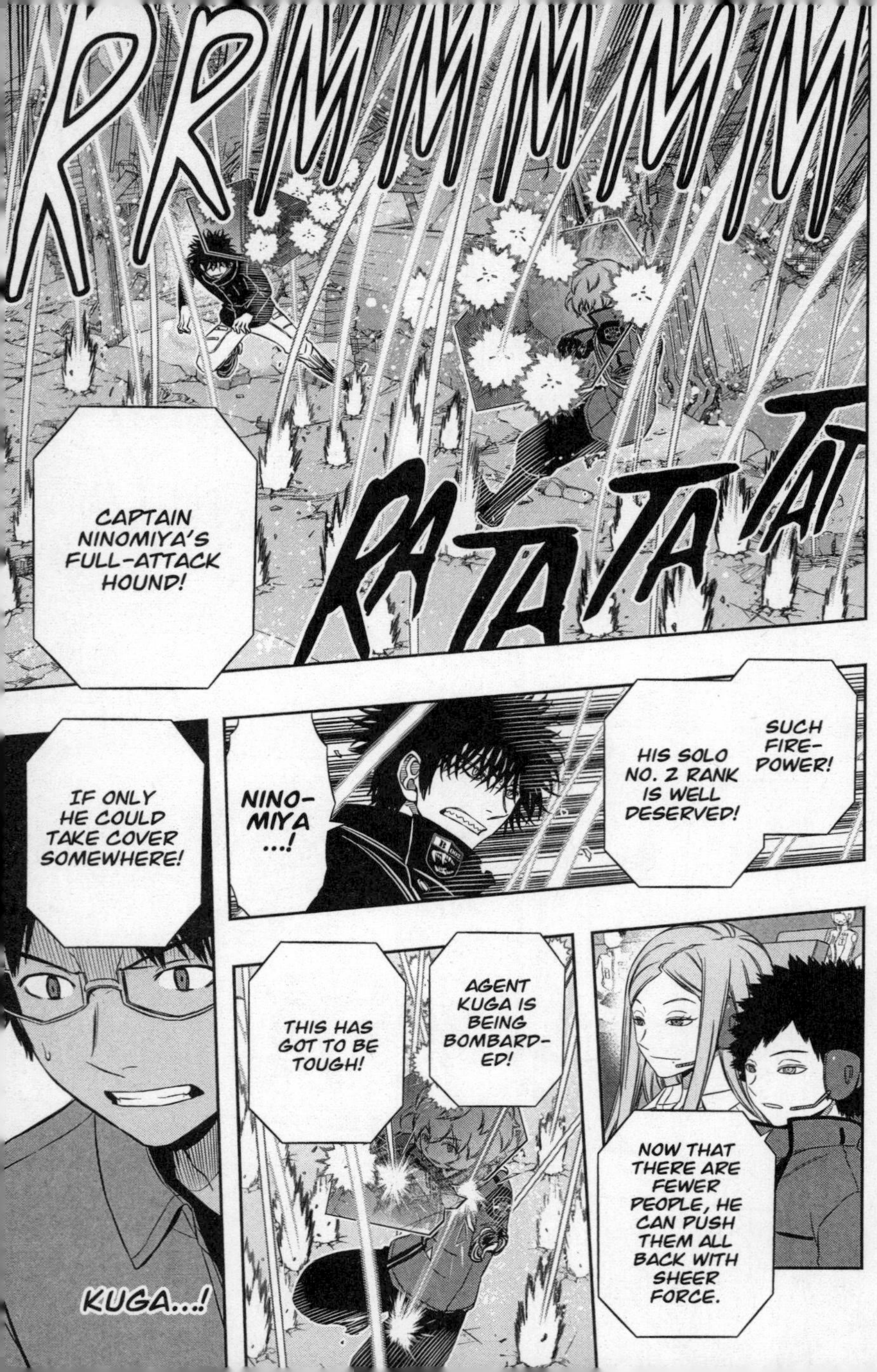
KRRMMMMMM
RATATATAT
CAPTAIN NINOMIYA'S FULL-ATTACK HOUND!
SUCH FIRE-POWER!
HIS SOLO NO. 2 RANK IS WELL DESERVED!
NINO-MIYA...!
NOW THAT THERE ARE FEWER PEOPLE, HE CAN PUSH THEM ALL BACK WITH SHEER FORCE.
AGENT KUGA IS BEING BOMBARD-ED!
THIS HAS GOT TO BE TOUGH!
IF ONLY HE COULD TAKE COVER SOMEWHERE!
KUGA...!

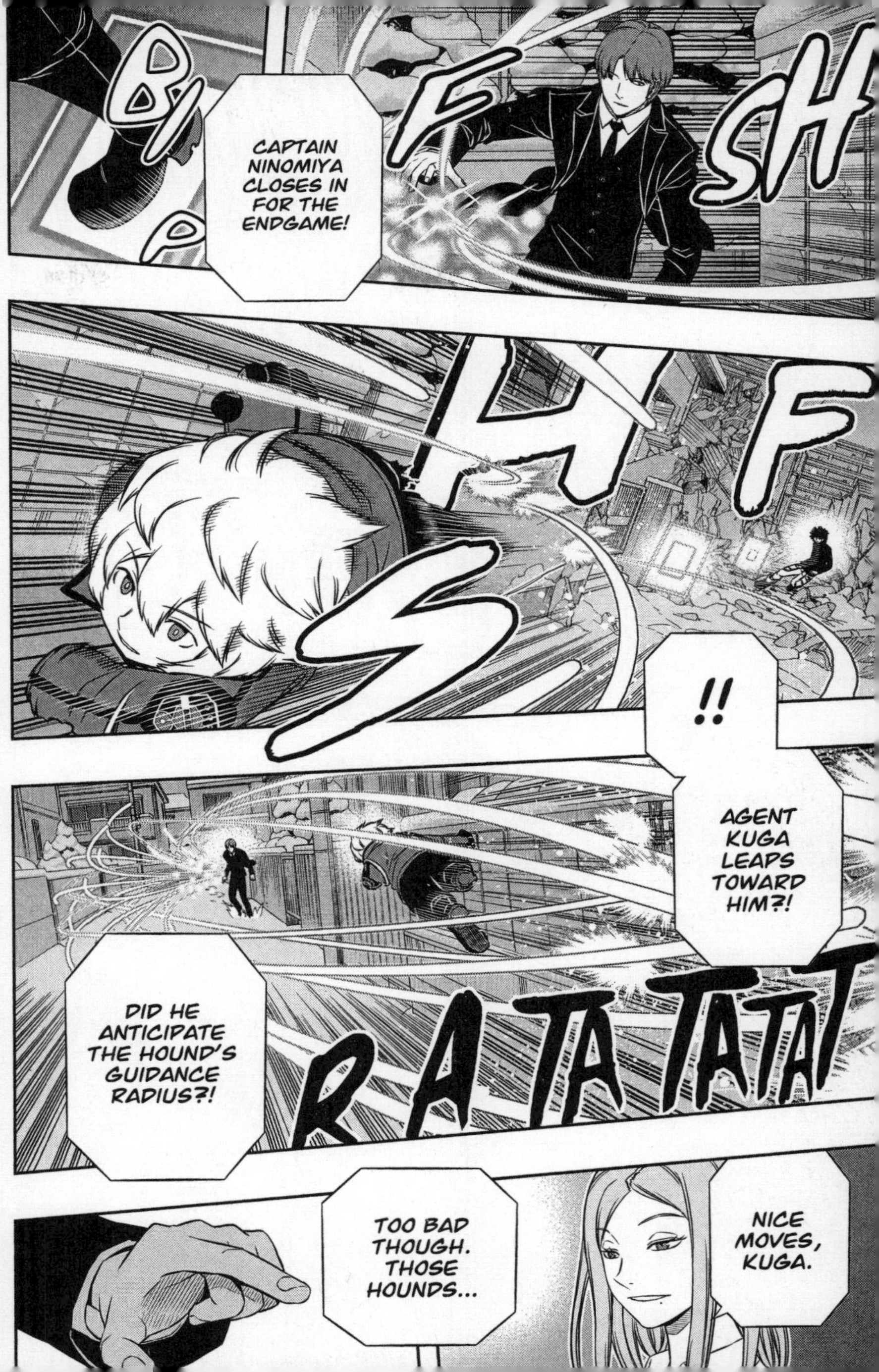
SH
F
CAPTAIN NINOMIYA CLOSES IN FOR THE ENDGAME!
B
P
HF
S
!!
AGENT KUGA LEAPS TOWARD HIM?!
RATATAT
DID HE ANTICIPATE THE HOUND'S GUIDANCE RADIUS?!
NICE MOVES, KUGA.
TOO BAD THOUGH. THOSE HOUNDS...

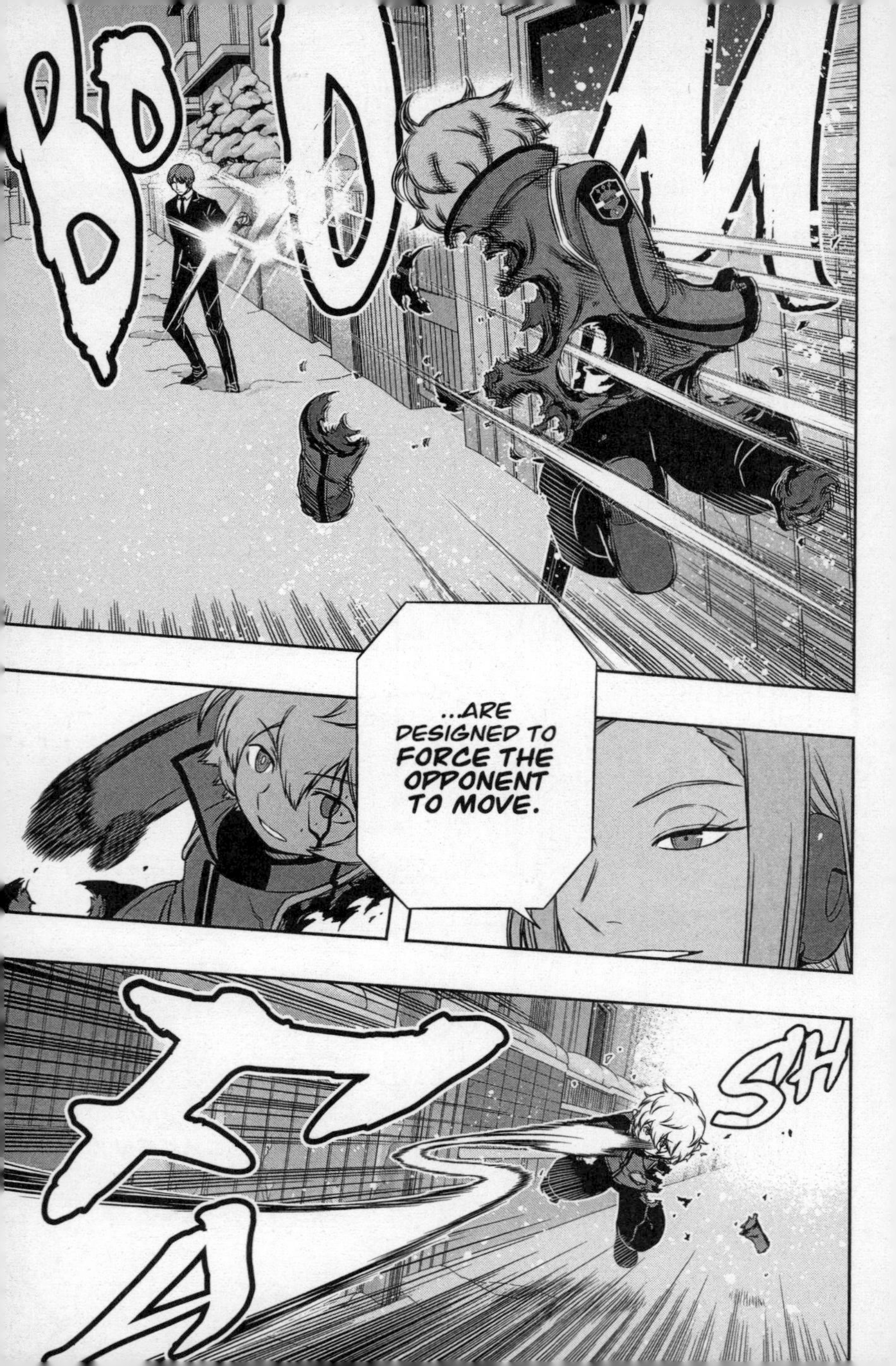
...ARE DESIGNED TO FORCE THE OPPONENT TO MOVE.
SH

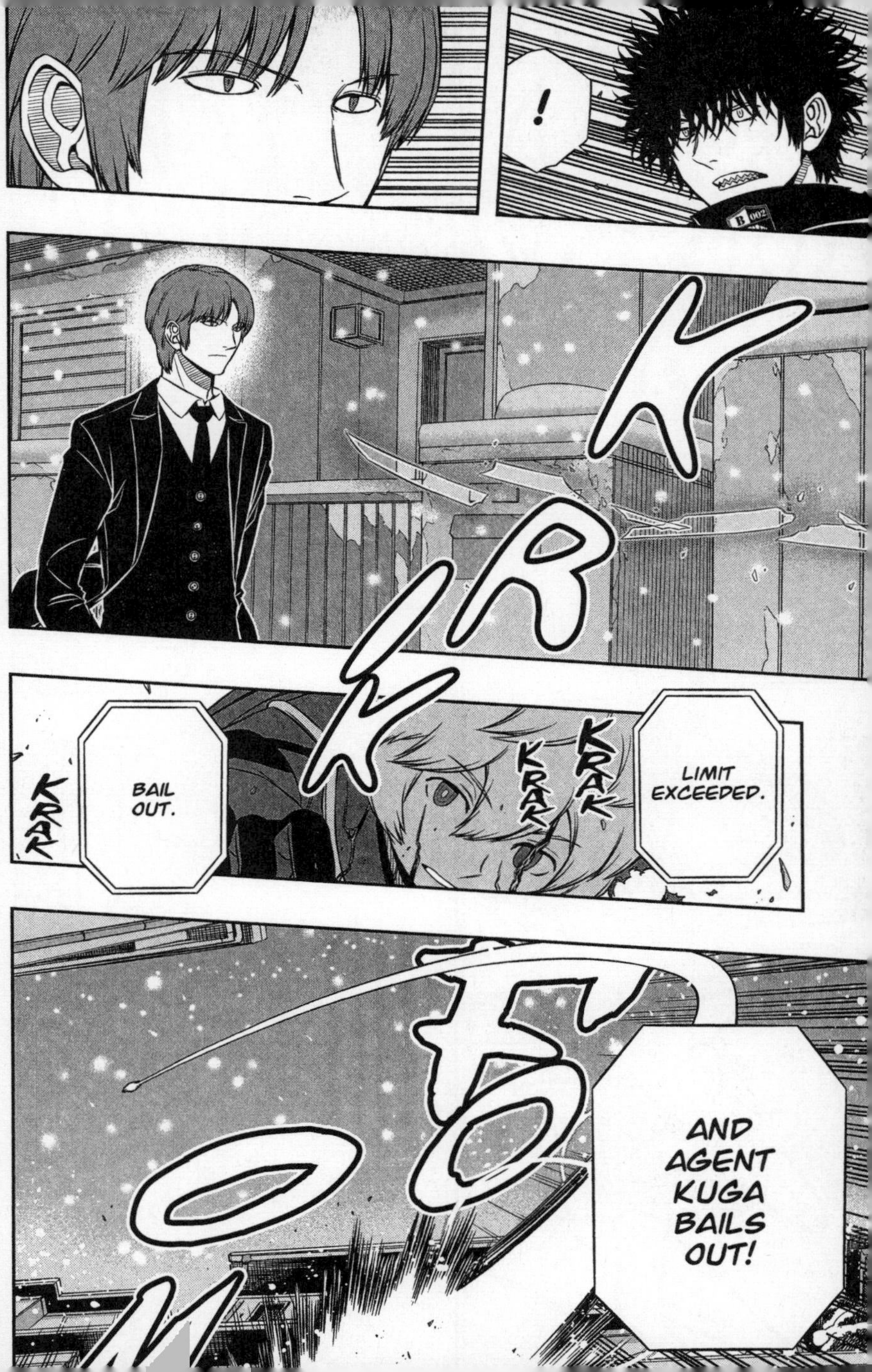
!
KRIK
LIMIT EXCEEDED.
KRAK
KRAK
BAIL OUT.
KRAK
AND AGENT KUGA BAILS OUT!

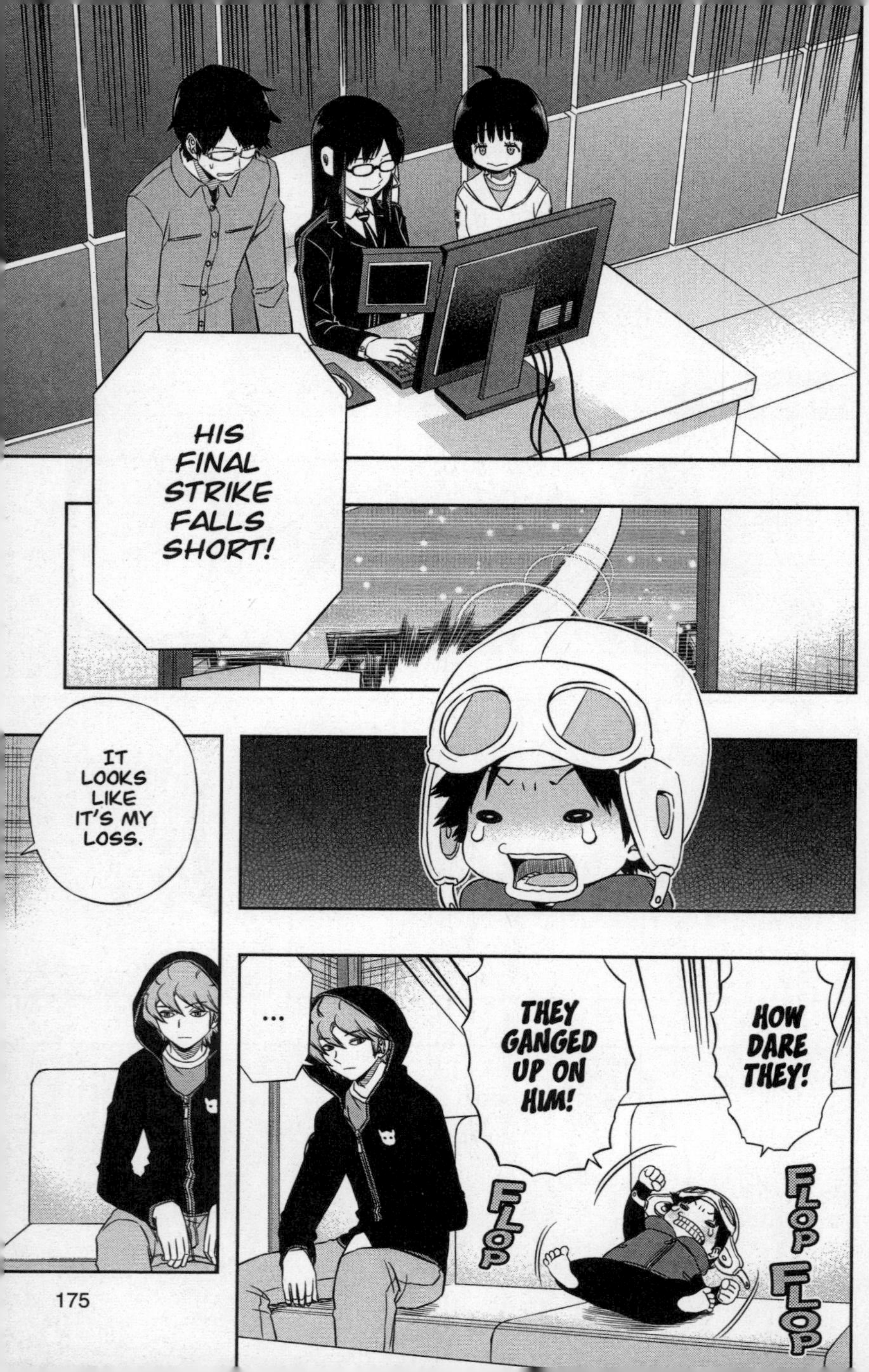
HIS FINAL STRIKE FALLS SHORT!
IT LOOKS LIKE IT'S MY LOSS.
HOW DARE THEY!
THEY GANGED UP ON HIM!
...
FLOP FLOP FLOP
FLOP

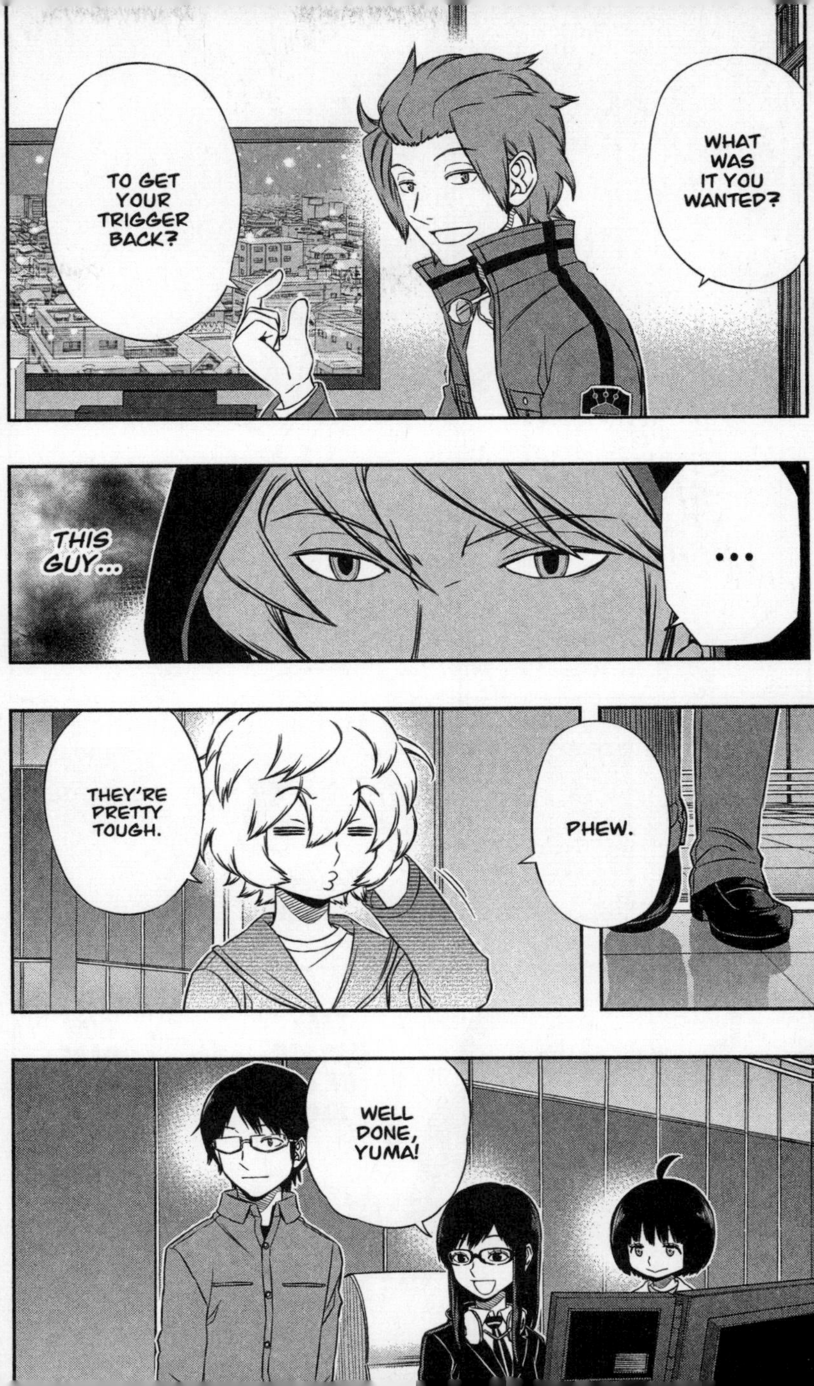
WHAT WAS IT YOU WANTED?
TO GET YOUR TRIGGER BACK?
...
THIS GUY...
PHEW.
THEY'RE PRETTY TOUGH.
WELL DONE, YUMA!

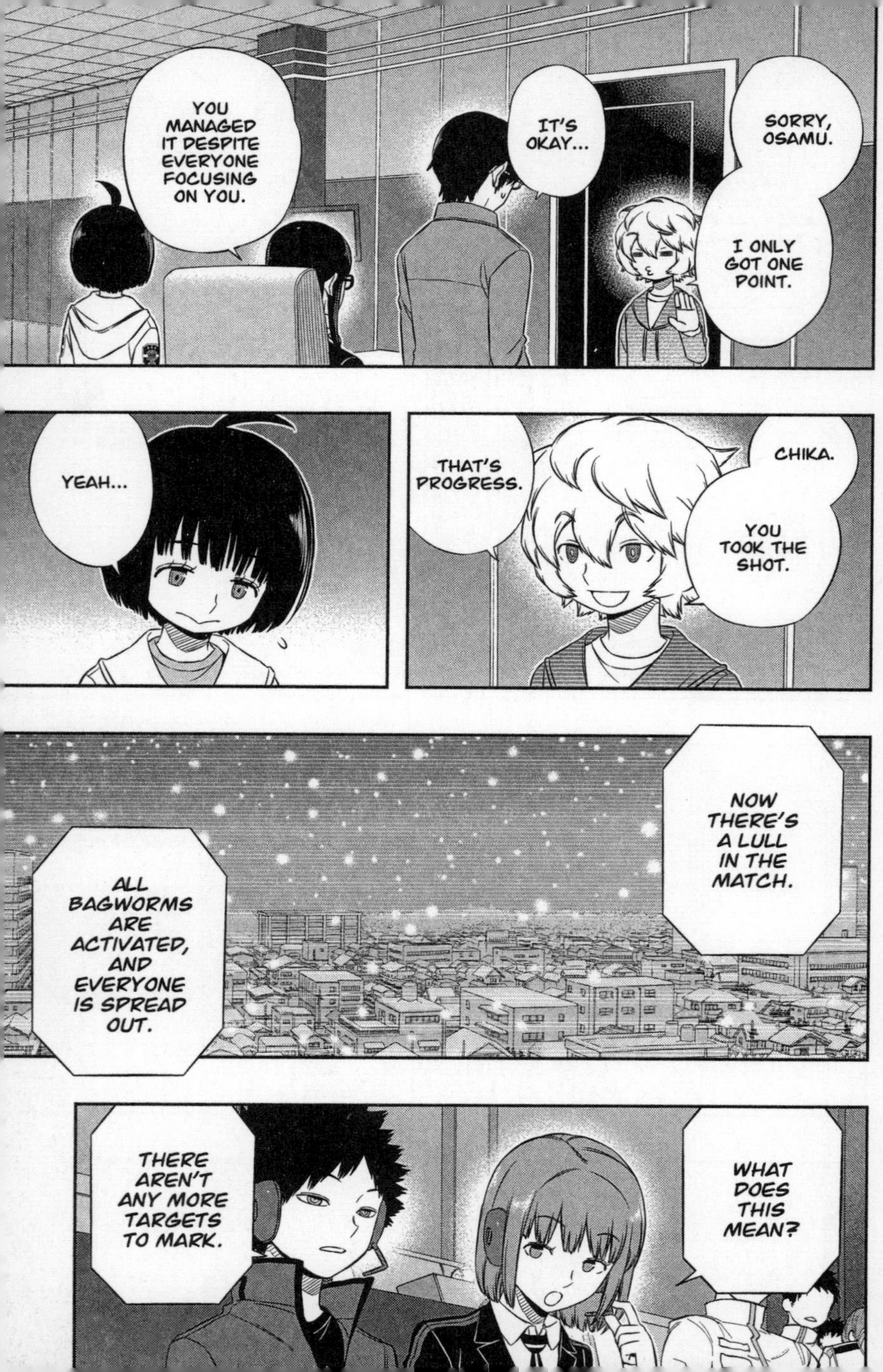
SORRY, OSAMU.
I ONLY GOT ONE POINT.
IT'S OKAY...
YOU MANAGED IT DESPITE EVERYONE FOCUSING ON YOU.
CHIKA.
YOU TOOK THE SHOT.
THAT'S PROGRESS.
YEAH...
NOW THERE'S A LULL IN THE MATCH.
ALL BAGWORMS ARE ACTIVATED, AND EVERYONE IS SPREAD OUT.
WHAT DOES THIS MEAN?
THERE AREN'T ANY MORE TARGETS TO MARK.

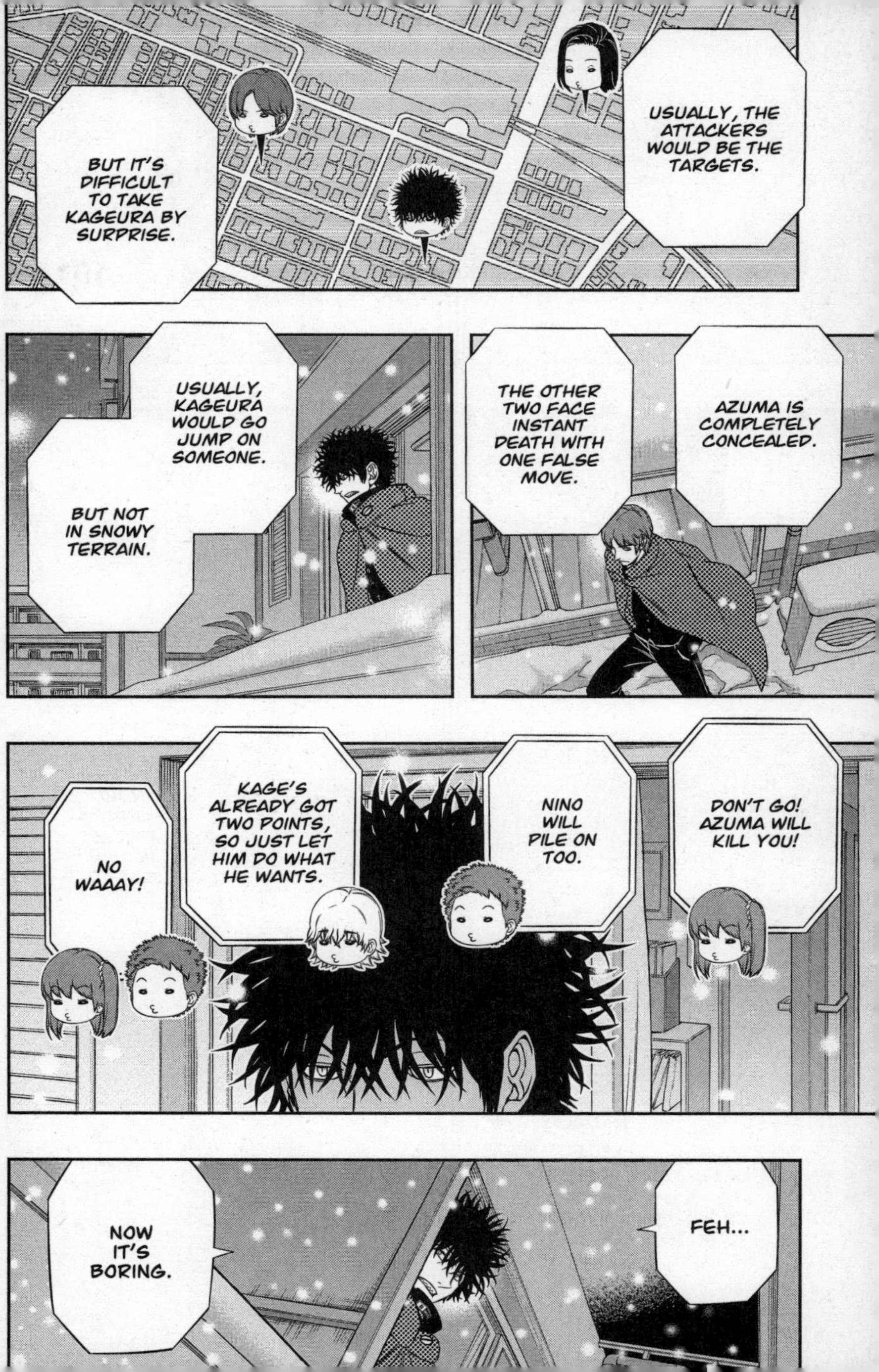
USUALLY, THE ATTACKERS WOULD BE THE TARGETS.
BUT IT'S DIFFICULT TO TAKE KAGEURA BY SURPRISE.
AZUMA IS COMPLETELY CONCEALED.
THE OTHER TWO FACE INSTANT DEATH WITH ONE FALSE MOVE.
USUALLY, KAGEURA WOULD GO JUMP ON SOMEONE.
BUT NOT IN SNOWY TERRAIN.
DON'T GO! AZUMA WILL KILL YOU!
NINO WILL PILE ON TOO.
KAGE'S ALREADY GOT TWO POINTS, SO JUST LET HIM DO WHAT HE WANTS.
NO WAAAY!
FEH...
NOW IT'S BORING.

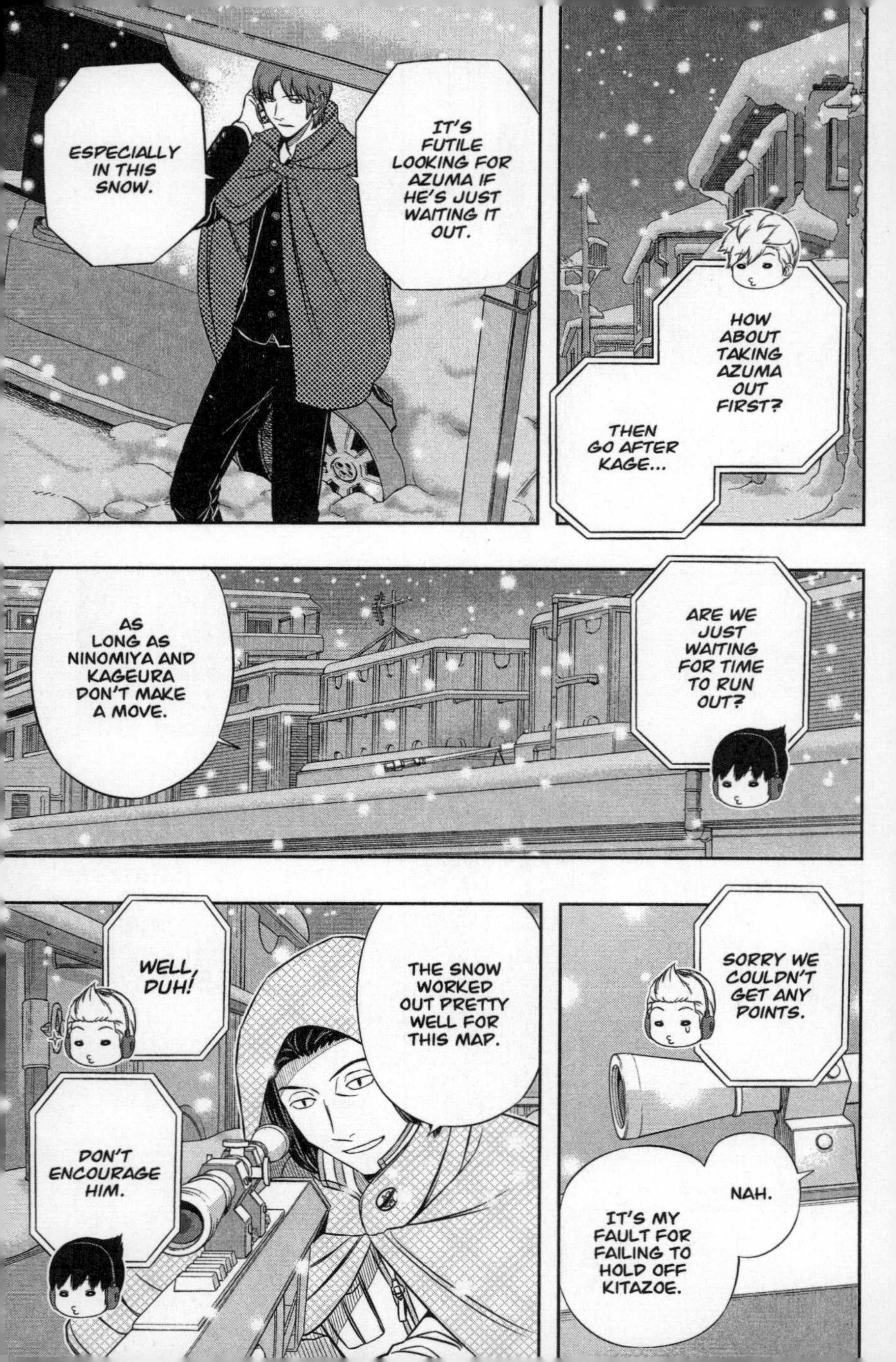
HOW ABOUT TAKING AZUMA OUT FIRST?
THEN GO AFTER KAGE...
IT'S FUTILE LOOKING FOR AZUMA IF HE'S JUST WAITING IT OUT.
ESPECIALLY IN THIS SNOW.
ARE WE JUST WAITING FOR TIME TO RUN OUT?
AS LONG AS NINOMIYA AND KAGEURA DON'T MAKE A MOVE.
SORRY WE COULDN'T GET ANY POINTS.
NAH.
IT'S MY FAULT FOR FAILING TO HOLD OFF KITAZOE.
THE SNOW WORKED OUT PRETTY WELL FOR THIS MAP.
WELL, DUH!
DON'T ENCOURAGE HIM.

NINOMIYA KNOWS THIS...

AZUMA IS IN EVACUATION MODE.

THE MATCH IS OVER.

...SO HE WOULDN'T RISK AN ATTACK.

WE'RE OUT OF TIME.

OKAY...

00:05

NINOMIYA SQUAD WINS!

THE MATCH IS OVER!

FINAL SCORE IS 3-2-2-1.

	Points	Survival	Total
Ninomiya Squad	3		3
Kageura Squad	2	None since multiple squads survived	2
Azuma Squad	2		2
Tamakoma-2	1		1

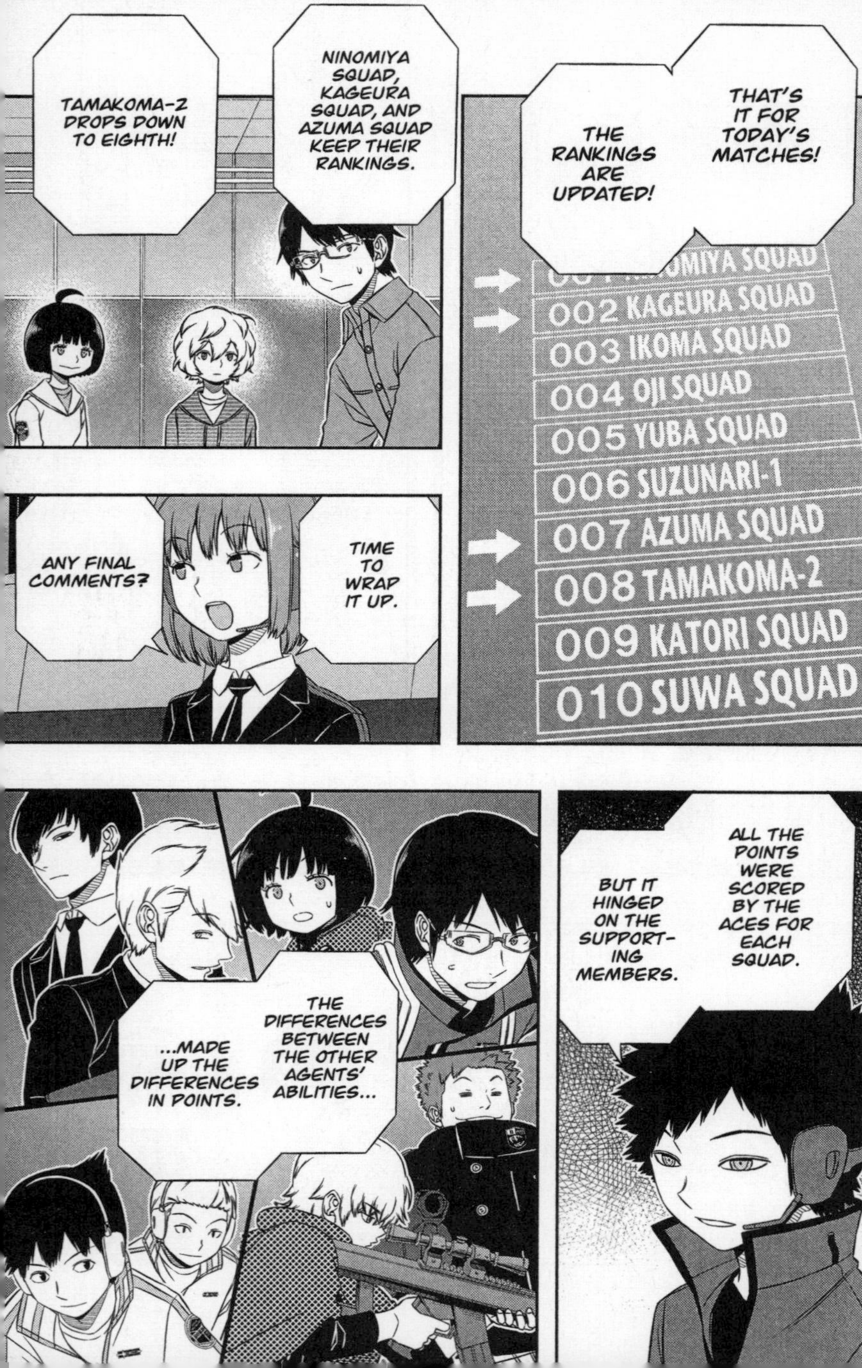
THAT'S IT FOR TODAY'S MATCHES!
THE RANKINGS ARE UPDATED!
002 KAGEURA SQUAD
003 IKOMA SQUAD
004 OJI SQUAD
005 YUBA SQUAD
006 SUZUNARI-1
007 AZUMA SQUAD
008 TAMAKOMA-2
009 KATORI SQUAD
010 SUWA SQUAD
NINOMIYA SQUAD, KAGEURA SQUAD, AND AZUMA SQUAD KEEP THEIR RANKINGS.
TAMAKOMA-2 DROPS DOWN TO EIGHTH!
TIME TO WRAP IT UP.
ANY FINAL COMMENTS?
ALL THE POINTS WERE SCORED BY THE ACES FOR EACH SQUAD.
BUT IT HINGED ON THE SUPPORTING MEMBERS.
THE DIFFERENCES BETWEEN THE OTHER AGENTS' ABILITIES...
...MADE UP THE DIFFERENCES IN POINTS.

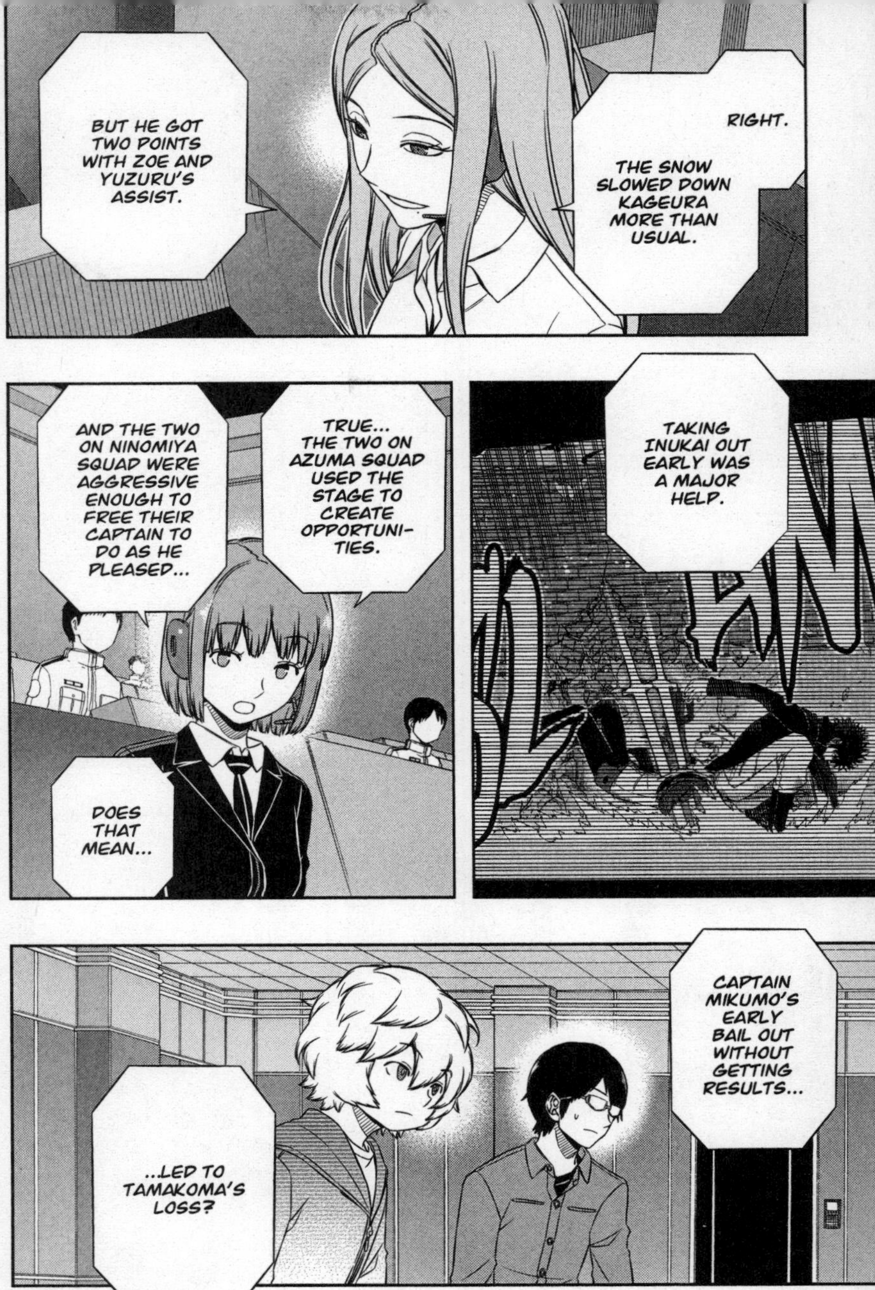
RIGHT.
THE SNOW SLOWED DOWN KAGEURA MORE THAN USUAL.
BUT HE GOT TWO POINTS WITH ZOE AND YUZURU'S ASSIST.
TAKING INUKAI OUT EARLY WAS A MAJOR HELP.
TRUE... THE TWO ON AZUMA SQUAD USED THE STAGE TO CREATE OPPORTUNI-TIES.
AND THE TWO ON NINOMIYA SQUAD WERE AGGRESSIVE ENOUGH TO FREE THEIR CAPTAIN TO DO AS HE PLEASED...
DOES THAT MEAN...
CAPTAIN MIKUMO'S EARLY BAIL OUT WITHOUT GETTING RESULTS...
...LED TO TAMAKOMA'S LOSS?

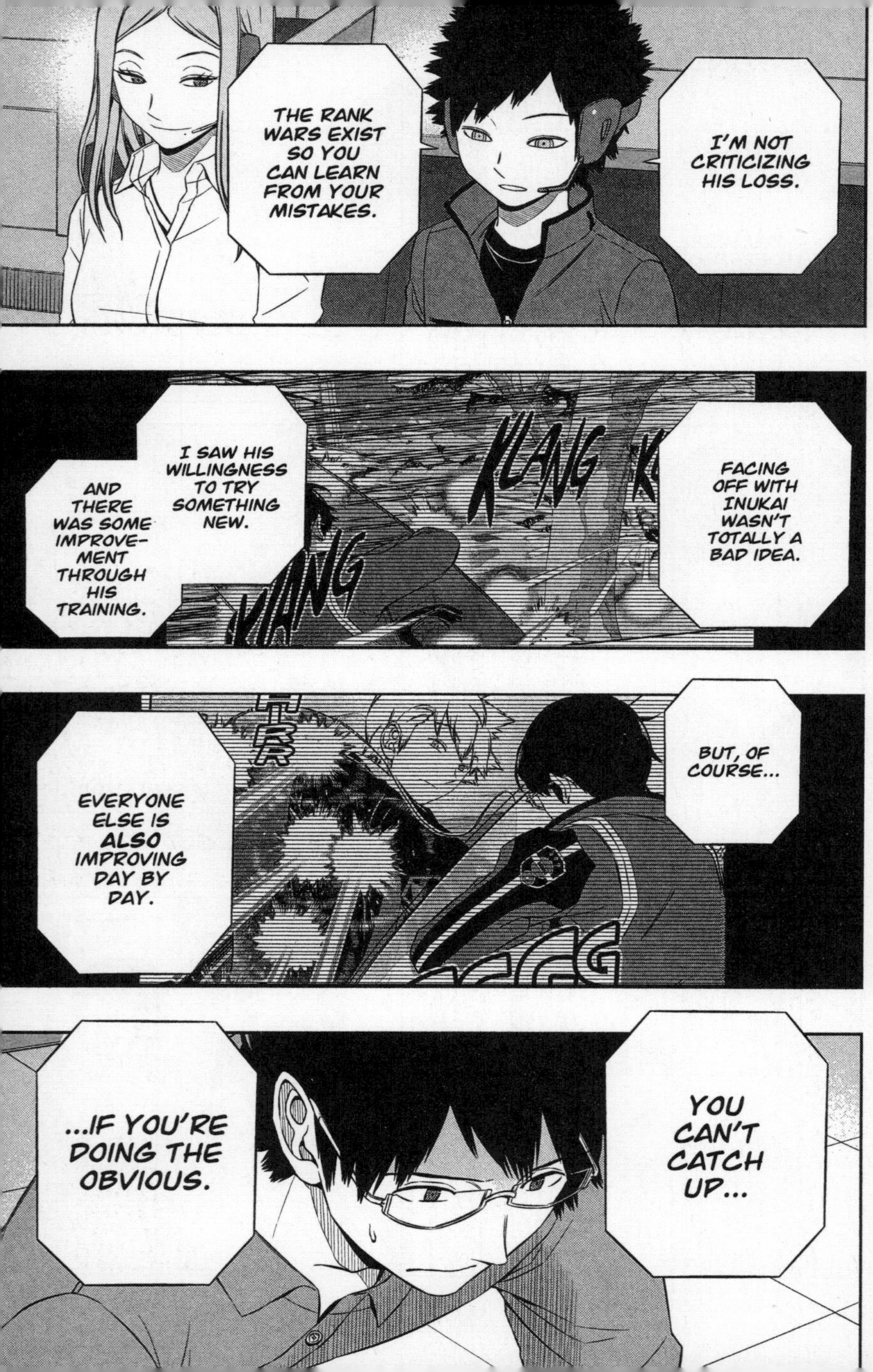
I'M NOT CRITICIZING HIS LOSS.
THE RANK WARS EXIST SO YOU CAN LEARN FROM YOUR MISTAKES.
FACING OFF WITH INUKAI WASN'T TOTALLY A BAD IDEA.
KLANG
I SAW HIS WILLINGNESS TO TRY SOMETHING NEW.
AND THERE WAS SOME IMPROVEMENT THROUGH HIS TRAINING.
KLANG
BUT, OF COURSE...
EVERYONE ELSE IS ALSO IMPROVING DAY BY DAY.
YOU CAN'T CATCH UP...
...IF YOU'RE DOING THE OBVIOUS.

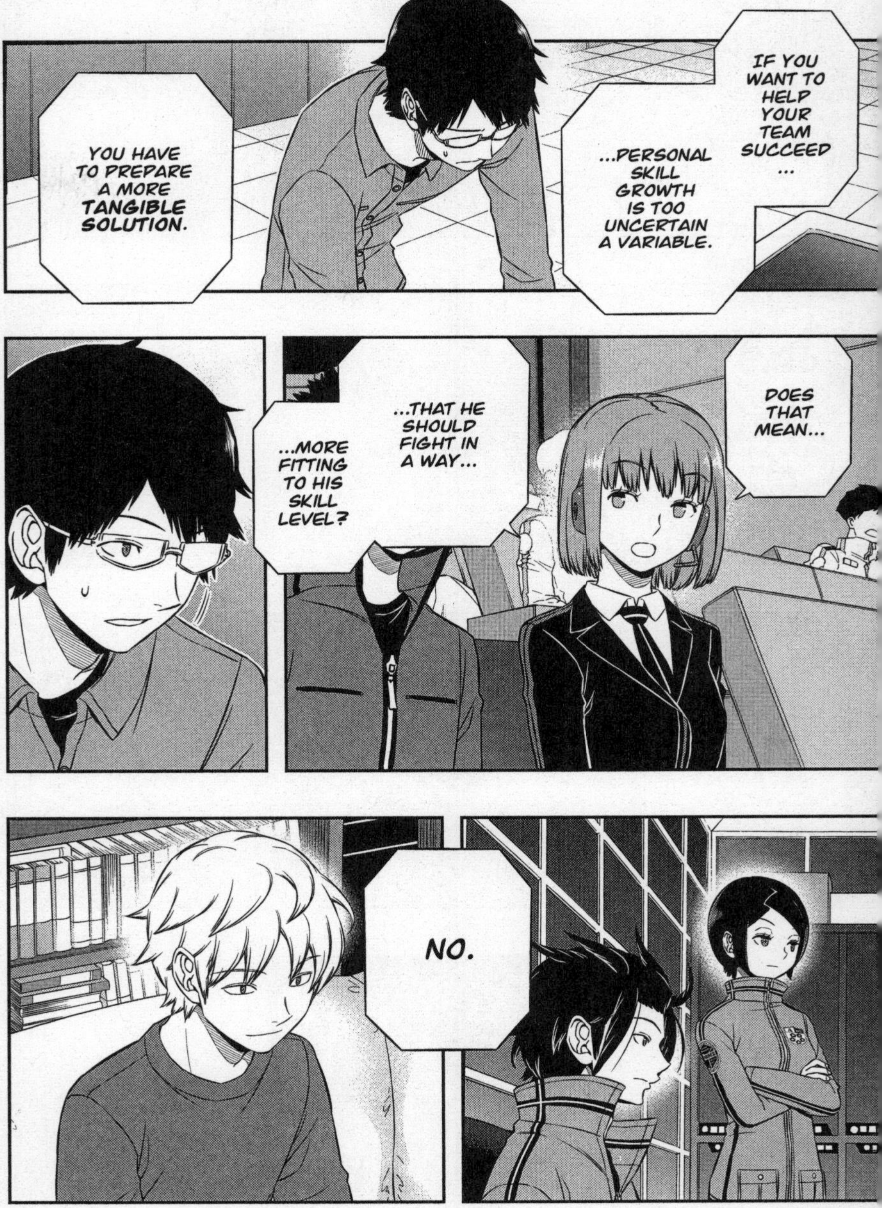

IF YOU WANT TO HELP YOUR TEAM SUCCEED...
...PERSONAL SKILL GROWTH IS TOO UNCERTAIN A VARIABLE.
YOU HAVE TO PREPARE A MORE TANGIBLE SOLUTION.
DOES THAT MEAN...
...THAT HE SHOULD FIGHT IN A WAY...
...MORE FITTING TO HIS SKILL LEVEL?
NO.

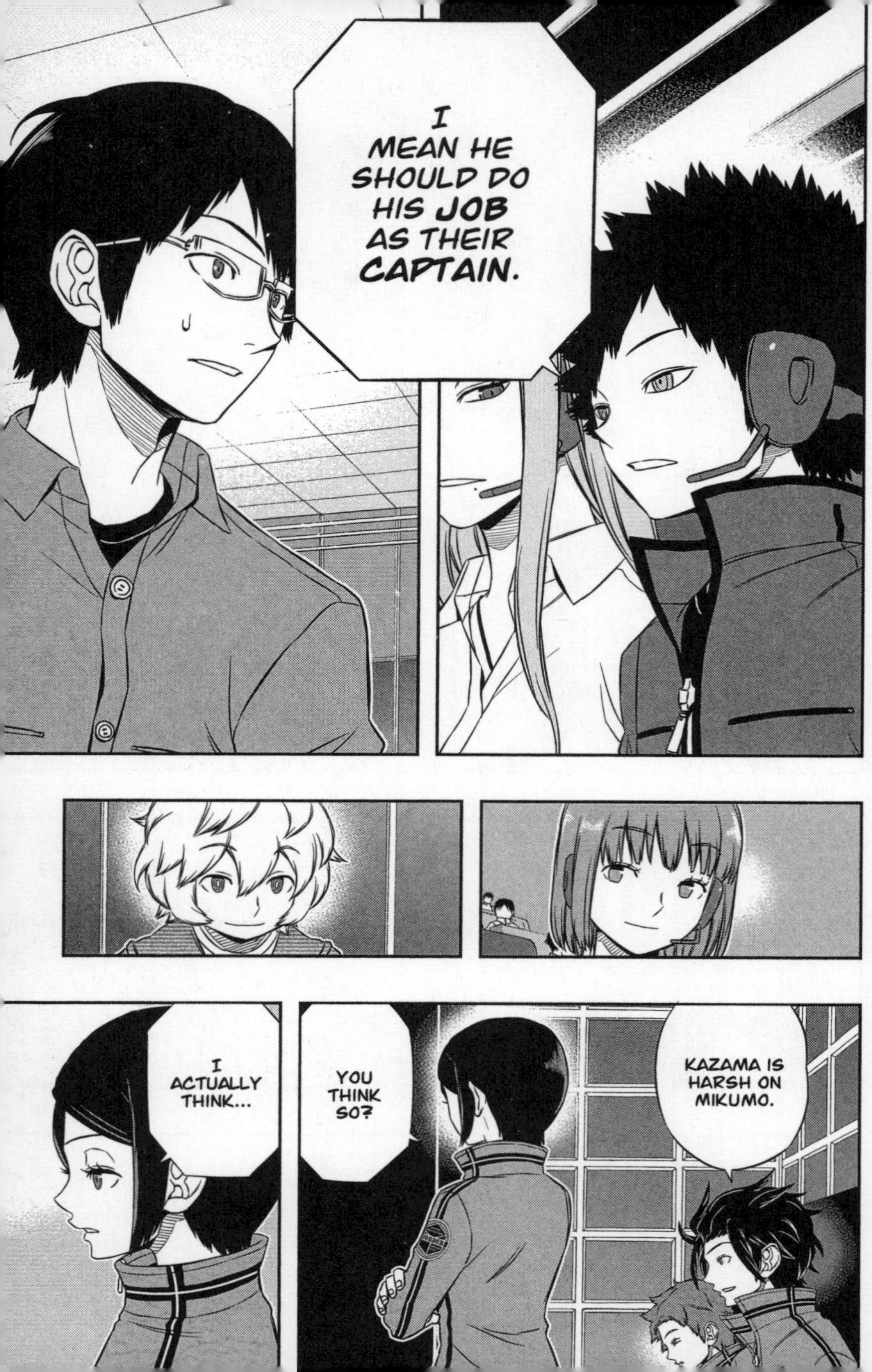
I MEAN HE SHOULD DO HIS JOB AS THEIR CAPTAIN.
KAZAMA IS HARSH ON MIKUMO.
YOU THINK SO?
I ACTUALLY THINK...

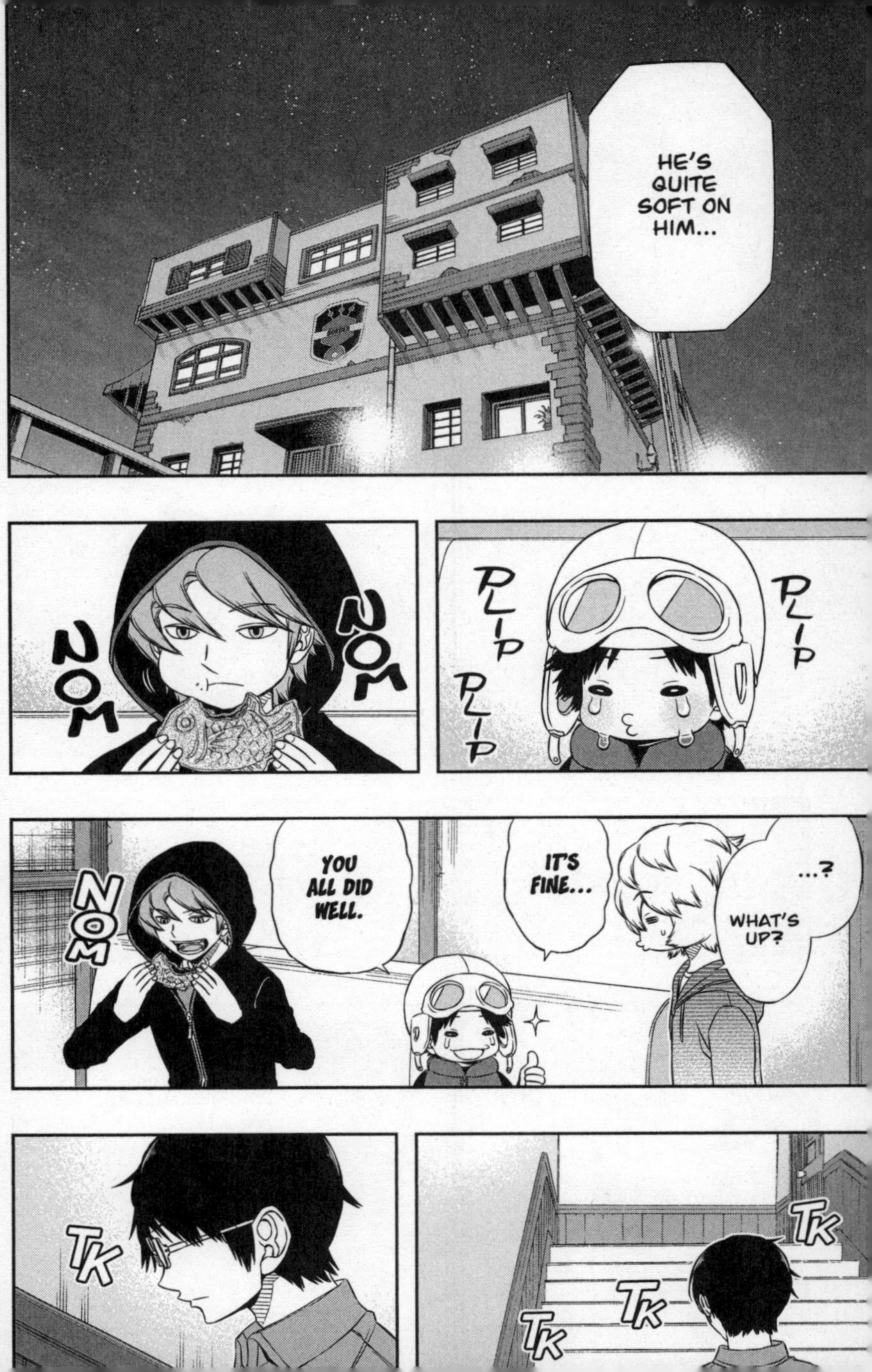
HE'S QUITE SOFT ON HIM...
PLIP
PLIP
PLIP
NOM
NOM
...?
WHAT'S UP?
IT'S FINE...
YOU ALL DID WELL.
NOM
TK
TK
TK
TK

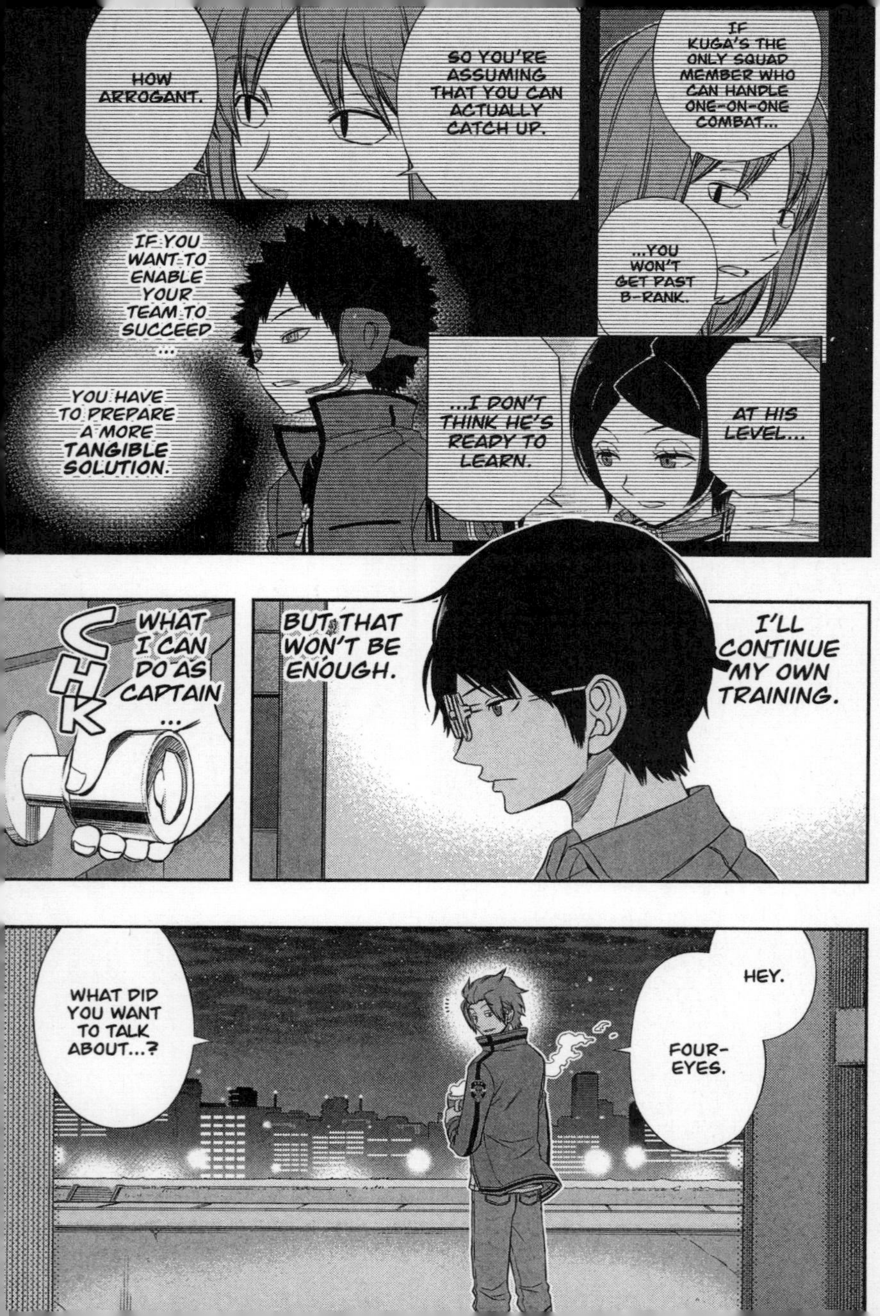
IF KUGA'S THE ONLY SQUAD MEMBER WHO CAN HANDLE ONE-ON-ONE COMBAT...
...YOU WON'T GET PAST B-RANK.
SO YOU'RE ASSUMING THAT YOU CAN ACTUALLY CATCH UP.
HOW ARROGANT.
AT HIS LEVEL...
...I DON'T THINK HE'S READY TO LEARN.
IF YOU WANT TO ENABLE YOUR TEAM TO SUCCEED...
YOU HAVE TO PREPARE A MORE TANGIBLE SOLUTION.
I'LL CONTINUE MY OWN TRAINING.
BUT THAT WON'T BE ENOUGH.
WHAT I CAN DO AS CAPTAIN...
CHK
HEY.
FOUR-EYES.
WHAT DID YOU WANT TO TALK ABOUT...?

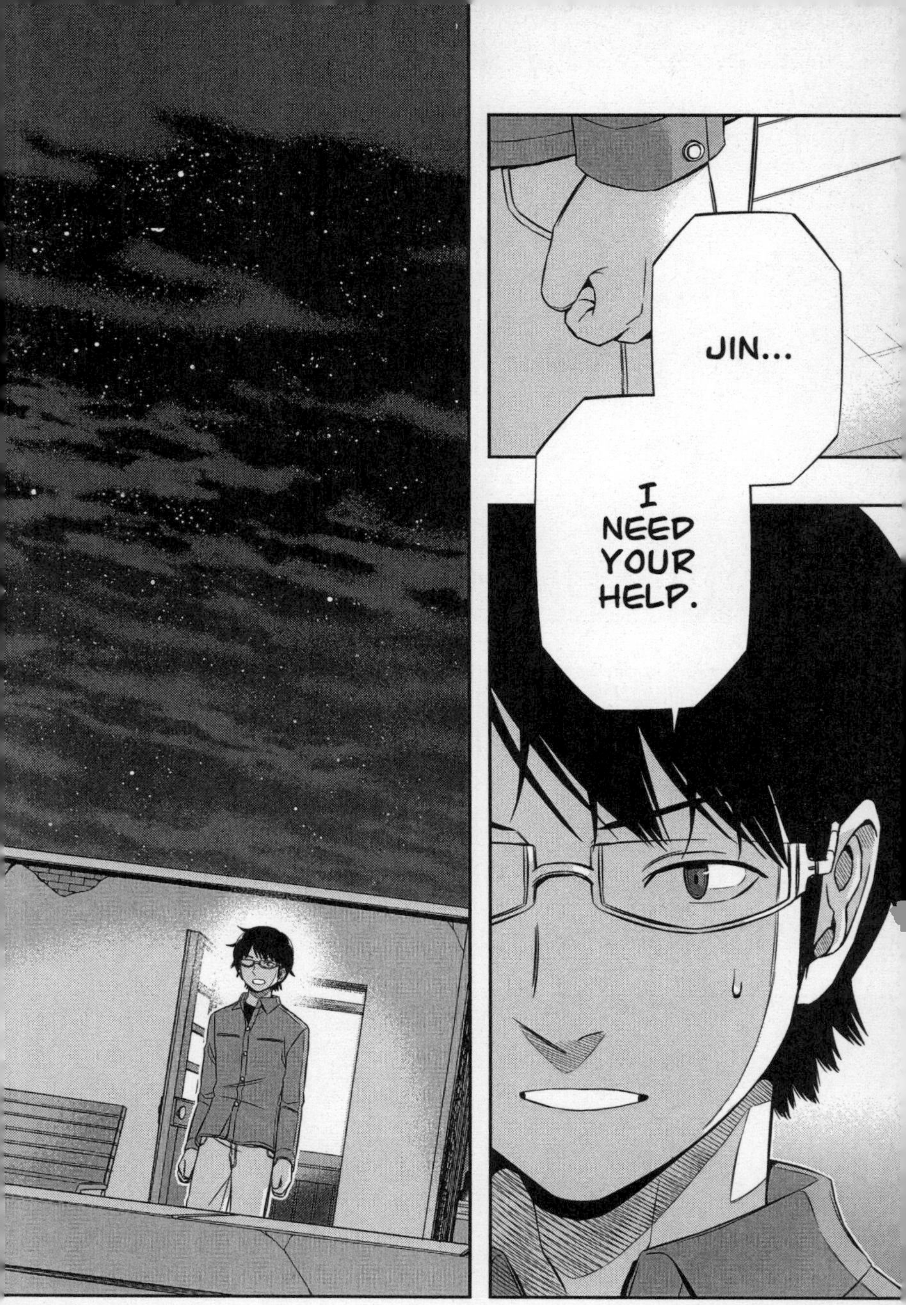
JIN...
I NEED YOUR HELP.

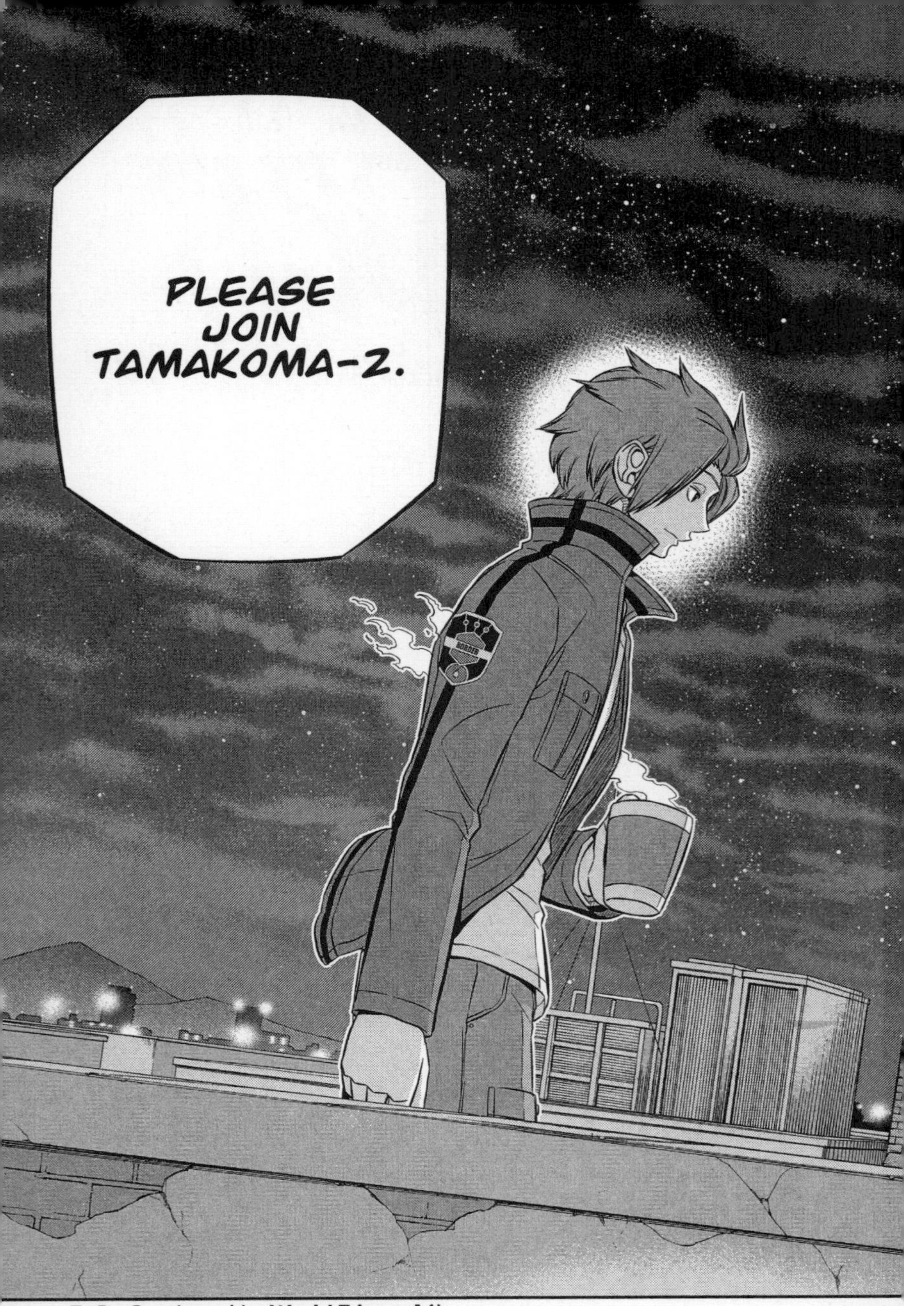
PLEASE JOIN TAMAKOMA-2.
BORDER

To Be Continued In ***World Trigger*** 14!

WORLD TRIGGER

Bonus Character Pages

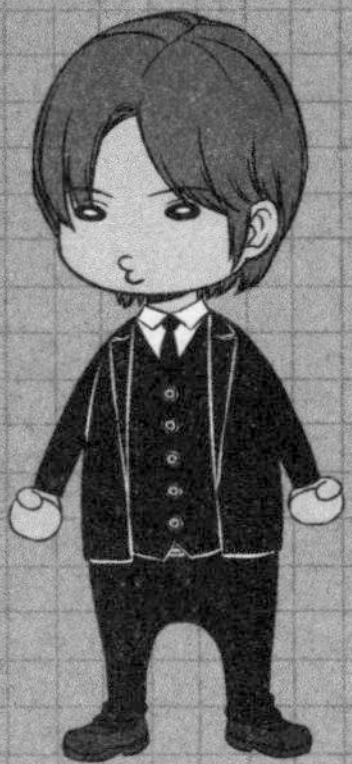

NINOMIYA

Bullet Elite

A hotshot who bragged to all who would listen that he had the highest trion levels of all time (at the time he joined Border). Shinoda schemed to toss him into Azuma Squad along with Kako and Miwa, thus schooling him in the ways of strategy. He's actually a bit of a simpleton. He picked black suits for his squad's uniforms to avoid the cosplay look of other squads. Little did he know that their uniforms were the most cosplay-like of all! I did say he was a simpleton.

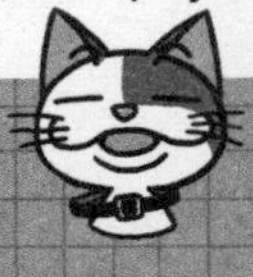

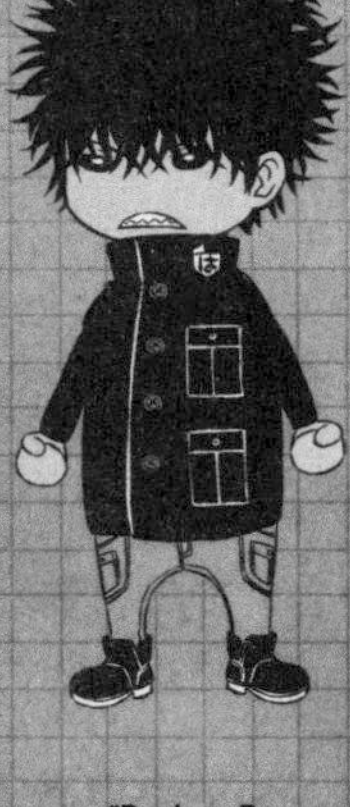

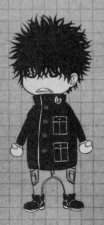

KAGE

Off With Their Heads!

He uppercutted Mr. Netsuki and was demoted to B-Rank. He's the second son of an owner of an *okonomiyaki* restaurant. His side effect is the most tiring in the manga, but his teeth were too pointy for him to be a nice guy and have people look at him with affection. His hair is super annoying to draw, so he may soon awaken to the wonders of baseball or Buddhism and shave his head.

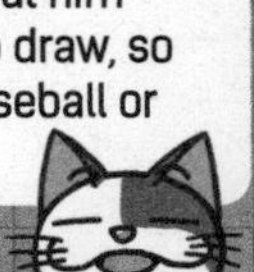

*Badge: Bo

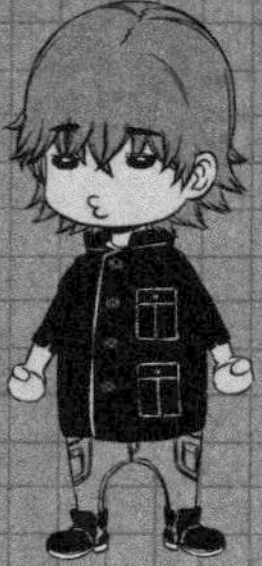

YUZURU
A Lock on Youth

Contrary to his naive appearance, he is a puberty black hole who was born with the natural ability to interact with girls. He comes complete with connections to high-ranking characters like Toma, Kageura and Ninomiya. Now all he has to do is start playing rugby, and the Business Director is confident he'll have a bright future. He's one of the few naturally gifted junior high schooler agents who can hold a top solo-rank spot...even if he slacks off during training.

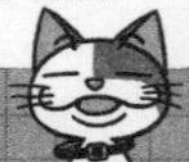

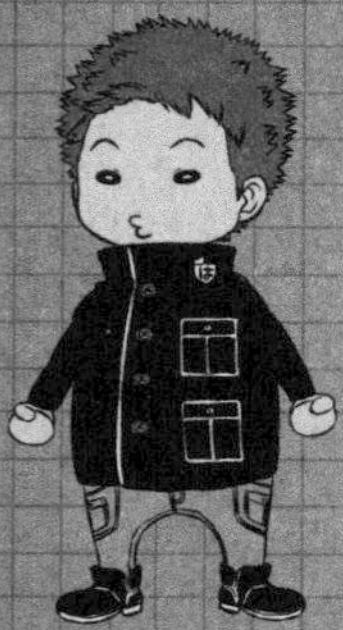

ZOE
Fat Lion

A physically fit hunk of meat who can run and dance. He's one of the top two along with Reiji in terms of raw physical strength. He and Kageura came to a mutual understanding after eight rounds in solo battle. He's a quiet hunk of meat who doesn't like to fight, but Kuruma's influence has nudged him toward acting like more of a do-gooder, increasing his empathy toward girls and younger kids and his respect for his seniors. He's grown to become a lovable mascot.

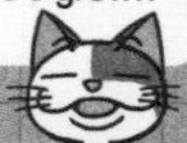

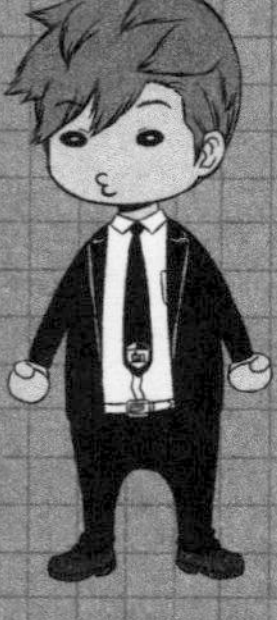

INUKAI
He Does NOT Own a Dog

He's the back of the head in Osamu's flashback. In Hatohara's yakiniku picture, he was cut off at the nose. He's second to none when it comes to only parts of him being visible. He's friendly to everyone because his two older sisters hammered communication skills into him. He's Ninomiya Squad's No. 2 and balancer. Kageura is the same age and holds a one-sided hatred against him, but he doesn't mind. He's bigger than that.

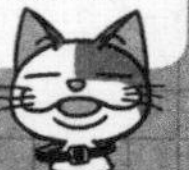

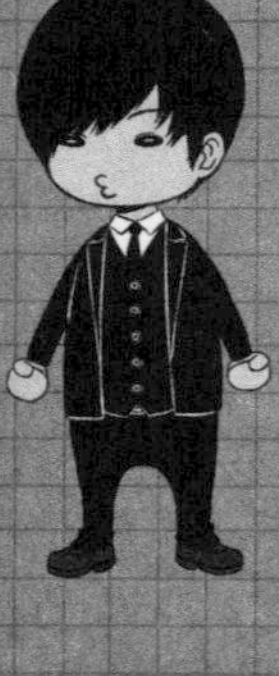

TSUJI
Wordless Kogetsu Whirlwind

The one who didn't get to show his face in Osamu's flashback. He's known for his great assists, just like Izumi and Tokieda. He's pretty good looking, but outside of his teammates he has difficulty even looking girls in the eye—let alone having a conversation with one! If he fought against Kako or Nasu Squads, he'd get crushed.

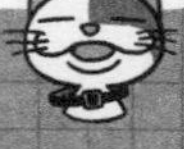

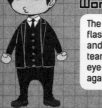

YOU'RE READING THE WRONG WAY!

World Trigger
reads from right to
left, starting in the
upper-right corner.
Japanese is read
from right to left,
meaning that action,
sound effects, and
word-balloon order
are completely
reversed from the
English order.

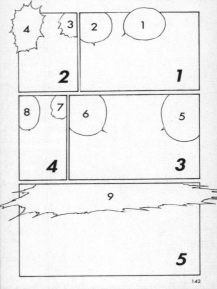